Mapping the Catholic Cultural Landscape

EDITED BY SISTER PAULA JEAN MILLER, FSE,
AND RICHARD FOSSEY

A SHEED & WARD BOOK

ROWMAN & LITTLEFIELD PUBLISHERS, INC.
Lanham • Boulder • New York • Toronto • Oxford

A SHEED & WARD BOOK

ROWMAN & LITTLEFIELD PUBLISHERS, INC.

Published in the United States of America
by Rowman & Littlefield Publishers, Inc.
A wholly owned subsidiary of The Rowman & Littlefield Publishing Group, Inc.
4501 Forbes Boulevard, Suite 200, Lanham, Maryland 20706
www.rowmanlittlefield.com

PO Box 317
Oxford
OX2 9RU, UK

Imprimatur, Most Reverend Joseph A. Fiorenza, Bishop of Galveston–Houston. *Nihil obstat*,
Reverend Terence P. Brinkman, STD. The photo of Lucie Christine (Mathilde Boutle) is used with
the permission of Sister Thérèse Emmanuel Le Roy of the Adoration Réparatrice Monastery, Paris,
France.

British Library Cataloguing in Publication Information Available

Library of Congress Cataloging-in-Publication Data

International Conference of Catholic Studies (1st : 2002 : University of
St. Thomas, Houston, Tex)
  Mapping the Catholic cultural landscape / edited by Paula Jean Miller
and Richard Fossey.
    p. cm.
  "A Sheed & Ward book."
  Includes bibliographical references.
  ISBN 0-7425-3183-X (cloth) — ISBN 0-7425-3184-8 (paper)
  1. Christianity and culture—History—Congresses. 2. Catholic
Church—History—Congresses. I. Miller, Paula Jean. II. Fossey,
Richard, 1948– III. Title.
BR115.C8 I495 2004
282'.09—dc22   2003021453

Printed in the United States of America

♾™ The paper used in this publication meets the minimum requirements of American National
Standard for Information Sciences—Permanence of Paper for Printed Library Materials,
ANSI/NISO Z39.48-1992.

Dedicated To Pope John Paul II:

For awakening the Catholic Church in its Mission
    To receive and to transform the secular world in all its potential;
For the challenge to enrich the Church as Sacrament of Unity
    By discovering and accentuating the gift of its cultural diversity;
And for the vision of the Catholic University in *Ex Corde Ecclesiae*,
    Calling us to Truth in the convergence of interdisciplinary studies.

Contents

Foreword
: The Most Reverend J. Michael Miller, CSB
: Secretary of the Congregation for Catholic Education of the Holy See   xi

Acknowledgments   xiii

Introduction
: Sister Paula Jean Miller, FSE
: University of St. Thomas, Texas   xv

PART I
Literature and Art:
Embodiments of the Faith

Overview
Catholic Culture in Literature and Art
: Clinton A. Brand
: University of St. Thomas, Texas   3

Chapter 1
Jane Austen's Catholic Sensibility
: Father Daniel Callam, CSB
: University of St. Thomas, Texas   9

Chapter 2
Shakespeare's *Measure for Measure* and the Art of Christian Mercy
: Patrick Kelly
: St. Thomas More College, Canada   19

Chapter 3
Story Theology in Flannery O'Connor's "The River," John Updike's
"The Christian Roommates," and Denys Arcand's *Jesus of Montreal*
    Patrick Harkins
    St. Mary of the Woods College, Indiana   33

Chapter 4
The Tree of the Choctaws:
Live Oaks in the Poetry of Father Adrien Emmanuel Rouquette
    Chris Michaelides
    University of Louisiana at Monroe, Louisiana   43

Chapter 5
The Theological Virtues in J. R. R. Tolkien's *Lord of the Rings*
    Kerry J. MacArthur
    University of St. Thomas, Texas   55

Chapter 6
Santiago in the Americas:
The Iconography of the Conqueror and the Infidel
    Kimberly Habegger
    Regis University, Colorado   63

PART II
Culture and Holiness

Overview
Mary as Human Exemplar
    Sister Paula Jean Miller, FSE
    University of St. Thomas, Texas   75

Chapter 7
Our Lady of Jasna Góra in Polish Catholicism
    Father Janusz Ihnatowicz
    Kielce, Poland   81

Chapter 8
Marian Devotion and Cultural Influence in the Naming of Churches
    Phil Lampe
    University of the Incarnate Word, Texas   91

Chapter 9

Literary Appropriation of Mary in the Spanish-Speaking World
Luis Eugenio Espinosa-González
Universidad de Monterrey, Mexico 103

Chapter 10
Marian Devotion in the Spiritual Life of Saint Rose of Lima
Father Alfred A. Brichta-López, O.P.
Dominican University of California 117

Chapter 11
Saints and Sanctity in France
Father Ted Baenziger, CSB
University of St. Thomas, Texas 129

Chapter 12
Lucie Christine: Nineteenth-Century Wife, Mother, and Mystic
Astrid O'Brien
Fordham University, New York 145

PART III
Transforming Interrelationships:
Catholic Faith and Secular Society

Overview
Secular Society and the Catholic Imagination
Richard Fossey
University of Houston, Texas 159

Chapter 13
The Import of Latino Spirituality for Twenty-First-Century
U.S. Culture, Politics, and Religion
John Francis Burke
University of St. Thomas, Texas 165

Chapter 14
"False Generosity" Toward Inner-City School Children:
Why the Fierce Opposition to Vouchers for "Sectarian" Schools?
Richard Fossey
University of Houston, Texas 183

Chapter 15
Journey to Faith: Isaac Hecker and Nineteenth-Century American Reform
Ruth M. Kelly
D'Youville College, New York   199

Chapter 16
Catholic Indian Boarding Schools and Sioux Catholicism
James T. Carroll
Iona College, New York   211

Chapter 17
Catholic Insight on Workplace Human Rights and Corporate Humanism
Michele Simms
University of St. Thomas, Texas   223

Chapter 18
Image and Social Responsibility:
Catholic Values and Fashion Advertising
Janice G. McCoart
Marymount University, Virginia   239

Chapter 19
Catholic Faith Between Secularization and Pluralism
Maria Clara Lucchetti Bingemer
Catholic University of Rio de Janeiro, Brazil   249

Chapter 20
Restoring All Things in Christ:
Some Reflections on the Pastoral Provision for the Anglican Use of
the Roman Rite
Clinton A. Brand
University of St. Thomas, Texas   259

Appendix A
Darkness into Light: *Guadalupe, Mother of All Mexico*   275

About the Editors   277

Foreword

L ack of confidence in man's future drains modern life of the *gaudium de veritate* essential to human creativity and culture. The contemporary malaise enveloping us can be overcome only through a rebirth of the human spirit—a cultural renewal built on a spiritual core. Because the Church is an "expert in humanity," she can foster dialogue with every culture. At the same time the Catholic Church understands how she has herself been shaped by and continues to shape the cultures of mankind.

Anchored in the heart of the Church, the Catholic university is responsible for discerning through its research the positive aspirations and negative elements of every culture. It is a place where "scholars scrutinize reality with the methods proper to each academic discipline" (*Ex Corde Ecclesiae*, 15) and should transmit to succeeding generations what is noble in all human experience, ensuring that Christ sheds his light on it.

As an institution committed to the liberal arts and to the religious, ethical, and intellectual tradition of Catholic education, the University of St. Thomas in Houston is honored to publish *Mapping the Catholic Cultural Landscape*. This selection of essays is the fruit of the first international conference held April 18-21, 2002 on the University campus. The Catholic Studies Program, in collaboration with the Department of Modern and Classical Languages, sponsored this three-day gathering of more than a hundred scholars from around the world. In addition to the numerous sessions which addressed the Catholic influence on culture during the first two millennia, the conference also included special liturgies, art exhibits, and exposure to the cosmopolitan diversity of Houston.

Mapping the Catholic Cultural Landscape responds to Pope John Paul II's call to foster the valuable dialogue between the Gospel and culture, a conversation that confirms the Church's catholicity. Faith's encounter and engagement with the splendid variety of cultures enriches human experience, leading it to deeper authenticity.

Firmly committed to implementing *Ex Corde Ecclesiae* faithfully and creatively, the University of St. Thomas launched its Catholic Studies Program under the direction of Sister Paula Jean Miller, FSE, as a way of celebrating the Great Jubilee of the Year 2000. Since the University's founding in 1947, St. Thomas has emphasized the study of the humanities and sciences for all our undergraduates. Indeed, our core curriculum still requires a combined total of eight courses in philosophy and theology. With the help of our Center for Thomistic Studies, the Philosophy Department promotes a living Thomism for the third millennium. Likewise, our

Theology Department fosters the dialogue between faith and reason by making available to our students the full riches of the Church's theological teaching.

The Catholic Studies Program at the University of St. Thomas was established to enhance the entire curriculum with the wealth of the Catholic intellectual tradition and to transmit this heritage to a new generation. It is a provocative program, challenging any notion that theology and philosophy, perhaps with English and history, can alone carry the weight for securing the University's catholicity. Rather, Catholic Studies integrates these and other disciplines to promote the dialogue between faith and culture and the pursuit of the ethical and moral implications of all learning. It is an interdisciplinary program which enables "students to acquire an organic vision of reality and to develop a continuing desire for intellectual progress" (*Ex Corde Ecclesiae,* 20). Our Catholic Studies Program is open to everyone who desires a deeper understanding of the mutual influence of Catholic thought and life upon cultures, the arts and sciences, medicine and law, education and business. It deepens in students a Catholic vision of the world, providing a lens through which they can view their chosen field of study and its practice. Catholic Studies is the new evangelization of the academy.

The chapters in this delightful volume furnish a vast and fascinating panorama of the wealth of the various cultural traditions within the Church. They also tell us of the need to evaluate contemporary culture in the light of faith, of the hard work yet to be done in establishing criteria for measuring the authenticity of a culture, and of the yet untold possibilities for culture to help the Church express and live the fullness of the truth.

The Most Reverend J. Michael Miller, CSB
Secretary of the Congregation for Catholic Education of the Holy See
Titular Archbishop of the See of Vertara

Acknowledgments

We thank our colleagues upon whom depended the success of the First International Conference for Catholic Studies: *Mapping the Catholic Cultural Landscape*:

Dr. Debra Andrist of Modern and Classical Languages, Co-chair of the Conference;

UST Catholic Studies Interdisciplinary Committee;

Father J. Michael Miller, CSB, UST President, who provided the financial security for this endeavor;

Dr. Jerome Kramer, Associate VPAA, mediator of all the administrative requirements for the conference and for the ongoing Catholic Studies Program;

Faculty who served as jurors and session moderators;

Bishop Ricardo Ramirez of Las Cruces, New Mexico, plenary speaker and celebrant of the Latino liturgy, Father Anthony Dao, O.P., celebrant of the Vietnamese liturgy, Father Romanus Muoneke, celebrant of the African liturgy, Father Ted Baenziger, CSB, celebrant of the French liturgy; and Reverend Doctor Laurence Cross, Liturgy of Saint John Chrysostom;

Tom Crow, Father Edward Bader, CSB, Mrs. Pat Collins, Dr. John Burke, and Sylvia Cameron who enriched our cultural experience through music and art;

Sandra Soliz and the Public Relations Department;

Facilities Operations, Media Services, and Dining Services;

Catholic Studies students who volunteered their services throughout the conference, especially Sister Anne Frances Le, O.P., Rachael Leland and Amber Martinez.

Particular thanks go to those Contributors who have worked beyond the demands of the initial conference to prepare their papers for publication in these Proceedings and to Monsignor Frank Rossi, Chancellor of the Diocese of Galveston-Houston, for facilitating the *nihil obstat/imprimatur* for this text.

Special acknowledgment and gratitude is due to Kim Fossey, UST Distance Learning Center Manager, who together with Jennifer O'Bryant, prepared the manuscript for camera-ready publication.

Introduction

T he Catholic creed is centered in the Incarnation of God; like Christ, the Church takes flesh in space and time, in particular lands and peoples. The Catholic Church is born from the cross of the Redemption; like Christ, the Catholic religion is irrevocably united with culture and is historically conditioned.

The Catholic faith is not a compendium of abstract concepts, but the belief and liturgy and life of a community of persons called to be the Body of Christ in history.

The Catholic Church is one; the Catholic faith is one; but the Church and the faith of the people of God exist in history, within cultures. Like Jesus Christ, the incarnate, historical Church is a scandal and a stumbling block, but simultaneously she stands as an invincible sign that God has irrevocably united himself with creation and with the continuing incarnation of divine faith within human cultures.

Catholic Studies is an academic discipline dedicated to unfolding the interpenetration of culture and faith, of worship and moral choice, as that is found embodied in persons and societies, expressed in their art, literature, theology, philosophy, sciences, and professions.

Catholic Studies was initiated in response to the vision of Pope John Paul II, particularly as expressed in the document *Ex Corde Ecclesiae* (1990). In that document, the Holy Father challenged Catholic universities to rededicate themselves to their mission to discover and share Truth, and to do so from an interdisciplinary perspective. Other professions (like medicine, for example) have moved in this century from direct generalized care (family doctor) into specializations, and now seek to integrate the knowledge gained through that in-depth study and experience into a multifaceted perspective again focused on the person in community. The university community, likewise diversified into loosely affiliated, specialized schools, is now called to incorporate complementary, but often isolated, perspectives of reality into a multidisciplinary approach to the discovery of Truth. For academic experts to attempt such an integration of specialized research, it is necessary for them to come together, share their findings, and be enriched and provoked by the learning of others in similar and different fields.

For this purpose, the first International Conference of Catholic Studies was held April 18-21, 2002 at the University of St. Thomas in Houston, Texas. Over one hundred university professors from Canada, Mexico, Brazil, Poland, Australia, and across the United States convened to share research on the status and the developmental process of inculturation of faith, as they discovered it in their representative cultures and within their respective disciplines. This Catholic Studies text,

Mapping the Catholic Cultural Landscape, compiles a significant representation of those papers, to provide a spectrum of cultural and multidisciplinary insights on the interrelationship between faith and culture.

What do we mean by *inculturation*? How does inculturation differ from the missionary approach of Christian Churches in past centuries? In his book, *Inculturation and Ecclesial Communion,* Francis Cardinal George, OMI, builds upon the vision of faith and culture of Pope John Paul II.

> The relation between faith and culture is a synthesis without syncretism, a unity in which the faith becomes culture and the culture becomes authentically human-istic. To this inculturation process, the faith brings the full truth about human reality, especially the truth of our origin and of our final destiny, of our openness to transcendence. Culture brings to the process human persons in their particular concreteness, as they exist in a determined context. From the faith-culture dia-logue and the synthesis issuing from it, the faith receives a new mode of expres-sion, a new maturity; and in this process, culture, in turn, is purified. Its genuine values are strengthened and it is opened to the full truth about humanity and respect for other cultures. Through synthesis with Christian faith, a culture can come to a greater understanding of human transcendence. Openness to our rela-tion to God makes a culture more open to all other cultures and ways of being human. Inculturation of the faith, as a cultural project, helps assure human sur-vival, guaranteeing respect for the fullness of human subjectivity, both personal and communal. It gives a new density to the unity of the human race and can help all men and women create a truly universal community.[1]

Mapping the Catholic Cultural Landscape is an initial attempt to do just that: to explore the inculturation of the Catholic faith within a global perspective. This single volume cannot hope to touch upon all the cultures of the globe, any more than could the first international conference—but it is a beginning. The papers in this volume include forays into French, Polish, English, American, Native Ameri-can, Canadian, Brazilian, and Spanish (Mexican, Peruvian) cultures. In the confer-ence, other cultures were also represented not only through academic research, but also through liturgy and in foods—African, Vietnamese, Filipino, and Austra-lian cultures. The entrance point into each of these cultures was their expression in literature, art, music, architecture; spirituality, Marian traditions, saints, liturgy; education, politics, business practices, and fashion.

This text seeks to discover the impact of the Catholic faith on cultures by ex-amining three primary subject areas: Catholic Culture in Literature and Art; Cul-tures and Holiness; and the Interrelationship between Faith and Secular Societies and Disciplines.

In Part One, Father Daniel Callam, CSB, University of St. Thomas, Texas, ex-plores the Catholic roots of the morality underlying the writings of Jane Austen. By examining her dependence upon the Book of Common Prayer, which retained Catholic belief and tradition (in spite of the acceptance in England of the Thirty-nine Articles), Callam is able to establish a Catholic influence on Austen's thought, even though she considered herself a staunch Protestant. Patrick Kelly, St. Thomas

More College, Canada, finds in Shakespeare's *Measure for Measure*, an expression of Catholic ethos in the person of the Duke, the "god" of the play and voice of its author. The Catholic characteristics of the play have raised the question of the religious affiliation of Shakespeare, who was active in England during the period of the Reformation and was himself under suspicion for his Catholic affiliation.[2] Kerry MacArthur of the University of St. Thomas, utilizes *allegoresis* to interpret each of the three main protagonists in terms of the theological virtues in *The Lord of the Rings*, by J. R. R. Tolkien. Through the actions and interactions of the heroes of Middle Earth, MacArthur is able to associate each of the theological virtues, Faith, Hope, and Charity, not only with a character and a symbolic color, but also with a correlative character symbolism in the work of Dante.

Patrick Harkins of St. Mary of the Woods, Indiana, examines the American scene and its capacity to express theological truths in storytelling: baptism in "The River" (Flannery O'Connor); true Christian life and sanctity in "The Christian Roommates" (John Updike); and call and conversion after Vatican Council Two in *Jesus of Montreal* (Denys Arcand). Chris Michaelides of the University of Louisiana explores the poetic landscapes of the nineteenth-century French missionary, Father Adrien Rouquette nicknamed *Chahta-Ima* by the Choctaws, because he was able to speak to them in their own tongue. Michaelides' treatment of the *Tree of the Choctaws*, a key symbol for the indigenous community Rouquette served during Western society's transition to modernity, tells us much about the struggle to reclaim sacred space in our own postmodern age. Kimberly Habegger of Regis University presents the iconography of Santiago (apostle, pilgrim, and warrior), its Spanish roots in Campostella and its adaptations in the Latin American world, particularly in regard to the expanding historical/cultural references for Conqueror and Infidel.

In Part Two, Father Janusz Ihnatowicz, a canon of the Cathedral of Kielce, examines the role of the icon of Our Lady of Jasna Góra in the life of Poland, a nation where eastern and western forms of Christianity meet. According to a manuscript dated from 1428, Saint Luke painted the icon on a table where the Holy Family ate their meals. The successful defense of the monastery against the siege of the Swedes in 1655 was attributed to her intercession and earned for her the title, Mother of God and Protectress of Poland. When Poland was later divided among nations, the icon became the symbol of national and religious unity.

In a contrasting relationship of culture and Marian devotion, Phil Lampe of Incarnate Word University, Texas, provides us with an insightful statistical study of the relationship between the naming of Marian churches in the United States, and the lack of due proportion to the cultural groups geographically represented. Since one measure of importance or influence is the frequency something is named or used within a culture, the dedication of churches under the patronage of Mary, as revered by a particular cultural group, is significant. Data gathered from 1926 to 2000 indicates a current lack of social acceptance in the United States of the ethnic groups with which Our Lady of Guadalupe is identified, in spite of the fact that she is the declared patroness of the Americas. Luis Eugenio Espinosa-González of the University of Monterrey, Mexico compares the appropriations of Marian tradition in several Spanish-speaking cultures over the course of seven centuries. Dogmas and disciplinary measures have been interpreted differently by local communities, casting light upon the cultural background, value system, and social expectations of each group. Images of Mary that emerge are as enthroned lady, as maternal ruler, and as biblical maiden.

Father Alfred Brichta-López, O.P., seeks to discover within the *procesos* of beatification and canonization, the influence of the Blessed Virgin Mary upon the spiritual life of Saint Rose of Lima. Franciscan, Dominican, and Jesuit missionaries each introduced a significant aspect of devotion to Mary into the life of Saint Rose. Father Lopez concludes that though Rose's spiritual life remained Christ-centered throughout her adulthood, she repeatedly turned to the Virgin Mary for the nurture she lacked from her biological parents. Her relationship to Christ through his mother became a source of profound spiritual and physical well-being for her, and for many others through her. Father Ted Baenziger, CSB, shifts our vision of holiness in the Spanish culture to that of France as the "home" of saints and sanctity over the centuries. France has been named *fille aimee de l'eglise* because she helped shape the Christian world from North America to Indochina, from the Holy Land to equatorial Africa. This article sketches out the ebb and flow of the life of the Church as it is exemplified in the saints of France. Astrid O'Brien of Fordham University focuses our attention next on the life of Mathilde Boutle, a French nineteenth-century wife, mother, and mystic. Mathilde's sanctity was achieved in the difficult circumstances of a marriage fraught with alcoholism, abuse, bankruptcy, and a meddling mother-in-law. Her mystical experiences were embedded in a tumultuous life, not unlike the challenges encountered by many young women today.

Part Three explores the impact and transformations that occur in the encounter of the Catholic Faith with secular society and disciplines. The changing Latino/American demographics in the United States, and particularly in the Southwest, is probably the most dramatic example of this transformative experience. John Burke of the University of St. Thomas, Texas, explores the possible impact upon the American political scene, as a culturally Catholic people becomes the majority in a societal system established by Anglo-Protestants. Burke applies Greeley's theory of a sacramental imagination (embodied by the Latino migration) vis-a-vis a dialectical imagination embodied by the Reformation/Counter-Reformation first wave of migration, to project changes in American society. Richard Fossey of the University of Houston, analyzes recent rulings of the U.S. Supreme Court on violations of the First Amendment clause by state voucher programs. Particular emphasis is placed upon the *Zelman case*, which shows an evolution in the Supreme Court's philosophy regarding the constitutionality of government aid to religious schools. Fossey's paper examines these discussions in light of Paulo Freire's notion of "false generosity" and the implications for sectarian prejudice within the nation's highest court.

Ruth Kelly of D'Youville College in New York, provides insight into the Catholic Church in America through the evangelization of Isaac Hecker, a Protestant convert to Catholicism, and the founder of the Missionary Priests of St. Paul the Apostle. Hecker saw the combination of the Catholic faith with the youthful energy of the American people as the opportunity to transform the entire Catholic world. Hecker's liberal, American style of Catholicism was offered as an alternative to the devotional Catholicism of immigrant America, unacceptable in his time but later received, in part, by the Second Vatican Council.

Michele Simms of the Cameron School of Business, University of St. Thomas, Texas examines the evolving role of corporate social responsibility in business practice as the business world is confronted with environmentalism, globalization, biotechnology, and bioterrorism. Issues of morality and justice that emerge from these contemporary issues are all issues of the human person, therefore Simms presents the relationship between Catholic thought and business practice, utilizing the encyclicals as support for workplace human rights and the corresponding relationship to corporate humanism.

Janice McCoart of Marymount University explores anti-Catholic sentiment and the shock tactics employed by the fashion industry to influence public values worldwide and to raise questions concerning Catholic belief. Since there is a growing tendency to define our sense of self by the images of advertising, the value of material goods threatens to take precedence over the traditional values of goodness, love, and religion. Maria Clara Lucchetti Bingemer of the Catholic University of Rio de Janeiro analyzes one aspect of the crisis of modernity, namely its impact on the manner of living out religion. The contemporary period is experiencing a multireligious explosion in the midst of a secularized society. Bingemer's work attempts to understand this desire for the experience of God, this thirst for mystery and the mystic, as a new emergence of values such as gratuity, desire, feeling, and the rediscovery, in a new dimension, of nature and of man's relationship with the earth. This new religiosity within secularized culture, poured forth in hours of religious rituals and celebrations, in a search for communion with the universe corresponds to a real search for a deep encounter and the desire to be affected by an *otherness*. This contemplative desire for an *other* emerging from the heart of the secular can become an opportunity for dialog between Christian religions, with other religious traditions, as well as with the modern world.

We conclude this text much as it began, by exploring the intimate relationship that exists in liturgy between the Catholic faith and English culture, through the historical sequence of separation, development, and reintegration. Clinton Brand, University of St. Thomas, Texas, reflects on the Pastoral Provision for the Anglican Use of the Roman Rite and the post-Reformation possibility it provides for restoring to the Catholic Church the spiritual patrimony of Anglicanism. Through this decree of the Sacred Congregation for the Doctrine of the Faith, Anglican clergy can be assumed into Catholic priesthood, Anglican laity confirmed, and "common identity" parishes established. Brand concludes that the Anglican Use provides an important model of "reconciled diversity" and the promise of enriching and building up the Body of Christ in the coming era.

This volume attempts to be truly Catholic in its approach. It is a vast undertaking and this work represents only that first delicious moment of plunging one's big toe into the vastness of a powerful and mysterious ocean. This action is recognizably limited, but within the human condition the longest journey indeed begins with a single step.

Our thanks to all those participants willing to take that step and launch out into the deep.

Sister Paula Jean Miller, FSE
Director of Catholic Studies
University of St. Thomas, Texas
July 22, 2003

Notes

1. Francis E. George, *Inculturation and Ecclesial Communion, Culture and Church in the Teaching of Pope John Paul II* (Rome: Urbania University Press, 1990) 46.

2. Paul Voss, "Assurances of Faith: How Catholic Was Shakespeare? How Catholic Are His Plays?" *Crisis* (2 July 2002).

PART I

Literature and Art: Embodiments of the Faith

Overview

Catholic Culture in Literature and Art

Clinton A. Brand

I t is not without significance that the discipline of Catholic Studies derives something of its ethos from the formative influence of two men of letters: John Henry Newman, the accomplished poet and novelist, and Karol Wojtyla, the equally talented poet and playwright. From Cardinal Newman's affirmation of a literary education in *The Idea of a University* (1873) to Pope John Paul II's warmly written *Letter to Artists* (1999), the Catholic Church in the modern world has championed the dialogue of faith and culture through the particular study and appreciation of art and literature.[1] In *Gaudium et Spes*, the Pastoral Constitution of the Church in the Modern World, the Second Vatican Council proclaimed the same idea, testifying that "literature and art are very important in the life of the Church":

> They seek to give expression to man's nature, his problems and his experience in an effort to discover and perfect man himself and the world in which he lives; they try to discover his place in history and in the universe, to throw light on his suffering and joy, his needs and his potentialities, and to outline a happier destiny in store for him. Hence they can elevate human life, which they express under many forms according to various times and places.[2]

The Council thus recognized not only the importance of literary and artistic creativity for the inculturation of the truth of the human person but also a remarkable historical phenomenon of our times: in an epoch that has witnessed widespread social fragmentation and the ongoing secularization of culture, with an attendant decline of the institutional authority of the Church, writers and artists have become more important than ever in their capacity to fathom and express the human yearning for transcendence. No less imperative is the academic study of art and literature from a Catholic perspective that seeks to honor and explicate the stirrings of the human spirit at the intersection of faith and culture.

Among the various disciplines that comprise the field of Catholic Studies, the critical appreciation of literature and the fine arts assumes a place of prominence, and it does so for a number of reasons. First, Catholic Studies as an academic discipline has grown out of the soil fertilized by the Catholic intellectual revival of the last century in Britain, America, and France. This broad-based renaissance while touching every aspect of Catholic and modern culture was pervasively literary in character, counting among its progenitors and followers a great many poets, novelists, playwrights, not a few artists, and an extraordinarily large number of converts.[3] (Indeed, it is scarcely an exaggeration to say that in the twentieth century literature and art served as an unparalleled school for conversions.) In addition to providing a context and both subjects and objects of inquiry for Catholic Studies, this literary resurgence also stimulated systematic reflection on aesthetic theory from a Catholic perspective—witness Jacques Maritain and Etienne Gilson's philosophy of art—not to mention the development of a distinctive style of literary criticism informed by Catholic principles—illustrated in the work of William F. Lynch, Walter J. Ong, and, among contemporary literary scholars, Denis Donogue.[4]

Quite aside from the critical study of Catholic writers and artists or literature and art addressed to specifically Catholic concerns, this scholarly work has induced a deeper appreciation of the ways in which non-Catholic, even nonreligious artifacts of the creative imagination can plumb the depths of human truth and answer to the Catholic impulse to wrestle with the human condition in its totality. As John Paul II puts the matter in his *Letter to Artists*,

> Even beyond its typically religious expressions, true art has a close affinity with the world of faith, so that, even in situations where culture and the Church are far apart, art remains a kind of bridge to religious experience. In so far as it seeks the beautiful, fruit of an imagination which rises above the everyday, art is by its nature a kind of appeal to the mystery. Even when they explore the darkest depths of the soul or the most unsettling aspects of evil, artists give voice in a way to the universal desire for redemption.[5]

This function of the arts in building "a kind of bridge to religious experience" may account for the capacity of literature and art, in our times, to mark a path for conversion, but it also bespeaks the way in which artistic and literary creation, in the most elementary sense, represents an act of faith and figures forth a bid for transcendence. As a virtue and habit of the practical intellect, artistic creativity entails the triumph of the imagination over oblivion in fashioning human artifacts that endure beyond the ravages of time, constituting unified wholes composed from the broken, scattered matter of human thought and feeling. Compassing the aspirations of the human spirit and leaping out from the specificities of time and place, literary and artistic experience gives voice to images and shape to actions and searches the interpenetration of the definite and the infinite, the temporal and the eternal, the universal and the particular. However historically conditioned and culturally grounded they may be, great works of human creativity in all ages invariably point beyond themselves to hint at what Alexander Pope called "a grace beyond the reach of art."

There are also other, more practical reasons that indicate the importance of literary and artistic criticism in the conspectus of Catholic Studies. Among these, the interdisciplinary nature of the academic analysis of art and literature provides a model for the integration of diverse subject matter and approaches characteristic of Catholic Studies. In the face of academic specialization, literary critics and art scholars have always sought to mediate and integrate the work of a liberal arts education. The study of art and literature, where it has not devolved into arid formalism or given way to ideological reductionism, involves an openness to the insights of history, philosophy, psychology, politics, economics, and theology— indeed, the full scope of human learning. Just as no single critical approach or methodology delimits a Catholic perspective on human creativity, so too Catholic Studies as a field takes much of its vitality from its ability to draw from and orchestrate a multiplicity of disciplines, methods, and critical techniques.

The essays in this section illustrate the diversity of approaches that can be brought to bear upon the study of art and literature as occasioned by the many angles of vision refracted through the prism of Catholic understanding. Ranging in subject matter from sculpture to film, including drama and fiction, from medieval Spain to twentieth-century Canada, these essays canvas the religious resonance of works by Jane Austen, William Shakespeare, J. R. R. Tolkein, Flannery O'Connor, John Updike, Denys Arcand, the statuary of Latin American *santeros* over the course of several centuries, and the sacred poetry of Father Adrien Emmanuel Rouquette who wrote in French in nineteenth-century Louisiana.

Father Daniel Callam substantiates Alisdair McIntyre's suggestion that Jane Austen is the last great exemplar of the classical tradition of moral reasoning. Yet Callam moves beyond McIntyre in arguing that Austen's anthropology of free and responsible agency derives not so much from a generalized Christian humanism but more particularly from the Catholic liturgical and devotional inheritance Austen imbibed second-hand as mediated in the Anglican Book of Common Prayer. Patrick Kelly explores another post-Reformation English writer shaped by vestigial Catholicism, offering a metadramatic reading of the problematic depiction of the Duke in Shakespeare's "problem play," *Measure for Measure*. According to Kelly, the character of the Duke functions in the drama as a kind of artistic secularization of Divine Providence to become a figure for "the providential dramatist," a reflexive figure of Shakespeare's rich theological and artistic imagination. The imaginative rendering of theological categories is also the concern of Kerry MacArthur's allegorical interpretation of the virtues of Faith, Hope, and Charity in *The Lord of the Rings*. MacArthur offers the compact outline of what augurs to be a more comprehensive, synoptic reading of Tolkein's work, one that provides compelling demonstration of the undoubted though elusive substance of Tolkein's deeply Catholic vision. In the next essay, Patrick Harkins, from a very different perspective, illustrates the ability of narrative to provoke and complicate religious reflection with concise readings of O'Connor's "The River," Updike's "The Christian Roommates," and Arcand's film *Jesus of Montreal*. Kimberly Habegger analyzes the complex, oddly versatile, and strangely durable iconography of Saint James the apostle, pilgrim, and warrior, as images of the saint were reconceived from Spain to the New World and across a number of cultural, political, and racial permutations. Continuing the theme of Catholic encounters with the New World, the essay by Chris Michaelides explores the fascinating sacred poetry of Father Rouqette, the nineteenth-century missionary priest who lived among the Choctaws of Louisiana. Father Rouquette's poem *L'Arbres des Chactas* (*The Tree of the Choctaws*), argues Michaelides, recuperates the sacred character of the landscape against encroaching modernization and finds in the great oak tree a rich symbol combining indigenous spirituality with the Catholic iconography of the ladder of heaven and the wood of the cross.

This last essay highlights something that all of the essays share in common, not only a keen appreciation of the diverse cultural expressions of Catholic tradition but also a sense of the endless adaptability and perennial relevance of Catholicism to the human imagination. Accordingly, the essays in this section also testify that we continue to find in the artistic mingling of faith and culture some taste of what Gerard Manley Hopkins called in his last poem, "The fine delight that fathers thought," that experience of aesthetic epiphany the poet elsewhere characterized as "the meaning motion" that "fans fresh our wits with wonder."[6]

Notes

1. See John Henry Newman, *The Idea of a University*, ed. Frank M. Turner (New Haven: Yale University Press, 1996), particularly Part II, Lecture 1, "Christianity and Letters"; see also *Letter of His Holiness Pope John Paul II to Artists*, April 4, 1999, available at http://www.cin.org/jp2/jp2artist.html.

2. *Gaudium et Spes*, Chp. II, Section 3, Para. 62, in *Vatican II: The Conciliar and Post Conciliar Documents*, ed. Austin Flannery, O.P. (Northport, NY: Costello Publishing, 1988), 967.

3. On the British experience of the line of literary converts stemming in part from the influence of G. K. Chesterton, see Joseph Pearce, *Literary Converts: Spiritual Inspiration in an Age of Unbelief* (San Francisco: Ignatius Press, 2000); and on the American experience, see Paul Elie's interwoven biographical study of Flannery O'Connor, Thomas Merton, Dorothy Day, and Walker Percy, *The Life You Save May Be Your Own: An American Pilgrimage* (New York: Farrar, Straus and Giroux, 2003).

4. See Jacques Maritain, *Creative Intuition in Art and Poetry* (New York: Meridian Books, 1955) and *Art and Scholasticism and The Frontiers of Poetry*, trans. Joseph W. Evans (Notre Dame, Indiana: University of Notre Dame Press, 1962); Etienne Gilson, *The Arts of the Beautiful* (New York: Scribners, 1965); William F. Lynch, S.J., *Christ and Apollo: The Dimensions of the Literary Imagination* (New York: Sheed and Ward, 1960); Walter J. Ong, S.J., *The Presence of the Word: Some Prolegomena for Cultural and Religious History* (New Haven: Yale University Press, 1967); and Denis Donogue, *Adam's Curse: Reflections on Religion and Literature* (Notre Dame, Indiana: University of Notre Dame Press, 2001).

5. *Letter of His Holiness Pope John Paul II to Artists*.

6. From "To R. B.," l. 1, and "Henry Purcell," l. 14, in *Poems and Prose of Gerard Manley Hopkins*, ed. W. H. Gardner (London: Penguin, 1953), 41 and 68.

Chapter 1

Jane Austen's Catholic Sensibility

Father Daniel Callam, CSB

A t the close of the eighteenth century, the Church of England was everything that an established Church should be: it provided a religious culture, inspired intellectual life, and formed the national ethos. As daughter
of the vicar of the village of Steventon in Hampshire, Jane Austen was immersed in
the rituals and liturgies of her national religion, absorbing its spirit with the very air
she breathed. An examination of the principles that govern the characters in her
novels, however, reveals a surprisingly Catholic approach to morality. She would
have been disquieted by this statement since she gloried in England's being thoroughly Protestant; in 1813 she wrote to her brother Francis: "I have a great respect
for former Sweden. So zealous as it was for Protestantism!"[1] There is obviously no
direct dependence on Catholic sources in her books, but there is an indirect one in
Anglicanism's Book of Common Prayer. Its influence on the church-going society
was immense. Sunday worship—matins and evensong were regularly attended—
would have etched its noble phrases on the memories of its participants, with daily
services and sacramental observance deepening the impression on the susceptible
mind. Jane Austen would have been early and continually under its influence. In
Mansfield Park, through the doubtful medium of Henry Crawford, she reveals her
close acquaintance with Anglican worship and, it may be, an item of religious

autobiography: "'Our liturgy,' observed Crawford, 'has beauties, which not even a careless, slovenly style of reading can destroy; but it has also redundancies and repetitions, which require good reading not to be felt. For myself, at least, I must confess being not always so attentive as I ought to be.'"[2]

That the Book of Common Prayer is Catholic in origin and contents is undeniable and well documented.[3] The prayers, the arrangement of the liturgical seasons, the forms of worship, and the very readings from the Bible all draw upon the pre-Reformation Church. Implied in these rites is an anthropology, the most striking feature of which is its view of man as a free and so responsible moral agent, able to fulfill the multiform and manifold obligations that society, honor, and friendship place upon him. This traditional datum of Catholic anthropology is confirmed in the *Catechism of the Catholic Church*:

> Coming to see in the faith their new dignity, Christians are called to lead henceforth a life "worthy of the gospel of Christ" [Phil 1.27]. They are made *capable* of doing so by the grace of Christ and the gifts of his Spirit, which they receive through the sacraments and through prayer.[4]

This view of the human condition contrasts strongly with the Calvinist doctrine of total depravity, which more than *sola fide* or *sola Scriptura* represents the novelty that divides the Reformation from the medieval and patristic Church. The doctrine begins well, with the recognition that the world has a redeemer. Since the redeemer is none other than God himself, the redemption he effected is universal. It follows that the whole of reality stood in need of redemption, both the vast physical universe and the equally vast internal universe of man's soul. Where Calvin and his party departed from traditional Christianity was in their regarding all human activity, including that of baptized Christians, as radically corrupt: "even the good works of Christians are intrinsically evil, though covered and not counted as sins through the imputed merits of Christ."[5] A strong Calvinist strain in Anglicanism is apparent in its authoritative Thirty-nine Articles:

> Original sin . . . is the fault and corruption of the Nature of every man, that naturally is engendered of the offspring of Adam; whereby man is very far gone from original righteousness, and is of his own nature inclined to evil. . . . And this infection of nature doth remain, yea in them that are regenerated.[6]

By honoring both the Book of Common Prayer and the Thirty-nine Articles Anglicanism became victim to a sort of religious schizophrenia, which accounts for its tolerance even today of a wide range of views in theology and morality. The optimism about man in the Book of Common Prayer represents the Catholic end of the spectrum, and the worldview of a Jane Austen would have been formed by her daily contact with the Prayer Book rather than by the Articles which were, literally, academic: until the mid-nineteenth century, undergraduates at Oxford and Cambridge were required to study and publicly to profess them.[7] The Anglican baptismal service, e.g., bespeaks the empowerment of the baptized person to follow Christ to the full: "he will renounce the devil and all his works, and constantly believe God's holy Word, and obediently *keep his commandments*."[8] Again: "WILT thou then obediently keep God's holy will and commandments, and walk in the same all the days of thy life? Answer. I will." The prayer is that the baptized person, "being buried with Christ in his death, may crucify the old man, and *utterly abolish the whole body of sin*." Many parallel instances could be produced, such as the collect for the feast of the Epiphany:

> O Lord, we beseech thee mercifully to receive the prayers of thy people which call upon thee; and *grant that they may both perceive and know what things they ought to do, and also may have grace and power faithfully to fulfil the same*; through Jesus Christ our Lord.[9]

Supremely among the Austen heroines, Elinor Dashwood (*Sense and Sensibility*), Fanny Price (*Mansfield Park*) and Anne Elliot (*Persuasion*) represent the capable moral agent. Elinor, for example,— "My Elinor"[10]—takes it for granted that Edward Farrars will marry her rival, Lucy Steele, because he said he would: "Nothing should prevail on him to give up his engagement. He would stand to it, cost what it might."[11] Elinor's heroic virtue also shows itself in her concealing from her family the torment she underwent in knowing that her beloved Edward was, with affection dead on both sides, still obligated by his engagement to Lucy.[12] Full recognition of Elinor's virtue comes at the end of the novel from her once self-indulgent, now repentant sister Marianne, "I compare [my behavior] with what it ought to have been; I compare it with yours."[13] It is in meeting one's obligations that true nobility is found, as Lady Russell observes in speaking to Anne Elliot of her father's reckless spending: "though a great deal is due to the feelings of the gentleman, and the head of a house, like your father, there is still more due to the character of an honest man." Anne agrees:

> This was the principle on which Anne wanted her father to be proceeding, his friends to be urging him. She considered it as an act of indispensable duty to clear away the claims of creditors, with all the expedition which the most comprehensive retrenchments could secure, and saw no dignity in any thing short of it.[14]

For Jane Austen the virtue that most clearly demonstrates man's power in the moral sphere is constancy. Edmund Bertram, eventually aware of its importance, lauds the behavior of his cousin Fanny to his father, Sir Thomas: "Fanny is the only one who has judged rightly throughout, who has been consistent. . . . You will find Fanny every thing you could wish."[15] The heroism of constancy is apparent in the heartrending dialogue between Anne Elliot and Captain Harville on the relative power of love in men and women. Anne, in refuting the Captain's conventional statement about women's inconstancy, says: "All the privilege I claim for my own sex (it is not a very enviable one, you need not covet it) is that of loving longest, when existence or when hope is gone."[16]

Altruism—what today would be called "social justice"—is another essential element of Christian life. In Jane Austen's world, men were the actors in public life, but women assessed their performance by the stringent moral code by which they themselves were guided in their more limited sphere. In *Pride and Prejudice*, for example, Mr. Darcy's management of the grand estate of Pemberley is described in glowing terms by his housekeeper: "'He is the best landlord, and the best master,' said she, 'that ever lived. . . . There is not one of his tenants or servants but what will give him a good name.'" Elizabeth Bennet reflects: "As a brother, a landlord, a master, she considered how many people's happiness were in his guardianship!— How much of pleasure or pain it was in his power to bestow!—How much of good or evil must be done by him!" She is not being altogether facetious, therefore, when she later tells her sister Jane that her affection for Mr. Darcy dated "from my first seeing his beautiful grounds at Pemberley."[17] The sincerity of Henry Crawford's courtship of Fanny Price is exhibited in his giving attention to Everingham, his estate in Norfolk, and if such seriousness had persisted he could well have won Fanny as his bride.[18] *Emma*'s Mr. Knightley is the paradigm of an upright landed gentry, and it is not the dependents of Donwell Abbey alone that benefit from his devotion to the common good. The penurious Miss and Mrs. Bates receive apples and eggs from the Abbey when he has none left for himself. That even Emma Woodhouse, self-centered and opinionated as she was, could be an effective minister to the needy assures the reader that her principles are sound and that, "faultless in spite of all her faults," she is hastening towards that perfect felicity which is the due of the heroine of a romantic comedy:

> Emma was very compassionate; and the distresses of the poor were as sure of relief from her personal attention and kindness, her counsel and her patience, as from her purse. She understood their ways, could allow for their ignorance and their temptations, had no romantic expectation of extraordinary virtue from those, for whom education had done so little; entered into their troubles with ready sympathy, and always gave her assistance with as much intelligence as good-will.[19]

And when the Elliot family goes to Bath, it is Anne, of course, who visits almost every house in the parish "as a sort of leave-take; I was told that they wished it."[20] The praise of practical charity and the condemnation of its neglect throughout the novels illustrate the importance for Jane Austen of a social responsibility and her conviction that such responsibilities could be met. Consequently, their neglect is reprehensible, even in the case of the genial and amusing Mr. Bennet whose carelessness about money left him without sufficient means "of prevailing on one of the most worthless young men in Great Britain to be [his daughter Lydia's] husband."[21]

No less than Catholicism—or Jane Austen—the Book of Common Prayer requires Christians empowered by the Holy Spirit to meet their obligations towards their dependents or those in need. Consider, for example, the prayer in time of dearth and famine: "Increase the fruits of the earth by thy heavenly benediction; and grant that we, receiving thy bountiful liberality, may use the same to thy glory, *the relief of those that are needy*, and our own comfort"; or that for the sovereign: " preserve thy people *committed to his charge*, in wealth, peace, and godliness." Or the exhortation before Communion:

> And if ye shall perceive your offences to be such as are not only against God, but also against your neighbours; then ye shall reconcile yourselves unto them; being ready *to make restitution and satisfaction*, according to the uttermost of your powers, for all injuries and wrongs done by you to any other; and being likewise ready to forgive others that have offended you, as ye would have forgiveness of your offences at God's hand.

A consequence of empowerment by grace is, therefore, the actual achievement of virtue and even the attainment of perfect righteousness. This expectation accounts for Catholicism's honoring the saints and, supremely, the Blessed Virgin Mary: they demonstrate validity of the Catholic system. But so in its way does the Book of Common Prayer. The saints have maintained a place in its liturgical calendar whence they summon the worshipper to perfection: "Mortify and kill all vices in us, and so strengthen us by thy grace, that by the *innocency of our lives, and constancy of our faith* even unto death, we may glorify thy holy Name" (collect for the feast of the Holy Innocents). A similar call to holiness is found in the third collect for grace— "grant that this day we fall into *no sin*, neither run into any kind of danger; but that all our doings may be ordered by thy governance, *to do always what is righteous* in thy sight"—and that for the first Sunday after Trinity— "Grant us the help of thy grace, that in keeping of thy commandments *we may please thee*, both in will and deed." A strongly Catholic note is sounded in the requirement that sinlessness be realized at reception of holy communion: "that ye may come *holy and clean* to such a heavenly Feast, in the marriage-garment required by God in holy Scripture, and be received as *worthy partakers* of that holy Table."[22]

Elinor Dashwood, Fanny Price, and Anne Elliot, as we have seen, represent the attainment of this Christian ideal, with Fanny—in that she strikes many readers as a first-class prig—its most striking instance:

> Fanny is charmless; she has only the virtues, the genuine virtues, to protect her, and when she disobeys her guardian, Sir Thomas Bertram, and refuses marriage to Henry Crawford it can only be because of what constancy requires. In so refusing she places the danger of losing her soul before the reward of gaining what for her would be a whole world.[23]

An echo of the Gospel is indeed heard in Jane Austen's depiction of Fanny: "Mrs. Norris fetched breath and went on. . . . 'Remember, wherever you are, you must be the lowest and last.' . . . Her niece thought it perfectly reasonable. She rated her own claims to comfort as low even as Mrs. Norris could."[24] The tolerance of misunderstanding and contempt by Fanny as also by Anne Elliot is almost Franciscan in its intensity. "Anne, with an elegance of mind and sweetness of character, which must have placed her high with any people of real understanding, was nobody with either father or sister: her word had no weight; her convenience was always to give way,—she was only Anne."[25] And yet Anne's worth is instinctively recognized by every right-minded character and supremely, if belatedly, by Frederick Wentworth: "Too good, too excellent creature!"[26]

These creatures are excellent because their judgments are in conformity with an objective moral standard, as Marianne acknowledges in comparing her behavior to Elinor's— "to what it should have been." The same point is made in *Pride and Prejudice*:

> "The wisest and the best of men, nay, the wisest and best of their actions, may be rendered ridiculous by a person whose first object in life is a joke."
> "Certainly," replied Elizabeth— "there are such people, but I hope I am not one of *them*. I hope I never ridicule what is wise or good. Follies and nonsense, whims, and inconsistencies *do* divert me, I own, and I laugh at them whenever I can."[27]

Throughout the novels the author measures the behavior of her characters with the scale of objective morality; frequently they are found wanting. A tragic-comic instance occurs at the beginning of *Sense and Sensibility* in the genteelly savage dialogue between John Dashwood and his wife, during which she convinces him that his dying father meant nothing when he asked his son to provide for his stepmother and his three half-sisters. There is scarcely a page of Jane Austen where the demands of truth and justice, of responsibility and charity are not affirmed either by praise when they are present or by ridicule when they are not. Such views are hardly limited to Catholicism. What is characteristically Catholic, however, is the conviction that moral excellence is an attainable goal and so an essential element of Christian life. In Jane Austen's Anglicanism, the general confession exhibits an awareness of sin along with a call to perfection:

> We have offended against thy holy laws. We have left undone those things which we ought to have done; And we have done those things which we ought not to have done. . . . Grant . . . that we may hereafter *live a godly, righteous, and sober life*.[28]

Thus, when an Austen heroine errs she must repent in order to overcome the effects of her wrongdoing and so be able successfully to discharge the obligations which she is about to assume. In a well-known essay[29] C. S. Lewis discusses the religious qualities of what could well be called the conversions of Marianne Dashwood, Elizabeth Bennet, and Emma Woodhouse. Elizabeth hardly recognizes herself after coming to grips with Mr. Darcy's letter: "How despicably have I acted!" she cried. "I, who have prided myself on my discernment."[30] Emma's repentance at the end of a farcical series of misunderstandings reaches the heroic level of her voluntarily calling on the excruciatingly boring Miss Bates. Marianne, too, with "time for atonement to my God"[31] after her illness, adopts a scheme of serious reading as ambitious as that of the young Emma, and somewhat more likely of realization.

Repentance is of course as important for Protestants as for Catholics. The Calvinist tradition, however, generally sees individual sins as the inevitable manifestations of a nature radically corrupt. Repentance is therefore a continuous characteristic of the believer's religious experience. The highly respected evangelical theologian Charles Ryrie provides a good account of this view:

> Total depravity . . . mean[s] that the corruption of sin extends to all men and to all parts of all men. . . . Walking in the light illumines areas of darkness which are immediately confessed; walking in that increased light illumines further areas of darkness, and so on and on through the Christian life.[32]

But for Catholics, true repentance combined with confession and expiatory penance removes all sin, restoring the person to his baptismal innocence; the intention of not sinning again is an essential part of the sacrament of reconciliation. Jane Austen's heroines are in this regard essentially Catholic, and her source for this shade of Catholicism was the Book of Common Prayer. In the confession, for example, one reads: "But thou, O Lord, have mercy upon us, miserable offenders. Spare thou them, O God, who confess their faults. *Restore* thou those who are penitent."[33] Similar is the exhortation before Communion: "Have mercy upon us. . ... Forgive us all that is past; and grant that we may ever hereafter *serve and please thee in newness of life*."

In Catholicism, one grows towards perfection by practicing virtue. The Aristotelian scheme of the moral life, baptized by Saint Thomas Aquinas, describes upright behavior as a skill that one gradually acquires by practice under the guidance of a wise mentor. Bad habits, barring a miracle of grace, will eventually corrupt the individual and when long indulged in are well nigh incorrigible. To this conviction Jane Austen frequently returns. John Willoughby's villainy, for example, is the fruit of

> the irreparable injury which too early an independence and its consequent habits of idleness, dissipation, and luxury had made in the mind, the character, the happiness, of a man who, to every advantage of person and talents, united a disposition naturally open and honest, and a feeling, affectionate temper.[34]

Not unexpectedly, the most profound examination of the effect of a misspent or neglected youth comes in *Mansfield Park*. Mary Crawford, for example, with every social grace has an atrophied moral sense: "Her's [*sic*] are faults of principle, Fanny, of blunted delicacy and a corrupted, vitiated mind."[35] Sir Thomas himself, in reflecting almost with despair on the failures of his children, recognizes his own negligence:

> Something had been wanting *within*, or time would have worn away much of the effect [of Mrs. Norris's influence]. He feared that principle, active principle, had been wanting, that they had never been properly taught to govern their inclination and tempers, by that sense of duty which can alone suffice. They had been instructed theoretically in their religion, but never required to bring it into daily

practice. To be distinguished for elegance and accomplishments—that authorized object of their youth—could have had no useful influence that way, no moral effect on the mind. He had meant them to be good, but his cares had been directed to the understanding and manners, not the disposition; and of the necessity of self-denial and humility, he feared they had never heard from any lips that could profit them.[36]

Appropriately, the exhortation after the baptism of infants proved the Anglican version of this Catholic doctrine.

> FORASMUCH as this Child hath promised by you his sureties to renounce the devil and all his works, to believe in God, and to serve him: ye must remember, that it is your parts and duties to see that this Infant be taught, so soon as he shall be able to learn, what a solemn vow, promise, and profession, he hath here made by you . . . that this Child may *be virtuously brought up to lead a godly and a Christian life*; remembering always, that Baptism doth represent unto us our profession; which is, to follow the example of our Saviour Christ, and to be made like unto him; that, as he died, and rose again for us, so should we, who are baptized, *die from sin, and rise again unto righteousness*; continually mortifying all our evil and corrupt affections and daily proceeding in *all virtue and godliness of living.*[37]

The Anglicanism that formed the society of Jane Austen's time did not survive the nineteenth century. Paradoxically, its disappearance owed as much to the Oxford Movement as to the corrosive effects of liberalism. While the former certainly honored the Catholicism of the Book of Common Prayer, it did so in a manner that robbed Anglo-Catholics of their influence on either public or ecclesiastical life. Furthermore, after the conversion of John Henry Newman to Catholicism the Movement lost its theological underpinnings, swirling off into the aesthetics of worship.[38] Anglican theologians thereafter tended to be liberal, even those professing Anglo-Catholicism. Given the substitution of liberalism for Catholic theology, it is apparent why moral relativism has overtaken Anglicanism in, e.g., its abandonment of the traditional understanding of family life. This article, then, is a plea for Anglicans to reinstate the Book of Common Prayer (1662 version) as their exclusive liturgical text and to interpret it in the light of their greatest theologian: Jane Austen. This designation is not altogether facetious: the Pope's recognition of Saint Thérèse of Lisieux as a Doctor of the Church invites some comparable action on the part of the Archbishop of Canterbury. There could be no better way to further effective ecumenism than by so honoring a Protestant thinker whose moral system is accepted and admired by Catholics and, indeed, by any right-minded person.

Notes

1. *Jane Austen, Letters 1796-1817*, edited by R.W. Chapman, *The World's Classics* 549 (London: Oxford University Press, 1955), 143. In her burlesque *History of England by a partial prejudiced and ignorant historian*, however, she praised the Catholic Mary, Queen of Scots, for "that steadfastness in the Catholic Religion which reflected on her so much credit."

2. *Mansfield Park*, ch. 34.

3. John Henry Newman, *Tract 90*: "our Prayer Book is acknowledged on all hands to be of Catholic origin"; cf. Massey Hamilton Shepherd, *The Oxford American Prayer Book Commentary* (New York: Oxford University Press, 1950).

4. *Catechism of the Catholic Church* (New York: Doubleday, 1994), § 1692 (Emphasis added). The Church highlights the superiority of man's condition in the new covenant: "The Symbol of the faith confesses the greatness of God's gifts to man in his work of creation, and *even more* in redemption and sanctification. What faith confesses, the sacraments communicate: by the sacraments of rebirth, Christians have become 'children of God' [Jn 1.12; 1 Jn 3.1], 'partakers of the divine nature' [2 Pet 1.4]." *Catechism of the Catholic Church*, § 1692.

5. *The Oxford Dictionary of the Christian Church*, 2nd ed., *s.v.* "Calvinism."

6. Article IX.

7. The plot of Newman's novel *Loss and Gain* pivots around the hero's inability to swear to, or even to comprehend, the Thirty-nine Articles. *Tract 90*, an unsuccessful attempt to overcome this theological schizophrenia, tried to legitimize a Catholic interpretation of the Articles.

8. Quotations from the Book of Common Prayer come from the 1662 version which was in use in Jane Austen's lifetime. It can be found at www.eskimo.com/~lhowell/bcp1662. All emphases in quotations from the Book of Common Prayer are added.

9. Cf. the preparation for Holy Communion: "Judge therefore yourselves, brethren, that ye be not judge of the Lord; repent you truly for your sins past; have a lively and stedfast faith in Christ our Saviour; amend your lives, and be in *perfect charity with all men*; so shall ye be meet partakers of those holy mysteries."

10. "Letter 70," 114.

11. *Sense and Sensibility*, ch. 37.

12. A similar situation occurs in *Persuasion* when Captain Wentworth finds himself expected and so bound to marry Louisa Musgrove at the moment his affection for Anne Elliot has been renewed.

13. *Sense and Sensibility*, ch. 46.

14. *Persuasion*, ch. 2.

15. *Mansfield Park*, ch. 20. Cf. Alasdair MacIntyre, *After Virtue: A Study in Moral Theory*, 2nd ed. (Notre Dame [IN]: University of Notre Dame Press, 1984), 222-26.

16. *Persuasion*, ch. 23.

17. *Pride and Prejudice*, ch. 43, 59.

18. *Mansfield Park*, ch. 41, 48.

19. *Emma*, ch. 50, 10.

20. *Persuasion*, ch. 5.

21. *Pride and Prejudice*, ch. 50; cf. Darcy's comment in his letter to Elizabeth: "a total want of propriety . . . occasionally even by your father"; *Pride and Prejudice*, ch. 35.

22. Cf. the Christmas preface: "Jesus Christ thine only Son to be born as at this time for us; who, by the operation of the Holy Ghost, was made very man of the substance of the Virgin Mary his mother; and that without spot of sin, to make us *clean from all sin*. . . ."

23. MacIntyre, *After Virtue*, 225. Kinsley Amis speaks for many critics in finding Fanny worse than a prig: "[*Mansfield Park*] is an immoral book. . . . Her judgement and moral sense were corrupted, and *Mansfield Park* is the witness of that corruption." *What Became of Jane Austen? and Other Questions* (London: Cape, 1970), 16-17.

24. *Mansfield Park*, ch. 23; cf. Matt 23.11: "He who is greatest among you shall be your servant; whoever exalts himself will be humbled, and whoever humbles himself will be exalted."

25. *Persuasion*, ch. 1. In Anne Elliot, Jane Austen succeeds in that most difficult of all literary endeavors: making virtue attractive. Another instance, of current interest, would be J. R. R. Tolkien's *Lord of the Rings*. That Fanny Price is *not* attractive, even to as perceptive a critic as C. S. Lewis (v. note 29), does not represent a failure on the part of Jane Austen, but another dimension of her art.

26. *Persuasion*, ch. 23.

27. *Pride and Prejudice*, ch. 11.

28. Cf. the Lenten form of morning prayers: ". . . at this time (in the presence of you all) should be read the general sentences of God's cursings against impenitent sinners, gathered out of the seven and twentieth Chapter of Deuteronomy, and other places of Scripture; and that being admonished of the great indignation of God against sinners, ye may the rather be moved to earnest and true repentance; and may walk more warily in these dangerous days; *fleeing from such vices* for which ye affirm with your own mouths the curse of God to be due."

29. C. S. Lewis, "A Note on Jane Austen," *Selected Literary Essays*, edited by Walter Hooper (Cambridge: Cambridge University Press, 1969), 176-79.

30. *Pride and Prejud*ice, ch.36.

31. *Sense and Sensibility*, ch. 46.

32. Charles Ryrie, *A Survey of Bible Doctrine* (Chicago: Moody Press, 1972), 111, 113.

33. Cf. the prayer for fair weather: "although we for our iniquities have worthily deserved a plague of rain and waters, yet upon our *true repentance* thou wilt send us such weather, as that we may receive the fruits of the earth in due season; and learn both by thy punishment to *amend our lives,* and for thy clemency to give thee praise and glory; through Jesus Christ our Lord. Amen."

34. *Sense and Sensibility*, ch. 44.

35. *Mansfield Park*, ch. 47. Cf. ch. 48: "Henry Crawford, ruined by early independence and bad domestic example, indulged in the freaks of a cold-blooded vanity a little too long."

36. *Mansfield Park*, ch. 48.

37. One could multiply such instances as in the collect for the first Sunday of Lent: "O Lord, who for our sake didst fast forty days and forty nights; Give us grace to use such abstinence, that, our flesh being subdued to the Spirit, we may ever obey thy godly motions *in righteousness, and true holiness*, to thy honour and glory. . . ." etc.

38. Cf. Christopher Dawson, *The Spirit of the Oxford Movement* (London: Sheed and Ward, 1934).

Chapter 2

Shakespeare's *Measure for Measure* and the Art of Christian Mercy

Patrick Kelly

E very reader or spectator of William Shakespeare's *Measure for Measure* must be struck by how the Duke of Vienna controls the plot of the play. Indeed, given how cryptic the Duke's statements of intention are, his actions are the primary evidence of his motives. Since the purpose of this article is to consider the Duke's role in light of the play's Christian themes, I would like to begin by presenting a brief summary of the baffling plot. Let us recall that in the opening scene, the Duke of Vienna chooses Angelo, an untried young man, to replace him for an unspecified time. Unknown to Angelo, however, the Duke remains in Vienna disguised as a monk in order to observe how his subjects, including Angelo, comport themselves in his absence. Reveling in his new power, Angelo applies the full rigors of the law to Claudio and Juliet, a young couple who are arrested for having sexual relations before marriage. In desperation Claudio sends for help to his sister, Isabella, who is about to enter a cloistered order of nuns, the Poor Clares. When Isabella comes to plead with Angelo for her brother's life, the deputy finds himself attracted to her, and tempts her with a foul bribe: her brother's life in exchange for her own chastity. Isabella vehemently rejects the bribe, and goes to her brother in prison to tell him of Angelo's treachery. Frightened by the prospect of death, Claudio begs his sister to accept the offer. Yet Isabella, revolted by both Angelo's impure designs and her brother's willingness to see her debased in order to save his own skin, remains unmoved.

Meanwhile the Duke, now attired as a monk, gives spiritual counsel to both Claudio and Juliet in the prison. There he also observes, unseen, the exchange between Claudio and Isabella. Largely an observer in the first half of the play, the Duke becomes in the second half the puppeteer who manages both the plot and the characters. As almost all critics have noted, the atmosphere of tragedy gives way to comedy when the Duke comes out of the shadows to intervene in the quarrel between brother and sister. He begins by telling Isabella of a woman named Mariana—a person totally unheard of in the play until this point—who was affianced to Angelo, but who was jilted by him when he discovered that her dowry had been lost.

The Duke then introduces the notorious bedtrick plot: Isabella is to pretend to agree to go to bed with Angelo; then, unknown to Angelo, Mariana is to take Isabella's place in the dark. And this is exactly what happens! The Duke hopes that Angelo will thus repent and save Claudio, who ironically stands condemned by Angelo for the very sin, which Angelo has just committed. This plan, however, misfires, when Angelo insists that the execution take place as planned. The Duke, who now has to scramble to save Claudio's life, comes up with the ruse of sending to Angelo as evidence of Claudio's death the head of a recently executed pirate. As well, he lies to Isabella by telling her that her brother has been executed. The Duke-Friar at last now chooses to reveal himself, although he does so with perplexing indirection.

First of all, with theatrical éclat, he returns to Vienna in his proper person as the Duke and greets Angelo in the public square. In accordance with the Duke's coaching, both Mariana and Isabella condemn Angelo at this time. When Angelo still does not confess his wrongdoing, the Duke exits and returns, disguised once more as the Friar, to denounce the corruption that is rife in Vienna. Then, when his monk's cowl is at last removed, the Duke immediately demands that Angelo be married to Mariana and, in spite of the pleas of both Mariana and Isabella, orders his execution. But let us not despair, for in the sixty lines or so that remain in the play the Duke resolves all complications into a happy ending. As in any comedy worth its salt, marriage and a happy society are the images that we are left with.

Even this bare bones of a plot summary may suggest just how important the Duke's role is. Except for Prospero in *The Tempest*, no character in Shakespeare is so clearly the stage manager of events. In the first systematic interpretation of the play—G. W. Knight's "*Measure for Measure* and the Gospels"[1]—the critic suggested that the Duke represented Providence. Knight had a large group of imitators, all of who viewed the Duke as the allegorical representative of either Providence or Christ himself. This interpretation of the play dominated the critical literature for at least two decades. Much of the criticism since has been an attack on the Christian allegorical approach, and often with good reason. With regard to the Duke, these critics have wondered how we can associate Godhead with a figure who uses deceit constantly, who resorts to the immoral bedtrick plan, and who makes his subjects suffer needlessly. The corrective to the Christian reading, however, has been unfortunately reductive. Most modern critics see the Duke as, at best, a comic image of Providence, at worst, a machiavellian figure who delights in psychological experiments.[2] Indeed, the once quasi-divine Duke of the Christian allegorists has shriveled into a much less inspiring figure. Consequently, he is little more than, to quote a slander used against him by Lucio, one of his own low-life subjects, "the old fantastical duke of dark corners" (4.3.156-57).[3]

Although the Christian allegorists do ignore the ambiguities in the Duke's role, the absence for the most part in recent commentary of the central place that the earlier critics gave to the play's Christian ideas is a real weakness. In no play of Shakespeare's are these ideas more directly presented than in *Measure for Measure*. And the central Christian mystery is that of Christ's wondrous mercy, which is most eloquently articulated when Isabella urges Angelo in his dealings with her brother to follow Christ's example:

> Why, all the souls that were were forfeit once,
> And He that might the vantage best have took
> Found out the remedy. How would you be
> If He, which is the top of judgment, should
> But judge you as you are? O, think on that,
> And mercy then will breathe within your lips,
> Like man new made. (2.2.73-79)

The Christian allegorists also rightly assumed that *Measure for Measure* must be understood on more than the literal level. In a play so full of cruxes, this strikes me as important. I would like to suggest an interpretation which is essentially a symbolic application of the Christian ideas in the play. The Duke stands for the god of the play—that is, for Shakespeare himself—and the Duke's relationship to his subjects mimics that of Shakespeare to his own characters. In this light, we might say that *Measure for Measure* is a play about the making of a play. As well, the Christian themes are central, for Shakespeare finds in Christ's mercy an emblem for the mercy that the dramatist of comedy bestows on his characters.

As far as I know, Francis Fergusson is the only critic to suggest the identification of the Duke with Shakespeare:

> But I think I see why Shakespeare could have wished to make such a character, who would be both inside the play, and so subject to its fictive situation, and also visible *outside* it, controlling and interpreting its course. He wished to show the *making* of the play at the same time as the play itself. So he presents Vienna, not as literal reporting in the manner of modern realism, but as a significant fiction; and so he modestly and as it were playfully confesses his own authorship, for it is clear that the Duke is a figure of Shakespeare himself. It is a problem in the metaphysics or epistemology of poetry, like that which Dante solved in the *Divine Comedy* by speaking both as author and as protagonist; or like that which Pirandello explores in *Six Characters*. (142-43)[4]

Beyond these useful hints, however, Fergusson does not go. In what follows I shall elaborate upon his suggestion by showing how it clarifies the cruxes of the play. My approach is what drama critics usually call metadramatic, for I seek in the play evidence for Shakespeare's view of his own art.[5]

The first crux relates to the Duke's motives in handing over his power to the untested Angelo. When the Duke asks permission from a certain Friar Thomas to take on the disguise of a monk, he tells the friar that he wants Angelo to apply more rigorously the very laws that the Duke himself irresponsibly had failed to apply. Yet if this were his only purpose, the Duke would have surely chosen Escalus, the older and experienced man, as his deputy. The main reason for the Duke's choice of Angelo is to test him, as he tells Friar Thomas:

> Lord Angelo is precise;
> Stands at a guard with envy; scarce confesses
> That his blood flows; or that his appetite
> Is more to bread than stone: hence shall we see
> If power change purpose, what our seemers be (1.3.50-54)

I would like to suggest that the Duke's curiosity as to how Angelo will conduct himself is akin to the dramatist's uncertainty about how the character that he has created will actually behave. At the outset of the play Angelo is merely a potential character. All that is known of him is his confidence in his own moral integrity. Yet Angelo cannot be regarded as truly virtuous since, as the Duke tells him, virtue is realized only in action: "Thyself and thy belongings/Are not thine own so proper as to waste/Thyself upon thy virtues, they on thee" (1.1.29-31). The Duke's testing of Angelo, therefore, parallels a similar exploration of Angelo's character by Shakespeare. Seen in this light, the Duke's experiment with Angelo, usually cited as evidence of his immoral manipulation, is not immoral at all, but metadramatic. The moral attack on the Duke, so common a feature in the psychological studies of his character, becomes irrelevant when we view the Duke's relation to his subjects as symbolic of Shakespeare's relation to his characters.

Although the Duke is largely an observer in the first half of the play, he is by no means a neutral observer. It is here that the Catholic motifs of the play need to be interpreted symbolically. We see the Duke in his disguise as friar visiting the prison and giving spiritual direction to the suffering couple, Juliet and Claudio. Yet the nature of the comfort he gives them is disturbing. More than one critic has remarked on the Duke's callousness in these interviews, for he appears resolved to deprive the young couple of all hope. His warning to Juliet not to be selfish in her penitence, for example, seems excessively rigorous; and his parting words to her would make him seem either deliberately cruel or completely oblivious to her suffering: "Your partner, as I hear, must die to-morrow,/And I am going with instruction to him./Grace go with you, *Benedicite!*" (2.3.37-39). Even more perplexing is the Duke's failure, in counselling Claudio, to balance his catalogue of *contemptus mundi* aphorisms (3.1.5-41) with the instilling of hope in a Christian heaven.[6] The Duke wishes to give Claudio the courage to face death, but his advice has the opposite effect. Claudio's bravado in the face of death—"Let it come on" (3.1.43)—soon gives way to a pagan terror of the horrors of life after death: "Ay, but to die, and go we know not where" (3.1.117-31). The prospect of eternity, which the Duke so conspicuously neglects in his speech, takes on a nightmarish quality for Claudio. But let us suppose that the Duke is the figure of the dramatist. In this light, he deprives Juliet and Claudio of all hope in order to explore whether, denied the consolation of a happy ending (a consolation that it is within his power to provide), they will heroically and independently confront their suffering. One recent commentator has pointed out how the Duke again and again forces ideal expectations upon his imperfect, all-too-human subjects.[7] This is the case, I believe, but the expectations need to be seen as those of the dramatist for his own characters.[8]

With the bedtrick scheme, the Duke becomes an active manipulator of plot and character, just as the dramatist's intervention is characteristic of comedy. The Duke is forced to introduce this plan only when the other characters reach an impasse: Claudio and Angelo want Isabella to sacrifice her chastity, but she adamantly refuses. No other aspect of *Measure for Measure*, not even the happy ending, has provoked more complaints than the Duke's ruse. But the bedtrick should be seen as evidence of what Francis Fergusson calls Shakespeare's "playful confession of authorship." Three objections are usually brought against the Duke's intervention with the bedtrick: that there is a sudden change in tone from tragic to comic; that the Duke's plan is immoral; and that we are bewildered by the introduction of a new player in the drama, Mariana.

The first objection that there is a change in tone derives from the complaint that Shakespeare grafts the happy ending of comedy onto a tragedy, and that the Duke's intrigues impede the free development of the characters. This argument implies that the characters would otherwise and inevitably have assumed noble dimensions through tragic suffering.[9] Yet a tragic situation does not necessarily create tragic characters. Without the Duke's intervention, *Measure for Measure* might very well have ended like that most disturbing of Shakespeare's works, *Troilus and Cressida*, where the characters remain caught in tragic situations that are resolved neither by a catharsis nor by the saving grace of a comic ending. The idea that characters should be left entirely alone to determine their fate goes against the grain of Shakespearean comedy, where the dramatist's intervention often leads his characters to new growth.

One can argue, therefore, that *Measure for Measure*'s change in tone, even its startling abruptness, is exactly right in conveying the dramatist's decision to invoke the conventions of comedy in rescuing otherwise intractable characters. What critics have faulted as meddling by the Duke is in fact Shakespeare's making conspicuous at this point in the play the need to usher in a comic universe, a characteristic feature of which is our awareness of the dramatist's controlling hand. This awareness is most acute at the happy ending, but an author's manipulation of comic characters can also be detected in the various means he uses to keep them in confusion and despair.[10] When Shakespeare intervenes in the person of the Duke, the suffering and bewilderment of the characters no longer result solely from their conflict with each other, but are in large measure caused by him. This is not to suggest, as critics often have done,[11] that the characters are no longer free after the Duke intervenes in their affairs. In his comparison of Prospero and the Duke, Harold S. Wilson perceptively notes that their maneuvers do not prevent others from acting:

> In each play, the action is set going and guided throughout by its duke; yet neither Duke Vincentio nor Prospero controls anyone else's choice; rather, they prepare the conditions in which others choose while taking precautions that no one shall give effect to a choice injurious to others.[12]

The second objection, the vexed question of the morality of the bedtrick plot, can also be resolved metadramatically. Twice, first to Isabella (3.1.256-58) and then to Mariana (4.1.70-74), the Duke argues that his trickery is a means which is justified by the end. Yet his two attempts to gloss over his deceit make it doubly conspicuous. I would suggest that by underlining the Duke's deception, Shakespeare intends to strengthen the parallel between the ruler's hoodwinking of others and the comic dramatist's method of keeping his characters in confusion until the moment of their happy illumination. The charge that the Duke delights in performing moral experiments on his subjects is irrelevant if the Duke is seen as Shakespeare in the process of testing his own characters.

Finally, even the most notorious crux in the play, the Duke's startling introduction of the unheard-of Mariana into the plot,[13] can be defended if the Duke is allowed to stand for the dramatist. Given that Angelo had callously abandoned Mariana, his fiancée, when her dowry was lost, critics have wondered why such a man's virtue, or lack of it, had to be tested at all. But, in a sense, Mariana does not exist until the Duke first mentions her. Such a position is arguable if one grants that, in addition to telling a particular story with a definite chronology, *Measure for Measure* also dramatizes the creation of a play, a process that has its own beginning and end. Within the time frame of the story, Mariana is pining at the moated grange when the play begins. Yet there is another time scheme, one that bears upon the dramatist's relation to his characters. Within this framework the Duke-dramatist, still unsure of what to expect of his characters, falls back upon impromptu devices both to correct the dangerous propensities of these characters and also to ensure the happy ending of comedy. Mariana is suddenly created by the Duke as playwright because a catalyst is needed for the development of the other characters. Near the end of the play, when the Duke has doffed his monk's habit, he casually states that he has "confess'd" Mariana (5.1.527). On the literal level, the statement is tantamount to an admission of blasphemy, for his taking on the disguise of a friar does not give the Duke the powers of ordination. But what if the Catholic practice of confession is viewed in symbolic terms? The Duke sounds the depths of Mariana in a way analogous to how a dramatist explores the inner workings of his character.

Let us return to the Duke's purpose in the bedtrick scheme, for his motive here remains obscure. His goal cannot be merely to save Claudio's life, since he could have done that in an instant simply by casting off his disguise and ordering the arrest of Angelo. The Duke is concerned, rather, to promote Angelo's moral growth through the bedtrick. Abetted by two willing though confused actresses, Isabella and Mariana, the Duke creates a play in which Angelo is allowed to act on his desire for Isabella without harming her. He expects that a chastening lapse on Angelo's part will teach him the universal need for mercy, thereby leading Angelo himself to be merciful to Claudio. The Duke in disguise, then, uses the dramatist's power to lead his characters to moral improvement by means of his craft. Both meanings of "craft" are apposite here, since the Duke's intrigues are founded both on guile and on the theatrical conventions of comedy available to Shakespeare. The dramatist in this case stands back as his character faces a moral challenge, hopeful that Angelo will act docilely according to his plan.

But Angelo does not repent; in fact, he sends a letter that Claudio be executed by a precise time, and that his head be sent as evidence of the event. One would think that now at last the Duke would relinquish disguise and use his power to save Claudio. But he still chooses to work indirectly by craft. First, he suggests to the provost of the jail that they perform what I would dub a "head-trick": instead of Claudio's head, the head of Barnardine, a brutal criminal who is to be executed that afternoon, will be sent instead. A new obstacle appears when Barnardine refuses to take spiritual counsel before his death, for the Duke cannot in good conscience send an unprepared soul to death. Then, in a wonderfully comic moment, the Provost informs the Duke that by good luck a notorious pirate named Ragozine was executed in the prison that morning. A head is available after all, and the Duke joyfully says: "O, tis an accident that heaven provides" (4.3.77). That line may be given a special weight if, as I am suggesting, the Duke is the figure of Shakespeare, the god of the play.

I have argued that the bedtrick plot is like a play-within-the play, with the Duke as both creator and director. This is even truer of the brilliant last scene of *Measure for Measure*.[14] This playlet demonstrates both the comic dramatist's power over his creation and the restrictions within which he must work. Much as he might want a straightforward resolution of conflict, the dramatist cannot simply impose it without the work seeming contrived and the characters wooden. Rather, he must respect, by recreating it in his art, the complex process by which a human being exercises free will, even when the result is arbitrary and even wrongful behaviour. In the Duke's sermons to Claudio and Juliet, we saw represented Shakespeare's own desire that his characters be ennobled through suffering. With the bedtrick, and especially in the last scene, the Duke now creates plays in which the major characters, Isabella and Angelo, are given the freedom to make difficult but virtuous choices. How first Angelo and then Isabella exercise free will in the last scene rewards scrutiny when interpreted metadramatically. The Duke gives each character a chance to achieve greatness through a heroic act of self-sacrifice: he wants to lead Angelo to a public confession and Isabella to the renunciation of the vengeance which is her due. In his capacity as dramatist, the Duke protracts his subjects' difficulties in order that their nobility in overcoming them might be the greater. But Angelo fails to meet this challenge as obviously as Isabella heroically succeeds.

With Isabella, the Duke's use of artifice to improve a character morally is vindicated. Tricked into believing that Angelo had executed her brother, Isabella received earlier from the Duke the promise of "revenges to your heart" (4.3.l35). She agrees to take part in the Duke's final play on the assumption that this promise will be kept. And indeed the Duke, maintaining the fiction of Claudio's death, seems almost to push her to demand revenge against the recently married Angelo. Thus he says to her:

> The very mercy of the law cries out
> Most audible, even from his proper tongue,
> "An Angelo for Claudio, death for death!" (5.1.407-09)

Although the Duke argues that "death for death" is beyond any doubt the penalty that Angelo deserves for ordering Claudio's death, he first asks Isabella to forgive Angelo's lecherous designs "for Mariana's sake" (5.1.403). Perhaps he is hinting to her that her pardon might include, for Mariana's sake, the greater crime: the murder of her brother. Remember how Isabella has been coached by the Duke to accuse Angelo of having violated her. (This of course has not happened, for the "trick" in the bedtrick was that Mariana took Isabella's place in Angelo's bed.) I would suggest that Isabella's playing the role of the betrayed maiden enkindles in her a genuine sympathy for the rejected Mariana. Remarkably, Isabella rejects the notion of "death for death" and seeks forgiveness for Angelo instead. When Mariana entreats Isabella to "take my part" (5.1.430), Isabella is able to respond sympathetically because, as an actress in the Duke's play, she has already taken the part of a woman betrayed by Angelo and learned something from it. Isabella's pleading for Angelo's life is the moral miracle of the play,[15] a miracle that the Duke has made possible by means of his craft, once again in both senses of the word. It is worth noting that in one of the play's most cryptic passages,[16] the Duke justifies his misleading of Isabella in religious terms:

> But I will keep her ignorant of her good,
> To make her heavenly comforts of despair,
> When it is least expected. (4.3.109-11)

The Duke's keeping his subjects in despair until almost the very end of the play parallels the work of the god in the play's universe, the comic dramatist who keeps his characters in confusion and even despair until the last possible moment, when all difficulties are resolved in the happy ending.

There remain two final cruxes in *Measure for Measure*, both of which relate to the artificiality of the happy ending. Consider first the Noah's Ark of couples that we have at the end of the play. Not surprisingly Claudio and Juliet are to be married, as well as Angelo and Mariana, but the Duke also orders the amoral Lucio to marry Kate Keepdown, the prostitute that he has got with child. Most amazing of all, however, the Duke proposes to Isabella. Except for the Claudio-Juliet union, the various marriages which occur at the end of the play elicit the complaint that these mates give no proof of loving each other. We may recall that the Duke had boasted earlier that he was safe against "the dribbling dart of love" (1.3.2). It is true that the marriages at the end of *Measure for Measure* are more implausible than any that are found in either the romantic comedies or the romances, but this very artificiality is by design: Shakespeare is pointing up the stock use of marriage at the end of a comedy, and, by extension, the comic dramatist's intervention with his happy ending.

Finally, how can we understand the Duke's extraordinary mercy at the end of the play?[17] We expect Claudio and Juliet to be released from prison, but it is surprising that the two reprobates, Angelo and Lucio, receive mercy. And most remarkable of all, the hardened criminal Barnardine is released. By even the most tolerant standard of mercy, the play's happy ending must be termed immoderate. A responsible ruler, one who is concerned about the stability of the state, should temper mercy with discipline. If we take the Duke's actions simply on the literal level as those of a Christian ruler, it is hard to see how mercy can be the only element in justice, for law and morality must be given their due. The Duke after all says to Angelo in the first scene: "Mortality and mercy in Vienna/Live in thy tongue and heart" (44-45). And the play as a whole suggests a dialectic of mercy and discipline.

But recall Isabella's eloquent words: "Why, all the souls that were were forfeit once,/ And He that might the vantage best have took / Found out the remedy" (2.2.73-75). For Isabella, our being redeemed from Original Sin by Christ's death and resurrection is the type of the highest mercy. From the metadramatic perspective in which the Duke stands for the dramatist, his imitation of Christ's wondrous mercy betokens the mercy, which the dramatist bestows on his own creatures in the happy ending of comedy. With greater authority than a head of state, the dramatist dispenses mercy within the world that he creates with a Christ-like extravagance.

In the final analysis, a metadramatic approach that sees the Duke as the representative of Shakespeare himself can give us a new appreciation of the Christian themes and the Catholic setting of the play. The conclusion of this argument is that the Duke is not Providence, but rather the providential dramatist. Consequently, the Duke is providential in the peculiar ways of the dramatist in relation to his characters: not merely in his providing a happy ending, but also in his resorting to deceit to lead his often intractable characters to new growth. In his fine analysis of *All's Well That Ends Well*, Arthur C. Kirsch posits a close link between metadrama and Providence, one that he finds illustrated as well in *Measure for Measure* and *The Tempest*:

> Shakespeare saw the extent to which the tragicomic dramatist could convert the audience's consciousness of the artifice of the playwright into an awareness of the artifice of Providence and thereby associate the workings of Providence with the dynamics of the play itself. This is a development which finds its fullest and most obvious expression in plays like *Measure for Measure* and *The Tempest*,

where the Duke and Prospero act simultaneously "like power divine" and like
theatrical producers" (*Jacobean Dramatic Perspectives*).[18]

In the end we may wonder whether Lucio's description of the Duke as
"fantastical" (4.3.157) has more than one meaning.[19] Lucio merely wants to suggest
that the Duke is an eccentric, but the root meaning of the word "fantastical" has
to do with imagination. Duke Orsino in *Twelfth Night* suggests this more positive
meaning of the term when he calls the spirit of love, so fecund in new shapes,
something "high fantastical" (1.1.15). It is in this sense that the Duke of Vienna in
Measure for Measure is fantastical, for ultimately he stands for the dramatist, the
loving shaper of character and illusion.

Notes

1. G. Wilson Knight, "*Measure for Measure* and the Gospels," *The Wheel of Fire: Interpretations of Shakespearean Tragedy With Three New Essays*, 4th rev. ed. (London: Methuen, 1949), 73-96. His allegorical approach to the Duke receives its most extended treatment in Roy W. Battenhouse, "'Measure for Measure' and the Christian Doctrine of Atonement," *PMLA* 61 (1946): 1029-59, which sees the Duke as working "as a sort of secret, omniscient, and omnipresent Providence" (Battenhouse, 1047). Elizabeth M. Pope, "The Renaissance Background of *Measure for Measure*," *Shakespeare Survey* 2 (1949): 66-82 is the first important study to question the allegorical method; she argues that it is unnecessary to interpret the Duke as God since a Renaissance audience would have assumed that any good ruler stood for God. Given the emphasis in recent studies on the Duke's limitations, it is not surprising that some critics have turned the allegorical approach on its head and view the Duke as a fallible or even comic image of Providence; cf. Richard S. Ide, "Shakespeare's Revisionism: Homiletic Tragicomedy and the Ending of *Measure for Measure*," *Shakespeare Studies* 20 (1988) 105-27 and Louise Schleiner, "Providential Improvisation in *Measure for Measure*," *PMLA* 97 (1982): 227-36.

2. For examples of the extreme psychological approach, see Carolyn E. Brown, "*Measure for Measure*: Duke Vincentio's 'Crabbed' Desires," *Literature and Psychology* 35 (1989): 66-88 and T. F. Wharton, *Measure for Measure* (London: Macmillan, 1989). It is not surprising that both of these critics take seriously Lucio's interpretations of the Duke. Some critics, more balanced in their approach, view the Duke to be in search of self-knowledge; cf. Donna B. Hamilton, "The Duke in *Measure for Measure*: 'I Find an Apt Remission in Myself,'" *Shakespeare Studies* 6 (1970): 175-83; Nigel Alexander, *Shakespeare: Measure for Measure* (London: Edward Arnold, 1975), 40-42; Eileen Jorge Allman, *Player-King and Adversary: Two Faces of Play in Shakespeare* (Baton Rouge: Louisiana State University Press, 1980), 183-97. Although these readings are not as reductive as the extreme psychological approaches to the Duke, they remain unconvincing for the reason that the Duke does not seem to be fully realized in human terms within the play. J. W. Lever, ed. *Measure for Measure* (London: Methuen, 1965), xcvii, writes well of how the Duke "failed as an authentic human being and remained a stage device, midway between personality and type." N. W. Bawcutt, ed. *Measure for Measure* (Oxford: Clarendon Press, 1991), 55, reaches essentially the same conclusion when he defines the Duke as "a collection of attributes which fail to coalesce."

3. Quotations from Shakespeare's plays are from G. Blakemore Evans *et al.*, eds., *The Riverside Shakespeare* (Boston: Houghton Mifflin, 1974).

4. Francis Fergusson, *The Human Image in Dramatic Literature* (New York: Doubleday, 1957), compares *Measure for Measure* to Luigi Pirandello's *Six Characters in Search of an Author*. In his 1925 "Preface" to the play, Pirandello is much concerned with the conflict between himself and his characters. For example, Pirandello comments on how his maidservant Fantasy creates characters who have a life independent of the author: " . . . she [Fantasy] amuses herself by bringing to my house—since I derive stories and novels and plays from them—the most disgruntled tribe in the world, men, women, children, involved in strange adventures which they can find no way out of; thwarted in their plans; cheated in their hopes; with whom, in short, it is often torture to deal." (Luigi Pirandello, *Naked Masks: Five Plays*, ed. Eric Bentley [New York: E. P. Dutton, 1952], 363.)

5. A plethora of metadramatic studies of Shakespeare's plays followed upon the publication of Anne Righter, *Shakespeare and the Idea of the Play* (London: Chatto & Windus, 1962). In the case of *Measure for Measure*, the critics who have taken a metadramatic approach note that the Duke acts like a dramatist, but almost always insist that he is distinct from Shakespeare. So, for instance, Richard Fly, *Shakespeare's Mediated World* (Amherst: University of Massachusetts Press, 1976), 79: "To see the Duke as a surrogate playwright is to suggest some kinship between him and Shakespeare. From the moment the Duke steps forward in Act III until he concludes the play, however, Shakespeare maintains a critical distance between himself as creator of *Measure for Measure* and the Duke as director of the play within the play." Among the metadramatic studies, the only extended attempt to view the Duke as Shakespeare is Josephine Waters Bennett, *Measure for Measure as Royal Entertainment* (New York: Columbia University Press, 1966), 135-50. Bennett's approach is a narrow one since she is concerned largely with the question of whether or not Shakespeare acted the part of the Duke. Other critics who have at least suggested parallels between Shakespeare and the Duke are Northrop Frye, *A Natural Perspective: The Development of Shakespearean Comedy and Romance* (New York: Harcourt, 1965), 69; Anne Barton [née Righter], "Introduction," *Measure for Measure*, in Evans, *The Riverside Shakespeare*, 549; Jonathan Goldberg, *James I and the Politics of Literature: Jonson, Shakespeare, Donne, and Their Contemporaries* (Baltimore: Johns Hopkins University Press, 1983), 232-33; Sidney Homan, *When the Theater Turns to Itself: the Aesthetic Metaphor in Shakespeare* (Lewisburg: Bucknell University Press, 1981), 146, 149; and Alexander Leggatt, "Substitution in *Measure for Measure*," *Shakespeare Quarterly* 39 (1988): 358-59.

6. One of the few critics to attempt a justification of the Duke's speech is Arthur C. Kirsch, "The Integrity of 'Measure for Measure,'" *Shakespeare Survey* 28 (1975): 89-105. He argues that the Duke's "whole purpose with Claudio, as with Angelo and Isabella, is not to set down what is in heaven, but the things in earth which inspire belief in heaven" (Kirsch, 98).

7. Jean E. Howard, "*Measure for Measure* and the Restraints of Convention," *Essays in Literature* 10 (1983): 149-58 does a good job of showing how the Duke is at war with "the intractable elements of life" embodied in his subjects. But she overstates her case when she claims that "as a playwright the Duke is inhibited by a schematic view of reality and a passion for well-made but reductive plots" (152). In fact, the Duke is most hesitant to intervene in the action; and, even when he does, he allows his subjects freedom of choice.

8. Cf. Mary Ellen Lamb, "Shakespeare's 'Theatrics': Ambivalence Towards Theater in *Measure for Measure*," *Shakespeare Studies* 20 (1988): 129-45, who comments on how critics attack the Duke for manipulating his subjects "as though they were characters" (140). Although Lamb's essay is one of the best recent studies of the Duke, she remains ultimately confined by the moral perspective when, concerning the ambivalent results of the Duke's giving roles to his subjects, she asks: "What do we have here? An immoral artist creating beneficial effects? A moral artist creating destructive effects?" (142). Lamb concludes that her questions are unanswerable because the play "withhold[s] from us the information necessary for a clear reading of the Duke" (142). But I would argue that a symbolic reading of the Duke as the figure of Shakespeare both closes the gaps found in realistic readings and makes irrelevant the moral questions to which such readings inevitably give rise.

9. This assumption is clearly present in Harriet Hawkins, *Likenesses of Truth in Elizabethan and Restoration Drama* (Oxford: Clarendon, 1972). She laments the Duke's "protection" in these terms: "At the very same time that it shelters the characters from the ultimate consequences of their own decisions and desires, it denies them the dramatic

magnificence which comes only from facing such consequences" (74).

10. The levels of awareness in the comedies, both of the audience and of the characters, are brilliantly examined by Bertrand Evans, *Shakespeare's Comedies* (London: Oxford University Press, 1967).

11. Cf. Philip Edwards, *Shakespeare and the Confines of Art* (London: Methuen, 1968), 117: "Responsibility for choice and for the consequences of choice are taken out of the protagonists' hands as the Duke steps in and labours to find an alternative female body for Isabella's and an alternative severed head for Claudio's."

12. H. S. Wilson, "Action and Symbol in *Measure for Measure* and *The Tempest*," *Shakespeare Quarterly* 4 (1953): 382. See also John Bayley, *The Characters of Love: A Study in the Literature of Personality* (London: Constable, 1960), 7-8: "What I understand by an author's love for his characters is a delight in their independent existence as *other people*, an attitude towards them which is analogous to our feelings towards those we love in life; and an intense interest in their personalities combined with a sort of detached solicitude, a respect for their freedom." Bayley's description of the author's relationship to his characters captures very well the Duke's relationship to his subjects.

13. In my view no critic has ever presented a satisfactory explanation of why there is no mention in the play of Mariana until the Duke introduces his bedtrick plan. On the realistic level, the only way of dealing with the inconsistencies that Mariana creates is to conclude that "the entire portion of the narrative concerning Mariana might have been an afterthought" (Larry S. Champion, *The Evolution of Shakespeare's Comedy: A Study in Dramatic Perspective* (Cambridge, Mass.: Harvard University Press, 1970), 152. But this is to attribute to Shakespeare a casualness that is simply not found in the play as a whole. Anne Barton (née Righter), "Introduction," *The Riverside Shakespeare*, 548, evaluates Mariana in these terms: "A kind of fairy-tale princess, the mechanism of a happy ending unlikely in more realistic terms, she is made to take Isabella's place in Angelo's bed an imaginary character substituting for a real one—and then to force a resolution that is contradictory and psychologically improbable, no matter how gratifying it may be in terms of the symmetry of the plot." But the very artificiality of Mariana that Barton notes here is appropriate if Shakespeare is concerned with showing the dramatist's making of the play, that is, character in this context must be subservient to plot.

14. A good analysis of the structure of the last scene can be found in Bennett, *Royal Entertainment*, 126-32.

15. Cf. David Richman, *Laughter, Pain, and Wonder: Shakespeare's Comedies and the Audience in the Theater* (Newark: University of Delaware Press, 1990), 140: "That Isabella can overcome her own pain and revulsion and second Mariana's plea for mercy is one of the greatest of the many miracles that Shakespeare's comedies depict."

16. See, for instance, Ernest Schanzer, *The Problem Plays of Shakespeare: A Study of Julius Caesar, Measure for Measure, Antony and Cleopatra* (New York: Schocken Books, 1965), 126-27. Edwards, *Confines of Art*, 118-19, is also quite critical of the Duke's justification for causing Isabella to suffer. However, Kirsch, "Integrity," 105, defends on religious grounds the Duke's "heavenly comforts of despair."

17. Hawkins, *Likeness of Truth*, 71, compares the Duke's dispensation unfavorably to that of Shakespeare's hero Henry V. But I think that Michael Goldman, *Shakespeare and the Energies of Drama* (Princeton: Princeton University Press, 1972), 173, is right to link the Duke's mercy to the aesthetic rather than the political realm: "The joy we feel at the play's end is a joy no exercise of government in this world can ever attain. Without comedy, the Vienna we are shown so realistically would remain boiling and bubbling in its corruption."

18. Arthur C. Kirsch, *Jacobean Dramatic Perspectives*, (Charlottesville: The

University Press of Virginia, 1972), 59.

19. In comparing Lucio and the Duke, both of whom she regards as artist figures, Lamb, "Shakespeare's 'Theatrics,'" 138, also comments on the root meaning of "fantastical." As well, in his discussion of Elizabethan views of the imagination David P. Young, *Something of Great Constancy: The Art of "A Midsummer Night's Dream"* (New Haven: Yale University Press, 1966), 132-33, quotes passages from John Marston and George Puttenham both of whom decry the negative sense of "phantasticall" and associate the word with the creative imagination.

Chapter 3

Story Theology in Flannery O'Connor's "The River," John Updike's "The Christian Roommates," and Denys Arcand's *Jesus Of Montreal*

Patrick Harkins

This chapter focuses on how story theology can help us understand theological concepts and the Catholic cultural landscape in the second half of the twentieth century. A short poem by Judith Ortiz Cofer, "Latin Women Pray," gives a good brief example of how story theology works. In this poem Cofer not only lays before us important dimensions of the modern Catholic cultural landscape, she also invites us to reflect on theological concerns as images not as propositions.

> Latin women pray
> Latin women pray
> In incense sweet churches
> They pray in Spanish to an Anglo God
> With a Jewish heritage.
> And this Great White Father
> Imperturbable in his marble pedestal
> Looks down upon his brown daughters
> Votive candles shining like lust
> In his all seeing eyes
> Unmoved by their persistent prayers.

Yet year after year
Before his image they kneel
Margarita, Josefina, Maria, Isabel
All fervently hoping
That if not omnipotent
At least he be bi-lingual.

Using ideas about story theology, this chapter explores the concept of baptism in Flannery O'Connor's "The River," the idea of living a true Christian life or what it means to be a saint in John Updike's "Christian Roommates,"and the definition of call and conversion in post-Vatican II Christianity in Denys Arcand's film *Jesus of Montreal*. The chapter is organized into a prologue about story theology, followed by the exploration of the stories in three acts, and concluding with a brief epilogue.

Prologue: Story Theology

Terence Tilley defines four main purposes of story theology:

1. to "uncover the stories which show what the Christian key words mean";
2. to "transform creatively (when necessary) the narratives of the tradition" in contrast with propositional theology that "presupposes that narratives are dispensable portrayals of religious faith";
3. to "make a religious tradition vibrant in a new context by telling new stories";
4. to "proclaim and manifest the Good News."[1]

Story theology is connected to stories in general, myth, simile, and metaphor. The truth of simile and metaphor lies not with exactitude but a breaking of expectations, a stretching of the imagination, and a challenge of assumptions. This sounds a lot like definitions of parables. Parables begin with simile and sometimes extend to metaphor and whole stories, even stories within stories. "Perhaps the greatest challenge of narrative theology," writes Tilley, "is that it requires that the hearer do some theology."[2]

William Bausch explains other reasons why story theology is so important by quoting Thomas Driver: "I find myself not only agreeing that theology originates in stories (and should itself tell more of them), but also thinking that all knowledge comes from a mode of understanding that is dramatic. Far from merely illustrating truths we already know some other way, the dramatic imagination is the means whereby we get started in any knowledge whatever."[3]

According to Bausch, four important historical developments help us appreciate story theology: (1) the shift from high to low Christology, (2) the importance of scientific thinking and how images play an important part of this mode of communicating scientific truth, (3) the exploration of dreams and the subconscious, and (4) the increasing appreciation for feminism and the importance of the feminine insight into the world. Bausch explains:

> So dreams, myths, imagination—all are related and find their best expression in art, especially in the art of story telling [. . .] [T]his truism is another reason why we are looking at a theology of story. As Flannery O'Connor says, "A higher paradox confounds emotion as well as reason and there are long periods in the lives of us and of the saints when the truth as revealed by faith is hideous, emotionally disturbing, down right repulsive."[4]

As Jean Cocteau begins his film version of *Beauty and the Beast*, we must remember the most important words, "Once upon a Time."

Act One: Flannery O'Connor's "The River" (1953)

In "The River," first published in 1953, Flannery O'Connor invites us to theological and cultural reflection using Biblical parallels, social satire, and symbolic expression. One of the important concepts she writes about is baptism. A five-year-old boy, Harry, is taken away from his party-loving parents by a fundamentalist Christian babysitter, Mrs. Connin, to the river to see Bevel Summers, a preacher and healer. At the river, Bevel

> lifted his head and arms and shouted, "Listen to what I got to say, you people! There ain't but one river and that's the River of Life made out of Jesus' Blood. That's the River you have to lay your pain in, in the River of Faith, in the River of Life, in the River of Love, in the rich, red river of Jesus' Blood, you people!"[5]

He baptizes Harry, but the experience is not the one Harry expected. Bevel no longer smiles and says, "'If I baptize you . . . you'll be able to go to the Kingdom of Christ. You'll be washed in the river of suffering, son, and you'll go by the deep river of life. Do you want that?' 'Yes,' the child said and thought, 'I won't go back to the apartment then, I'll go under the river.'"[6] Bevel plunges his head in the water and tells Harry, "You count now." Harry is already thinking about changing his life by running away.

But O'Connor drives home the point about how people misunderstand true baptism. Mrs. Connin asks the preacher to pray for Harry's mother. When Bevel asks what her problem is,

> "She hasn't got up yet," he [Harry] said in a high dazed voice. "She has a hang-over." The air was so quiet he could hear the broken pieces of the sun knocking on the water. The preacher looked angry and startled. The red drained out of his face and the sky appeared to darken his eyes. There was a loud guffaw from the bank and Mr. Paradise shouted "Haw! Cure the afflicted woman with the hangover!" and began to beat his knee with his fist.

Next, Mrs. Connin brings Harry back to his parents who are having another drinking party. His mother is annoyed that her son was baptized. People are interested in the heirloom book of *The Life of Jesus for Those Under Twelve* that Mrs. Connin gave Harry, not for its subject, but as a collector's item. Harry wants out. The next day he makes his way back to the river. There "he intended not to fool with preachers anymore but to Baptize himself and to keep on going this time until he found the Kingdom of Christ in the river."[8] Once in the water the current catches him and pulls him along and "all his fury and fear left him."[9] Harry floats away.

In "The River" O'Connor calls for us to reflect on the theology of baptism by creating characters who in parable fashion misunderstand. Harry wants to swim in the river of life. But he mistakes the metaphoric and spiritual river for the physical river. He is, as are so many, a literalist of the theological imagination. Mrs. Connin and others mistake baptism as an occasion for physical healing. In spite of Bevel's denial of the connection, people did come and did testify to being healed. Sallie McFargue describes O'Connor's Catholicism as "in many ways old-style, pre-Vatican II. Good and evil, the battle, often violent, of God and the devil for the individual soul is central. She is concerned not with the salvation of the world in social or economic terms—no agricultural experts here!—but the baptism of idiots."[10] How fine are the metaphors of water, life, and blood; but how confusing they can be as well. This is story theology because it asks the readers to do their own theology. O'Connor makes clear that, as confused as the adults are, it still takes more than a child's view to understand. Experience without reflection is only raw data that can lead us to drown rather than swim.

Act Two: John Updike's "The Christian Roommates" (1964)

John Updike's "The Christian Roommates," first published in 1964, reflects much of the cultural climate of that decade. Updike's world is the intellectual milieu of Ivy League intelligentsia. In this context, Updike explores what it means to be a good Christian, even a saint. The main characters, and the roommates in their first year at Harvard, are Orson Ziegler and Henry "Hub" Palamountain. Orson is a Methodist from South Dakota majoring in pre-med and would be recognized as the good Christian—orderly, hardworking, concerned for correctness. His nickname is "Orson the Parson," and in Updike fashion he is teased in verse: "One midnight, Orson distinctly heard Dawson sing, 'My name is Orson Ziegler, I come from South Dakota.' There was a pause, then Kern sang back, 'I tend to be a niggler, and masturbate by quota.'"[11]

Hub challenges everything that Orson stands for. He is committed to vegetarianism and pacifism. He goes to concerts and other activities and does not get good grades. More than once Hub offers Orson the shirt off his back. He does not want to interfere with another person's freedom, and in an existential way refers to it as "dreadful freedom." He is an amalgam of beliefs. He spins on a spinning wheel "for a half hour a day, after Yoga." He says, "I consider myself an Anglican Christian Platonist strongly influenced by Gandhi."[12] But others see Hub closer to Catholicism when they describe his prayer as medieval or Counter-Reformation because he prays facedown on his bed with his arms outstretched.

> "He's a saint," Kern said.
> "He's not," Orson said. "He's not intelligent. I am taking Chem 1 with him, and he's worse than a child with the math. And those Greek books he keeps on his desk, they look worn because he bought them secondhand."
> "Saints don't have to be intelligent," Kern said. "What saints have to have is energy. Hub has it."[13]

Three other scenes focus on the values of being a good Christian, a modern saint. First, Orson and others challenge Hub's vegetarian principles because he eats eggs and wears leather shoes. He is referred to as "Saint Henry Palamountain." He is persecuted for his beliefs. He tries to explain, but finally admits, "My feet are tender; I have compromised. I apologize [. . .] I am covered with blood, and pray daily for forgiveness." Orson admits, "I hate him."

Second, there are conflicts over women and sexuality. At a poetry reading by Carl Sandburg, Hub sits behind a girl with long red hair. She cuts it off and gives it to Hub to spin and save as a love knot. Orson cannot believe that she would do this, but Hub says he is acting out of kindness because she was going to cut her hair anyway. "I didn't talk her into it. I merely offered, and she thought it was a lovely idea. Really, Orson, I don't see why this should offend your bourgeois scruples."[14] Orson thinks about his girlfriend, Emily. He had taken her virginity clumsily in the summer, and at Christmas break they have another unpleasant sexual encounter. Orson also begins to fantasize that she is having sex with a Native American. He even has some homoerotic visions of himself and Hub. Instead of praying as usual, Orson becomes obsessed. Hub was like a "poisonous food Orson could not stop eating."[15]

Third, when Hub obtains the head of a parking meter full of coins from an accident and wants to give the money to charity, Orson argues with Hub, "'You give it back or we'll both go to jail.' Orson sees himself ruined, the scarcely commenced career of his life destroyed. Hub turned serenely. 'I am not afraid. Going to jail under a totalitarian regime is a mark of honor. If you had a conscience, you'd understand.'"[16] After a fight that Hub wins, Hub reluctantly returns the money.

Orson and Hub graduate. Orson returns to South Dakota, marries Emily, and cares for people as a doctor. He slips away from his beliefs and begins favoring Voltaire's Enlightenment skeptical views toward religion. He gives up praying altogether, something described as "a kind of scar he carries without pain and without any clear memory of the amputation."[17] Hub becomes a speaker for pacifism, avoids jail, does missionary work in Africa.

In "The Christian Roommates," Updike leads us to ask who is the real Christian roommate. At first, Orson has a religious faith in rules and order; but this faith is like seed in poor soil or choked by weeds. He has to deal with his sexual life. He is no prodigal son who goes to the big city and loses his faith and inheritance as an example of return and forgiveness. He does return home and heals people as a doctor and leads a respectable and respected life, but he no longer practices his faith. Hub symbolizes a radical Christianity familiar in the 1960s, with hints of liberation theology. He lives out his faith in action. He does not join a religious community, but is committed to justice. Updike's dichotomy may be too simplistic for today, but he does have a sense of comic and tragic irony to prick our conscience.

Act Three: Denys Arcand's *Jesus of Montreal* (1989)

Jesus of Montreal, released in 1989, is part satire, part drama, and part parable. Arcand leads us to reflect on the meaning of call and conversion. He explains that he wanted to:

> make a film full of discontinuities, going wildly from comedy to the most absurd drama; in the image of the world around us it was to be fragmented, contradictory, banal. A little like in the supermarkets where in ten meters of displays you can find Dostoevsky's novels, *eau de cologne*, the Bible, porno videos, the complete works of Shakespeare, pictures of the earth taken from the moon, astrological predictions, and posters of actors or Jesus.[18]

At the request of Father Leclerc, Daniel Coulombe, an actor and playwright, revises a script of a forty-year-old passion play based on Mark's gospel to make it modern and relevant. Daniel bases his revision on theological, Biblical, historical, and archeological research as well as inventive theatrical techniques. Daniel calls together actors who are working at other jobs but want to act in a real play. Constance is working in a soup kitchen, Martin is doing voiceovers for pornographic films, René is doing commentary for educational films, and Mireille is working in commercials.

The play is well received by a public that is both agnostic and skeptical and deeply believing. Father Leclerc, however, fears repercussions from his superiors and wants to return to the old script that he wrote. During the last performance, a fight breaks out; and Daniel, playing Jesus, is hurt and dies from the injuries. Doctors use his heart and eyes to heal the sick in need of transplants. The actors decide to form a theatre group named for Daniel and to continue his work.

The screenplay has much in the way of creating parallels to gospel situations. There are images of meals, miracles, teaching, and coming to faith, as well as opposition and satire against the modern world's secular values. In particular, Arcand asks us to theologize about the idea of call and conversion. He argues that people's faith and prayers for healing that might seem shallow are as effective and cheaper than drugs or psychiatrists. He would like to keep faith alive and believes the passion play needs updating, a sense of the rightness of Vatican II theology.

Father Leclerc once heard the call to a priestly vocation, but had long since stifled it. When Daniel catches him in a sexual tryst with his mistress, Constance, he admits that he is not a very good priest. In the seminary he was attracted to Broadway theatre and prostitutes. He also rejects the script that is so popular and moving even to people who are not practicing Catholics. He is afraid, he says, of being criticized and sent to an old folks home in Winnipeg. Mostly he fears being isolated and alone. His response is a very human one. As John Dominic Crossan has said of the disciples in Mark, the disciples did not lose their faith but their nerve.[19]

Father Leclerc's mistress, Constance, follows her heart. Her main concern is to comfort those in need. Daniel finds her working in a soup kitchen. About her affair with Father Leclerc, she comments, "Oh well, it makes him happy and it really doesn't hurt me."[20] Her constant care of people and lack of moral values display a Christianity that is only horizontal.

Mireille is a beautiful ingénue acting in commercials, even appearing to walk on water to capture the "unbearable lightness of being." She is sleeping with her director, who exploits her body. By choosing to do the play that her lover calls "mystical theatre," Mireille changes dramatically. At first, she is afraid and unsure of herself. She does not believe she can go out in public without makeup. At an audition for a commercial when she is about to take off her clothes, Daniel stops her. He cleanses the studio by destroying equipment. Mireille is changed. She is faithful to the vision of the passion play, and she and Constance stay with Daniel as he is being shuttled from one hospital to the next and through an apocalyptic scene in a subway station. At one point she explains,

> Don't you know how I used to be? My idea of paradise was the beach of Bora Bora. I never met any guys who did not wear Rolex watches or drive BMWs. I did not know that there were still men whose first thought wasn't to jump on me. . . . What we have is very precious, we have to keep going.[21]

This is concrete theology.

Daniel plays the role of Jesus. In a sense he becomes Jesus. He is thoughtful, kind, creative, sees the best in his friends. When he plays the role of Jesus and speaks the words of Jesus in the play, it is as if we are hearing the words from Jesus himself. This is the transforming power of drama and the word. He is calm when faced with a lawsuit or a lawyer's offers of riches and fame. Yet his anger causes him to break up video equipment that leads to his arrest. He leads his acting friends to become more loving, more sympathetic, and better people. At least they want to try. The movie asks us to consider the complex relationship of assuming a new role in life, acting differently, and really living out principles and being true to them and one's calling. Conversion does mean acting, and a dramatic conversion can lead to new roles, new relationships, and a new sense of self.

Theologically, this has the ring of truth. The stories told in *Jesus of Montreal* make it a complex parable. This movie tells the passion story for our time in a theatrical way. The play told in bits and pieces includes bits and pieces of Jesus' teaching from before and during the last supper. This is effective story theology.

Epilogue

To conclude, Tilley's four main purposes of story theology are "to uncover the stories which show what the Christian key words mean," "to transform creatively (when necessary) the narratives of the tradition," "to make a religious tradition vibrant in a new context by telling new stories," and "to proclaim and manifest the Good News." The stories that we have explored are examples of theology that challenge, run against the grain, and use techniques of parables. They are interesting narratives that extend our understanding and raise questions whose answers may disturb us or lead to other questions. They create human faces, even though they are fictional faces, on aspects of Catholic culture. In them we can map the Catholic cultural landscape of the second half of the twentieth century, and they do help us do our own theology about baptism, what it means to be a saint, and call and conversion.

Notes

1. Terence W. Tilley, *Story Theology* (Collegeville: The Liturgical Press, 1985), 11-15.

2. Tilley, *Story Theology*, 217.

3. William J. Bausch, *Storytelling, Imagination and Faith* (Mystic [CT]: Twenty-Third Publications, 1989), 17.

4. Bausch, *Storytelling, Imagination and Faith*, 21-25.

5. Flannery O'Connor, "The River," in *The Complete Stories* (New York: Farrar, Straus, Giroux, 1985), 165.

6. O'Connor, "The River," 168.

7. O'Connor, "The River," 168.

8. O'Connor, "The River," 173.

9. O'Connor, "The River," 174.

10. Sallie McFague, *Speaking in Parable: A Study in Metaphor and Theology* (Philadelphia: Fortress Press, 1975), 136.

11. John Updike, "The Christian Roommates," in *American Short Story Masterpieces*, edited by Raymond Carver and Tom Jenks (New York: Bantam, Doubleday, Dell, 1987), 469.

12. Updike, "The Christian Roommates," 469.

13. Updike, "The Christian Roommates," 476.

14. Updike, "The Christian Roommates," 479.

15. Updike, "The Christian Roommates," 481.

16. Updike, "The Christian Roommates," 483.

17. Updike, "The Christian Roommates," 486.

18. Denys Arcand, *Jesus of Montreal* (1989), *Screenplay*, translated by Matt Cohen, in *Best Canadian Screenplays*, edited by Douglas Bowie and Tom Shoebridge (Kingston [ON]: Quarry Press, 1992), 339-40.

19. John Dominic Crossan, *Parables: The Challenge of the Historical Jesus* (New York: Harper and Row, 1973).

20. *Best Canadian Screenplays*, 355.

21. *Best Canadian Screenplays*, 413.

Chapter 4

The Tree of the Choctaws:
Live Oaks in the Sacred Poetry of
Father Adrien Emmanuel Rouquette

Chris Michaelides

The writings of poet and missionary Father Adrien Emmanuel Rouquette occupy a prominent place in nineteenth-century Louisiana Francophone literature, a rich cultural landscape that is just beginning to be explored and in a sense rediscovered by scholars and teachers throughout the state. Landscape itself is of course a subject that for several decades has attracted much attention in cultural studies; in keeping with the theme of this conference, then, I would like to focus here on the treatment it receives both in Father Rouquette's literary work and through his ministry. Central to his poetic landscapes is the live oak, which was deeply symbolic within the indigenous community he served and, by extension, within his own life and work. My intention is to show that, writing to us as a missionary priest in late nineteenth-century America, and therefore witness to the beginnings of modernization, Father Rouquette has much to tell us about the place of the sacred in our own postmodern age.

The name Rouquette was by the mid-nineteenth century well known in New Orleans and Paris. Adrien's older brother François-Dominique published a collection of poetry, *Les Méchacébéennes* (*Mississippian poems*), in 1839 to critical acclaim in Paris; Adrien followed his brother's success with his own first volume of poetry, *Les Savanes* (*The Savannas*), in 1841;[1] and his younger brother Térence also published verse.

Moreover, the Rouquettes, linked by marriage with the prominent Cousin and Carrière families, were among the most powerful landowners in Louisiana during the first half of the nineteenth century; their mansions and large plantations covered the north shore of Lake Pontchartrain, across from New Orleans. Adrien spent his early childhood in the city, where his father, Dominique Rouquette, a wine merchant, had emigrated from Bordeaux. After the death of his father, Adrien moved with his family to a home on the north shore, along Bayou St. John, where there were large encampments of Choctaw Indians. His contacts with the Choctaws and the friendships he formed with children his age, made a lasting impression on him and probably influenced decisions he made later in life.

As an adolescent, Adrien attended middle school at Transylvania College in Kentucky, where he was inspired by stories of Daniel Boone and John James Audubon. He received there the sad news of his mother's death, and after a brief return to New Orleans made his first voyage to France. There he would attend the College de Rennes in Brittany and, later, law school in Paris. As a restless young man he made the Atlantic crossing a total of nine times, and eventually abandoned his half-hearted law studies to enter the seminary in New Orleans. He became the first native Louisianian to be ordained a priest, and served as secretary to Bishop Antoine Blanc and as an assistant priest at St. Louis Cathedral.

Despite his success, Father Adrien Emmanuel Rouquette was never happy with his duties in the city; his dream was to return to the forests of the north shore and establish a hermitage, where he hoped to be joined by other enlightened Christians seeking an escape from the ills of modern commercialism. He later altered this ambition; in the absence of a steady stream of Christian hermits to Bayou Lacombe, he would seek to establish a mission community among the Choctaws, who then numbered several thousand.[2] Granted leave from his duties by Bishop Antoine Blanc on several occasions, Father Rouquette constructed small two-room cabin chapels (eventually there were five) where he would sleep, write, gather with family and friends, and conduct Mass.[3] These were placed near, sometimes directly under impressive live oaks, which he considered sacred and to which he was deeply attached. In 1859 he was accorded the honor of attending the Feast of the Dead, after which he addressed the gathering in Choctaw and earned the name Chahta-Ima, "Like a Choctaw." Father Rouquette adopted this name with great pride: he used it to sign many of his writings—which included poems, articles and a novel, *La Nouvelle Atala* (*The New Atala*), whose title harks back to the classic work by Chateaubriand.

One discovers in Father Rouquette an enigmatic figure situated at the intersection of conflicting worlds and changing times—somewhere between France, where he was educated, and his native Louisiana; between the growing city of New Orleans and the forests of Lake Pontchartrain's north shore; between white Creole feudal society and the modernizing American republic. He was a writer who remained obsessed with becoming a second Chateaubriand decades after the echo of Romanticism had died in Europe. Indeed, he appears as such an anachronism that it is still an open question whether his rewriting of Chateaubriand is reactionary or, if read as parody, avant-garde. As a young man he fancied himself a melancholy traveler tossed from shore to shore like the wandering romantic hero René, yet he is to this day revered as a kind of founding father in the Louisiana parish of St. Tammany, where he did his missionary work.

Such contradictions are symptomatic of the poet-priest's struggle to find his bearings in a society making the transition to modernity. I would like to focus here on his response to this challenge, the ways in which he drew from his Catholic faith and poetic imagination in order to transform the Louisiana landscape—that is, the ways he attempted to reclaim sacred space. Over the past several decades, postmodern cultural studies have offered new critical perspectives on landscape in relation to European colonialism and the appropriation of non-Western societies.[4] Such an approach clearly lends itself to Rouquette's work, at least as a point of departure. Both his writing and his ministry were predicated on the desire to inhabit a certain kind of space—to which, as a native Creole, he could feel he was returning, but which was also very much a product of the exotic American landscapes he encountered in French Romanticism.

Chateaubriand had written in the preface to his 1802 novel, *Atala*, that "we are everywhere reduced to the worn-out forms of an aged civilization," to which he contrasts the example of newly forming civilizations among Native Americans. Rouquette's inclusion of this statement in the opening paragraph of the preface to his 1879 novel, *La Nouvelle Atala*, establishes this notion of Western decadence, the exhaustion of European culture, as the primary motivation behind his entire literary project.[5] Indeed, here Chateaubriand's initial premise has turned into violent rhetoric. The Daniel Boone-inspired character, Hopoyouksa (Wise Man), is a French nobleman who has fled Europe to live among the Indians.

"Quand un edifice vermoulu s'affaisse et s'écroule," he says in defense of his self-imposed exile, "l'oiseau prend son vol: Fuyons comme l'oiseau, pour n'être pas ensevelis sous un amas de débris et de poussière! Tout homme a le droit d'abandonner une société, qui tombe en dissolution; un cadaver, qui exhale la peste; une sentine d'infection contagieuse!"[6] ("When a worm-eaten edifice weakens and crumbles, the bird takes flight: Let us flee like the bird, in order not to be buried under the pile of debris and dust! Every man has the right to abandon a society that falls into dissolution; a cadaver, which exudes the plague; a mass of contagious infection!") He goes on to extol the virtues of the Louisiana forests: "Dieu fit les déserts pour nous servir d'asiles, quand tous les autres asiles ont été détruits ou fermés: Allons là où se trouve Dieu! O ombrages des grands arbres séculaires, sombres profondeurs des forêts primitives, . . . ô vierge nature, que tu as de charmes pour celui qui s'est séparé de cette prétendue civilization!" (God made the wilds to serve as our refuge, when all other refuges have been destroyed or closed off: Let us go where God is found! O shade of the great ancient trees, somber depths of the primitive forests, . . . O virgin nature, how great are your charms for he who has separated himself from that so-called civilization!")

Such had also been the logic behind Father Rouquette's *Apologie de la vie solitaire et contemplative* (*Apology of the solitary and contemplative life*), which he had published in 1852 in order to convince Bishop Blanc to allow him to establish a hermitage in Lacombe.[7] Since the Church and its monasteries could no longer offer European society a refuge from itself, he reasoned, it would be necessary to flee to the American wilderness:

> Oui, lors même que tous les cloîtres seraient détruits ou fermés, le *grand cloître du désert* sera toujours ouvert pour les âmes fatiguées du monde et de ses vaines agitations. Il restera, ce *cloître indestructible*, avec ses cavernes profondes, ses grottes mystérieuses, ses vallons ombreux, ses hautes montagnes, ses retraites inaccessibles, ses rochers connus de l'aigle et battus des flots, et ses îles verdoyantes qui rappelle Lérins.[8] (Yes, even when every cloister is destroyed or closed, the *great cloister* of the wilderness will always be open for souls tired of the world and of its vain agitations. It will remain, this *indestructible cloister*, with its deep caverns, its mysterious caves, its shady valleys, its tall mountains, its inaccessible recesses, its rocks familiar to the eagle and lashed by the waves, and its verdant islands reminiscent of Lérins.)

This rejection of European modernism and search for unspoiled natural havens corresponds rather neatly to what postmodern critics interpret as an elaborate fiction, the creation of an exotic other in dialogue with the colonizing subject. As J. Michael Dash puts it in his study of Caribbean literature, *The Other America*, "As modern technology and rapid urbanization took its toll on the capacity to have a profound, authentic experience for the individual, an exoticist project emerged that allowed for escape from the atrophied, industrialized world of Europe in the realm of adventure outside Europe."[9]

Yet Father Rouquette is almost too late even for this kind of adventure: Daniel Boone, Audubon, Chateaubriand have already walked this ground; the steam engine and the telegraph are shrinking distances, as the modern world encroaches more and more on what lies beyond it. The anxiety we read in Father Rouquette's work belongs to the mid- to late-nineteenth century: it is the great *fin de siècle* malaise—the feeling that there are no more worlds to conquer, that everything has already been done, everything has already been written. Indeed, a fundamental lack of essence implies that, in the absence of an original Word, there is nothing but *re*-writing. This is evident in the rather curious project of writing something called *La Nouvelle Atala*, an openly unoriginal novel that is in many respects a rewriting of Chateaubriand's *Atala* (in fact, the original novel actually figures in the story), and in the *Apology*, which is made up entirely of quotations—hundreds of them—from European authors. Father Rouquette was an inveterate collector of quotations: his work spaces were strewn with books and clippings from newspaper articles he saved for use in correspondence, reviews, or writings for publication.[10]

These symptoms of postmodern malaise (that "plague," as Rouquette called it) intensify the search for virgin landscapes, ancient forests of live oaks, and exotic birds. Nowhere does Rouquette express this more clearly than in the poem, "Souvenir du Kentucky," from his first volume of poetry, *Les Savanes*.[11] The poem begins by recalling the tragic moment in 1825 when the young Adrien, then at boarding school far from home, received news of the death of his mother, Louise:

Enfant, je dis un soir: Adieu, ma bonne mère!
Et je quittai gaîment sa maison et sa terre.
Enfant, dans mon exil, une lettre, un matin,
(O Louise!) m'apprit que j'étais orphelin![12]
(A child, I said one night: Farewell, my good mother!
And merrily I left her home and her land.
A child, in my exile, a letter, one morning,
(O Louise!) informed me that I was an orphan!)

Young Adrien did have comrades at his school and was looked after by wealthy friends and family; he most certainly was not abandoned in the wild after the death of his mother. Yet, transformed as poetic landscape some fourteen years later, the event takes on new meaning. The loss of maternal home and land leads not to despair but to the dream of a solitary existence in a great primitive forest, the Kentucky woods. The ancient trees, the Indian lore, the spirit of Daniel Boone, evoke an Edenic wilderness in which the poet is the sole inhabitant, "unlearned" and thus prior to civilization—he is in essence the first man. In the poem's mystical climax, the forest becomes a vast cathedral resounding with the harmonies of a divine music, a "universal organ," at whose sound the poet, as Adamic representative of all humankind, falls on his knees and, awestruck, finds God in solitude.

Elsewhere in *Les Savanes*, Rouquette likens this first man to the "happy Choctaw," primitive, simpler, and therefore closer to God's creation. In "Regrets d'un étudiant Créole exilé à Paris" ("Sorrows of a Creole Student exiled in Paris"), he longs to return to Lacombe: "I must have my woods back," he writes, "I must have my oaks." Lost among the decadent pleasures of the great capital city, he dreams of fleeing "all trace of civilization":

Oh! surtout, il me faut ta hutte, heureux Chactas;
Il me faut la prairie où s'égarent tes pas!
Oui, fils de la forêt, ton sort me fait envie;
Je voudrais, avec toi, recommencer ma vie:
Libre alors, je vivrais, comme l'oiseau dans l'air,
Ayant pour nid de l'herbe, et pour toit un ciel clair;
Libre alors, je vivrais, voyageur solitaire,
N'ayant qu'un chien chéri qui m'aime sur la terre;
Libre enfin, je mourrais sur de sauvages bords,
Étendu sur le sol comme les arbres morts

Oui, Chactas, je le dis ; je voudrais être toi. . . .[13]

(Oh! Above all, I must have your hut, happy Choctaw;
I must have the prairie where your footsteps wander!
Yes, child of the forest, I envy your fate;
I should like with you to begin my life again:
Then, I would live free as a bird in the air,
Having the grass for a nest, and the clear blue sky for a roof;

Then, I would live free as a lone wanderer,
Having on this earth only a faithful dog to love me;
Then, at last, I would die free upon wild shores,
Stretched on the ground like a fallen tree;

Yes, Choctaw, I say it now; I should like to be you. . . .)

We see in this early poem a foreshadowing of Father Rouquette's future missionary work among the Choctaws, as well as a hint of the Choctaw name, Chahta-Ima, that he would later acquire. Only here his ambition goes beyond simile: more than being *like* a Choctaw, he longs to *be* a Choctaw.

There is another image in this passage that goes hand in hand with that fantasy: the comparison of his lifeless body to a fallen tree. Together with the scandal Rouquette caused in New Orleans for having "gone native," there was a persistent rumor in the city that he actually lived in an oak tree. Although this local belief amused the young priest, it was based on his well-known fascination with and love for the St. Tammany oaks, near which he built his cabin chapels.[14] His favorite of these locations he called the Nook, a place he considered sacred. The subject of a poem in his English volume of poetry, *Wild Flowers*, the Nook was surrounded by impressive live oaks, under which he wished to be buried:

The nook! O sacred, deep retreat,
Where crowds may ne'er intrude;
Where men with God and angels meet
In peaceful solitude;

O paradise, where I have flown;
O woody, lovely spot,
Where I may live and die alone,
Forgetful and forgot![15]

Rouquette's most eloquent and ambitious evocation of sacred space is without doubt *Les Savane*'s three-part poem, *L'Arbre des Chactas* (*The Tree of the Choctaws*), whose central figure is the great oak itself. In the first stanza the poet describes the immense tree: it is likened to a twisting boa, human veins, a tall ship, a giant, a king, a cathedral dome, an obelisk, Noah's Ark, and Jacob's ladder stretching from earth to heaven. The number of similes and metaphors alone attests to the difficulty of making the description: the poet is confronted with something so vast, so sublime, that it cannot be contained by language. The tree of the Choctaws comes to represent the infinite: its branches are "ageless" and "without number," its roots have "a thousand knots," a large number expressing the uncountable. The great tree encompasses the created universe itself, and as a "ladder to heaven" represents an unbroken mediation between creation and Creator, between earth and heaven.

The poem's second stanza introduces a tragic rupture. A woodsman fells the immortal oak:

Eh bien! cet arbre-roi, ce géant des forets, / Cette arche, cette échelle aux infinis degrés, / Un homme aux muscles forts, un homme à rude tâche, / Suant des mois entiers, l'abbatit de sa hache! / Il l'abattit enfin; et puis, s'assit content; / Car, dans l'arbre, il voyait quelques pièces d'argent![16] (Well then! this king among trees, this giant of the forests, / This Ark, this ladder with steps to infinity, / A man with strong muscles, a man at his rude task, / Sweating for months, cut it down with his axe! / At last he cut it down; and then sat down contented; / For, in the tree, he saw a few pieces of silver!).

The reference to the Gospel of Matthew is quite deliberate, for this woodsman is not just a thoughtless brute; he is Judas. And for Father Rouquette his betrayal is ushered in by the American world of commerce, modern science, and calculation. The infinite gives way to the finite, the "uncountable" is destroyed for the sake of the "countable"—a *few* pieces of silver. Again we hear the refrain that echoes throughout Rouquette's life: his lamentation of the loss of the sacred in modern society.

There is however a third stanza, a third and final act of this drama, that is triumphant: the Choctaws' Tree is reborn as the tree of the Cross and, more than that, as the very body of Christ:

Car c'est l'arbre de vie et d'immortalité,
Qui nourrit de ses fruits toute l'humanité;
Oui, c'est l'arbre sacré, dont la puissante sève
Est le sang pur du Christ, fils d'une seconde Ève. . . .[17]
(For 'tis the tree of life and immortality,
Which feeds with its fruit all humanity;
Yes, 'tis the sacred tree, whose mighty sap
Is the pure blood of Christ, son of a second Eve. . . .)

This is the most comprehensive and revealing expression of Father Rouquette's response to the loss of essence in the modern and postmodern world. The function of poetry is for him to make sacred, and in this the power of the poet is likened to that of the priest. It is a small step indeed from writer of sacred poetry to ordination and missionary work in St. Tammany. Both as poet and as priest, Rouquette sanctifies the land through Eucharistic transformation: this tree is the body, this sap is the blood. Chateaubriand had considered the priesthood, but ultimately his Catholicism was literary, based on Romantic aesthetic pleasure and the cult of the sublime. A generation later, however, at the height of positivist progress and modernization, Adrien Rouquette would have to realize this dream, to become a priest in order to make literal the grounding of his beloved forest upon the original Word.

For this he was viewed both as a saint and as something of a wild man during his lifetime, and is now accorded the status of a founding father in the area of Lacombe, home of the Choctaws and their trees. Interestingly, a local tradition surrounding Father Rouquette reinforces this status in a way that resonates with his poetry, and that at the same time provides perhaps the ultimate realization of his dream to live and die in harmony with the great primitive forest. It is something between local belief and local legend that Father Rouquette's body does not lie in St. Louis Cemetery No. 3, where it had been moved from Cemetery No. 2 in 1966, and that it was not even to be found in its original tomb. The Bayou Lacombe Commemorative Booklet issued in 1976 by the Heritage Committee of the Bayou Lacombe Bicentennial Commission contains an article on Father Rouquette in which the author, local historian Tom Aicklen, treats the priest's burial site as an open question:

> Despite his repeated requests to be buried at the Nook among the people he served and along the bayou he loved, his wish was disregarded. The wish of this man who had denied nothing to others was denied.

Yet another indignity was to befall him.

> His rest was disturbed and his remains moved from the tomb. Unfortunately the records of 1887 show only a large X scratched across his name and notation as to where he was taken. Supposedly he was placed in the new tomb of the priests in St. Louis Cemetery No. 3, but his name is not listed among other priests, the earliest of which died in 1902, fifteen years after Rouquette was buried. It is incredible that the remains of such a great man should be missing, but numerous inquiries inevitably lead back to the old book with the large X.[18]

A later publication issued by the St. Tammany Historical Society revisits the story of Rouquette's death and burial and, while dismissing the historical validity of the claim, makes mention in an extensive note of the belief that Father Rouquette's body now rests in Lacombe:

> Mel Leavitt, *Great Characters of New Orleans* (San Francisco: Lexicos, 1984) p. 5, claims Rouquette is "buried where he wished to be, a small graveyard off Squeezing Bayou (Bayou Lacombe)." This is obviously incorrect, though it is popular folklore still alive in St. Tammany.[19]

The mystery surrounding Rouquette's death and burial, then, is in one sense an especially revealing example of cultural appropriation: to lay claim to this original source, this founding father, is to preserve the cultural heritage of an entire community. As such, local beliefs and legends on this subject take different forms, the most fascinating of which was communicated to me by St. Tammany Historical Society president Tom Aicklen during my first visit to Lacombe. According to this version, Choctaw friends stole Rouquette's body shortly after the funeral ceremony in New Orleans and brought it back to Lacombe, where it was buried beneath or actually sealed within a live oak near the site of the Church of the Sacred Heart, which he founded. As confirmation I was shown the tree in question—reputed to be the oldest in Lacombe—which serves as the priest's final resting place. Aicklen explained that Rouquette's request to be buried in Lacombe was based not only on his own attachment to the forest but also on his familiarity with the Choctaw practice of burying their dead near ancient oaks: merging with the immortal tree constituted eternal life. The story also resonates with Father Rouquette's Christianization of that tradition, as the Tree of the Choctaws becomes the body and blood of Jesus Christ. Merging with the live oak in this context would represent participation in the body of Christ—communion with God. In any event, it seems fitting to conclude that the present-day heirs to Father Rouquette's spiritual and cultural legacy have reinforced his original poetic and missionary enterprise by making their founding father quite literally part of the Louisiana landscape that produced in him such a deep sense of the sacred.

Notes

1. Like "Les Méchacébéennes," "Les Savanes" was well received in Paris, counting among its admirers Hugo, Lamartine, Chateaubriand, and Saint-Beuve. See J. A. Reinecke, "Les Frères Rouquette, poètes louisianais." *Comptes-Rendus de l'Athénée Louisianais* (1920) 12-85, and G. William Nott, "Adrien Rouquette: Poet and Mystic." *Louisiana Historical Quarterly* 6 (1923): 388-94.

2. See discussion of Choctaw population figures in Dagmar Renshaw LeBreton, *Chahta-Ima: The Life of Adrien-Emmanuel Rouquette* (Baton Rouge, LA: Louisiana State University Press, 1947), 8-11.

3. The first of these was constructed on land given to Rouquette by the Choctaws at the site of their largest settlement, Buchuwa, and was destroyed during the Civil War. Subsequent chapels were Chuka Chaha or the Night Cabin, Kildara or the Cabin of the Oak, Our Lady of the Wilderness, and the Nook. See LeBreton, 238-66.

4. See for example Antonio Benítez-Rojo, *The Repeating Island: The Caribbean and the Post-modern Perspective*, trans. James Maraniss (Durham, NC: Duke University Press, 1992); Chris Bongie, *Exotic Memories: Literature, Colonialism, and the Fin de Siècle* (Stanford: Stanford University Press, 1991); J. Michael Dash, *The Other America: Caribbean Literature in a New World Context* (Charlottesville, VA: University Press of Virginia, 1998); Edward W. Said, *Culture and Imperialism* (New York: Vintage Books, 1993); and Hayden White, *Tropics of Discourse: Essays in Cultural Criticism* (Baltimore: Johns Hopkins University Press, 1978).

5. Adrien-Émmanuel Rouquette, *La Nouvelle Atala ou La fille de l'esprit: Légende indienne par Chahta-Ima*. Édition critique, ed. Elizabeth Butcher Landry (Lafayette, LA: M.A. thesis, Southwestern Louisiana University, 1994) 58. All translations of writings by Rouquette cited in this article are my own.

6. *La Nouvelle Atala*, 137.

7. Adrien Rouquette, *La Thébaïde en Amérique ou Apologie de la vie solitaire et contemplative* (New Orleans, 1852).

8. *Apologie 7*. Lérins, now Saint-Honorat, is an island located off the coast of southern France. It is the site of an abbey founded in the fifth century by St.Honoratus, a hermit whose followers came from Roman Gaul and Brittany.

9. Dash, 28

10. "Hermit though he was, he had a passion for newspapers. He read them exhaustively, building up from them his store of knowledge with clippings of actualities, varying from congressional speeches and a notice of Bryant's birthday to scientific articles on the eucalyptus tree. A file of fifteen or more newspapers, most of them marked Bee and dated 1881, suggests that he picked up the exchange from the Bee's office, read them and clipped them as he found articles or opinions of value in their columns. Catholic in his interests, he constituted for himself a reserve of information from which he could draw, when the moment presented itself, for the benefit of others or which he kept as his own rich background against which to check his views and opinions," (LeBreton, 330-31).

11. Adrien Rouquette, *Les Savanes, poésies américaines* (Paris and New Orleans, 1841).

12. *Les Savanes, 75-76.*

13. *Les Savanes, 123.*

14. LeBreton, 136-37.

15. Adrien Rouquette, *Wild Flowers, Sacred Poetry* (New Orleans, 1848) 21-23.

16. *Les Savanes* 53-54.

17. *Les Savanes* 56.

18. Tom Aicklen, ed. "Bayou Lacombe Commemorative Booklet," (Lacombe, LA: 1976). Quoted material uncredited.

19. Blaise C. D'Antoni, *Chahta-Ima and St. Tammany's Choctaws* (Mandeville, LA. St. Tammany Historical Society, 1986) 163.

Chapter 5

The Theological Virtues in J. R. R. Tolkien's *Lord of the Rings*

Kerry J. MacArthur

Many commentators have noted certain Catholic features in J. R. R. Tolkien's *Lord of the Rings*, such as Eucharistic symbolism in the elves' *lembas*, also called "waybread," a fair translation of *viaticum*; or the Marian imagery associated with Elbereth and even Galadriel. And many commentators have discussed the question of the figure of the hero in *The Lord of the Rings*, even including the dismissal of Frodo as a hero by Harold Bloom.[1] But little has been made of Tolkien's heroes as Catholic figures. I would propose that the Catholic view of the Theological Virtues—Faith, Hope, and Charity—can shed light on the heroes of *The Lord of the Rings* and can provide a rationale for the peculiar division of the role of hero in this work.

Before proceeding, it may be desirable to address the problem of allegory in Tolkien. In the preface written for the paperback edition of *The Lord of the Rings*, Tolkien claims that he "cordially dislike[s] allegory in all its manifestations."[2] This statement, taken at face value, might seem to preclude the enterprise I intend to carry out, because it could fairly be called an allegorical reading. Tolkien's cordial dislike, however, needs to be understood in the context of his other works and of the state of allegorical understanding at mid-twentieth century.

The first thing to be noted is that in spite of his dislike of allegory, Tolkien wrote at least one story that is patently allegorical, "Leaf by Niggle," and "Smith of Wooton Major" certainly lends itself to allegorical interpretation. Thus it seems that Tolkien was at least occasionally willing to overlook his dislike.

Further, it needs to be kept in mind that Tolkien retired from teaching in 1959 and therefore was away from most academic pursuits before the modern revival of interest in allegory had established itself. Probably the two most influential books in this revival were Northrop Frye's *Anatomy of Criticism* (1957) and D. W. Robertson's *Preface to Chaucer* (1962), which clarified many misconceptions about how allegory actually works.

It is clear from remarks in his article "*Beowulf*: the Monsters and the Critics" (1936) that Tolkien used the term allegory to refer to what may be called simple or transparent allegory—writing that contains labeling that enables the reader to interpret readily the symbolic significance. There, in asserting that *Beowulf* is not an allegory, Tolkien says "the iron shield [Beowulf] bore against the serpent . . . was not yet the breastplate of righteousness."[3] In Tolkien's view, allegory seems to require clear labeling and a one-to-one correspondence of character, object, or action to abstract meaning. These requirements would come naturally to one of Tolkien's generation and nationality, to whom the first work to come to mind when hearing the word allegory would be *Pilgrim's Progress*. Even for an educated individual, allegory would primarily indicate Spenser's *Faerie Queen*, Langland's *Piers Plowman*, the *Pearl*, and medieval drama such as *Everyman*. All of these works operate by a more or less transparent allegorical machinery, though the subtlety of the use varies from work to work.

The research of D. W. Robertson and Bernard Huppé and others, along with the increasing awareness of sign theory, has enabled a later generation to recognize that *allegoresis* (at least potentially) is more important as a technique of reading than allegory is as a literary genre.[4]

Tolkien's objection to allegory in the "Foreword" is directed primarily toward those who read the book as an allegory of World War II, and who presumably interpreted the coalition of Gondor, Rohan, Rivendell, etc. as the allies while Sauron stood for Hitler. Tolkien points out some of the obvious flaws in this interpretation, but then goes on to distinguish between "applicability" and "allegory," applicability "resid[ing] in the freedom of the reader, and [allegory] in the purposed domination of the author."[5] His distinction between "applicability" and "allegory" matches closely the distinction drawn by D. W. Robertson and Bernard Huppé between *allegoresis*, allegorical reading, and *allegory*, the writing of transparent allegory.

My focus today is on the role of the theological virtues in *The Lord of the Rings*, and that is a subject that is inseparable from a discussion of Tolkien's "divided protagonist." One peculiarity of *The Lord of the Rings* is the dividing of the action of the book into two main actions, one of which is further subdivided into two actions. In each of these three actions, one of the members of the Fellowship acts generally as protagonist. The first sundering of the company occurs at Gandalf's fall in Moria. Thereafter he performs significant deeds in the rehabilitation of Theoden, the confrontation with Saruman, the sustenance of Minas Tirith, and the Battle of the Morannon. The second parting (aside from the death of Boromir) occurs when Aragorn leads Legolas and Gimli in the pursuit of the Orcs that have captured Merry and Pippin. Aragorn's subsequent acts include leadership at Helm's Deep, the challenge to Sauron using the *palantir*, the muster of the dead, the defeat of the Southron fleet, the succour of Minas Tirith, and the Battle of the Morannon.

The second parting also involves the beginning of Frodo's march to Mordor. Although Sam assumes an increasingly important role as this section continues, Frodo remains the protagonist of this action. Although he performs fewer actions than Gandalf or Aragorn, those he does are of highest significance. They include the taming of Gollum, the negotiations with Faramir, and the carrying of the Ring to the Cracks of Doom. Furthermore, though Sam performs many crucial acts, such as the defeat of Shelob and the rescue of Frodo from the guard tower, it is always Frodo who makes the decisions about which actions to follow.

The Lord of the Rings thus features a division of its most important actions among three chief characters, and most of these actions cannot be coordinated in the reader's mind until the three leading characters are reunited after the destruction of the Ring. Although this tripartite division may be seen as serving practical purposes in advancing the plot, it is certainly legitimate to ask whether a triple protagonist may have a function beyond the literal plot level.

Anyone asking such a question may very likely begin by tracing certain clues related to the character of Aragorn. A reading of this character's background, relationships, and actions leads one to consider the possibility that Aragorn has something to do with the virtue of Hope. In the first place we find that he is a man of many names. As a youth, as we read in Appendix A, he was called Estel to disguise him from his enemies.[6] In Lorien he receives at Galadriel's hand the gift from Arwen of a brooch with a green stone, along with his foretold name *Elessar*, Elfstone.[7]

The name Estel means "hope" in Elvish, and the story of Aragorn's youth contains many references to him as representing hope: Ivorwen prophesies concerning the marriage of Aragorn's parents, "If these two wed now, hope may be born for our people."[8] When Aragorn and Arwen betroth themselves to one another, Arwen expresses her confidence in Aragorn's future part in bringing about the downfall of Sauron. Aragorn answers, "with your hope I will hope."[9]

Further, when Arwen's father Elrond learns of their love for one another, he imposes a condition on their future union, namely that they may not marry until Aragorn has established himself as king of both Arnor and Gondor, incidentally using the word "hope" twice in his charge.[10] By terms of this condition, indeed, Aragorn must live the next long stage of his life in hope.

One more citation from Aragorn's younger days will round out the text-references identifying Aragorn with hope. When Aragorn's mother is about to die she says to her son, "Onen I-Estel Edain, ú-chebin estel anim," ("I gave Hope to Dunedain, I have kept no hope for myself.")[11]

One more citation seems to establish an association between hope and the elf-stone given to Aragorn at the hand of Galadriel. Galadriel says, "This stone I gave to Celebrian my daughter, and she to hers; and now it comes to you as a token of hope. In this hour take the name that was foretold for you, Elessar, the Elfstone of the house of Elendil."[12]

All of these passages refer primarily to hope as a natural human attitude, and not as a Christian virtue. They refer to hope in relation to such matters as success against enemies, the restoration of a legitimate dynasty, and betrothal. Is it possible to connect these natural hopes to the supernatural virtue of Hope?

If we consider valid the proposed connection between Elfstone and the idea of Hope, then it may profit us to consider the symbolism of the Elfstone. The Elfstone is "a great stone of a clear green, set in a silver brooch that was wrought in the likeness of an eagle with outspread wings."[13] At this point I would like merely to suggest that the green color of the stone (identified as a beryl[14] the green form of which is called emerald) associates the stone with the theological virtue of Hope. For example, in Dante's *Purgatorio*, in the allegorical procession that represents the Church, three women appear who represent the three theological virtues: one is red, the second green, and the third white. The green woman represents the virtue of Hope. Of interest is that the green woman is actually described not as simply being green but as "di smeraldo fatte"—"made of emerald."[15]

If this hint suffices, then it remains to consider whether Aragorn embodies the virtue of Hope in his person and actions within the story. First of all there is the matter of the "return of the king." Aragorn reestablishes a kingship that has been "in exile" for 1045 years in Arnor and for 969 years in Gondor. It is possible that Aragorn's "return" is meant to evoke the Arthurian myth of the return of the king in a time of need. That myth, whether associated with Arthur or Barbarossa, seems to be intended to provide a people with hope for the future, and it tends to take on semi-messianic overtones. When we consider that Aragorn, in riding to fight against the southern enemy, raises the dead, and that in the aftermath of battle he goes through the city healing the wounded, we discern that the hope associated with Aragorn's return takes on the appearance of a messianic hope.

Furthermore, we can see in regard to the *palantir* a textbook lesson in three parts on the virtue of Hope. The *palantiri* are seeing stones, originally seven in number, that were brought from Numenor to Middle Earth by the Dunedain. At the time of *The Lord of the Rings*, all are thought to have been lost. Two turn up in the course of the story, however, one at Orthanc and one at Minas Tirith. It is also evident that Sauron has obtained at least one. Through the *palantiri* people can see things and communicate at great distances.

Although Gandalf initially takes charge of the *palantir* gained from Saruman at Orthanc, it is shortly made clear that it belongs to Aragorn as the heir of Isildur, for Gandalf surrenders it to him with respect, though he warns against trying to use it.[16]

Three characters make substantial use of the *palantiri*—Aragorn, Denethor, and Saruman. Aragorn's use of it is successful, though quite taxing. His right to the *palantir* is established quite clearly by his ability to overcome Sauron's control of it, though Sauron is of a much higher nature of being and, in himself, far more powerful.

We discover, shortly before Denethor's death, that he has habitually used the *palantir* of Minas Anor to gain knowledge of events in the world. However, Sauron has been able to manipulate Denethor's vision so that he sees only what Sauron wants him to see. Denethor's ultimate response to what he sees in the *palantir* is despair. In fact, it is at the height of Denethor's despair, when he declares, "The West has failed. It shall all go up in a great fire, and shall be ended. Ash! Ash and blown away on the wind," that his possession of the *palantir* is revealed.[17] Denethor himself associates the *palantir* with his despair when he tells Gandalf, "I have seen more than thou knowest, Grey Fool. For thy hope is but ignorance."[18] Seeing, specifically far-seeing (the meaning of *palantir* is "far-seer") is directly associated here with despair.

The other character who uses a *palantir* is Saruman. As in the case of Denethor the reader sees the effect before the cause. Gandalf reports Saruman's betrayal at the Council of Elrond. As Gandalf reports it, that betrayal consists of a grandiose plan to claim the Ring for himself and place himself over all of Middle Earth as a wise and powerful ruler. At the time Saruman claims extensive knowledge of Sauron's activities and plans, and it is this knowledge that motivates him to presume to aspire to absolute power himself. Thus Saruman's use of the *palantir* leads him to presumption.

As we can see, the use of the *palantir* by two characters who have no right to it leads to either despair or presumption, the two traditional sins against the virtue of Hope.

If we turn back to the three women in Dante's *Purgatorio*, we find that the one representing Faith is white. The character in *The Lord of the Rings* most associated with white is Gandalf after his return from seeming death. Indeed he is now called Gandalf the White instead of Gandalf the Grey. Although his change in color comes about because of his succession to Saruman's abdicated position at the head of the Council, an examination of his actions shows that they can be consistently interpreted as evoking primarily Faith.

A significant shift takes place in Gandalf's role after he has returned as Gandalf the White. Before his fall in Moria he primarily served as a counselor and a leader. We see him as a counselor primarily in his account to Frodo of the history and importance of the Ring, and in his contributions to the Council of Elrond. We see him primarily as leader in the Fellowship's journey south from Rivendell. After his return Gandalf still performs these functions, but a new or enhanced function begins to take center stage—the function of instigator or inspirer. This function first manifests itself in Gandalf's handling of Theoden in his despondent state. Theoden has been brought to a state of doubt through the treacherous advice of Grima Wormtongue. In this state he doubts his own prowess, the loyalty of Eomer, and the good intentions of his friends, including Gandalf himself. Ostensibly through words alone Gandalf is able to restore Theoden to a more youthful vigor and to a more confident frame of mind.

Later, at the siege of Minas Tirith, Gandalf performs the same task on behalf of the defenders of the city: "Wherever he came men's hearts would lift again, and the winged shadows pass from memory."[19] It is here that Gandalf's power to dispel fear and doubt becomes associated specifically with his raised hand. First at Faramir's return from Ithilien and later in the retreat from Osgiliath, Gandalf rides out to repulse the pursuing Nazgul. When he does, "a shaft of white light" issues from his raised hand that repels the Nazgul.[20]

The conclusion of the book (The Grey Havens) reveals that one source of Gandalf's power to encourage his allies and repulse his foes is the Elf-ring Narya, known as the Kindler, given to him by Cirdan.[21] Though the gem of this ring is red, it issues a white light, as seen in the passages cited above.

Interestingly, the two characters who sin against Hope in their dealings with the *palantir* also sin against Faith in their relationship to Gandalf. Saruman, a colleague of Gandalf's on the White Council, betrays this council and the mission on which the wizards (Istari) were sent to Middle Earth. He can thus be seen as guilty of apostasy.

Denethor's despair seems to be based on doubt, a doubt both in the ability of normal human beings to accomplish their task of defense, and a doubt in Providence, a doubt that those agents sent by the Valar have the ability to defeat Sauron. It may be that the artifact linking Gandalf, Saruman, and Denethor is the staff. The two wizards have staffs that serve as both tools and badges of office. Denethor, as steward of Gondor, has as his only badge of office a white rod with a gold ball at the top.

The remaining member of Dante's troupe of three women is red. Can we associate the color red with Frodo? Although the primary artifact associated with Frodo is a plain gold Ring, this Ring evokes the color red in several ways. First, the Ring is initially identified by Gandalf by reviving, through exposure to fire, its red lettering. In addition, much of the discussion that takes place about the Ring refers to its forging in the fires of Mount Doom. From the beginning, then, fire is associated with the Ring, giving a red overtone to the gold.

Incidentally, as an expert in Anglo-Saxon language and literature, Tolkien would have been aware that the usual color-word used to describe gold in Old English is "red" (*ræd*). It is possible that Tolkien's normative color word for gold, through habituation to Old English, was red, rather than yellow.

In the closing chapters of the book the red coloring associated with the Ring grows even stronger as Frodo sees it in his mind as a burning wheel of fire.[22] As he approaches Mount Doom, this vision begins to exclude all else and becomes almost the only thing he sees. Thus, increasingly, red is all that Frodo sees.

Furthermore, Frodo bleeds more than any member of the Fellowship (other than Boromir at his death). Of all of the surviving members of the Fellowship, Frodo is the only one seriously wounded—stabbed by the Nazgul, stung by Shelob, and his finger bitten off by Gollum. These wounds, though I have introduced them in order to show Frodo's association with the color red, bring us beyond color to action. One of Frodo's primary actions is to suffer. Indeed the fact, previously mentioned, that Frodo is the only seriously wounded member of the Fellowship highlights his suffering. Furthermore, his woundedness becomes an almost essential part of his being. He never fully recovers, in Middle Earth, from any of his wounds, and they produce incapacitating pain on the anniversaries of his having received them.

But the most important action of Frodo is his sacrifice of himself on behalf of others. It is clear that Frodo loves many goods in the world. He loves his foster-father Bilbo, his companions Sam, Merry, and Pippin, and he loves the Shire. He does not, however, cling to these goods in order to possess them. He sacrifices himself to the extent that he can in love for all of them, and that is one good definition of Charity. By the end Frodo has given almost all of himself and cannot himself enjoy the benefits attained or the goods preserved through his sacrifices.

It may be possible to see two characters in the story as sinning particularly against Charity—Gollum and Sauron. Both of them violate Charity through avarice, but each is avaricious in a different direction. By this I mean that Sauron's avarice seems to be directed outward—he desires the whole world, and he desires the Ring as a means to attain all the world. Gollum, on the other hand, desires only the Ring as an end in itself. Gollum practices avarice as a miser, but Sauron as a tyrant, as Chaucer explains in *The Parson's Tale*.[23]

Although this treatment does not exhaust the subject, I hope I have been able to suggest that the three protagonists in *The Lord of the Rings* evoke the three Theological Virtues, that this evocation is associated with specific colors and specific artifacts, and that in relation to each virtue two characters are presented as sinning in different ways against each virtue. These considerations raise hopes that further study will elucidate additional structural and symbolic patterns that will serve to unfold the meaning of *The Lord of the Rings*.

Notes

1. Harold Bloom, "Introduction," *Modern Critical Interpretations: J. R. R. Tolkien's The Lord of the Rings*, (Philadelphia, PA: Chelsea House, 2000), 2.

2. J. R. R. Tolkien, *The Lord of the Rings*, 1 vol. paperback edition (NY: Houghton Mifflin, 1994), xvii.

3. J. R. R. Tolkien, "Beowulf: The Monsters and the Critics," in *An Anthology of Beowulf Criticism*, ed. Lewis E. Nicholson (Notre Dame, IN: University of Notre Dame Press, 1963), 74.

4. See, for example, D. W. Robertson, Jr., *A Preface to Chaucer* (Princeton, NJ: Princeton University Press, 1962) and Bernard Huppé, *A Reading of the Canterbury Tales* (Albany, NY: SUNY Press, 1964) 3-9.

5. Tolkien, *LOTR*, xvii.

6. Tolkien, *LOTR*, 1032.

7. Tolkien, *LOTR*, 366.

8. Tolkien, *LOTR*, 1032.

9. Tolkien, *LOTR*, 1035.

10. Tolkien, *LOTR*, 1036.

11. Tolkien, *LOTR*, 1036.

12. Tolkien, *LOTR*, 366.

13. Tolkien, *LOTR*, 366.

14. Tolkien, *LOTR*, 196.

15. Dante Alighieri, *Purgatorio*, ed. G. A. Scartazzini (Milano: Ulrico Hoepli, 1896), *Canto 29*, lines 121-9.

16. Tolkien, *LOTR*, 580.

17. Tolkien, *LOTR*, 834.

18. Tolkien, *LOTR*, 835.

19. Tolkien, *LOTR*, 806.

20. Tolkien, *LOTR*, 792.

21. Tolkien, *LOTR*, 1007.

22. Tolkien, *LOTR*, 898.

23. Geoffrey Chaucer, "The Canterbury Tales," in *The Riverside Chaucer*, ed. Larry D. Benson (Boston: Houghton Mifflin, 1987), 313-4.

Chapter 6

Santiago in the Americas:
The Iconography of the Conqueror and the Infidel

Kimberly Habegger

While religious art tends to focus on the portrayal of a given faith's protagonists' tenets and values, the representation of the religious *other* personifies what a religion opposes such as evil, polytheism, etc. The juxtaposition of the protagonist and the *other* offers a vivid didactic example for the viewer of the ceremonial artifact. The religious art to be analyzed in this study is produced within the framework of (Spanish) Roman Catholicism. The ideological *other* that collides with Catholicism often appears in these artifacts alongside the protagonists. Originally taking the form of the Muslim during the Middle Ages, the conceptualization of the infidel expands to include the Protestant and other heretics as a consequence of the Counter-Reformation. The *other* eventually encompasses the indigenous peoples of the Americas.

With the entrenchment of the Spanish presence in the New World, the enemy of the faith is represented visually through the religious art produced in both Europe and the American continents. Among the Latin American artifacts, some iconographic elements can be traced to Spanish sources while others more accurately reflect the Latin American world and its belief systems. The infidel can be represented symbolically or more literally: the image of Saint George slaying the dragon exemplifies the symbolical while that of Saint James slaying the Moors illustrates the more literal. In this study we will analyze images of Saint James, or Santiago Matamoros. As Santiago had crusaded against the Moors in the Middle Ages in the peninsula, he subsequently fought to convert the indigenous peoples of the Americas. Santiago's influence in his adopted land manifests itself through iconographic renditions, anecdotal evidence and ceremonial practices throughout the centuries and in numerous locations in the Spanish Empire. As evidenced in the Cathedral of Santiago de Compostela, Saint James has been portrayed in three distinct manners in the Spanish tradition: as apostle, pilgrim, or warrior. A representative sampling of New Mexican artifacts reveals that *retablos* and *bultos* featuring Santiago as warrior in combat with the infidel far outnumber Santiago's other manifestations.

Characteristic portrayals of Santiago, with particular emphasis on New Mexican examples, will illustrate the methods in which the infidel has been depicted in Spanish and Latin American religious art.

Patron saint of Spain, Santiago (San Iago in Old Spanish) underwent numerous reincarnations and adaptations until he was exported to the New World. This medieval Santiago consisted of a conglomeration of historical and mythical figures including, but not limited to, James the apostle of Christ, the Roman deities Castor and Pollux, and the early Christian thinker Prisciliano. He also embodied the response to Islam's Mohammed. After arrival in the New World, Santiago continues to adapt to his new environment; eventually the causes for which he fights and those he challenges in battle evolve to reflect the space and the time he occupies. A study of his depiction in American art would be incomplete without first acquiring an understanding of his Spanish manifestations.

Donna Pierce details the evolution of the iconography depicting Saint James in terms of the three phases of development mentioned in the introduction: James the Apostle, James the pilgrim, and Santiago Matamoros the warrior. Historically, Santiago was represented first as apostle, then as pilgrim, and finally as warrior. Despite this overall evolution, these different interpretations can appear simultaneously. Located in the Cathedral of Santiago de Compostela, the main altar displays the three roles of Santiago in vertical organization: "Tenemos en la capilla mayor tres imagenes de Santiago. De abajo a arriba la de Santiago Maestro, obra del taller de Mateo; luego las de Santiago Peregrino y Santiago Caballero, esta última de Mateo de Prado."[1] Santiago, the warrior, is placed above the other two images; all are positioned over what are believed to be the physical remains of the disciple of Christ known as James the Greater. Before entering into the portrayal of the conqueror and the vanquished of Santiago Matamoros imagery, let us briefly summarize the iconography of these three manifestations of Santiago.

During Christianity's earliest years, Christians employed a symbolic iconography in order to avoid persecution. After the conversion of Roman emperor Constantine in A.D. 312, the apostles were portrayed as a group of twelve identical men in the company of Christ; any identification of individuals was achieved by the use of inscriptions.[2] In the iconography depicting the disciples after the dispersal, identification occurs through the portrayal of the corresponding form of martyrdom (in the case of James, a beheading). As the apostles begin to be represented as individuals, they are attributed with specific physical characteristics such as white hair for Saint Peter, clean-shaven youthful looks for Saint John, and dark hair and a beard for Saint James, a man in the prime of life.[3]

As of the sixth century, the disciples are depicted with individual characteristics and symbols of their martyrdom and/or miracles: the sword associated with James references his beheading. Beginning during this period, Saint James often appears as a pilgrim with the characteristic pilgrim's staff, cloak, and cape, wide-brimmed hat, knapsack, and water gourd. Eventually, a scallop became associated with the saint and was added either to his hat or his cape. As the result of the many pilgrimages to the holy Galician site, the faithful give witness to many miracles that allegedly transpired en route and attribute them to Saint James. These occurrences, such as the miracle of the fowls and the origins of Saint James' shell, are eventually represented iconographically as well.[4]

The *Crónica general*, written under the direction of Alfonso el Sabio, offers the physical description of Santiago Matamoros on which later iconographic representations will be based. The *Crónica* attests to Santiago's first apparition at the Battle of Clavijo circa 813. The saint promises King Ramiro I that he will intervene in the impending battle against the Moors; in so doing, he describes the appearance that he will assume: "Et por que non dubdes nada en esto que te digo yo, veerem'edes cras andar y en la lid, en un cavallo blanco, con una seña blanca et grand espada reluzinet en la mano."[5] The iconographic elements of Santiago Matamoros typically include the following: the apostle is dressed as a warrior mounted on a white steed; in one hand he carries a sword, in the other a white banner emblazoned with the red cross of Santiago. The most evocative aspect of the imagery is the presence of the fallen, often beheaded, infidels.

The various visual signs described above have both unifying and differentiating functions with regard to the Santiago myths. For example, the headgear depicted (halo, pilgrim's hat, knight's helmet) aids the viewer in relating the image to its corresponding myth. Signs such as the sword and decapitated heads establish a connection between the myths of the apostle and the warrior, while the pilgrim's gear references both the travels and ministry of Saint James the Apostle as well as the pilgrimage to Santiago.

Based on strong oral, literary, and iconographic traditions, Santiago is transported to and readily assimilated in the Americas. New World literary sources describe Santiago's intervention on behalf of the Spaniards and/or Christians in at least fourteen confrontations, primarily with the Indigenous population. Oñate's raid on the Acoma Pueblo in 1599 was reportedly one of these instances. According to Gaspar Pérez de Villagrá's *Historia de la Nueva México*, during the aftermath of the battle, Indians described having witnessed "a noble Spaniard who was foremost in every encounter. They say he was mounted on a white steed. He had a long white beard, bald head, and carried a flaming sword in his right hand."[6] Villagrá's description appears to be either lifted from a medieval Spanish chronicle or the result of the Indians describing the imagery on the banners the Spaniards carried into battle.[7] The transference of the mentality of the *Reconquista* to the American arena justified the military struggle with and the eventual conquest of a people of different practices and spiritual traditions. The protectors of the faith were obliged to convert or vanquish the *other*.

Despite Santiago's initial preference for defending Spaniards and spreading the faith, later renditions reveal a gradual transformation as Santiago becomes an American crusader fighting for increasingly profane or popular causes. Spain's patron saint eventually becomes deeply entrenched among the indigenous groups as well: María Concepción García Sáiz summarizes the phenomenon:

> Thus it is not surprising that he (Santiago) should lend his image to Illapa, the god of thunder of the Peruvian mountain communities. Nor is it surprising that he should lend his image to the Chunchos, their traditional enemies, nor even, no matter how paradoxical it may seem, that he should join the American armies and appear in the nineteenth century against the Spaniards.[8]

García Sáiz concludes that Santiago is "no longer one of the pillars of Spanish history, but instead the clearest representation of one of the keys of Spanish culture, syncretism."[9]

Far removed from Spain and the colonial centers of the empire, the northern-most region of the colonies also adopted the saint as their own. As Thomas Steele explains: "And so, domesticated in New Mexico as he had been in Spain, and with the ready transfer from Moors to uncooperative Indians made in the first year of the new colony's experience, Santiago is ready to serve the outlying colony as he had the mother country, as patron of soldiers attacking the unchristian enemy."[10] Yet, as in South America, the saint found followers among the indigenous groups, particularly the Pueblo Indians of New Mexico. Santiago, along with San Rafael, the patron of fishermen, are the only two Catholic saints truly integrated into the Tewa mind. Alfonso Ortiz explains that the Pueblo Indians' interest in Catholic saints was limited because the Pueblo gods and goddesses already adequately covered the needs of their people. Yet the Tewa did assimilate Santiago and San Rafael as the horse and new fishing techniques became integrally woven into their culture and they had no native spirits for either.[11] According to Steele's inventory of 1000 authentic New Mexican *santos*, Santiago was the fifteenth most represented image of colonial New Mexican manufacture. Perhaps the New Mexicans' *santero* interest in the portrayal of Santiago derived, in part, from the neighboring Pueblos' assimilation of the saint.

Of the Apostle, pilgrim, and warrior types, it is this last version of Santiago that is transported and adopted most readily in the Americas; in New Mexico Santiago Matamoros is represented to the exclusion of the other two. The portrayal of the infidel in Spanish-American religious art is of particular interest due to the simultaneous continuity and adaptations of the Santiago legend to the American cultural environments. The iconography of the infidel can be analyzed in terms of the infidel's existence or absence in a given work, with regard to the physical distribution of the bodies, and with attention directed towards the infidel's ethnic identity or historical origin.

The disposition of the bodies/body parts of the infidel offers one method of classification. The enemy may be in the process of being slain, the cadavers may be at rest, or the bodies may be decapitated. If decapitated, the heads may be dispersed randomly, in a grid pattern, or the heads may merge with the hooves of the warrior's charger. In certain instances, Santiago's foes are not represented. In figures in the round, this may be a result of the structural complexity of the replication of extra figures. Or perhaps, this is the result of a stylistic choice on the part of the *santero* in order to emphasize the saint's other attributes. The ethnic identity of the infidel tends to reflect that of the immediate historical enemy at the time of production. Spanish iconography identifies the Moors through the incorporation of turbaned heads, dark beards and *musyaches*, and Middle Eastern garments. Although American iconography applies these methods of identification, *santos* portraying clearly indigenous enemies also exist. An etching of Santiago Matamoros executed by Guaman Poma during the early colonial period in Peru offers a clear example of this phenomenon. The obviously Andean headdress and garments indicate that the military foe is a fallen Inca warrior; this ethnic identification correlates to the historical enemy of the Faith from the vantage point of Guaman Poma, a Christian Indian. Other historical variations and/or inaccuracies in the portrayal of the enemy are common; some of which will be illustrated subsequently.

These same variations occur in the representation of Santiago, whose standard iconography has been established previously. At times there exists a kind of historical dissonance between the Santiago and his corresponding enemy portrayed in a given artifact. For instance, the Santiago may reflect dress of the *santero*'s epoch yet the enemy appears to be a Medieval Moor. The *santero* does not always modernize/Americanize both images evenly resulting in interesting and complex iconography.

A body of significant scholarly contributions by Rolena Adorno has centered on the life and work of Guaman Poma. Her work analyzes the written text and accompanying iconography used in *El primer nueva crónica y buen gobierno* authored by Guaman Poma circa 1615 and explicitly written for King Phillip III of Spain. Through the analysis of the vestimentary code and the code of pictorial background representation, Poma's work demonstrates how "native Andean and conventional European icons can be combined in a pictorial construct to create a syntactically complete statement that is intelligible to the viewer."[12] Adorno's study offers compelling insights into how signs from two different cultures coexist to impart a rich and complex message. Although her approach has been adapted in this study, it does have certain limitations for our purposes. The iconography of the Santiago *santos,* and of all religious subjects, varies little as it used for didactic purposes for a largely illiterate faithful; thus ease of recognition is imperative. In contrast, Guaman Poma portrays a wide variety of subjects without the limitations of a preexisting iconographic code. In addition, Guaman Poma wrote during a historical period approximately seventy years after the conquest; consequently the signs of the Andean world were still in existence and had suffered limited transformation as a result of European contact. However, the typical New Mexican *santero* produced his *santos* approximately two hundred years later in an environment far from the powerful cultural influences (with its corresponding iconography) of a civilization such as the Incan. As a result, the contrasts and the complexity that Adorno discovers in Guaman Poma's work cannot be equaled in the analysis of the Santiago imagery.

The church of San José de Gracia is located in Las Trampas, New Mexico, along the High Road to Taos. The altar is clearly defined against the stark whiteness of the adobe walls. To the left of the altar hangs a large *retablo* of Santiago. The central image of the composition is the holy personage portrayed with typical European characteristics: light skin, a beard, etc. The dress of the saint is contemporary to the period of production and also regional in style: the military uniform mimics that of a mid-nineteenth-century Mexican officer. The saint possesses the obligatory sword, banner, (although it is not held in his hand) and white charger—note the particularly human quality of the horse's eye. Santiago also carries a shield in his left hand. The dominant aspect of the background is the presence of the fallen infidels. Despite the American and historical modifications to the protagonist, the antagonists are portrayed as Moors, not as indigenous warriors. Nevertheless, the infidels are not decapitated nor are they wearing the turban, two common identifying traits. To the modern eye, the nineteenth-century hero appears out of place framed by his fallen Moorish enemies.

Another noteworthy representation of Santiago is located farther south on the High Road in the Santuario de Chimayó. Unlike the *retablo* of Las Trampas, this image is a *bullto*, or statue. Authentic New Mexican examples of Santiago *bultos* are rare, perhaps due to the technical difficulty of producing the horse, much less the infidels. This *bulto* has no background figures to be analyzed therefore only the vestimentary code can be examined. This work was carved by an anonymous *santero* and it appears in a church inventory in 1818. The clothing of *Señor Santiago*, as he is known, suggests that of the conquistador, not that of the period of manufacture. Nevertheless, the image possesses two sombreros of Mexican style and rustic quirts and a short sword somewhat indigenous in appearance and certainly unlike the long medieval knight's sword typically depicted. *Señor Santiago* carries no banner, which is not uncommon among authentic examples. However, by his positioning it seems that a banner was part of the original design. The saint appears at rest, not in battle, and his enemies are not referenced. The pensive, even spiritual quality of the saint is emphasized in this artifact at the expense of his war-waging image.

Found in the New Mexican Museum of International Folk Art, a *retablo* by well-known New Mexican *santero* Molleno (1815-1845) offers another rendition of the infidel. Only the severed heads of the infidel appear in this *retablo*. Due to the beards and *musyaches*, the heads are most likely of Moors although there are no turbans to aid in identification. The four heads are clustered around the horse's hooves although they do not touch the animal. The heads are dispersed in a black trellis pattern. Within each space formed by the trellis there are two to four quotation-like marks and red highlights run throughout the field. The red color suggests the enemies' bloodshed in battle. Santiago's cloak evokes his role of medieval pilgrim more than that of conquistador or late-colonial military officer. Nevertheless, the hat, while crudely portrayed, seems to be contemporaneous with the period of manufacture as similar depictions frequently appear in New Mexican iconography.

An additional *retablo* by Molleno located in the same museum, illustrates how the infidels' heads can merge with the charger's hooves. The saint is clothed in garb nearly identical to that of the previous example; here the spur is more clearly discernable. It is difficult to determine if the heads are severed or if they are still connected to their bodies. Imploring hands raised to the heavens appear to be connected to torsos dispersed in a sea of red leaf-like or *bota* shapes; the portrayal of the human suffering of the infidel is not typically of concern in the iconography of Santiago Matamoros. The conical headgear may crudely reference Moorish turbans yet it seems more similar to either the ceremonial hoods used by *penitentes* or the headdress portrayed in chronicles created after the conquest. An illustration from the *Codex Durán* (chapter 6) portrays Quetzalcoatl whose identifying iconographic traits were his beak and "pointed miter of paper."[13] Of course, one can only speculate as to what source may have served as Molleno's model for the infidel's headgear in this *retablo*.

The iconography of the infidel can be abstract or representative. Through the act of representation, the infidels' ethnic identity (and consequently their religious beliefs) takes shape. The evolving and/or ambiguous ethnicity of Santiago's foes reflects the historical environment of the *santero*. New Mexican religious art is characterized by a syncretistic iconography typical of that produced in an environment of multiple ethnicities (much less an environment where one segment of the population was brutally subjugated by the other). Among some of the more provocative questions remaining is why the infidels are typically portrayed as Moors and not as Indians, particularly when Mexican and New Mexican written testimonies clearly indicate that Santiago's opponents are indigenous people. Another question lies in the frequent historical dissonance resulting from incongruous portrayals of Santiago and the infidel. Is this the result of an uneducated artist imitating models from different sources or could there be a symbolic intent behind the imagery? The consideration of the ethnic identity of both the artist and the intended recipient of the work of art must be considered as well: New Mexican icons were created by and for mestizos who are simultaneously the vanquished and the victors (the beneficiaries and the disinherited) of the cultural/religious conquests resulting from the encounter between the European and American continents. Given this, it may seems ironic that Santiago would appeal to the New Mexican faithful, yet despite its mestizo heritage, this population as a whole has identified strongly with its Spanish roots. Steele elaborates: "However much the Spanish in New Mexico may have been racially an Indian-Spanish mixture or even in some cases pureblooded Indian, they thought themselves to be both culturally and racially Spanish."[14]

While the mestizo embrace of Santiago may seem problematic, certainly the Indian incorporation of the saint would be more so. While not iconographically represented, the ceremonial activities of the indigenous populations in South America, Meso America, and the Southwestern United States reveal a Santiago transformed once more. In such ceremonies the Christian/infidel battle is recreated with a twist: Santiago is either appropriated or conquered by the indigenous people.

In brief, those who revere Santiago view him as the representation of nationhood or the faith in conflict with (and eventually in defeat of) the *other*. The result of syncretism over the centuries and across continents, Santiago and his crusade have adapted to reflect this struggle among numerous antagonistic peoples.

Notes

1. Jesús Precedo Lafuente, *Guía de visita: Catedral de Santiago de Compostela* (Aldeasa, 1998) 23.

2. Donna Pierce, "Santiago Through the Centuries in Art," in *Santiago: Saint of Two Worlds.* Joan Meyers, Photographer (Albuquerque: University of New Mexico Press, 1991) 33.

3. Pierce, 36.

4. Pierce, 42.

5. Américo Castro, *España en su historia: Cristianos, Moros y Judíos.* (Buenos Aires: Editorial Losada, S.A., 1948) 113.

6. Gaspar Pérez de Villagrá, *Historia de la Nueva México, 1610.* Eds. Miguel Encinas, Alfred Rodíguez and Joseph P. Sánchez (Albuquerque: University of New Mexico Press, 1992). Quote from Thomas J Steele, S.J. *Santos and Saints: The Religious Folk Art of Hispanic New Mexico.* (Santa Fe: Ancient City Press, 1994) 114.

7. Emilio Choy, "De Santiago Matamoros a Santiago mata-indios," in *Antropologia e historia.* Ed. Emilio Choy (Lima: Universidad Nacional de San Marcos, 1979) 421.

8. María Concepción García Saíz, "Constructing a tradition," in *Folk Art of Spain and the Americas.* Ed. Marion Oettinger, Jr., (New York: Abbeville Press Publishers, 1997) 156.

9. Saíz, 157.

10. Steele, 114.

11. Alfonso Ortiz, *The Tewa World.* (Chicago: University of Chicago Press, 1969) 156 and Steele 110-11.

12. Rolena Adorno, "On Pictorial Language and the Typology of Culture in a New World Chronicle," in *Semiotica* 36.1-2 (1981): 53.

13. Serge Gruzinski, *Painting the Conquest.* (Paris: Flammarion, 1992) 61.

14. Steele, 105.

PART II
Culture and Holiness

Overview

Mary as Human Exemplar

Sister Paula Jean Miller, FSE

On May 20, 1982, Pope John Paul II founded the Pontifical Council for Culture and formulated its goals. In the letter of foundation, the Holy Father stated that "man lives a fully human life thanks to culture."[1] He became even more specific, proclaiming that the future of humanity depends upon culture; that we discover ourselves in the ground of culture, the fundamental reality that unites us; and that culture is that by which and in which each person becomes ever more human. If holiness is indeed "wholeness," and as fully alive women and men we are "the glory of God" as Saint Irenaeus declares, then culture is integral to human holiness as the perfection of the divine image and likeness, and personal and communal holiness is the medium for the conversion and transformation of culture. Each and every culture is constituted by human persons who have not yet reached perfection, who are still plagued by the effects of sin—and therefore each culture, like each individual, stands in need of purification and authentic development in the full truth about the human person. This is what the Gospel brings to culture: "a specific vision of love as self-sacrifice, an experience which prods men and women to explore the heights and the depths of human relationships."[2]

While Faith is independent of any culture, each and every dimension of human life, every concrete situation must be touched by the faith of the believer, for as the

Pope states, "a faith which does not become culture is a faith not fully received, not entirely thought through, not faithfully lived."[3] As the Holy Father states again and again in *Christifideles Laici,* the challenge to the Church laity is to vitiate the separation between faith and life, to eliminate the "compartmentalization" of faith in society, to fulfill culture as the "substratum waiting for the incarnation of Christianity."

This section of *Mapping the Catholic Cultural Landscape* explores the intimate relationship between holiness and culture as that is embodied in the lives and lands of the saints. Particular emphasis is placed upon the "Queen of all Saints," the Virgin of Nazareth, who is now known as the Lady of Jasna Góra (the Black Madonna), the Aztec pregnant maiden of Guadalupe, Our Lady of Lourdes, and Fatima, and Knoch. Virtually every Christian culture has come to possess and name her as its own and depicted her with its own ethnic face. Mary is our exemplar because she is the fully human one who has been filled with grace, and because she said her human "yes" to the Incarnation, the body of humanity is able to participate in the divinizing grace of Christ. Mary is earth giving its *fiat* to the God of heaven. Unlike her Son, she is not divine by nature but is like us: called to be the Woman of Faith and to transform the world by preparing peoples for the mystery of the Incarnation: God become flesh.

Diverse cultures celebrate Mary as an enthroned queen, a maternal ruler, yet the biblical maiden. Each member of the communion of saints who constitute the court of this Queen celebrate her intercession in their human need under a proliferation of titles of devotion: Our Lady of perpetual help, gate of heaven, help of the sick, refuge of sinners—Mother of us all. The contributors to this section have chosen to look closely at the lives of three women who were able to perceive a pattern in the way of relationship of this Woman to human culture and to apply the principles learned to their own time and place: Rose of Lima, Peru—a Dominican religious; Jehanne d'Arc, the warrior maiden of France (the Church's "eldest daughter"); and Mathilde Boutle (Lucie Christine), a wife, mother, and mystic in modern France.

The relationship between faith and culture is not static nor is it even consistent; cultures go through cycles of development and the inculturation of the Faith ebbs and flows through the growing pains of humanity. The saints that emerge from each culture, and in relation to the strengths and weaknesses of a culture within a particular historical period, radiate the meaning of sanctity, of holiness, as that is called forth by the human crises of the day. Sanctity emerges in the cloister and the streets, in times of war and days of peace, in relationships of love and in the sufferings of marital discord.

The first three chapters examine holiness in the particular cultural expression of its relationship to the Blessed Virgin Mary. Father Janusz Ihnatowicz, a canon of Kielce, Poland, traces the history of the icon of Our Lady of Jasna Góra and explains the powerful devotion of the Polish people to Mary as she is depicted in this icon over a period of hundreds of years. Poland as a land is the gateway between East and West and this icon expresses the unique assimilation of both Catholic traditions within a single culture. Devotion to Our Lady of Jasna Góra is intertwined with

Polish nationalism throughout the centuries, and so it was natural for her image to become associated with the Poles' Solidarity strike in the Gadansk shipyard in 1980. This devotion to Mary, Father Ihnatowicz asserts, partly explains why Poland did not succumb to the Protestant Reformation.

Phil Lampe of Incarnate Word University, Texas, provides us with an insightful statistical study of the relationship between the naming of Marian churches in the United States, and the lack of due proportion to the cultural groups geographically represented. Since one measure of importance or influence is the frequency something is named or used within a culture, the dedication of churches under the patronage of Mary, as revered by a particular cultural group, is significant. Data gathered from 1926 to 2000 indicates a current lack of social acceptance in the United States of the ethnic groups with which Our Lady of Guadalupe is identified, in spite of the fact that she is the declared patroness of the Americas.

Within the Catholic tradition, Luis González of the Universidad de Monterrey, Mexico explains that "It is interesting to note the flexible reception of Mary by local communities." Perhaps Mary is subjected to a wider range of popular interpretations than the figure of Jesus because Mary's "incorporation into tradition is perhaps less complicated or dangerous than the appropriation of Christ." The author proposes that studying Marian literature in the context of community reinterpretation reveals that some "popular devotions existed long before any official theological statement was promulgated." In other words, "A religious discourse was alive in literature and art, and this form of catechesis probably taught the faithful long before any statement was given." González observes that "Mary's appropriations in the literature of Spanish-speaking countries can easily reveal to us the cultural backgrounds, the value systems and even the social expectations of their authors."

The second half of this section develops the relationship of the communion of saints to the Queen of Saints. Utilizing contemporary texts, Father Brichta-López, O.P., examines the Marian devotion of Saint Rose of Lima. "Although Rose's spiritual life remained Christ-centered throughout her adulthood," Father López writes, "she repeatedly turned to the Virgin Mary for the nurturance lacking in her biological parents." It was through the Virgin, Father Lopez believes, "that Rose approached Christ, the Virgin's son, who as the Infant Jesus visited [Rose] early in her life while she prayed and embroidered in the silence of her hermitage and who subsequently betrothed himself to her with the words, "*Rosa de mi corazon, sea mi esposa!*" Later in life, while racked with bouts of painful illness, "[Rose] identified with the crucified Christ." Nevertheless, the author concludes, "it was always the Virgin Mary who led Rose to Christ, whether as child or adult."

Father Ted Baenziger of the University of St. Thomas traces "some of the *grande lignes* of the history of the saints and culture in that country [France] so closely tied to our own United States." The history of canonized saints in France is also important because of its long and close (if tumultuous) relationship with the Church of Rome. France has been dubbed the Church's "eldest daughter,"since she was converted to Christianity early in her history, and then "helped to shape the Christian world from North America to Indochina, from the Holy Land to Equatorial Africa." Father Baenziger places the concept of sanctity into its broader theological context by explaining its meaning in terms of liturgical worship and the developing theological understanding of *dulia* and *hyperdulia*: the distinctions between the worship of God (*Sanctus*: the Holy One), our honor of the saints (*dulia*) and the special reverence given to Mary, the Mother of God (*hyperdulia*). Within this framework the cycles of sanctity and culture within France are readily intelligible.

Finally, Astrid O'Brien of Fordham University introduces us to Mathilde Boutle (Lucie Christine), a nineteenth-century housewife and mother who became a mystic "in the spiritual family of Julian of Norwich, Angela of Foligno, and Saint Theresa," even while experiencing the "joys and trials of family life." The author has written a moving and inspirational essay on Boutle, relying on two earlier and little known sources on Mathilde Boutle's life. The essay is a gentle challenge to spirituality for those caught up in the stresses and strains of an active secular life.

Notes

1. Pope John Paul II, "Letter to Cardinal Casaroli," May 20, 1982, in *Inculturation and Communion, Culture and Church in the Teaching of John Paul II*, (Rome: Urbana University Press, 1990), 42.

2. Francis Cardinal George, OMI, *Inculturation and Communion*, 42.

3. Pope John Paul II, Address to the Congress of the "Movimento Ecclesiale de Impegno Culturale," January 16, 1982, *La Traccia* 3, #1, February 15, 1982, 55-57, 2.

Chapter 7

Our Lady of Jasna Góra in Polish Catholicism

Father Janusz Ihnatowicz

The icon of Our Lady preserved in the Monastery of Jasna Góra in Czêstochowa (in recent years often addressed as Black Madonna) plays an important role in Polish religious and national life. Every year millions of pilgrims come to the shrine, many of them on foot. The largest assemblage is the annual pilgrimage from Warsaw, generally involving several thousand persons. The longest covers the distance of over 800 kilometers. There are very few Poles indeed who have never visited this sanctuary. Copies of this icon are found in all Catholic churches and in most homes. I suspect that when many Poles think of Mary, they see her with the features of this icon. (It is striking how many images of Mary produced by folk-artists have the features of Our Lady of Jasna Góra, even when they were not consciously meant to be copies.) Moreover, this icon is a powerful national symbol. One need but remember the picture of Our Lady of Jasna Góra on the gate to Gdansk shipyard and in the lapel of Lech Walesa during the strike in 1980 that led to the formation of Solidarity.

In this essay I wish to consider briefly some factors in Polish history and spirituality that, I believe, cooperated to bring about and to shape the special prominence of Our Lady of Jasna Góra.

Sanctuary of the Nation

In 1382, a wooden parish church, dedicated to the Blessed Virgin Mary, on a hill close to the town of Czêstochowa, was given to the monks of St. Paul the First Hermit. Within a few years the church, to become known as Jasna Góra (the Bright Mountain), became a center of Marian devotion. And we know that an image of Our Lady was venerated there prior to 1430. That year the monastery was robbed and the icon heavily damaged. It was then restored in Kraków, and returned to the monastery.

This is how the icon appears after that restoration. It is painted in tempera on canvas spread over a linden-tree (lime-tree) board consisting of three sections. It is 122.2 cm (49 inches) by 82.2 (33 inches) in size, and 3.5 cm (1.5 inches) thick. It represents the hodigitria style. Mary wears a blue dress and a cloak of the same color that covers her head. Both are decorated with Anjou lilies (fleur de lis). Over her forehead on the veil there is a six-rayed star. Her right hand is placed on her breast; with the left she supports the Infant Jesus. Jesus is dressed in a red tunic (also decorated with Anjou lilies); his right hand is raised in blessing. In his left hand he holds a closed book, resting on his knees. Both Mary and Jesus have gold nimbi in relief. On Mary's right cheek two cuts are evident; these cuts are probably evidence of the damage done during the robbery in 1430.

Yet this is not what the pilgrim sees. Only faces and hands of Jesus and Mary are visible; the rest is hidden with a jeweled replica of the figures' vestments, with golden crowns placed on their heads. It has been like that for centuries. When in 1966 Polish bishops had the cover removed and the icon shown in its original form, they faced a popular rebellion at this "strange" image that suddenly appeared, and they had to cover it again. It has stayed that way since. However, due to many copies of the actual painting circulating in the world and even placed in churches, the original image has become more familiar and accepted. (This is the way it appears in the private chapel of Pope John Paul II at the Vatican; while at Castel Gandolfo a copy placed there by Pope Pius XI is one "covered.")

How extensive were the interventions of the fifteenth-century restorers? Scholarly opinions differ widely. Some argue that the painting was simply touched up, with damage painted over; others think that the image was repainted. One such theory was inspired by the sixteenth-century account of the restoration. Apparently restorers tried in vain to cover up the damage to the picture by painting over in tempera, only to find that each time the paint would run after a few hours. Why would it run? This could be explained by the fact that the previous painting was done in the older encaustic technique, by that time long forgotten. Putting tempera on wax would make the paint run. Thus, to solve the problem, the restorers used a completely new canvas. The author of this theory appealed to evidence produced by modern photographic techniques and to the fact that he could find no traces of previous paint on the canvas. Also, the board shows holes from nails in places where there are no such holes in the canvas. However, other scholars question this theorist's conclusions and his evidence.

Yet, whatever the extent of restoration, it is safe to assume that the result closely resembles the original painting. And this leads us to a much more difficult question: where and when was this original produced? As there is little external evidence, scholars have had to fall back on criteria of style and technique. So far, their efforts have produced no solid agreement. Places as far apart as Syria and the Czech kingdom, and dates between the twelfth and fourteenth centuries have been proposed. If the theory about the encaustic technique of the original is true, it makes a date between the sixth and ninth century possible. But is it?

When art history can give no answer, piety produces its own. Already in the early part of the fifteenth century an account of the icon's origin and the itinerary that brought it to Jasna Góra were recorded. (A text from 1428, found in a manuscript from 1474.) According to this account, Saint Luke painted the icon on a table where the Holy Family ate their meals. According to the same story, after escaping the destruction of Jerusalem in A.D. 72, it was taken to Byzantium, and ultimately to Kievan Rus. When it was being moved once more—this time to Silesia—the icon, which had already shown its miraculous powers, by another miracle chose the hill of Jasna Góra as its resting place.

Whatever we might think about the historical veracity of this account, it witnesses to the reverence that the image enjoyed already. This was also the story that the restorers of 1430 must have known. It would explain why they made an effort to preserve not only the likeness but also the very wood on which the canvas was stretched.

In the sixteenth century the cult of Jasna Góra increased. Numerous pilgrims came to the shrine. This explains why the siege of the monastery by the Swedes in 1655 outraged the whole nation. Its successful defense was ascribed to the miraculous assistance of Mary. In the siege's aftermath, the popularity of the shrine grew steadily. Before the end of the eighteenth century the icon of Jasna Góra was believed to represent Mary as the Protectress of Poland in a special way. This was expressed clearly in a 1764 declaration by the Polish Parliament: "The Republic is devoted to its Holy Queen the Blessed Virgin, in her image of Czêstochowa famous for her miracles, and in its needs receives her protection."

This importance increased even more in the nineteenth century when Poland was divided among Russia, Prussia, and Austria. Jasna Góra became a symbol of national and religious unity. People from all three parts of Poland, often against the prohibitions of the occupying powers, journeyed there. The same was true during World War II, and especially under communist rule. It was a place of national hope. What Pope John Paul II said of himself, may be said of the whole nation: "I am a man of trusting faith, I have learned it here."[1]

Poles have gotten used to linking all their affairs and all-important moments of their lives with this place, with this Sanctuary.[2] It has indeed become, as Pope John Paul II called it, "the sanctuary of the nation."[3] For the Pope this means more than just the fact that so many Poles come to Jasna Góra to find spiritual renewal. He spoke from the perspective of events in the twentieth century, events in which he himself took part. When the Polish Republic was restored after the First World War, building on the religious and national importance of the Shrine during the Partitions and its unifying role, Polish bishops enlisted the icon and sanctuary of Jasna Góra in their pastoral programs of spiritual renewal. It was also so in the 1930s with a program to reach university students. In 1956 it was there that the Polish Church celebrated its emergence from the dark night of Stalinism.

Especially comprehensive and effective was the program of the Great Novena, a nine-year preparation for the celebration of the Millennium of Christianity in Poland in 1966. This program had a two-fold connection with Our Lady of Jasna Góra. First, it centered on the Shrine itself. It was inaugurated and brought to conclusion there, and pilgrimages to it were an essential part for the whole program. It also had an "external" side. A faithful copy, blessed by Pope Pius XII in 1957, began its "peregrination" at the Shrine: during the next twelve years or so, the icon visited every parish in the country. During 1966 it was taken to every diocesan celebration.

Or perhaps it should be said that it was meant to be taken. Communists made this goal impossible to achieve. Halfway through the year, they "arrested" the icon and imprisoned it in a church in Warsaw, forbidding its removal to any further celebrations. This action might seem silly and was rather counter-productive, for more than anything else it focused the people's and the world's attention on the picture. But it was also, from their point of view, logical. This image, associated with Mary as the Queen of Poland, by its presence alone reminded the Polish people who is the legitimate authority in Poland, and further undermined any claims of legitimacy on the part of the Communist regime.

The great Novena program was as effective as it was, in part at least because it appealed to the role that Our Lady of Jasna Góra already played in the life of Polish Catholics. At the same time, as Cardinal Wyszynski observed in 1966, and Pope John Paul II speaking in 1979 confirmed, it both revealed and gave a new and powerful dimension to her power. "More happened than we intended . . . . It was revealed that Jasna Góra is an integrating factor of Polish life, a force that grasps the hearts of the whole people." But it was really, the Cardinal added, the disclosure of how great the power of the Queen of Poland is in the nation.[4]

Mary, Mother and Queen of Poland

Here Pope John Paul touched the heart of the matter: Mary's role in Polish Catholicism. Christianity was introduced in Poland in 966, but took root fully only two or three centuries later, at a time when devotion to the Mother of God in the Church was especially strong and her role was one of the central issues of discussion. Hence Mary dominated Polish religiosity. Protestant critiques did not manage to dislodge it. One may suspect that this critique was, in part at least, what alienated Poles from the Reformation.

It is not accidental that perhaps the earliest extant poetic text in Polish is a hymn to the Mother of God (*Bogurodzica*), ascribed to Saint Adalbert (Wojciech), a tenth-century bishop of Prague and then missionary in Poland, but certainly composed before the fifteenth century. A fifteenth-century historian called it the "national anthem" of the Polish kingdom. A sixteenth-century theologian called it the "Polish catechism." Pope John Paul II said that it is not a cultural monument, it is a document of life; it is a confession of faith, a Polish *Credo*. This song, said the Pope, "gave Polish culture its basic, original framework."[5] It expressed what Poles thought of themselves as a nation, but it was also a means by which they appropriated the Gospel.

Catholic devotion to Mary flows from the Church's teaching on her Motherhood. She is the Mother of God, but at the same time is given to us as our mother. Poles tend to understand Mary's motherhood in analogy to a mother's role within the family. The father is the ultimate authority and source of security in a traditional family, but also a rather remote figure, away from the daily life of his children, an authority whose task it is often to judge and punish wrongdoers. The mother is accessible, and provides care and protection. At times she might be seen as an intermediary between the father and the children.

Being the Mother of Christ gives Mary a special access to him, a special intercessory power: what son would refuse his mother's pleas? This finds expression in an old song: "Hear us for your Son cannot refuse you anything." Her intercession is powerful.

Mary is willing to intercede for us because she is our mother. What mother would not do all she could to keep her children from harm, even from consequences of their own foolishness and disobedience? Emotionally Polish religious life is centered on a trust in Mary. Mary's maternal love, not God's righteous anger is at the center. Neither Calvinism nor Jansenism could take root easily in the Polish soul. This gives Polish Christianity a certain "softness," a certain optimism.

At the same time there is always the danger that Simon de Monfort's formula, taken up and popularized by Cardinal Wyszynski, "through Mary to Christ" will be misunderstood, that somehow we shall see Mary as closer to us than Jesus himself. (And for many Poles emotionally this might be true.) This may go as far as imagining that we need the loving Mother Mary as an intermediary between us and the angry God. A hymn, once quite popular, seems to voice such an idea: "But when the angry Father punishes/happy is he who runs to mother's protection."

Mary's motherhood has a strong social and national dimension. Poles see themselves under the special protection of Mary not only as individuals but also as the nation. This understanding found its expression in the idea of Mary as the Queen of Poland. She was proclaimed as such by King John Casimir Vasa in 1656. This choice found its liturgical expression and confirmation in the establishment of a solemnity of Mary under the title Queen of Poland. It is an additional reason why many national initiatives (such as the Solidarity movement) are placed under Mary's patronage and protection. In Poland, patriotism and respect for Mary may be identified with each other.

As a result there is such a thing as nonbelieving reverence for Mary among Poles. Even people far from Catholicism somehow share in the respect for Mary. The great Romantic poet, Adam Mickiewicz, expresses this situation well in his play "Dziady" (The Forefathers Eve). A political prisoner in a Russian jail sings a song suggesting that Jesus and Mary have abandoned Poland. Another prisoner, the hero of the play, protests:

> I will not have these names used in revelry
> Long I do not know where my faith is gone,
> All the saints of the litany are nothing to me
> But I will not let you blaspheme Mary's name.

All this, as we saw earlier in this essay, found its special focus at Jasna Góra. Pope John Paul II summed it well in a homily during his 1979 visit to the shrine. "The image of Jasna Góra" (whose tradition in Poland goes back 600 years), the Pope said, "has become the expression of a more ancient tradition, of an older language of faith in our history." By this the Pope means the text of the medieval Marian hymn already mentioned. "She who spoke in the song on the lips of our forefathers, spoke in her own time by means of this Image, through which her maternal *presence* in the life of the Church and the Fatherland is manifested."[6]

This language about the relationship of an image and its prototype might appear a little overdrawn to the ears of many western Christians, but it expresses well the common feeling of Poles. That it is quite natural for a Pole—even one who is Pope—to speak that way, is due, I submit, to an influence of Byzantine theology of the icon.

Icons in Polish Catholicism

Poland is one of the places where eastern and western forms of Christianity meet. For centuries, Byzantine and Latin Christians lived side by side, especially in the eastern provinces. Even small villages would often have a Latin and a Byzantine church. This led to an extensive interchange of forms of devotion, religious sensitivities, and customs.[7] One result of eastern influence on Latin rite Catholics in Poland is their attitude toward holy images.

Christian thought on the role of images developed in two stages. The first question was the very legitimacy in the Church of representational art, that is, of pictures and sculptures of human figures. Already in antiquity, in spite of sporadic negative attitudes, tradition accepted its legitimacy. Old Testament prohibitions were not seen as applying to such images. From earliest times, biblical scenes, images of Christ, Mary, and later of saints decorated Christian sacred places. In the fourth century, Saint Basil described their role: "what the word transmits through the ear, the painting shows through the eyes."[8]

The Latin Church generally understood this in a "weak" sense. Images are a good catechetical and inspirational tool, especially for the unlettered; they recall to the people events of salvation and holy persons. Byzantium, however, went further. In the eighth and ninth centuries several emperors attempted to ban images from Christian worship and devotion. Defending the traditional teaching, Orthodox theologians gave a "strong" interpretation to Basil's words. Icons may be called "a theology in color." As Scriptures or decrees of ecumenical councils reveal and explain the divine truths in words, icons do it through color and form, through images. Holy icons are "windows into eternity"; that is, by looking at them we get a glimpse of the glorified condition of those depicted in them.

Moreover, they are quasi-sacramental. They represent holy persons depicted in them in the strongest sense of the word: icons not only remind us of them, or tell us something about their present condition, they somehow make them present, make them really available, serve as a means of contact with them. When I pray before an icon, and this is the only legitimate use of them, I am actually standing in the presence of the one depicted.

This theology was never officially taught by the Polish Latin Church, but the attitude toward holy images flowing from it has certainly influenced Polish religiosity. This, I believe, explains in part at least why Poles reacted so violently when Communists ordered the removal of crucifixes from classrooms and other public buildings such as hospitals. It was perceived as an attack at the very soul of Catholic Poland. More, as a sacrilege. High school students were willing to risk prison, when they organized occupational strikes of school buildings in defense of these holy images. The nation was filled with horror. (One may contrast this with the weak reaction in the United States, even by Catholics, when religious symbols are removed in public places by court orders or even, on bad advice by lawyers, from classrooms in Catholic colleges. Some people complain that this detracts from the Catholic character of the institution, but few consider it as somehow striking at the heart of Catholic religion.)

In the Presence of Mary in her Icon

This influence explains, I believe, why Poles are accustomed, as Pope John Paul II says, to come to Jasna Góra to speak to their Mother about everything. They believed that "She does not merely have her revered Image here . . . in some special manner she is here. She is present here."[9] And these words are not for the Pope, or for the average Pole, a mere metaphor. (This explains why Poles can see the visitation of a copy, blessed by the Pope, as a true visit of Mary in their parish or home.)

This is why for a Pole coming to the Shrine is an experience of such profound depth and power. As they come there by the millions, most do not seek any other healing than spiritual regeneration. Hence, going to confession is for most an important act when there. But, with the heart purified by the sacrament, the most moving time is praying before the icon, praying often merely by looking into Mary's eyes, which seem to look back at you.

There is a great power in the icon. Something that no copy, not even the most faithful one, can accomplish. Most people, who come before it, are moved. It is not merely something emotional, though surely emotions play a role. It is not simply the question of being moved by the fervor of pilgrims around one, or the concentrated sense of wonder and holiness, that the centuries of devotion have given it.

There is something in the icon itself. Is it its greatness as a work of art? (No copy quite gets it.) Mary's face is beautiful, but solemn and strangely sad; her eyes seem to look at one directly with certain care and sadness. This look breaks the heart. There is a sense of contemplation and peace flowing from the icon.

But is that all? At the risk of appearing to be influenced unduly by the reputation of the place, its high emotional tone, I will claim that when one stands or kneels before the icon in prayer, there is a strong sense of presence there. This icon does in an almost experiential manner, what icons are believed to do—to put us in touch with the person of the saint, becoming a window through which we are given a glance of the glorified bodies of Jesus and Mary. That experience is what a pilgrim takes away. And that experience is somehow invoked and recalled whenever a copy of the icon is presented, and that recollection somehow moves us closer to God.

Notes

1. John Paul II, *Homily at Jasna Góra,* June 4, 1979; AAS 71 (1979), 757.

2. John Paul II, *Homily at Jasna Góra*, 764.

3. John Paul II, *Homily at Jasna Góra*, 761.

4. Quoted by John Paul II, *Homily at Jasna Góra*, 758.

5. John Paul II, *Allocution to young people in Gniezno*, Poland, 3 June 1979; AAS 71 (1979), 754.

6. John Paul II, *Homily at Jasna Góra*, June 4, 1979; AAS 71 (1979), 757 (italics in the original).

7. We are concerned here with the eastern influence on Latin rite Catholics, but I am told that spontaneous latinization of easterners, especially Catholics, occurred. Ukrainian clergy, especially those of American origin trained in western universities, fall into conflicts with the faithful, when they try to eliminate such western customs in the name of ritual purity.

8. Basil the Great, *Sermon 19*, on forty martyrs.

9. John Paul II, *Homily at Jasna Góra*, June 4, 1979; AAS 71 (1979), 758.

Chapter 8

Marian Devotion and Cultural Influence in the Naming of Churches

Phil Lampe

The Catholic Church has a tradition of publicly recognizing and honoring its saints. It is believed that by honoring God's creatures, glory and honor is given to God the Creator. Mary, considered to be the most perfect of God's creatures, is also the most honored and revered of the saints. It is this recognition and honor given to her which is one of the more obvious differences between Catholics and Protestants.

Some social commentators have expressed the opinion that the importance and devotion given to Mary by the Catholic Church has actually been detrimental to women. They contend that it has served to impose a conservative, traditionalist, familial, sexual ethic which has condemned women to early marriage, large families, subservient roles and household drudgery.[1] Such charges appear to be seriously questioned, if not refuted, by the findings reported in the study entitled *Young Catholics in the United States and Canada*. Individuals who scored high on the Madonna scale (seeing Mary as gentle, warm, patient, and comforting) also scored high on sexual liberation, social commitment, marital happiness, sexual fulfillment in marriage, support for the ordination of women, and opposition to racial segregation. In addition, they were more likely to pray every day, attend Mass every week, be active in their parish, believe in life after death, and return to the Church if they ever leave it.[2] Thus, it appears that devotion to Mary serves the individual, the Church, and society.

Catholics throughout the world have a special devotion to the Virgin Mary as the Mother of God. However, some countries are more closely identified with her than others. Many countries have their own special image and title of Mary which is widely known and recognized such as Our Lady of Guadalupe (Mexico), Our Lady of Czêstochowa (Poland), Our Lady of Lourdes (France), Our Lady of Fatima (Portugal), and Our Lady of Knoch (Ireland). Nevertheless, honoring Mary and observing her many devotions such as feast days, devotional liturgy, prayers, and doctrinal beliefs are shared with Catholics worldwide.

In order to determine the influence of culture on Marian devotion in the United States, a longitudinal study was conducted on the naming of churches dedicated to her. This is because, unlike most Church devotions which are universal, the naming of churches within an area, diocese, or country, is a decision proper to that area. Names of churches were obtained from *The Official Catholic Directory* for the years 1929, 1950, 1980, and 2000. Of special interest was the pattern of general acceptance of Our Lady of Guadalupe exhibited over the years as reflected in the naming of churches in her honor.

Number of Dedications

One measure of importance or influence is the frequency with which something is mentioned or appears in a culture. Therefore, the frequency of dedications of churches to Mary may be taken as an indication of her importance. The *Catholic Directories* indicate that over the years more churches have been dedicated to her than to any other saint and, unlike other saints, there is no diocese that does not have multiple churches dedicated in her honor. The number of churches dedicated to Mary was compared for the years 1950 and 1980. The year 1950 was selected because it was pre-Civil Rights, but post-World War II and the Church was well distributed throughout the nation with most of the present dioceses already established. It was also pre-Vatican II, which allowed a comparison with 1980, a year that was selected because it was post-Vatican II and post-Civil Rights era, with a wide geographic distribution of ethnic minorities. Furthermore, in 1950 there were no Hispanic bishops in the United States and none had been appointed for over a century.[3] By 1980, however, there were more than a dozen Hispanic bishops in various parts of the country. This was an important consideration because bishops must approve the final selection of a church title in their dioceses.

In 1950 there were 122 Roman Catholic dioceses in the United States. Located in these dioceses were approximately 14,921 churches, with 3,066, or 21 percent, dedicated to Mary. By 1980 there were 161 dioceses with approximately 18,436 churches of which 4,098, or 22 percent, were dedicated to her. Thus, in the 30 years between 1950 and 1980 there was an increase of 39 dioceses, and 3,515 churches, but virtually no difference in the percentage of churches dedicated to Mary. These numerical increases in the number of dioceses and churches are due to population growth and expansion, the splitting of existing dioceses creating new ones, and the addition in 1959 of two new states, Alaska and Hawaii.

Frequency of Dedications

Every diocese has numerous churches dedicated to Mary. The percent of churches dedicated to her varied between seven and twenty-five percent. Overall, more churches in the United States are dedicated to Mary than to any other person, including Jesus. Given the difference between Catholics and Protestants in the recognition and honor shown to Mary, and the consequent criticism this has engendered, it may be expected that there would be a direct relationship between size of the Catholic population in an area and the number of churches dedicated to her. Thus, cities with a much larger number of Catholics would have more Marian churches than those with a much smaller number. However, such was not the case. For example, while the dioceses of two major southern cities, Atlanta and Memphis both had the same size Catholic population (three percent) in 1980, the former had fourteen percent of its churches dedicated to Mary, while the latter had twenty-seven percent. Meanwhile, the dioceses of two major northern cities—Buffalo and Pittsburgh, both had Catholic populations of forty percent, but very different percentages in churches dedicated to Mary (seven percent vs. twenty-six percent). Thus, Atlanta, which had a small Catholic population of only three percent, had fourteen percent of its churches dedicated to Mary while Buffalo, which had a large Catholic population of forty percent, had only seven percent of its churches dedicated to her.

There was also an absence of any clear and consistent geographic pattern in the distribution of Marian churches. Regions of the country that have historically been identified as Catholic or as having a strong Catholic influence, such as the Northeast, parts of the Midwest, and the Southwest, are no more likely to dedicate churches to Mary than the Protestant Bible Belt. Comparing the age of the dioceses also failed to reveal any consistent differences in dedications. There were no significant differences between more recently established dioceses and those that were established at an earlier time.

Variety of Dedications

The variety or variation with which something appears in a culture is another recognized measure of importance. Thus, in addition to examining the frequency of dedications, it is relevant to examine the variety of titles under which churches are dedicated. A review of the names of Marian churches in 1980 reveals there were approximately 391 different titles. Some of these are variations on the same basic title, such as Star of the Sea, Saint Mary Star of the Sea, and Our Lady Star of the Sea.

The various titles were classified into the following eight categories: nominal, devotional, honorary, inferential, regional/identificational, ethnic/national, historical/doctrinal, and shared dedication.[4] Nominal refers to the simple use of the name (e.g., Saint Mary). Devotional refers to titles which are meant to instill or generate devotion based on commonly recognized qualities or attributes (e.g., Mother of Mercy). Honorary titles are those which bestow an honor and/or ceremonial recognition (e.g., Queen of Heaven). Inferential titles do not directly refer to Mary but are commonly understood as such (e.g., Holy Rosary). Regional/identificational refers to titles which identify Mary with a particular place or geographical setting (e.g., Our Lady of the River). Ethnic/National are titles which represent or symbolize a particular people or nation (e.g., Our Lady of Guadalupe). Historical/doctrinal titles are based on a historical event or Church doctrine (e.g., Assumption). Shared dedication is where two or more names are specified in the title (e.g., Sacred Hearts of Jesus and Mary).

The single most common title is Saint Mary. Every diocese has one or more churches which bear this title. The most common category of titles is historical/doctrinal, which is closely followed by the nominal title. These two categories account for over half of all churches dedicated to Mary. Table 8.1 shows, in descending order, the most common categories, together with the most frequent example of each:

Historical/Doctrinal	*Immaculate Conception*
Nominal	Saint Mary
Devotional	Our Lady of Perpetual Help
Ethnic/National	Our Lady of Lourdes
Honorary	Saint Mary Star of the Sea
Regional/Identificational	Our Lady of the Lake
Inferential	Holy Rosary
Shared Dedication	Saints Mary and Joseph

Table 8.1

Cultural Influence in Dedications

Religion is part of culture and, like it or not, culture is part of religion. Culture's influence on religion can be seen in the naming of churches, particularly those classified as ethnic/national. Ordinarily it may be expected that preference in the naming of a church would be given to a local, regional, or national saint over a foreign one. In the case of ethnic/national madonnas, Our Lady of Guadalupe is the American madonna. There are three reasons for this statement. First, Our Lady of Guadalupe is the only recognized Marian apparition in North America; second, her miraculous image is enshrined in North America; and third, Pope Pius XI named her "Patroness of the Americas." Regardless of these compelling reasons for special devotion and recognition as the American madonna, she has been less accepted in the United States than other "foreign" madonnas. The following indicates the level of acceptance given to various ethnic madonnas over the last twenty years, as measured by the naming of churches in their honor.

	Lourdes *1980-2000*		*Mt. Carmel* *1980-2000*		*Fatima* *1980-2000*		*Guadalupe* *1980-2000*	
Dioceses	95	103	78	68	57	59	52	65
Churches	130	144	140	131	71	74	106	119

Table 8.2

As shown in table 8.2, in 1980 fewer dioceses honored Mary under the title Our Lady of Guadalupe than any of the other three ethnic/national madonnas. In the number of churches dedicated, Our Lady of Guadalupe received fewer dedications than Our Lady of Mt. Carmel and Our Lady of Lourdes but more than Our Lady of Fatima. However, it should be remembered that while the apparition of Guadalupe dates back to 1531, that of Fatima only occurred in 1917. Thus, while older churches could have been dedicated to Guadalupe, they could not have been dedicated to Fatima. The acceptance of the latter was obviously very recent, quick, and wide-spread.

In 2000, the situation was similar. Once again greater acceptance was shown to Our Lady of Lourdes and Our Lady of Mt. Carmel in the number of dioceses dedicating churches to them and in the total number of churches dedicated. However, Our Lady of Guadalupe did surpass Our Lady of Fatima in both the number of dioceses and the number of churches. The number of dioceses dedicating churches to ethnic madonnas is more indicative of general acceptance than number of churches dedicated. This is because the latter number can be inflated, and therefore misleading, due to strong devotion expressed in certain dioceses or regions of the country. Such is the case with Our Lady of Guadalupe.

Number and Percent of Dioceses Dedicating Churches to Our Lady of Guadalupe				
	1929	*1950*	*1980*	*2000*
Dioceses	104	122	160	176
Southwest U.S.	12 (43%)	16 (48%)	25 (48%)	31 (48%)
Rest of U.S.	16 (57%)	17 (52%)	27 (52%)	34 (52%)
Total	28 (100%)	33 (100%)	52 (100%)	65 (100%)

Table 8.3

Over the years there has been a steady, albeit slight, improvement in the number and percent of dioceses dedicating churches to Our Lady of Guadalupe. In 1929 and 1950 only twenty-seven percent of all dioceses in the United States had at least one church dedicated to her, but by 1980 the percentage had risen to thirty-three percent and by 2000 it was thirty-seven percent. However, as can be seen in table 8.3, there has been no change in the last half-century in the relative percentage of dioceses in the Southwest and the rest of the country with regard to such dedications. Virtually half of all dioceses honoring Our Lady of Guadalupe through the dedication of a church are located in the largely Hispanic Southwest.

The relationship between size of Hispanic population and dedication of churches to Our Lady of Guadalupe can be further seen in the following table (table 8.4). By 1990 over fifty percent of the faithful were Hispanic in thirteen dioceses located in seven states. In an additional twenty-eight dioceses throughout the United States between twenty-five and fifty percent were Hispanic.[5] These were the dioceses most likely to have churches dedicated to Our Lady of Guadalupe. It should be pointed out, however, that Our Lady of Guadalupe is not equally identified with nor accepted by all Hispanics. She is specifically identified with Mexicans and Mexican Americans. Each Hispanic nationality has its own particular Madonna. Hispanics in the Southwest are overwhelmingly of Mexican descent and so Our Lady of Guadalupe is widely accepted and honored with numerous churches dedicated in her honor. Meanwhile, the diocese of Miami which also has a large Hispanic population, but primarily of Cuban descent, has only one church dedicated to Our Lady of Guadalupe.

Number and Percent of Churches Dedicated to Our Lady of Guadalupe			
1929	*1950*	*1980*	*2000*
Southwest U.S. 35 (64%)	61 (75%)	76 (72%)	83 (70%)
Rest of U.S. 20 (36%)	20 (25%)	30 (28%)	36 (30%)
Total 55 (100%)	81(100%)	106 (100%)	119 (100%)

Table 8.4

Interpreting the Data

Data presented appear to indicate a preference for European madonnas. Interpreting the reasons for this apparent preference is sure to be controversial, not just because the focus will be limited, therefore ignoring some causes, but because there may be other possible interpretations for the data. Two questions, however, come to mind. First, does this noted difference in acceptance derive from ethnic prejudice? Second, does this difference constitute discrimination?

These are two separate questions and the answers are not necessarily related. As Merton pointed out, discrimination may occur with or without prejudice, just as prejudice may exist with or without discrimination.[6] Prejudice is a prejudgment which affects, and is affected by, one's beliefs, feelings, and possible actions. Discrimination is an unfair or differential treatment based on irrelevant criteria. Thus, both prejudice and discrimination can be either for or against. Therefore, it is possible to be a victim of either one or both because it is directed against a person or group, or because it unjustly favors someone over a person or group.

From the beginning it appears that most of the churches dedicated to Our Lady of Guadalupe have been located in the Southwest. Nevertheless, some slight improvement has occurred since 1950. It should be noted that the large differences between the regions of the country may indicate positive prejudice in the Southwest and/or negative prejudice in the rest of the country. However, it may also be interpreted as indicative of a proper appreciation and recognition of the American madonna in the southwestern part of the country and a lack of such in the rest of the country.

This apparent lack of general acceptance of *La Morenita* (a common Spanish term of endearment which means "the little dark one," used in Mexico to refer to Our Lady of Guadalupe) is generally reflective of the lack of acceptance of those with whom she is most closely identified. A longitudinal study conducted at ten-year intervals by Bogardus for the period 1926 through 1966 reveals the extent of ethnic prejudice which she has had to overcome.[7] (See table 8.5.)

Social Acceptance of Specific Ethnic Groups
with Whom Our Lady of Guadalupe May Be Identified

Ethnic Group	Rank of Group*			
	1926	1946	1956	1966
Spanish	11	15	14	14
American Indian	18	20	20	18
Mexican American	22	22	22	23
Mexican	21	24	28	28

National ranking in a list of 30 different ethnic groups.

Table 8.5

Results of the study revealed the existence of an ethnic/racial hierarchy reminiscent of the class hierarchy. Just as there is a class structure commonly referred to as upper, middle, and lower, based on socioeconomic status, so there are upper, middle, and lower levels among ethnic groups based on degree of social acceptance. At the top are those groups which are composed of the descendants of white, western Europeans; in the middle are those of white, eastern Europeans; and at the bottom are those of non-white, non-Europeans

Data in the table above reveal that the ethnic groups with whom Our Lady of Guadalupe could be most closely identified, with the exception of the Spanish, which is possibly the weakest connection, are among the least socially accepted. This is reminiscent of her original identity as an indigenous maiden in a Spanish-dominated society. She appeared to, and identified with, those at the bottom of the social hierarchy rather than those at the top. Three of the four groups are non-European and usually referred to as non-white. All three were legally discriminated against until after 1950, and although *de jure* discrimination has ended, *de facto* discrimination has not. Thus, from the beginning the Virgin of Guadalupe has been identified with minority groups who are among the least socially accepted in the United States.

This identification can, consciously or unconsciously, be a source of the relative lack of acceptance for the Virgin who should be loved and honored by all Catholic Americans. As the Mother of God, she is the antithesis of a member of a minority group which is characterized as composed of low-status, inferior individuals who possess minimal power. Conversely, the European madonnas are identified with members of the dominant group who are characterized as high status, superior individuals possessing power. These latter characteristics are appropriate for the "Queen of Heaven."

Unlike the other madonnas, Our Lady of Guadalupe left an image of herself. Ironically, what should be one of her greatest advantages may actually be a disadvantage. The image is of a short dark-skinned indigenous maiden. In a culture that identifies female beauty with slender light-skinned Europeans it is less likely that she would be selected to represent Mary the "Mystical Rose," renowned for her beauty and grace. The desire to represent Mary, the most perfect of God's creatures, in the most favorable way possible affects our representations of her. Consequently, discrimination can result which is unconscious and unintended.

Future Dedications

Anyone with even a rudimentary knowledge of American history knows that both prejudice and discrimination are deeply embedded in American culture. Fortunately, they are no longer legal or as widespread, overt, and socially accepted as they once were. Unfortunately, they still exist, and can be found to some degree in all social institutions, including religion. This is because the same people with the same prejudices are members of all the institutions.

The noted general reduction in prejudice and discrimination can be traced to several factors. First, there is increased interaction and acceptance among the different ethnic/racial groups. Members of minority groups are now found in greater numbers at higher levels of all the major social institutions. Success of individual members of a group affects the overall image of the entire group. Before 1970 there were no Hispanic bishops, whereas now there are over twenty. Increases are also found in government, business, education, entertainment, and the military. These increases are accompanied by more interethnic/interracial relationships resulting in an increase in friendships and marriage.

Second, there is a dramatic increase in the number of non-whites and non-Europeans as well as non-Protestants and non-Christians. Americans can no longer be identified simply as WASPs (white Anglo-Saxon Protestants). Third, these groups are no longer segregated into ghettos and enclaves, but are more generally distributed throughout the country. In the United States the Southwest has been the region of the country most closely identified with Hispanics, particularly Mexicans and Mexican Americans, who comprise over sixty percent of all Hispanics. Two states, California and Texas, have the largest population of these two groups, and the largest number of churches dedicated to Our Lady of Guadalupe. It is no coincidence that these same two states have approximately three-fourths of all the dioceses in the Southwest and one-third of all the dioceses in the entire nation with churches dedicated to her. In 2000 they had fifty-seven percent of all such churches in the United States.

The United States is undergoing a dramatic change, which promises to significantly enhance the acceptance of Our Lady of Guadalupe. In 1950, there were approximately 2.5 million Hispanics in the country. By 2050, according to Census Bureau projections, they will increase to nearly 100 million, which is one of every four Americans.[8] According to the Secretariat for Hispanic Affairs, the (arch)dioceses of Brownsville, Brooklyn, El Paso, Los Angeles, Las Cruces, Lubbock, Miami, Santa Fe, San Angelo, San Antonio, Tucson, and Yakima are all over fifty percent Hispanic.[9] In addition, according to the 2000 Census, Hispanics accounted for sixty-two percent of the population increase in the nation's five largest states from 1990 to 2000, and eighty-one percent of all the growth in the 100 largest cities. Currently one of every eight Americans and one of every three U.S. Catholics is Hispanic. Before the end of this century Hispanics are projected to comprise one-half of all U.S. Catholics,[10] and they, together with other non-white minority groups will outnumber non-Hispanic whites. This so-called "Browning of America" promises to help Our Lady of Guadalupe, *La Morenita*, fit in and receive the recognition and honor she is due.

Notes

1. M. Warner, *Alone of All Her Sex*, (New York: Random House, 1983).

2. J. Fee, A. Greeley, W. McCready and T. Sullivan, *Young Catholics in the United States and Canada*, (New York: Sadlier, 1985).

3. Gilbert Cadena and Lara Medina, "Liberation Theology and Social Change: Chicanas and Chicanos in the Catholic Church," in *Chicanas and Chicanos in Contemporary Society*, R. DeAnda, ed., (Boston: Allyn & Bacon, 1996), 99-111.

4. Philip Lampe, "Honoring Mary in the United States," *Listening* 22 (Autumn, 1987), 196-203.

5. *National Survey on Hispanic Ministry*, (Washington, D.C.: NCCB/USCC Secretariat for Hispanic Affairs, 1990).

6. Robert Merton, "Discrimination and the American Creed," in *Discrimination and National Welfare*, R. H. MacIver, ed., (New York: Harper and Row, 1949), 99-126.

7. Emory Bogardus, "Comparing racial distance in Ethiopia, South Africa and the United States," *Sociology and Social Research* 52 (1968), 149-56.

8. *Reflecting an American Vista*, (Washington, D.C.: National Community for Latino Leadership, Inc., 2001), 1.

9. Cadena and Medina, 100.

10. Cadena and Medina, 100.

Chapter 9

Literary Appropriation of Mary in the Spanish-Speaking World

"Ex ore infantium et lactantium perfecisti laudem" (Psalm 8, 3)

Luis Eugenio Espinosa-González

The study of the concept *inculturation* provides us with a changing definition of culture and a new vision of the culturally conditioned heritage of Christianity.[1] Leaving aside the difficulties of defining the term *inculturation*, the relationship between Christ and culture seems to depend on unspecific rather fluid definitions, for which we have to include here both terms of the equation: Christianity and culture.

The term *inculturation*, originally intended as a description of the process of the reception of the Gospel message by local churches, has lately been used to describe a sophisticated, culturally-sensitive evangelization methodology. My research has focused on the earlier process describing the reception of the Christian message by particular communities. Dogmas and disciplinary measures have been appropriated differently by different groups in different moments. Research indicates that the *Biblia pauperum*[2] has, in fact, been more influential in the shaping of popular religion in Latin America than the official definitions or statements lying behind it. Does the reason lie in a more attractive content, in its earlier rooting in a people through familial and cultural traditions, or is resistance to official teaching due to pastoral and pedagogical approaches that are insufficiently "fitted" to a particular people and culture?

Within the Catholic tradition it is interesting to note the flexible reception of Mary by local communities. Mary seems to have been subjected to a wider range of popular interpretations than the figure of Jesus. Her incorporation into tradition is perhaps less complicated or dangerous than the appropriation of Christ, at least in terms of dogmatic exactitude or risks of heresy. Some popular devotions existed long before any official theological statement was promulgated. A religious discourse was alive in literature and art, and this form of catechesis probably taught the faithful long before any statement was given.

Mary's appropriations in the literature of Spanish-speaking countries reveal to us the cultural backgrounds, the value systems, and even the social expectations of their authors. In this essay, we will limit ourselves to three examples in this process of mutual enrichment between culture and Christianity. The first one goes back to the early thirteenth century and focuses on a tale written or rewritten by Gonzalo de Berceo. A second one focuses on a seventeenth-century text in Nahuatl language telling the story of Mary's appearance at the Tepeyac hill, near Mexico City.[3] In both cases these publications represent the printing moment of previous traditions made by nonhierarchical members of a Christian group or subculture. In both cases we find an attempt to use "popular" language in order to make the story accessible to new audiences. In both cases as well, the similarities and the discontinuities with other pieces of Marian literature show the author's main contributions to the understanding of Mary.

A third textual approach to Mary is presented almost as a counterexample: the twentieth-century attempts to redirect Marian popular devotion so as to be more consistent with Catholic tradition. This attempt is found in Pope Paul VI's apostolic exhortation *Marialis cultus,* but is more directly available to Latin American audiences via the documents of the third general assembly of CELAM (Episcopal Council of Latin America) at Puebla. In this last example, we can witness the attempts made by the hierarchy to "correct" or nuance the popular devotion.

An Enthroned Lady

Mary's presentation in Gonzalo de Berceo, Milagros de Nuestra Señora[4]

It is the first half of the thirteenth century and we are now in Northeastern Spain. Gonzalo de Berceo is writing a manuscript in Castilian, thus distancing himself from his predecessors who wrote in Latin. His poetic style reminds us of the techniques used by the authors of the *mester de clerecía.*[5] Gonzalo, like some other contemporaries, takes as source of inspiration a collection of miracles performed by the Glorious Mother of Christ, already in circulation throughout Europe.[6] As such, Gonzalo adds commentaries to existing material: his work includes a general introduction and a last miracle (*la iglesia robada*) that do not exist in previous Latin versions.

Berceo is deeply influenced by both the Spanish traditional piety, as promoted by the writings of Ildephonsus of Toledo, and the Marian revival of the twelfth century, particularly under the leading role of Bernard of Clairvaux.[7] Gonzalo's use of typology in his introduction closely follows Bernard's style. The author of *Milagros de Nuestra Señora* joins those pious devotees of our Lady who had always considered themselves servants of the Glorious One. It is not surprising then that of 371 nouns applied to Mary studied in this text, "Glorious" is the most frequently used (118 or almost thirty-two percent) and "Mother" is the second one (108 or twenty-nine percent).[8]

Mary is described by Berceo following the general medieval tendency to use the saints and their powers as intercessors. As stated by T. Head in the electronic version of his article on medieval veneration of relics, "[I]n exchange for their services and gifts, the saint provided his or her friends with intercession in the divine court and protection against disease and enemies in this world."[9] Gonzalo describes several miracles where we find in Mary not only an intercessor but an incomparably powerful one. In several cases she had to supplement the "salvation-tasks" previously and unsuccessfully attempted by some angels,[10] by saints,[11] or even by apostles like James[12] or Peter.[13]

The *Milagros de Nuestra Señora* reveals how Marian piety was colored and shaped by medieval social practices. According to this source, Mary is the powerful Lady who stands close to her imperial Son. The Byzantine mosaics in Ravenna, Italy had already depicted this parallelism between the Roman emperor and his wife on the one hand, and Jesus and his mother on the other. Mary is in the midst of the heavenly court—depicted very much as a feudal household or a kingly court—the influential mother whose petitions cannot be rejected by God,[14] even in severe cases of sin and denial of the Faith.[15]

So far, orthodoxy cannot be questioned. Mary has been recognized as *Theotokos* since the council of Ephesus in the fifth century. Visually, Mary was the chair (*sedes*) where Jesus sat down to rule the world. Gonzalo explicitly includes this portrayal in his description of an image of Our Lady preserved miraculously from the fire: "Estaba la imagen en su trono posada, so—cosa es costumnada—Fijo en sus brazos, los Reÿs redor ella, sedié bien compañada, como rica Reïna de Dios santificada."[16] We might even consider certain biblical background, supported by no more than a thin exegetical line, to this intercessory role. We are referring to John's passage about the wedding at Cana (Jn 2).

However, there are other cultural depictions that today we would hardly consider "divine" qualities. In one miracle story Mary is presented as a cruel ruler—strangling Bishop Siagrius because he dared to use Ildephonsus' chasuble, a personal gift from Mary.[17] In another, Our Lady seems less than friendly with those who have stolen Church property.[18] In this case, Mary's anger is followed by divine fire that burns the bodies of those burglars without consuming them. In a third story Mary tells Teophilus that she is tired of his prayer.[19] These descriptions may sound irreverent to us but the author helps us understand this anger in light of the medieval concept of authority that implied a certain amount of wrath, when he describes the virtues of a new bishop: "león para los bravos, a los mansos cordero; guiava bien a su grey, non como soldadero, mas como pastor firme que está bien facero."[20] However, one may wonder if Mary's wrath is justified when directed toward a bishop who had called her attention to a poorly prepared cleric.[21] Mary is evidently favoring her unconditional followers, even those who are simple minded or those whose only merit was to praise her daily. Mary is depicted in the collection of miracles as a moody Lady, very much in line with the feudal *dammes*.

An even more interesting behavior is shown by Mary when one of her devotees decides to get married.[22] Mary's jealousy in this scene seems incredibly human. She is an infuriated Lady who feels rejected by this man's decision. Our Lady's behavior can only be understood when it is placed in the context of courtly love of Medieval Europe. The excellence of chivalric ideal love should not be displaced by mortal love affairs! One hears minstrels' songs behind Gonzalo's tales. In Mary's hands, the ability to touch Christ's heart is a double-edged sword. As both a temperamental woman and a merciful intercessor—even beyond logic—Mary belonged to that time. It is evident that the medieval understanding of love, authority, family ties, and serfdom played a role in the reshaping of Mary's face. The woman of Nazareth is obscured by the shadow of new cultural influences.

A Maternal Ruler

The story of Mary of Guadalupe's appearance at the Tepeyac

We now move to the mid-seventeenth century. L. Lasso de la Vega worked as chaplain at Guadalupe, Mexico. With his native aides he wrote a book called *Huei tlamahuiçoltica* in the Nahuatl language.[23] In Mexican colonial times, scholars discovered the connection between two sections of this work and a book published a year earlier in 1648 by the *criollo* priest, M. Sánchez.[24] Moreover, due to their literary genre, both books could be placed in line with similar Spanish accounts from previous centuries.[25]

The section of the *Nican mopohua* that describes Mary's appearances at the Tepeyac leaves us with the certainty that it is the result of an evangelization process.[26] The main idea seems to be similar to other legendary accounts as mentioned by W. Christian Jr., namely, to justify the privileged position of Guadalupe's image and temple.[27] It is possible that the author, or the editor or editors, was not only trying to validate a sacred place, but also to purge it of syncretistic memories. The *Nican mopohua* stresses the significance of this "divine" newcomer in the description of Our Lady. This is confirmed by the almost certain connection between the pre-Hispanic literary expectations of the Nahuatl poem, the *cuicapeuhcayotl*,[28] and the answer offered by Christianity. In this text, Mary is clearly distinguished from any pre-Hispanic deity.

The author's vision concerning divinity and Church life concurs with the early Christian evangelization in New Spain. The acceptance by the native protagonists, Juan Diego and Juan Bernardino, of Mary's healing role, and even their participation in sacramental and catechetical practices seem to be not only familiar to the author but he also seems to suggest these as appropriate or orthodox religious practices and behaviors. We also notice certain attempts in the *Nican mopohua* to sketch model pastoral attitudes in Juan Diego's behavior. Juan Diego goes through a process of maturing in his Christian commitment, something expected of any native attending the *doctrina*. These elements lead us to conclude that we are not looking at a missionary text. The literary style suggests an author trying to reach either a catechetical community, or a group of preachers or teachers committed to those who were already Christians.

M. Rojas insisted that the *Nican mopohua* has a christocentric character.[29] He suggests that our text is trying to delimit the specific role of Mary in salvation. She is not a deity, but the Mother of the true God. However, if the author of the *Nican mopohua* was interested in limiting Mary's role in the economy of salvation, the titles given to her in the text would certainly have had counterproductive results. Such titles were applied in pre-Hispanic times to the highest deity of some Nahua groups, *Ometéotl*. Rojas himself comments on the potential confusion generated by Mary's presentation as "Mother of God," for any Nahuatl audience. A strict, literary approach to the *Nican mopohua* does not yield enough significant information about Jesus Christ to consider the text christocentric in emphasis.

Attention then centers on Mary of Guadalupe to better understand the author's meaning of "divinity." Analysis will proceed from three different angles: What are the narrator's comments about her? What kind of relationship does Juan Diego have with Mary? What does Mary say about herself in the *Nican mopohua*?

Every time the narrator refers to Mary, he centers his attention on two aspects: first, she is a Noble Lady or a Ruler; second, she is a Maiden, a Virgin.[30] The narrator mentions Mary in our apparition story twenty-four times. Thirteen times she is presented as the noble lady coming from heaven (*ilhuicac cihuapilli*).[31] Once, the adjective "precious" is added (*ilhuicac tlaçocihuapilli*).[32] The noun "Lady"[33] is used alone once, and in combination with the term "ruler" once more (*tlatoca cihuapilli*).[34] In conclusion, sixty-six percent of all titles given to Mary by the narrator concentrate on that reverential term.

If we consider Sánchez' work as the main source of our text,[35] it is strange that the Spanish term *Señora* that could work as a direct translation is not often found in the parallel passages of M. Sánchez. The shift from "María," or "María Virgen," omnipresent in the *criollo* rendition of the story, to "Heavenly Lady" in the *Nican mopohua* could be considered a statement. The most direct and almost familiar tones in the Spanish book are transformed into a deferential way of approaching Mary in Nahuatl. Is the distance created something intended by the author or implied by the Nahuatl way of speaking? The Marian title "heavenly ruler" was part of the Nahuatl vocabulary since the sixteenth century. It seems to translate the noun "Queen" used in some Marian prayers, and has been used since the early years of evangelization in the printed catechetical books.[36]

A second aspect underlined by the narrator's presentation of Mary is her virginity. The repetitive use of the adjective "perfect" to refer to the Maiden (*cenquizca ichpöchtli*)[37] seems to stress the fact that we are not talking about a common young girl-maiden. We are talking about the *intact one* that always remained in the same condition: the ever virgin. The stress on Mary's virginity was a common feature in colonial Mexican religious literature. The authors I have used to discover the presence of Marian titles in early evangelization concur in using the same, almost insistent, terminology regarding Mary's virginity.

Our author, either an Indian himself or someone trying to stand in the native's place, uses Juan Diego as his speaker. At first sight there are no significant differences between Juan Diego's perception of the "divine" Lady, and the terminology employed by the narrator. Juan Diego recognizes and calls Mary with the same titles of *Cihuapillé* (Lady) and *Nochpochtziné* (my Maiden, my Virgin) that we have found in the narrator's words. Both of those titles appeared in different combinations, nine times each, the most frequented titles to describe the heavenly Maiden.[38] The exact mention of the "heavenly Lady" (*ilhuicac cihuapilli*) appears in Juan Diego's mouth only twice, and in both cases during conversations with Bishop Zumárraga.[39] It is certainly not a title used when addressing Mary directly.

We notice in Juan Diego's speeches a tendency for a repetitive use of Marian titles, next to each other. Lady (*Cihuapilli*), Queen (*Tlacatlé*), and Mistress (*Notecuiyoé*)[40] are written one after the other just to emphasize the recognition of Mary's role in relationship to Juan Diego. She is a person in a privileged place, a person with authority. Similar use of repetitive sequences are frequently present in Sahagún's *huehuehtlahtolli* directed to the gods.[41] We may conclude that those repetitions constitute a literary device derived from polite or formal Nahuatl conversations. The author, who had never used this technique during the narrative parts, reproduces this typical Nahuatl way of speaking in Juan Diego.

Another novelty is introduced by Juan Diego's speeches. He did not limit himself to the more official titles given to the Lady. Our native protagonist adds certain expressions that we could call "familiar." I refer here first to the term "my youngest daughter" (*Noxocoyouhé*) that appears five times,[42] normally in combination with the more formal titles, with the exception of the scene describing the last encounter. It is quite telling that the expression is never used during Juan Diego's first encounter with Mary. It is present in the second conversation. Finally, during the third encounter, when Juan Diego was trying to avoid Mary, the title is joined to the second familiar term, "my dearest little child" (*Nopiltzintziné*), leaving aside the formal titles.[43]

This increasing familiarity has attracted commentators on the account to affirm the close relationship between Mary and Juan Diego implied by the text. Those names could certainly either refer to a closer, more family-like relationship between our protagonist and the "divine" Lady, or simply to another existing literary source at hand. A girl could call her mother, "my older sister";[44] or a king refer to his relationship to the people saying, "I am your mother, I am your father."[45] I discount the idea that Juan Diego is having an unusually affectionate and familiar conversation with the celestial Lady. The changing tones may well reflect the native's attempt to remind the Lady about the maternal role included in her authority. However, she is more than a mother in the strict sense of the term; neither Juan Diego nor Juan Bernardino, Juan Diego's uncle, ever address Mary as "mother."

No single case can be found of stories concerning Nahuatl gods being engaged with their devotees in conversations similar to the ones we read in the *Nican mopohua*. In Nahuatl literature, supernatural beings were perceived as frightening.

There are written accounts concerning those deities guiding people to places and appearing in visions to ask the group to continue searching for a location. People interpreting signs and omens were part of the Nahua groups' religious tradition, but not a single testimony has been found of a conversation between deities and priests or emperors. Hence, in contrast with those *huehuehtlahtolli* directed to *Tezcatlipoca*, whose language was borrowed by Juan Diego, our protagonist seems quite comfortable in the presence of someone he immediately recognized as a "divine" ruler.[46]

This approach to "divinity" is a novelty for indigenous literature, but also indicates the strong Spanish personality of Mary, the *asistente conquistadora*, as Sánchez called her.[47] Juan Diego felt attracted to her, commented the narrator.[48] Diego's response to Mary's wishes denotes that he considered her trustworthy, as becomes obvious at the end of the story. She remains a powerful person while at the same time stays close to him, interested in him. We cannot say that this kind of vision of Mary is exclusive to this text. We can state that when compared with the publication of Sánchez in 1648, the native character has gained confidence in his treatment of this powerful Lady. This new relationship between our protagonist and the "divine" being can be more paradigmatic than real. It may well represent an approach desired by the author of the text for his audience or readers. Is the author making Mary approachable for his audience? Is he making her more human while still remaining respectful?

Every time Mary speaks in our text, two features are underlined. She presents herself with full credentials. She is the "entirely Virgin Holy Mary, Mother of the true God," who insistently presents herself also as mother of the people in general,[49] and mother of Juan Diego in particular.[50] Her attitude and promises reveal an attempt to make Juan Diego feel comfortable with her.

Mary's words play between the literal meaning and the literary style of royal speeches. She wants a temple in order to listen to the cries of the people and their sadness. Like the *Mexica* kings, Mary is willing to pay Juan Diego for his services. Also like those rulers, she protects our protagonist and Juan Bernardino between her arms; she is the source of happiness. In all those ambivalent words, Mary seems prompted to get closer to her people. Either as a familiar mother or as a bright politician, she asks for a residence, which immediately implies for Nahuatl mentalities a fresh starting point and a will for permanence. She is not a distant foreigner, at least not anymore. The Christian Mary is replacing not only pre-Hispanic deities, but she is also making herself available as a source of compassion, of healing, of happiness in the midst of these people. One gets the impression the text invites us to walk together with our protagonist in the full discovery of Mary's *real* (in both Spanish senses of the term) character.

The intrinsic cultural dynamism and the ambivalent character of Nahuatl language have offered a "more gentle" understanding of Mary's authority. She has gained a more tender and sweet character when compared to Spanish medieval accounts. The diminutive, reverential terminology that dominates the entire text certainly reveals Nahuatl cultural influence. The attitude of Juan Diego, peaceful and fearless, in front of something considered by the text as "divine" deviates from any reference we have from pre-Hispanic records. The more traditionally found "terrifying" character of the supernatural disappears from the scene, which favors an almost paradigmatic context: the native that comes closer without any fear to the one who calls him.

The Biblical Maiden
Mary's presence in the document of CELAM Puebla

The characteristics surrounding the presence of the heavenly Lady in the *Nican mopohua* (no mask on her face, standing in front of Juan Diego) and the "divine" power of the Glorious One contained in the *Milagros de Nuestra Señora,* could be considered typical of Christian literary tradition. We will now compare these accounts with the model of a "descendent christology."[51]

As in Karl Rahner's explanation, the presence of Mary at the Tepeyac, as the presence of Christ on earth, is a sign of Divine love. Normally this sort of christology "implies a doctrine concerning the cosmic and (…) transcendental significance of the Incarnation."[52] Both Mary's intercession and Guadalupe's message come from above, and her will and wishes affect human lives. She is metaphorically incarnated in her image and in a culture. In the texts studied, Mary is first and foremost presented as a "Divine Being" to replace the pre-Hispanic deities. In Berceo's book we see how she can perform miracles and change the natural course of events, either human or in the cosmic realm. In the *Nican mopohua*, we read how she makes a decision in the upper world and comes to ask for human collaboration to realize it. Those "salvific" moments are not responses to explicit human desires but they are free gifts from heaven. Rahner warns about this metaphysical type of Christology:

> which, if, as is usual, it is presented in isolation and without connection with the first (he refers here to the *'saving history'* type, or ascending Christology), all too easily gives the impression of mythology, and seems to run counter both to historical experience and to any genuine idea of God.[53]

This kind of presentation of miraculous apparitions looks like mythological narrative to contemporary eyes. Positivistic minds read the stories dismissing any kind of historicity or veracity. Just as the christology "from above" risks obliterating the concrete human experience of the man Jesus of Nazareth, our texts give us few traces of the human face of Mary. Her historic character seemed irrelevant in our stories. The woman of Nazareth has been surpassed by the allegoric Apocalyptic Lady in Sánchez' work and by the Glorious heavenly intercessor.

That exaggerated role attributed to Mary in the economy of salvation represents nevertheless, a well-known belief in some Latin American countries still. Some Catholics may have not understood very clearly which teachings are dogmas of faith. In many Latin American contexts, the acceptance of Mary is synonymous with Catholicity. This faith emphasizes an emotional bond instead of a rational one and often circumscribes Mary's relevance in religion to domestic spheres.[54]

Latin American bishops and Pope John Paul II have written several documents and delivered speeches that show not only special deference to popular religiosity and Marian devotion in general, but also to the image and message of Guadalupe in particular. The first traces of this effort to reinforce the Guadalupe event as a unique moment in Latin American salvation history occurred in 1978. The final document after the CELAM meeting in Puebla contains a paragraph that, although it represents a historical challenge to find evidence to support it, exemplifies my statement concerning the relevance given to Guadalupe:

> En nuestros pueblos, el Evangelio ha sido anunciado presentando a la Virgen María como su realización más alta. Desde los orígenes—en su aparición y advocación de Guadalupe—María constituyó el gran signo, de rostro maternal y misericordioso, de la cercanía del Padre y de Cristo, con quienes ella nos invita a entrar en comunión. María fue también la voz que impulsó a la unión entre los hombres y los pueblos.[55]

Although no one would dare to deny the relevance of Mary in the preaching of the Spanish missionaries in Mexico, the inherent connection between her and the rest of the Gospel seems to be far less clear to the people than stated in the document. After the reading of the *Nican mopohua* it becomes evident that parts of the above-quoted statement are more in line with romantic views of the role of the image and even of Mary than with historical accuracy.

In the final document of Puebla, the traditional role of intercessor played by Mary is complemented with a more biblical and christocentric understanding of her relevance. In a section dedicated entirely to her,[56] Mary is presented above all as a role model for any Christian. Puebla sees in Mary's relationship with Christ a paradigm to be followed, not simply admired, by the Church.[57] Mary's human and active participation is underlined by the Latin American bishops.[58] Mary is the perfect disciple of Jesus. She listened to and trusted God.[59] Even the Marian dogmas are reinterpreted as an invitation to every person.[60]

These statements about Mary were incredibly disruptive of Latin American tradition. She had been rarely praised for being a good listener, an excellent disciple, or for being a woman.[61] In Puebla, there is a new interpretation that enhanced the example of Our Lady as a human being more than as a "divine" intercessor. These statements can be quoted as one more example of the twentieth-century theological interest in models "from below." The support given by the Episcopal gathering to the apparition of Guadalupe in a Mexican city seems like a pastoral acknowledgment of popular devotions, however the emphasis has been changed.

The woman of Nazareth present in the document of Puebla is not a product of that gathering of bishops. This "reading" of Mary can be discovered already present in Pope Paul VI's apostolic exhortation *Marialis cultus*. This exhortation is frequently quoted in the document of the Latin American bishops. Pope Paul VI had singled out the need to renovate some traditional forms of piety.[62] He insisted that Marian veneration should clearly express her trinitarian and christological connections.[63] The Second Vatican Council and the liturgical renewal that followed thereafter demanded a biblical note in all forms of cultic action. Indeed, Pope Paul VI's presentation underscores Mary's biblical role. His analysis presents Mary as a good listener, a praying woman, and an offering Mother. Pope Paul VI took good care to connect his statements to biblical references.[64]

Today, theologians seem to have rescued the biblical Mary. However, the main cultural trends in popular religiosity seem to leave aside these "corrections" and to remain loyal to a more supernatural understanding of Mary. While the first two studies are clear evidence of theological appropriation that started from the understanding of the people, the pontifical document and the CELAM concluding statement are intended as catechetical tools to correct those popular visions. The presentation of Puebla seems, indeed, much more profound and prophetic to us, but it has not yet touched most of the faithful. It is possible that we will have to wait for the adequate artistic and literary devices to successfully present the biblical Mary to the *pauperum*.

By the 1970s, inculturation sought to reinforce the Christian message in order to become victorious in its confrontation with the non-Christian elements and the more secularized order of Western societies. Trust in the content of Jesus' message has been the common conviction of most theologians: it is still a word of hope for every culture. The missionary effort, nevertheless, lost the political support of the Western countries. The initial trust in the power of ideas over cultural systems today is far less than evident.

The conflicting but complementary mariological models present in our texts could be a better starting point for understanding that there is no one single message or that there is no single way of being Church. In spite of the discussions, inculturation continues both to challenge and to integrate the response of the local communities. Until now, the official Church has paid insufficient attention to the receiver of the message. The process of communication, although improved by cultural awareness, continues mostly as a top-down process in order to inform people about the Good News. The conviction that we have something important to say reinforced the missionary endeavor but distracted us from the basic pedagogical question: Are the faithful learning? Our preaching and teaching styles have made us forget that a message is intended to be heard and understood.

The term "spontaneous inculturation" could provide a term for that specific appropriation of foreign elements made by members of a group, in a more neutral way than acculturation.[65] Such a digestive moment, as in physiology, takes place mostly unconsciously. The reception and translation of new elements is filtered by the receivers' perception of the world. Such an apprehension of reality is mostly shaped by a set of common or shared viewpoints; value systems; ideals; prejudices; and the economic, political, and religious interests that we call culture.

However, not every single element in any culture is "salvific." Texts are reproductions of social and personal contexts. In such "scripts" the believer finds signs of hearts longing for a better understanding of the ultimate mystery. Traditional approaches seem to be insufficient. Perhaps now is the time for the Church to listen to those children and infants who speak through popular devotions and piety, raise their voices, and offer guidance for a more effective pastoral approach.

Notes

1. L. E. Espinosa González, "Los primeros pasos de la inculturación. De Lovaina a Roma," *Voces. Revista de Teología misionera de la Universidad Intercontinental* 10 (1997) 133-51. A lengthy study of the term "inculturation" in the first chapter of my doctoral dissertation, *In principio erat appropriatio. An evaluation of the Nican mopohua as a model of inculturated evangelization.*

2. Name given to all forms of sacred art that works as a catechetical tool for the people.

3. In Nahuatl, this piece of literature was also known in Spanish since the seventeenth century. Today the *Nican mopohua* is considered by some authors to be the foundational story or the original source behind the devotion of Our Lady of Guadalupe.

4. I use the edition prepared by F. Baños and I highly recommend the preliminary study of Isabel Uría. G. De Berceo–F. Baños (ed.), *Milagros de Nuestra Señora*, (Barcelona: Crítica, 1997).

5. The book mentioned in our previous footnote provides an excellent bibliography for the study of this group of writers.

6. F. Baños clearly mentions the latest findings in terms of sources of Gonzalo de Berceo's work. The relevance of the previously considered main source, the manuscript Thott 128 of the Royal Library of Copenhagen, has been questioned after the discovery of the alcobacense 149 of the Portuguese National Library at Lisbon and the codex 110 of the Spanish National Library at Madrid.

7. The influence of Bernard seems undeniable in the introduction of Berceo's book. There is a clear tendency to accept and use Bernard's typology.

8. Santa María appears 61 times, Queen appears 29 times, immediately followed by Virgin (28) and Lady (20).

9. His article in ORB: *The Online Reference Book for Medieval Studies*. http://orb.rhodes.edu/encyclop/religion/hagiography/hagindex.html.

10. Miracle II, §87-88. El sacristán fornicario.

11. Not even three saints acting together can replace the force of Mary's love, as in miracle X, §242-57.

12. Miracle VIII, §198-206. El romero de Santiago.

13. Miracle VII, §164-68. El monje y San Pedro. Mary is even capable of changing Jesus Christ's previous decision.

14. In miracle XXIV, § 798. "Tú eres pora todo, ¡grado al Criador!, por rogar al tu Fijo, tu Padre, tu Señor; quequiere que tú mandes e ovieres sabor, todo lo fará Él de muy buen amor."

15. Miracle XXIV. Teófilo.

16. Miracle XIV, §319. La imagen respetada por el fuego. G. De Berceo–F. Baños (ed.), *Milagros de Nuestra Señora*, 79.

17. Miracle I, §72.

18. Miracle XVII, §384. La iglesia profanada. "La Reïna de Gloria tóvose pro prendada, porque la su eglesia fincava vïolada; pesó-l de corazón, fo ende despechada, demostrógelo luego que lis era irada."

19. Miracle XXIV, §778: "Sobre yelo escribes, contiendes en locura; harta só de tu pletio, dasme grand amargura, eres muy porfidioso, enojas sin mesura."

20. Miracle XIII, §314.

21. Miracle IX, §231: "si tú no li mandares decir la missa mía como solié decirla, grand querella avría, e tú serás finado, hasta'l trenteno día: ¡desend verás qué vale la saña de María!"

22. Miracle XV. La boda y la Virgen.

23. L. Lasso De La Vega–P. F. Velásquez (trans.), *Huei tlamahuiçoltica omonoxiti ilhuicac tlatoca cihuapilli Sancta Maria totlaçonantzin Guadalupe in nican huei altepenahuac México itocayocan Tepeyacac*, (México: Imprenta de Juan Ruyz, 1649).

24. M. Sánchez, *Imagen de la Virgen María, Madre de dios de Guadalupe. Milagrosamente aparecida en la ciudad de México. Celebrada en su historia, con la profecía del capítulo doce del Apocalipsis*, (México: Imprenta De la viuda de Bernardo Calderón, 1648). The first commentary was made by L. Becerra y Tanco in 1666. He suggested that the Nahuatl text should be considered the work of a native hand. Sánchez' book could use it as source, but certainly Lasso de la Vega was publishing something that was not entirely his work.

25. As commented by R. Nebel in *Santa María Tonantzin. Virgen de Guadalupe. Continuidad y transformación religiosa en México*, (México: Fondo de cultura económica, 1995), Original in German, 1992.

26. A broader analysis of the Nahuatl text in my doctoral dissertation mentioned above.

27. W. Christian Jr., *Apparitions in Late Medieval and Renaissance Spain*, (Princeton: Princeton University Press, 1981), 7.

28. The comparison can be easily made by reading M. León-Protilla, *Tonantzin Guadalupe*, (Mexico: El colegio nacional-Fondo de cultura económica, 2000).

29. M. Rojas, *Nican mopohua*, (México: Ideal, 1978), 41-42.

30. The idea of this analytical approach was taken from S. C. Espinosa González, "La dimensión misionera del Nican Mopohua," *Revista interdisciplinaria Extensiones*, VI/1-2 (2000) 4-16. This magazine is a publication of the Universidad Intercontinental in Mexico City.

31. NM 43, 48, 72, 78, 103, 122, 124, 134, 143, 189, 194, 195, 200. Paragraph numbers taken from M. Rojas publication of the *Nican mopohua*.

32. NM 212.

33. NM 14. One of Sahagún's favorite expressions in his sermons, see S. Klaus, *Uprooted Christianity: the Preaching of the Christian Doctrine in Mexico Based on Franciscan Sermons of the 16th Century Written in Nahuatl*, (Bonner Amerikanistische Studien, 33), Germany: Anton Saurwein, 1999, 96.

34. NM 211

35. Thesis supported by L. Sousa, S. Poole, J. Lockhart (eds.), *The Story of Guadalupe*, (Los Angeles: Stanford University Press, UCLA Latin American Center Publications, 1998.)

36. We have selected as study samples some Nahuatl works of P. de Gante, A. de Molina and the Dominican's *doctrina chiquita*, found in J. Cortés Castellanos, *El catecismo en pictogramas de Fr. Fedro de Gante*, (Madrid: Fundación Universitaria Española, 1987.) Two sermons of Juan de la Anunciación, in *Sermonario en lengua mexicana*, Antonio Ricardo, México, 1577. And two more sermons of Juan Bautista, *Sermonario en lengua mexicana*, (México: Diego López Dávalos,1606-07).

37. NM intro., 73, 75, 117, 183, 208.

38. *Cihuapilli*: NM 24, 38, 50, 54, 55, 63, 66, 101, 110; Nochpochtziné: NM 24, 50, 54, 55, 63, 66, 110, 111, 115. A quick comparison of the paragraphs makes us see that both names appear frequently next to each other.

39. NM 80, 165.

40. The different English renditions can be misleading. The three Nahuatl names were used to refer to a Nahuatl woman who was acting as a ruler; a *cacica* in later colonial Spanish (word borrowed from the Caribbean languages), the English terms can be exchanged and it would make no difference.

41. See B. De Sahagún, *Historia general de las cosas de la Nueva España*, Book VI, the first verses of chapters 1, 2, 3, or 4.

42. NM 50, 55, 66, 110, 116.

43. NM 110, 116.

44. See M. León-Portilla and L.Silva Galeana (eds.), *Huehuehtlahtolli: Testimonio de la antigua palabra*, (México: Comisión Nacional del V Centenario del Encuentro de Dos Mundos, 1988), 99.

45. M. León-Portilla and L.Silva Galeana (eds.), Huehuehtlahtolli, 173.

46. NM 13.

47. M. Sánchez, *Imagen de la Virgen María*, 179. (in E. De La Torre Villar and R. Navarro De Anda, *Testimonios históricos guadalupanos*, México: FCE, 1999).

48. NM 22.

49. NM 29.

50. NM 119.

51. We refer here to the Metaphysical Christology described by K. Rahner in "The Two Basic Types of Christology" in *Theological Investigations*, vol. XIII, (London: Darton, Longman & Todd, 1975), 213-23. (Original in German from 1972).

52. Karl Rahner, *Theological Investigations*, vol. XIII, 218.

53. Karl Rahner, *Theological Investigations*, vol. XIII, 221.

54. A. González Dorado, *De María conquistadora a María liberadora*, (Santander: Sal Térrae, 1988), 63-73.

55. Pue 282.

56. Pue 292-303.

57. Pue 292, 296.

58. Pue 293.

59. Pue 296-97.

60. Pue 298.

61. Pue 299.

62. MC 24.

63. MC 25.

64. MC 17-20.

65. V. Neckebrouck, *Paradoxes de l'inculturation. Les nouveaux habits des Yanomami*, (Leuven: Leuven University Press, 1994), Chapter 4.

Chapter 10

Marian Devotion in the Spiritual Life of Saint Rose of Lima

Father Alfred A. Brichta-López, O.P.

As a mystic whose life embraced both active and contemplative dimensions, Saint Rose of Lima (1586-1617) subscribed to a Christ-centered spirituality. Following the example of her fellow Dominican Tertiary and spiritual model, Saint Catherine of Siena, Rose placed paramount importance upon nurturing her impassioned relationship with Christ, whom she situated at the apex of her spiritual paradigm. In the course of constructing a spirituality on this foundational relationship, she immersed herself in intense prayer and engaged in such ascetic practices as rigorous fasting, abstinence from meat, sleep deprivation, and flagellation, all of which were consistent with penitential disciplines of the time. Whether in the confines of her hermitage, begging for alms, attending to the needy, or in a prayerful position before the altar of the chapel dedicated to Nuestra Señora del Santísimo Rosario in the Dominican Church of Santo Domingo in Lima, Rose continually experienced a unitive communion with God that enabled her to achieve a balanced mix of the active life of charitable works and the contemplative life of intense prayer and meditation

Although she assiduously endeavored to pattern her spiritual life after that of her Dominican model, Rose's spirituality, unlike Saint Catherine's, included an especial devotion to both the Christ Child and the Virgin Mary under several titles and their corresponding images celebrated in certain neighborhood parishes in the city of Lima. In this paper, I will identify these titles and images and describe Rose's devotion to the Virgin and Christ Child as represented by them. I will also attempt to evaluate the significance of Marian devotion in Rose's unique spirituality by discussing aspects of her life that account for her repeated manifestations of deference toward the Virgin.

The original documentation forming the basis of this paper is part of the 1617 and 1630 *procesos*[1] undertaken in support of the cause for Rose's beatification and canonization. Although Rose's principal biographers, such as Leonard Hansen, Andrés Ferrer de Valdecebro, Domingo Angulo, Luis G. Alonso Getino, Rubén Vargas Ugarte, and Noé Zevallos, relied on these *procesos* either directly or indirectly, they ignored accounts of her devotion to the Virgin Mary in favor of her more spectacular mystical experiences and ascetic practices. For the most part, the documentation of the 1617 and 1630 *procesos* consists of the testimony of witnesses who either had known Rose personally, or had knowledge of her, during her lifetime and/or who had experienced miracles attributed to her intercession after her death. The testimony of one of the witnesses of both the 1617 and 1630 *procesos*, Doctor Juan de Castillo, a noted medical doctor and theologian of Lima, captured the attention of a number of Rose's biographers because of its vivid, precise detail regarding the sophisticated mystical dimension of her spirituality. However, nowhere in Castillo's account is there any mention of Rose's more mundane Marian devotion.

The several titles of the Virgin Mary that served as the focus of Rose's Marian devotion reflect the influence of the religious orders in Lima with which she came into contact at different times in her life. Foremost among these titles are Our Lady of the Angels (Nuestra Señora de los Angeles), which identifies a Franciscan devotion; Our Lady of the Most Holy Rosary (Nuestra Señora del Santísimo Rosario), which names a Dominican devotion; and Our Lady of Montserrat (Nuestra Señora de Montserrat), which refers to a devotion of great significance to Jesuit founder Ignatius of Loyola. In addition, Rose revered the Virgin in her representations as Our Lady of Loreto (Nuestra Señora de Loreto), Nuestra Señora de los Remedios, and Nuestra Señora de Atocha. All of these Marian devotions were expressions of a strictly Spanish European mariology, since both the various images of the Virgin and their respective traditions were introduced to the New World by early representatives of the various religious orders in colonial Peru. Neither the 1617 *proceso* nor the 1630 *proceso* mentions any of the native regional South American Marian devotions contemporary with Rose, such as Our Lady of Copacabana (Bolivia, 1583), Our Lady of Chiquinquirá (Colombia, 1562), Our Lady of Quinche (Ecuador, 1604), Our Lady of the Mercedes of Caacupé (Paraguay, early 1500s), Our Lady of Coromoto (Venezuela, 1591), and Our Lady of Luján (Argentina, 1630).

During her childhood, Rose was initially attracted to Franciscan spirituality, to the extent that she wore a garment patterned on the habit of the Franciscan Order for a period of eleven years prior to her investiture as a Dominican Tertiary. Later on in her life, Rose was delighted to learn of the existence of a medieval saint with the name of Rose, who had been a Franciscan Tertiary of Viterbo, Italy (1234-1252).

According to Fray Pedro de Loaysa, one of her Dominican confessors, Rose sought spiritual direction from an unidentified Franciscan friar very early in her life. This friar served as her first known confessor but later convinced her to pursue Dominican spirituality.

Acting upon the advice of her early Franciscan confessor, Rose sought out at least nine accomplished and celebrated Dominican priests as confessors over the course of her life. Of these, she manifested the greatest esteem for and confidence in Fray Juan de Lorenzana. Somewhat later, Rose's pursuit of Dominican spirituality led her to seek a more formalized commitment to Dominican ideals. Over a period of time, some of her influential friends repeatedly petitioned the Dominican authorities of the Peruvian province of San Juan Bautista for permission for her to become a Dominican Tertiary. Only then did these authorities in turn appeal to Dominican superiors in Spain for the required permission, which was eventually granted. In a private ceremony at the Dominican *convento* of Nuestra Señora del Santísimo Rosario in Lima, Rose made her formal profession of vows as a Tertiary to Fray Alonso de Velázquez, the prior of the Dominican community there. Along with these private vows, Rose's vesture in the habit of a female Dominican Tertiary served to formalize her installation as a member of the Third Order of Saint Dominic.

Toward the end of her life, Rose took up residence in the household of her lay spiritual counselor and friend, El Contador de la Santa Cruzada Gonzalo de la Maza, and his wife, María de Uzátigui, both of whom were prominent residents of Lima. Uzátigui introduced Rose to Jesuit priests from the neighborhood parish church of San Pablo Apóstol, which the Maza family regularly attended. Seven Jesuit priests complete the list of Rose's confessors.

According to Padre Antonio de la Vega Loaysa, one of Rose's Jesuit confessors who testified in the 1617 *proceso*, Rose held an appreciation for and received many favors from the Virgin of Loreto. Rose, along with others, devoted time to changing the clothing and adornments of the statue of the Virgin of Loreto located in the chapel of Nuestra Señora de la Candelaria in the Jesuit church of San Pablo Apóstol. Vega Loaysa also stated that Rose had been devoted to the Virgin Mary under her title of Nuestra Señora de los Remedios, whose statue was centrally located in a niche high above the main altar in the church of San Pablo Apóstol. According to Luisa (Barba) de Santa María, a friend of Rose who also testified in the 1617 *proceso*, on one occasion while Rose was in the Jesuit church of San Pablo Apóstol, she remembered that she had failed to put away some of the instruments that she had used to mortify her body earlier that day. Rose was very upset because she was afraid that others would see the instruments; and so, positioned on her knees, she intently prayed before the image of Nuestra Señora de los Remedios, petitioning the Virgin to hide the instruments for her in one of two places that she indicated. After making her supplication, Rose felt relieved, and when she returned home later that day she found the instruments stored in the second location that she had suggested to the Virgin.[2]

Although the documentation of the *procesos* fails to reveal many details of Rose's affiliation with the Franciscan Order in Lima during her childhood and early adolescent years, it is likely that she would have been introduced to Our Lady of the Angels and the Franciscan devotional traditions surrounding this title of the Virgin Mary through contact with Franciscan religious. This assumption is based on the fact that when Rose turned to Dominican spirituality she not only sought spiritual counsel from Dominican confessors but also incorporated various Dominican devotions into her repertoire of spiritual observances. One particular Dominican devotion that Rose especially treasured involved the Virgin under the title of Nuestra Señora del Santísimo Rosario, after whom the principal Dominican *convento* in Lima was named. Interestingly, witnesses who testified in the 1617 and 1630 *procesos* recounted stories about and/or interactions with Rose in which she frequently referred to Nuestra Señora del Santísimo Rosario as Nuestra Señora de los Angeles. The fact that Rose interchanged these titles in addressing the Virgin suggests a confused devotional piety on her part. However, further scrutiny of the witnesses' testimony reveals that they believed Rose to be truly knowledgeable of both Franciscan and Dominican spirituality, fully aware of the traditions behind the titles of the Virgin whom she frequently invoked, and thus deliberate in her practice of interchanging the two titles.

The following four situations related by witnesses in the 1617 *proceso* demonstrate Rose's reliance upon the Virgin Mary as an advocate to whom she deferred in soliciting counsel and succor under the title of Nuestra Señora del Santísimo Rosario. The first incident occurred while Rose was in her early teens. One Sunday morning, María de Quiñones, a professed religious of the *monasterio* (convent) of La Encarnación in Lima, met with Rose's crippled and bedridden grandmother, Isabel Herrera, to persuade her to encourage Rose to enter the *monasterio* of Santa Clara. Herrera agreed that her granddaughter should become a nun. Nevertheless, Quiñones pleaded with Herrera to refrain from discussing the matter with Rose's mother, María de Oliva, who was also ill at the time.

Accompanied by one of her brothers, Rose left home to attend mass at the Dominican church of Santo Domingo. Entering the church, she approached the altar in the side chapel dedicated to Nuestra Señora del Santísimo Rosario. Poised before the statue of the Virgin holding the Christ Child, Rose attended mass and prayed for the Virgin's blessings as she set out to join the *monasterio* of Santa Clara. As she prayed before the image, Rose suddenly found herself transfixed and unable to move, as if nailed to the floor. Realizing that the hour was late and that her brother had been repeatedly coming into the church to see if she was ready to leave, Rose remained steadfast in prayer, conversing with the Virgin. She decided that her decision to enter the *monasterio* of Santa Clara did not please either the Christ Child or his mother. Rose begged forgiveness of the Virgin and promised not to follow through with her proposed plan. Instead, she committed herself to returning to the home of her parents and to caring for them for as long as they or she lived. After making this promise, Rose found herself able to move freely and thus capable of going home in the company of her brother. Upon arrival, Rose discovered that Isabel Herrera had been crying over her granddaughter's decision to enter the *monasterio* of Santa Clara ever since she had left the house earlier in the day. María de Oliva, who was also present when Rose returned home, failed to comprehend Isabel Herrera's surprising change of heart.[3]

The second situation illustrates the Virgin's persistent, nurturing support of Rose's prayer life. Given her many responsibilities, Rose spent most of the hours in the day engaged in fulfilling her commitments. Thus, she slept no more than two to three hours out of twenty-four and would have slept even less if her principal Dominican confessor, Fray Juan de Lorenzana, had not intervened. Because Rose did not set aside any specific time for sleeping, Lorenzana, in consultation with other confessors from whom she sought counsel, ordered her to devote the hours from twelve midnight until four in the morning to sleep. This newly devised schedule ensured Rose of a regimen that included additional hours of rest.

Waking up at four o'clock in the morning in order to resume praying proved to be no easy task for Rose, who found the new schedule fatiguing. Another complicating factor interfering with her adjustment to the new regimen was that of anxiety. In her conversations with María de Uzátigui and Fray Pedro de Loaysa, Rose explained that one day in the course of meditating she had gazed upon the statue of Nuestra Señora del Santísimo Rosario in the church of Santo Domingo and had noticed an intense sadness in the faces of the Christ Child and the Virgin. This sadness, according to Rose, stemmed from two sources—transgressions perpetrated by Dutch Protestant forces who were believed to have disembarked at the port of Callao with the intention of invading Lima and, secondly, problems arising from the scandalous behavior of some Dominican religious in the Peruvian province of San Juan Bautista. Although Loaysa would have liked to know more concerning the scandal, he could not bring himself to question Rose further on the matter, since she did not broach the subject other than to mention it in passing. According to Loaysa, Rose anguished over the state of affairs in which the lives of various Dominican friars were embroiled. After all, they were members of the order that she so dearly loved. In her anguish, she cried long and hard and was unable to eat, drink, and sleep sufficiently.

Since Rose had been accustomed to beginning her sleep around four in the morning, she found sleeping before that hour almost impossible. She explained to her intimate friends that she fared better with fewer hours of sleep. Now, mindful of Fray Juan de Lorenzana's dictates, she was committed to sleeping more hours. However, Rose found herself sleeping beyond the hour at which she had intended to rise. Her inability to wake herself in time to begin her proposed daily routine saddened her, especially since oversleeping interfered with the time she had allotted for her morning prayers.

In a valiant attempt to comply with the prescriptions of her confessor, Rose sought help from the Virgin Mary under her titles of Nuestra Señora del Santísimo Rosario and Nuestra Señora de los Angeles. With the assistance of her motherly advocate, she ultimately prevailed in accommodating her pattern of sleep. Rose reported that just before four in the morning, the time when the church bells generally sounded, Nuestra Señora del Santísimo Rosario would approach and awaken her with the words, "Daughter, wake up! It is now time to pray!" At times, Rose failed to awaken at the Virgin's call. On these occasions, the Virgin would again attempt to awaken her, saying, "My daughter, it is now time to wake up!" Then there were times when Rose felt utterly unable to overcome her urge to remain sleeping. When she overslept, the Virgin would approach her and call a first time, after which the Virgin would issue a second call, to which Rose would respond, "Yes, I am getting up," but, instead of acting upon her response, would fall back into sleep. Gently taking hold of Rose's hand, the Virgin would call her a third time in an attempt to rouse her from slumber. On the occasions when Rose awoke at the Virgin's first call, she enjoyed a face-to-face vision of her heavenly visitor. However, when the Virgin had to call her a second and third time, Rose glimpsed only the back of her visitor, a view that she interpreted as representing the Virgin leaving the scene.[4]

The third incident illuminating Rose's relationship with the Virgin Mary proved to be instrumental in her resolution to undertake a spiritual marriage with the primary object of her devotion, Christ. One evening during the year before her death, Rose joined María de Uzátigui at the latter's home, where Uzátigui was in the process of dressing an image of Nuestra Señora de Loreto from the Jesuit church of San Pablo Apóstol. It was Good Friday night, and Rose informed both Uzátigui and her husband, Gonzalo de la Maza, that she intended to marry her beloved Christ on Easter Sunday morning. Uzátigui questioned Rose about her proposed marriage, whereupon Rose began to describe the events that had transpired in a mystical encounter between her and the image of Nuestra Señora del Santísimo Rosario in the church of Santo Domingo on the previous Sunday, which happened to be Palm Sunday. On this occasion, after the blessing of the palms, Rose waited to obtain some fronds. However, since all of the palms had already been distributed to people attending the services and procession, Rose was not able to acquire any as she had in previous years. Distressed at not receiving any fronds, she went to the chapel of Nuestra Señora del Santísimo Rosario and pouted, informing the Virgin that she did not want palms given by human hands. Rose then repented for having said that and asked for palms from the hands of the Christ Child whom the Virgin held in her arms. While absorbed in prayer before the Virgin, Rose noticed that she had turned her head to her son, the Christ Child, whereupon he looked toward the Virgin's face and then tenderly addressed Rose, saying, "Rosa de mi corazón, sea mi esposa!" to which she affectionately responded in the affirmative.[5]

In their testimony in the 1617 *proceso*, two of Rose's Dominican confessors, Fray Pedro de Loaysa and Fray Francisco Nieto, related very similar accounts of a situation in which Rose had sought help from the Virgin under the title of Nuestra Señora del Santísimo Rosario. Stirred by her own disquieted spirit, Rose declared to her mother, María de Oliva, that she wished to build a hermitage in the recesses of the backyard patio of her parents' home. Rose was denied permission to construct the refuge. María de Oliva refused to allow her daughter to immerse herself in a life of silence by retreating from family and friends.

Realizing that she was failing in her attempt to convince her mother of her need for the hermitage, Rose turned to her heavenly advocate for help. One day, Rose called upon Fray Francisco Nieto at the Dominican *convento* of Nuestra Señora del Santísimo Rosario. She gave him a rosary and asked him to place it around the neck of the statue of Nuestra Señora del Santísimo Rosario in the church of Santo Domingo adjacent to the *convento*. Nieto took the rosary and that same day, during the siesta hours, attempted to drape it around the neck of the Virgin. Unable to complete the task, he left it for another day.

The following day, Rose went to the church and, after entering and approaching the chancel, immediately noticed that the rosary had not been situated on the statue as she had requested. This disturbed and disappointed her greatly, whereupon she asked to see Nieto and queried him as to why he had been remiss in accomplishing the task. The friar responded without providing a reason, simply stating that he had been unable to place the rosary on the statue. Rose then asked him to return the rosary to her. After he complied, she gave it to the head sacristan of the *convento* with the same instructions that she had given Nieto. That very day, the sacristan situated the rosary around the neck of the statue. On the following day, however, he discovered that the rosary originally placed around the neck of the Virgin was now arranged in the hands of the Christ Child.

While attending mass at the *convento* on the feast of the Purification of Mary, the day after the sacristan found the Christ Child holding the rosary, Rose immediately noticed the position of the rosary. She called for Nieto and asked him who had taken the rosary from the neck of the Virgin and placed it in the Infant's hands. He stated that he did not know and that when he had asked all the sacristans why the rosary had been repositioned they responded that they had not done so, since there had been absolutely no reason for any of them to move it. Rose interpreted the rosary in the hands of the Christ Child as a sign that God would dispose María de Oliva to permit her to construct the hermitage she so desperately wanted. That afternoon, Rose, accompanied by Fray Juan de Lorenzana, María de Uzátigui, and her husband, Gonzalo de la Maza, approached her mother with the plea to allow her to construct the hermitage. The fact that María de Oliva now acceded to her petition was no surprise to Rose, since, as a result of the above-described incident, she firmly believed that God had disposed her mother to grant her request.[6]

While consistent with Marian piety of the time, Rose's devotion to the Virgin Mary reveals a noticeably urgent need for the affection and nurturing that she failed to receive from either parent and particularly from her mother. Throughout her adolescent and adult life, Rose's father, Gaspar Flores, held the lowly but secure post of harquebusier soldier (*arcabucero*) in the detachment of viceregal guards in Lima. He also participated in military campaigns in the course of his service as an arcabucero and later served as an administrator of a work project in the town of Canta. In all likelihood, Flores married Rose's mother, María de Oliva, when he was in his late fifties; very probably he was sixty when Rose was born and ninety-one when she died in 1617. His testimony in the 1617 *proceso* reveals that he adopted a passive role as a parent, deferring to his wife in the rearing of his children. In a poignant statement Gaspar Flores admitted that throughout Rose's life he had remained indifferent to her spiritual aspirations, primarily, he said, because he understood little when it came to matters of mystical significance.

The testimony provided by María de Oliva in the 1617 and 1630 *procesos* describes the Flores family as poor but possessing cultural values that were almost exclusively Spanish in origin. The fact that María de Oliva continued to plot, although without success, to arrange a marriage for Rose with a suitor from a wealthy family supports the depiction of her as a social climber. The testimony of many of the *procesos*' witnesses corroborates the characterization of Rose's mother as a shrewd, determined woman who utilized the limited resources available to her to stabilize and/or better the Flores family's economic position in colonial Lima society.

Rose's profound appreciation of the Virgin as "mother," so clearly evident in the *proceso* documents, is not surprising in view of the fact that the relationship between Rose and her biological mother was one of mutual edginess. María de Oliva exercised her maternal role in a formidable manner by meddling into almost every aspect of Rose's life. Feeling enveloped by her mother's imposing designs but ever mindful of her responsibility to contribute to the support of her parents and siblings, Rose continually searched for opportunities to ease the oppressive effects of her mother's machinations. Her quest for solitude led her to build, with the help of her brother, Hernando Flores de Herrera, two years her senior, a much desired hermitage in the backyard of her parents' home. Within the confines of this meager refuge, Rose intermittently escaped her mother's controlling tendencies and engaged in intense prayer to the Christ Child. [7]

Five years before her death, Rose accepted the invitation of María de Uzátigui to live as a guest in the Maza household. In time, an intimate spiritual relationship began to develop between Rose and the members of the Maza family, which included Uzátigui's husband, Gonzalo de la Maza, and their two daughters, Micaela and Andrea de la Maza. As their friendship deepened, Rose disclosed to Uzátigui that she felt constrained at her parents' home. In particular, she revealed that her mother's brooding presence seriously interfered with her ability to exercise her pious devotions to the fullest extent. In response, the Maza family provided Rose with a room in their home. Although she frequently participated in household chores such as sewing, the Mazas, ever attentive to her predilection for solitude, concertedly strove to afford her the privacy that she so greatly treasured. During the five years that she resided with the Maza family, Rose intermittently returned to her parental home for a week at a time. [8]

The incidents involving the titles and corresponding images described above provide an insight into Rose's repeated deference to the Virgin. It was the immeasurable, reciprocal love that she observed between the Virgin Mary and her son, the Christ Child, that encouraged Rose to defer to her celestial mother and seek not only maternal affection and affirmation but also consolation and counsel from her. Approaching the Virgin as an advocate allowed Rose to achieve communion with Christ, the quintessential object of her spirituality, with confidence, a quality that she sorely lacked because of her pronounced, self-imposed scrupulosity. This scrupulosity led Rose to consult numerous Dominican and Jesuit confessors who ultimately failed to impart the spiritual confidence and assurance she so fervently desired and sought.

While ultimately occupying a subordinate role in the hierarchy of Rose's spiritual life, the Virgin Mary nevertheless continued to fulfill a key position, that of a nurturing mother. Rose's devotion to the Virgin and loving adoration of the Christ Child fortified her spiritual life. At times, Rose did not hesitate to pray for needs that she believed would help her in her own relationship with God. Nevertheless, her perception of the Virgin as a nurturing mother inspired her interaction with and on behalf of others. In the course of her communication with two of her Dominican confessors, Fray Pedro de Loaysa and Fray Francisco Nieto, Rose disclosed that she had continuously received favors (*mercedes*) from the Virgin and the Christ Child that were destined for the spiritual and physical well-being of others.[9]

The *proceso* documents suggest that Rose became absorbed in the dynamic of the mother-son relationship between the Virgin Mary and the Christ Child by observing the various representations of the Virgin under her favorite titles—Rosario, Los Angeles, Loreto, Los Remedios, and Atocha. These images, all of which depicted the Virgin with a pleasant disposition and a nurturing pose, tenderly holding the Infant Jesus in her arms, became the focus of Rose's Marian devotion. The life-size image of Nuestra Señora del Santísimo Rosario, centrally located in a side chapel of the church of Santo Domingo in Lima, portrays an impressive, compassionate, loving image of the Virgin, affectionately clutching the Christ Child to her left breast. This image of a doting mother holding the Infant to herself while at the same time presenting him to the world mesmerized Rose. The image not only led Rose to ponder and comprehend the motherly love of the Virgin for the Christ Child, it also embodied the nurturing love that the Virgin manifested for all humankind and especially for individuals such as Rose herself who needed only to beseech the Virgin for motherly love to obtain it.[10]

The path that led Rose to Christ, the core of her spiritual life, drew upon the spirituality of great women and men in the history of Western Christianity. Throughout most of her adulthood, Rose relied heavily upon the example of Dominican saints, especially Saint Catherine of Siena and Saint Dominic Guzmán, in enacting a life centered on spiritual ideals in which she steadfastly persevered until the day she died. However, as a Dominican Tertiary, Rose never abandoned her early regard for Franciscan spirituality, embracing Saint Francis of Assisi and Saint Rose of Viterbo along with Saints Dominic and Catherine as models whose lives she emulated in her endeavor to establish and fortify an intimate relationship with Christ. Later on, when introduced to the Jesuits at the Mazas' parish of San Pablo Apóstol, Rose integrated aspects of their spirituality into her personal piety.

Although Rose's spiritual life remained Christ-centered throughout her adulthood, she repeatedly turned to the Virgin Mary for the nurturance lacking in her biological parents. Neither her aged, passive father nor her manipulative, controlling mother was able to provide her with the quality of spiritual and emotional sustenance that she sought and received from her heavenly advocate. It was through the Virgin that Rose approached Christ, the Virgin's son, who as the Infant Jesus visited her early in her life while she prayed and embroidered in the silence of her hermitage and who subsequently betrothed himself to her with the words, "Rosa de mi corazón, sea mi esposa!" Later on, in her adulthood, during her bouts with the tormenting illness that inflicted excruciating pain and drained her life's energy, she identified with the crucified Christ. Nevertheless, it was always the Virgin Mary who led Rose to Christ, whether as child or adult.

Throughout her life, Rose never failed to honor the significance of her relationship with the Virgin. During her childhood, not long after receiving the sacrament of confirmation from the archbishop of Lima, Toribio Alfonso de Mogrovejo, she affixed the phrase "de Santa María" to her name. Rose often spent prolonged periods of time in prayer in the side chapel dedicated to Nuestra Señora del Santísimo Rosario in the church of Santo Domingo. The loving interaction between the Virgin and Rose enabled the latter to approach the object of her spiritual quest, her beloved Christ, with confidence and ultimately attain the level of intensity that characterized her unitive communion with him.

Notes

1. A *proceso* is an official transcript of the testimony of witnesses in a juridical case. As used here, the term refers to the official documentation sent to Rome in support of a candidate for beatification and canonization; it can also refer to the actual juridical process of compiling that documentation.

2. Riti 1570, 160/1, 128/1.

3. Riti 36/1-37/1.

4. Riti 83/1-84/1; Lilly Library transcription, 87/2, 103/2, 21/2.

5. Riti 1570, 85/1-85/2.

6. Riti 188/1-189/2, 199/1-200/1.

7. Riti 46/1, 127/2, 82/2, 160/2-161/1.

8. Dominican College microfilm, Roll 8, Vol. 1, Santa Rosa de Lima, 69/2-70/2.

9. Riti 1570, 188/1-189/2, 199/1-200/1.

10. This statue of Nuestra Señora del Santísimo Rosario dates from the sixteenth century. According to the Dominican priest and chronicler Juan Meléndez Ramírez (1633-1710), King Charles V of Spain presented the statue to the Dominican church of Santo Domingo in Lima.

Archival Sources:

Archivio Segreto Vaticano Processus: Riti 1570: "Traslado de la Vida, Muerte, Milagros de Santa Rosa de Santa María: Traslado Auténtico de las Informaciones de la Vida Sanctidad, Muerte y Milagros de la Bendita Rosa de Santa María, Natural de la ciudad de los Reyes del Perú, del Abito de la Orden de Sancto Domingo de Pedimiento del Procurador original de ella por man^do del Illmo Señor Don Bartolomé Lobor Guerrero Arçobispo de la d^ha Ciudad del Concejo de su Mag^d Juez de la Causa, Sacado por Hayme Blanco Notario Público de Su Cámara y Govierno, Escrito en trescientas y treinta y tres ojas/ Jayme Balnco Not° Pub°."

Dominican College Library, Dominican College, Washington D.C.: Dominican College microfilm, Roll 8, Vol. 1, Santa Rosa de Lima and Dominican College microfim Roll 9, Vol. 1, cont., Santa Rosa de Lima constitute a *proceso* which is entitled "Investigaciones de la Vida y Milagros de la Dicha Beata Rosa de Santa María."

Lilly Library, Indiana University, Bloomington: "Proceso Original de la Vida, Santidad, Muerte y Milagros de la Bendita Soror Rosa de Santa María del Hábito de Tercera de la Religión de Santo Domingo, Criolla de Esta Ciudad de los Reyes," (167, September 1-1630, April 14).

Chapter 11

Saints and Sanctity in France

"Que tes œuvres sont belles, que tes œuvres sont grande"

(Hymne Français)

Father Ted Baenziger, CSB

God blesses this world with many saints, men and women who inspire us to holiness, and nowhere more strikingly than in France, This paper traces some of the *grandes lignes* of the history of saints and culture in that country so closely tied to our own United States.

Sanctus, the origin of the word saint, means holy, and includes the notion of purity and goodness. "Toi seul es saint," says the Sanctus of the Mass in French; God alone is good, quoting from Jesus' remark to the young man who calls him "good Master" (Mark 10:17). The worship given to God alone, *latria*, is that recognition of God's holiness. All Catholic liturgy is based on our praise, petition, thanksgiving, and asking pardon of the most Holy One, and God alone is fully Holy.

By the direct action of God, however, we are made holy as the People of God, through inheritance (the Chosen People) and through adoption (as believers in Jesus Christ). For the Jews, the people are holy, the tribe of Levi is set apart for holiness, holy is the city of Jerusalem, the Temple, and the Holy of Holies where the Ark was kept. For Christians, the Church militant is part of the Communion of Saints: all those who seek holiness and are in union with God.

Certain persons, after a remarkable life or an extraordinary witness (called *martyr* in Greek, referring to giving one's life blood) are considered *Sancti* or *Benedicti*

(Blessed: the terms are equivalent in Church literature until the thirteenth century). These form the Church triumphant and are in Heaven. Honor (*dulia*) is given them and prayers may be addressed to them (for Mary, *hyper-dulia*). This devotion is called cult, from the same root as culture, and cultivation, the practice or correct way of doing actions. Thus we talk of the cult of saints, Mary's cult, etc. Only later distortions have made cult into a word with negative connotations.

What exactly do we admire in saints? What do we expect from them and how do we go about getting what we expect? Saints are with God and enjoy the ultimate happiness of heaven. We really cannot expect them to be concerned with our business, and yet, time and again, we have had proof that the Body of Christ, the struggles of the saints on earth, the smaller and larger questions of our life here, do indeed call for and receive a response. Whether in the crisis of France's near destruction in 1427 and the mysterious voices given to a young virgin Jehanne (Joan of Arc), or in the case of illness (Bernadette and Thérèse calling on the Virgin Mary's help and receiving it), or in the case of countless prayers answered, these holy men and women come to our aid.

We come with our own sets of preconceptions: that the saints are living and interested in us, the struggling faithful. We come with an attraction towards heroes and heroines, those of special lives, the winners, who, like Christ, gave their lives out of love. These individuals interest and fascinate us, through reputation, relics, or simple curiosity. We name our children for saints, we take them as patrons. How many of us are named for saints?

Of course the first saints are from the primitive Church: Mary and Joseph, John the Baptist (and his parents), the Apostles and Paul, the Disciples, Mary Magdalene, Martha, and Lazarus. Many were the martyrs of that time (Stephen being the first) and continuing into the persecutions by a series of governors and emperors. Virgin martyrs, especially, often gather quite a following (Agnes, Agatha, Cecilia, etc.). Not many of these ever came to France or were from this part of the world. It was with the generalized christianization of Roman Gaule that a new form of sanctity was recognized, that of confessors—Martin of Tours being the first in the West.

But why should we be concerned about France at all, since it is only a small country in this Europe newly born to Christ? I think there are a number of reasons to celebrate France as the home of saints and sanctity. First, the history of the Church is written largely into her history. As these people grew fervent, the Church drew its strength from them. What was to become France, *fille ainée de l'église*, the Church's eldest daughter, helped shape the Christian world from North America to Indochina, from the Holy Land of Jesus' birth to Equatorial Africa. Texas' first bishops were French, as were those of Sénégal, Tahiti, Québec, and Louisiana.

The French have loved saints and named their towns after them; 4,376 communes (twelve percent of the total) and 242 towns bear the name of Martin alone! The favorites today we may judge by given names (Marie and Louis being the most popular in 1999) and by informal preferences, Geneviève, Thérèse Martin de Lisieux (called the Little Flower in English, but not in French), Vincent de Paul, Jean-Marie Vianney (le Curé d'Ars), Bernadette Soubiroux, Jeanne de Chantal, and Louis de France, the king. During the dictatorship of Napoleon III, the newly formed Postal

Service, les PTT, issued its first Almanac, a list of saints for every day of the year (including FêteNat, July 14, which is not a saint, and quite a few others we cannot recognize today). Indeed saints are popular even today in a dechristianized land. France has sent more missionaries than any country its size, especially since 1800; hundreds of these have faced martyrdom in Africa, Indonesia, and most recently Algeria. We have all heard of the Canadian martyrs, Jean de Brébœuf and others. They are heroic men and women.

This legion of saints did not emerge from the culture at once, but rather appeared in cycles. The "boom bust" mentality, which is a very sketchy image of reality, does seem to be repeated in France. Before 400, there was little activity except Martin; with the invasions of 410-510 there was a vast conversion of the country. Before Charlemagne there was a near collapse of the Church in France, then from 800 to 900 a minor resurgence. Before the Black Death in 1330-1400, the Church went through a renaissance and a sort of Golden Age, when the monarchs became saints and the people were profoundly pious. The Wars of Religion (from 1540) brought some heroes to the fore, such as Jean-François Régis and the Jesuit Order (until they were suppressed after 1714). This fervor died down under Kings Louis XV and XVI. The Révolution brought its martyrs and its renewal after 1800. In this period, the Basilian Fathers were founded, along with hundreds of small communities that stretched across the world, including the Cenacle Sisters and the CCVI (Incarnate Word Sisters), all from France. Before 1918 and the Armistice, France experienced its worst-ever persecution; a new sanctity came from the streets, but new hatreds as well. It was the time for Thérèse de Lisieux, patroness of the missions, and Father Charles de Foucault (recently beatified) who disappeared in Tuareg territory (1858-1916). The writings of both became widely available after the First World War.

Lastly, we will look at the present situation in France, a place of hope and discouragement. Every generation needs its teachers and charismatic leaders. Are they there today? Is the Church in retreat; has France become pagan again? But let us first look more closely to the past—to five periods of saints and sanctity.

Beginnings to 800

The story of Saint Pothin and his companions, the proto-martyrs of Gaul (the land that became France), was one of terror and great courage. Blandine, the last of them, was a widow of 81 years who faced her executioners with extraordinary faith. Denis, the first bishop of Lutecia (later Paris), is supposed to have carried his head to the other side of the Martyrs Mountain (Montmartre) to present-day Saint Denis, where all the kings and queens of France have wanted to be buried. The first apostle of France, Martin of Tours, was a friend of Saint Patrick, who also has very important French roots.

850-1500 France as Political Unity

This international period, before the rise of nationalism, saw France welcoming such great figures as Dominic and Thomas Aquinas (also a Dominican), and Bruno (founder of the Grand Chartreux), but there were native-born saints by the hundreds, including Bernard of Clairvaux, Louis IX, Joan of Arc, Roch (or Roc), patron of lepers, and Yves, patron of lawyers.

1513 Réforme and Counter-Reformation

Francis de Sales comes at the head of the list, but who can forget Vincent de Paul (d. 1660) and his co-founder of the Sisters of Charity, Louise de Marillac; Jean-François Régis, apostle of the Cévennes; Jean de Brébœuf (of the Canadian Martyrs); Jeanne de Chantal (Visitation Sisters); and Jean-Baptiste de la Salle, who founded the Christian Brothers.

1789 Révolution and Its Aftermath

Great women come from this period, some of them martyrs, such as the Carmelites of Compiègne. Madeleine-Sophie Barat founded the Madams of the Sacred Heart, along with her companion Rose-Philippe Duschene, who was the superior in America. This period of great missionary activity has many martyrs from France in foreign lands, such as Jean-Gabriel Perboyre, a Vincentian killed in China in 1840.

1880-1918 Anti-Cléricalisme

Saint Thérèse de l'Enfant Jésus de la Sainte Face was the most spectacular of the courageous defenders of the faith in France at this time. A cloistered carmelite from a saintly family, her writings electrified France, much as the devotion to illiterate Joan of Arc inspired the soldiers in the trenches. Paul Claudel, Raissa and Jacques Maritain were converted; Charles Péguy, the poet, died in battle.

Conclusion

So where is France now? Are there saints in the making, faith in action, hope for the future? Many cast a jaundiced eye on the secularist society of Europe and say the Church is dying. But there are living saints of our day: l'Abbé Pierre de Paris, Cardinal Lustiger, and dedicated sisters and lay people are working with all their strength against the indifference and hostility of the ambient "culture of death." Granted, this is a time of low ebb, and many churches are empty, but the same can be said for Assisi in the time of the young Francisco (whose nickname means Frenchy), when all of northern Italy was practically lost to the faith.

A bad ending to our survey of French saints would be the extreme view that everyone should convert to Catholicism and become holy, a saint. A better ending would read as a prayer to God: that all your children become wholly yours, O Lord, that you bless us and make us holy as you are holy. All is grace; thy will be done.

French Saints

First Name	Last Name or (Translation)	Year of Birth/Death	Year Beatified/Canonized	Feast Day	Comments
Agnès	Galand de Langeac, O.P.	1602-1634	b. 1994	19 Oct.	
Albert	le Grand, (the Great), O.P.	1206-1280	b. 1622, c. 1931	15 Nov.	Bishop of Köln (Cologne), taught at University of Paris
Anselme	Anselm	1033-1109	b. 1720	21 April	Bishop of Canterbury, abbot of Bec-Hellouin in Normandy, theologian[1]
Anne	(Mother of Mary) Joachim, husband	2nd c. legend		26 July	Patronesse of Bretagne and Québec; apparitions (1624 in Bretagne, then to sailors in Quebec)
Barbe	(Barbara)	3rd c. martyr		4 Dec.	No dates, no place; martyr; her father was struck by lightning; she is patroness of firemen, artillerymen, miners
Bernadette	Soubiroux	1844-1879	b. 1925, c. 1933	18 Feb.	Virgin, religious, Lourdes, 18 apparitions[2]
Bernard	de Clairvaux	1090-1153	c. 1174	20 Aug.	Founder of l'Abbaye de Cîteaux, avec Robert de Molesmes (Cisterciens)
Bonaventure	Giovanni di Fidenza	1221-1274		14 July	Franciscan, 2nd General Superior, taught at the University of Paris; cardinal bishop of Albano, died in Lyons at a Council
Bruno		1035-1101		6 Oct.	Founder, Carthusians (Chartreux), see Hughes
Catherine	Jarrige, O.P. (third order)	1754-1836	b. 1996	4 July	
Catherine	Labouré	d. 1876	c. 1946	28 Nov.	Virgin, Fille de la Charité, rue du Bac, miraculous medal given by Mary in 1830
Charlemagne	emperor	756-813(?)	c. 1165[3]	28 Jan.	Patron of the University of Paris since 1661
Claude	de la Colombière, S.J.	1641-1682	c. 1992	15 Feb.	Spiritual Director of Ste Marguerite-Marie Alacoque

First Name	Last Name or (Translation)	Year of Birth/Death	Year Beatified/Canonized	Feast Day	Comments
Claudine	Thévenet (Sœur Marie de Ste-Ignace)	1774-1837	c. 1993	3 Feb.	Foundress
Clotilde	(Chlothilde)	474-545		3 June	Wife of Clovis, daughter of Chilperic, king of Burgundy; widow in 511, she saw much murder.
Denis	and Rusticus and Eleutherius, comparisons	235(?)-275		9 Oct.	Bishop Basilique from 400; huge cemetery; burial of French monarchs for 1000 years.[4]
Dominique	(Dominic Guzman)			4 Aug.	Founder, Dominicans, Dominicaines (Sisters of St Sixtus of Rome) 1206 à Prouilhe (Aude), 5,000 moniales (cloistered); 32,286 apostoliques; 1216 men's order in Toulouse, Paris, Madrid, Rome, Bologna
Eloi	de Rouen	590-659		1 Dec.	Jeweller to the King, Bishop, confessor, missionary to Flanders, patron of goldsmiths, jewellers and blacksmiths
Emilie	de Rodat	1787-1852	c. 1950	19 Sept.	Foundress, Sainte Famille, 1816, 4,766 members
Emilie	de Vialar	1797-1856	c. 1951	24 Aug.	Foundress, Sœurs de St. Joseph de l'Apparition, 999 members
Eugène	de Mazenod	1782-1861	c. 1995	21 May	Founder, Oblates de Marie Immaculée (missionaries) 1816, bishop of Marseille 24 years, had the Cathedral and ND de la Garde built

First Name	Last Name or (Translation)	Year of Birth/Death	Year Beatified/Canonized	Feast Day	Comments
Eugénie	Joubert	1876-1904	b. 1994	7 Feb.	Sister of Holy Family Sisters (de Sacré-Cœur), worked in poor sections of St. Denis, Liège
Félicien	(and Primus) in Rome	d. 304		9 June	A good French cheese from the town of St. Félicien is named after the saint.
François	de Sales	1567-1622	b. 1661, c. 1665	29 Jan.	Bishop of Génève (Geneva), never entered it (Calvin); friend of Jeanne de Chantal
Frédéric	Ozanam	1813-1853	b. 1997	9 Sept.	Professor at the Sorbonne, Franciscan (third order), Founder, la Société de St Vincent de Paul
Genest	(Genêt)	d. 286(?)		26 Aug.	A mimic in Roman theatre. Patron of actors. Name of a play by Corneille.
Geneviève		419(?)-512		3 Jan.	Virgin, patronness of Paris;[5] One of the great libraries of the world is at Collège Saint Geneviève
Germain	d'Auxerre	378-448		31 July	Bishop, married to Eustache; in 418, becomes celibate, completely poor; friend of St. Patrick, St. Loup (both bishops); died at Empress Constance's court in Ravenna[6]
Gilles	(Giles) Aegidius	7th c.		1 Sept.	Athenian hermit at Nîmes; symbol: the stag
Hilaire	d'Arles (Hilarius, Hilary)	401-449		5 May	Quarrelled with Leo the Great
Hughes	de Grenoble (Hugo)	1053-1132	c. 1134	1 April	Bishop at 27, he ran away, came back, set St. Bruno up in the Grande Chartreuse, became a Carthusian himself
Hyacinthe	Cormier, O.P.	1832-1916	b. 1994	17 Dec.	Master of the Dominicans at the Marie beginning of 20th c.

First Name	Last Name or (Translation)	Year of Birth/Death	Year Beatified/Canonized	Feast Day	Comments
Inigo Lopez	de Loyola (Ignace or Ignatius)	1491-1556	c. 1622	31 July	Founder, les Jésuites (Société de Jésus) with Jean de Polaco en 1540 à Montmarte (Paris) where they were students
Isaac	Jogues, S.J.			19 Oct.	See Jean de Brébœuf; Canadian martyr, by Iroquois tomahawk, on 18 Oct. 1646
Jean	Eudes	1601-1680	c. 1927	19 Aug.	Founder, Eudistes and Sœurs du Bon Pasteur (Good Shepherd Sisters)
Jean	de Brébœuf, S.J.	d. 1649		19 Oct.	Canadian Martyrs (also Gabriel Lalemant)
Jean-Baptiste	de La Salle	1651-1719		7 April	Founder, Frères des Écoles Chrétiennes (Christian Brothers)
Jean-Baptiste	Souzy et 63 compagnons	1734-1794	b. 1955	18 Aug.	Martyrs at Rochefort (French Revolution)
Jean-François	Régis, S.J.	1597-1640	c. 1737	16 June	Apostle of the Cévennes (Ardèche), parish priest
Jean-Gabriel	Perboyre, C.M. (Vincentien)	1802-1840	b. 1889, c. 1996	11 Sept.	Martyr, missionary
Jean-Marie	Vianney	1786-1859	c. 1925	4 Aug.	Curé d'Ars (parish priest at Ars, near Lyon)
Jeanne	de Lestonnac	1556-1640	c. 1949	2 Feb.	Foundress, Compagnie de Marie-Notre Dame, 1606, 1,940 members
Jeanne	Jehanne d'Arc, Joan of Arc	1412-1431	b. 1909, c. 1920	30 May	Vigin, burned at the stake;[7] Patroness of France (1925)
Jeanne	de Valois	d. 1505	b. 1505, c. 1950	4 Feb.	Queen of France, Foundress, les Annonciades
Jeanne-Antide	Touret	1765-1826	c. 1934	23 May	Forced out of the convent at the Revolution, Foundress, Sœurs de la Charité en 1799, 4,815 members
Jeanne-Françoise	Frémiot de Chantal[8]	1572-1641	c. 1767	21 Aug.	Foundress, Visitation, (to pray and care for the sick, now contemplative) in 1610, 4,000 members

First Name	Last Name or (Translation)	Year of Birth/Death	Year Beatified/Canonized	Feast Day	Comments
Louis	Louis IX, King of France	1214(?)-1270	c. 1297	25 Aug.	Married to Marguerite de Provence, 11 children, (Mother Blanche de Castille [1188-1252], ruled until he was 28). Established the Sorbonne in 1257
Louis and Zélie	Martin	1823-94 and 1831-77	b. 1994		Parents of Thérèse de Lisieux
Louise	de Marillac	1591-1660	c. 1934	15 March	Foundress with Vincent de Paul, la Congrégation des Sœurs Servantes (les Filles de la Charité, the Daughters of Charity), 25,000 members
Louis-Marie	Grignion de Montfort	1673-1716	c. 1946	28 April	Founder Montfortians in 1705, then the Sisters de la Sagesse, Brothers of St. Gabriel
Madeleine	Barat	1774-1865	c. 1925	24 May	Foundress, Madames du Sacré-Cœur, 3,473 Sophie members[9] in America since 1853
Marcellin Joseph Benoît	Champagnat	1789-1840	c. 1999[10]	6 June	Founder, Frères Maristes
Marie	(Mary, Myriam)			15 Aug.	Mère de Dieu, patronne de France (promise of 1638 by Louis XIII) Mother of God (*Theotokos*)
Marie-Louise	Trichet	1684-1759	b. 1993	28 April	Foundress, Filles de la Sagesse
Mary Magdalen;	Martha et Lazarus			22 July	Les-Stes-Maries-de-la-Mer is named after as a hermit, lived in the Grotte de la Ste Baume 30 years, or in Auxerre (see Saint Louis, who had to decide where she died)

First Name	Last Name or (Translation)	Year of Birth/Death	Year Beatified/Canonized	Feast Day	Comments
Marie-Victoire Thérèse	Couderc	1805-1885	b. 1970	26 Sept.	Foundress, La Société de Notre-Dame du Cénacle, à La Louvesc (Ardèche), (with Jean-Pierre-Étienne Terme, 1826); Houston, Texas 1892
Marguerite	Alacoque	1645-1690	c. 1940	17 Oct.	Virgin at the Visitation convent of Marie Paray-le-Monial; devotion to the Sacred Heart (Sacré-Cœur de Paris)
Martin	de Tours	315(?)-397		11 Nov.	Patron of France, bishop, first "confessor" saint; the cape[11] 500 villages in France have his name, 3,000 churches.
Michel	(Michael) l'archange			29 Sept.	Patron and Protector of France
Nicolas	de Flue	1426-1487		22 March	National Hero of Switzerland, father of 10 children, hermit at 51, judge, statesman; the cathedral of Fribourg is named after him.
Nicolas	Barré	1621-1686	b. 1999	27 May	Minime, Founder of Congregation of the Infant Jesus
Odile		d. 740		13 Dec.	Patronness of Alsace; Foundress, the abbey at Hohenburg (Odilienberg); legend has it she was born blind and was cured at baptism.
Ouen	(Audoenus), Owen	d. 684		24 Aug.	Bishop of Rouen; a famous church in Paris
Paul	de la Croix	1694-1775			Founder, Passionistes 1720
Pétronille		1st c. Roman		31 May	Patronnesse of France in relation to the papacy, as "daughter" of Peter
Pierre-Julien	Eymard	1811-1868	c. 1962	1 Aug.	Founder, Saint Sacrement 1856, "Apostle of the Eucharist"

First Name	Last Name or (Translation)	Year of Birth/Death	Year Beatified/Canonized	Feast Day	Comments
Pothin	Blandine and companions	d. 177		2 June	Martyrs (of Vienne/Lyon)[12]
Rémi	Remigius	437-523		1 Oct.	Bishop of Rheims at age 22, baptized Clovis
Robert	de Molesmes	1029-1111		29 April or 7 June	See Bernard de Clairvaux. Cîteaux. 21 March 1098.
Roch	Roc	1295-1327		16 Aug.	A healer, pilgrim, and 3rd order Franciscan perhaps; died in jail, patron of lepers
Romaric		d. 850(?)		10 Dec.	Founder, Chanoinesses de Remiremont: oldest community of women in France
Philippine	Duchesne	1769-1852	c. 1988	18 Nov	Superior Madames du Sacré-Cœur en Rose Amérique
Sainte Ampoule (vial of oil)	de Hincmar, évèque de Rheims				Carried to Rémi by a dove to baptize Clovis; shattered in 1793, fragments saved; remade 1820; kept in Reims since 1906 (separation of Church and State)
Sainte Chapelle (saintly room built 1250)	of Louis IX				Crown of thorns, bought from a Beaudoin (cousin), king of Constantinople, through Venice, brought from Provence to Paris by the barefoot king (now in Notre-Dame de Paris)
Siméon			c. 1042[13]	1 June	Bishop of Trèves
Ste Cène (holy room)	le Cénacle				Where Christ ate the last supper.
Sulpice	Sulpicius "the Debonair"	580-646		17 Jan.	Chaplain of the army for Clotaire, then Bishop of Bourges, the church in Paris is named for him

First Name	Last Name or (Translation)	Year of Birth/Death	Year Beatified/Canonized	Feast Day	Comments
Symphorien		d. 178		27 Aug.	Patron of Autun; very popular saint; Foundation of the Basilians at St.-S.-de-Mahun, 1799.
Thérèse	Martin, de Lisieux; as a Carmelite her name was Thérèse de l'Enfant Jésus de la Sainte Face	1873-1897	c. 1925	1 Oct.	Virgin, Patroness of France and of all missionaries
Thomas	d'Aquin (Aquinas)	1225-1274	c. 1323	28 Jan.	Italian philosopher and theologian, taught at University of Paris, had a famous dinner with Bonaventure and King Louis IX; died in France while travelling to the Council of Lyon
Vincent	de Paul	1581-1660		19 July	Founder, Congregation de la Mission (C.M.), Les Lazaristes, (Vincentiens) in 1625 (approved 1633); la Prieuré St. Lazare was the Mother House[14]
Yves Ives		1253-1303	c. 1347	19 May	Patron of Bretagne and lawyers;[15] lawyer, University of Paris 1267, Franciscan tertiary, "official" judge for the Bishop of Tréguier, ordained parish priest (Tredrez 1285, Louannée 1293).

Notes

1. There is still a very strong link between the two places and Anglican monks from Canterbury often stay at the Abbey in (Catholic) Bec and vice versa.

2. First saint whose photo we have (taken by the Curé Bernadou in 1862).

3. Although he was canonized by an anti-pope, subsequent popes made no objection (Benedict VI says he is Blessed).

4. Carried his head from Montmartre to Seine St. Denis. Not the Areopagite and not Pseudo-Dionysius, in spite of misidentification for the entire middle ages (see Hilduin, "Areopagitica," 836). Catholic Encyclopedia On-Line: http://www.newadvent.org/cathen/04721a.htm

5. Saved Paris from Attila the Hun, 451; knew Simon the Stylite (Eastern Church); friend of St. Germain; was present at the conversion of Clovis in 486 or 496; he had her body placed in the new church of Sts. Peter and Paul (presently St. Étienne du Mont and the Pantheon) in 512.

6. http://perso.wanndoo.fr/orthodoxie/STGermain.html

7. Twenty-four years later her mother's insistence brought a new trial and "réhabilitation."

8. Chantal has become a popular first name for girls in France.

9. See Rose Duchesne.

10. Presently in the Curia: Robert Schumann (1886-1963), Ministre des affaires étrangeres (Foreign Minister), 1948-1953; case from 1983. Also Edmond Michelet (1899-1970), Minister of Culture 1969-70, third order Franciscan. Not yet in for examination: Marie Antoinette, Jacques et Raïssa Maritain, and the founders of the Basilian Fathers. Charles de Foucault has been named blessed by Pope John Paul II.

11. "La Chape de Martin," one half of a legionnaire's cloak, was cut by him to protect a poor man from cold. Christ appeared to Martin that night and it changed his life. He resigned, joined a monastery under Hilaire, was named bishop of Tours, established monasteries in the South of France (Ligugé, Marmoutier). Although he died in October, he was buried in Tours on November 11, his feast day. The chape was placed next to the cathedral, called the "Chapelle," and the responsibility for the chapel fell to Hugo, the Duke of France who was known as Hugues Capet, became king and the first of the Capetian dynasty. During the Wars of Religion, in 1562, the relics were burned. In 1996, Pope John Paul II made a pilgrimage there.

12. Both were very aged. He died in prison; forty-six others died (we only have ten names, Gregory of Tours gives the other thirty-eight), Blandine, an old slave of eighty years, showed extraordinary courage in her martyrdom. Well-documented account, worth reading.

13. First French saint officially canonized by a pope (Benedict VIII).

14. Sacked 13 July 1789, became Paris' first train station in 1850.

15. "Sanctus Ivo erat Brito, Advocatus et non latro, Res miranda populo," http://www.newadvent.org/cathen/08256b.htm

Notes

Recommended Readings:

Calvert, J., et F. Martin. *Calendrier catholique*, (Paris: Bernard Grasset, 1953).

Collombet, F. B. *Vies des Saints du diocèce de Lyon*, (Lyon: M. P. Rusand, Halles de la Grenette, 1835), 446 p., laid paper, In.8. Precious tome for the local saints of the primatial See of France.

Frémy, Dominique et Michèle. *Quid 2001*, (Paris: Éditions Robert Laffont, 2002), 2158. See the articles on Catholic saints and the History of France especially. The newest volume (2003) is available and has the same information.

Gaudibert, Pierre. *Du culturel au sacré*, collection *Synthèses contemporaines*, (Tournai, Belgique: Casterman, 1981), 164

Giry, Reverend Père François, éd. *Vie des Saints*, (Paris: 1859). A two volume reduction of the work of the Boullangistes, covering all the saints from the beginning of christianity, begun by the Jesuits of Lyon in 1830 and never finished.

Hourcade, Janine. *Sainte Geneviève*, (Paris: Mediaspaul, 1998), 111. A bibliography and some striking images, as well as a preface by the archbishop of Reims, Mgr. Defois, complete this charming history.

Livre des Jours. Office romain des lectures, (Paris: Le Cerf–Desclée de Brouwer, 1976). This one volume accompaniment to the Office of the Hours, has many primary sources from the writing of the saints, especially on their feast day.

Meslin, Michel, ed. *Mystique, culture et société*, actes du colloque (Groupe histoire comparée des religions), (Université de Paris–Sorbonne, 1983), 109. The article *Thérèse de l'Enfant Jésus ou la mystique du quotidien*, by Nguyen- Tri-Minh, holds the most interest for Christians, but the entire work deals with mysticism across the ages and cultures of the world.

Rocquet, Claude-Henri. *Petite Vie de saint Martin*, (Paris: Desclée de Brouwer, 1996). A small bibliography caps this dramatization of the life of Saint Martin.

Tincq, Henri. *Pour le ciel. Le Monde*, mercredi 25 décembre 2002, Paris. 463 saints and 1,284 beatified Christians, all by Pope Jean-Paul II, to give an example to all the faithful, no matter what their status. How saints are *made* by this pope.

West, V. Sackville. *The Eagle and the Dove*, A study in contrasts, (Mermaid books), (London: Michael Joseph, Purnell and Sons, Ltd., 1943), 1953. This study of Teresa of Avila and Thérèse of Lisieux is a classic.

Chapter 12

Lucie Christine:
Nineteenth-Century Wife, Mother, and Mystic

Astrid O'Brien

I n Evelyn Underhill's *Mystics of the Church* there is an account of a nineteenth-century French woman, a devoted wife and mother, who was also a mystic "in the spiritual family of Julian of Norwich, Angela of Foligno and Saint Teresa."[1] The source of Underhill's information was *The Spiritual Journal of Lucie Christine*, which appeared in English in 1915;[2] the French original, edited by Auguste Poulain, S. J., was first published in 1910.[3]

Poulain had come to know of the existence of the journals from the nuns of Adoration Réparatrice, a contemplative religious order whose mission is prayer and Eucharistic adoration in reparation for both individual and collective human sinfulness. The foundress, Mother Marie Thérèse, had envisioned, besides the enclosed sisters, a secular fraternity whose members, fully immersed in the political, economic, cultural, and social concerns of the time, would nevertheless share in the mission of the order so far as their state of life allowed.[4]

The author of the journals was a member of this fraternity; after her death they were given to the monastery by her daughter. The latter stipulated that they were not to be shared with any of the family who might request them, no doubt because they revealed so much family tragedy.[5] The nuns, however, were not so restricted. Awed by the depth of the author's union with God, they had sought Poulain's advice regarding the possibility of publication. He was convinced that making available significant portions of the journal would "excite devotion in many hearts."[6]

The family, however, opposed the publication of any identifying information, or even "the trials and joys of family life."[7] Therefore, all proper names were either omitted or changed; Poulain chose to call the woman Lucie Christine, i.e., Light of Christ.[8] He focused on her mystical experiences, with the result that she appears less as a real woman than as a plaster saint, so immersed in her visions that her feet barely touched the ground, an impression Poulain's footnotes, stressing the rarity of her gifts of grace, only heightens. She was, however, nothing of the kind. She was a woman with all the courage and practical wisdom of a modern Joan of Arc, though her weapons were love, prayer, and suffering; her battlefield was her home. Living at a time when the belief that mystical experience was given only to clerics and religious was virtually unchallenged, she reached full union with God while carrying out all the duties and obligations of her state, often under very difficult circumstances.

The very existence of the journals was kept from her descendants until after the deaths of her daughter and son-in-law, when reference to them was found in a box containing other family mementos.[9] Four of her great grandsons then petitioned the nuns for access to the notebooks in order to complete a family history. Since, with the passage of so many years, the reasons for maintaining secrecy seemed no longer relevant; the nuns agreed.[10] Her great grandson has compiled a Little Family Chronicle, and since both he and the nuns are now willing for the full story to be told, he has graciously provided me with a copy. All information regarding Lucie Christine in this paper is from either Poulain's edition or the family chronicle.

Her real name was Mathilde Bertrand; she was born in Paris on February 1, 1844, to an upper middle class couple who were cultured and devoutly Catholic. Although she had had, even in childhood, a great attraction to prayer,[11] and seven of her eight first cousins entered religion, there is no evidence that she ever considered entering the monastery herself. Nor is there any evidence of a conversion experience; rather, there seems to have been a progressive deepening of her prayer life as she matured.

Of superior intelligence and studious disposition,[12] she received the education customary for girls of her class at that time, most likely at a school taught by nuns.[13] Catechism was taught by the parish priest who, recognizing her intellectual and spiritual gifts, predicted that "she would make her mark" in the future.[14] Formal education for girls ended with First Communion;[15] Mathilde, according to a childhood friend, prepared herself in a very edifying manner, impressing her cousins and companions with her intelligence and piety. Although only eleven-years-old, she seemed to them quite grown up, skilled in giving advice and arranging their games and amusements[16]—a gift that, later, her own children and she herself, recognized with gratitude.[17]

All the men in her family were well-educated professionals; the women, like their husbands, were refined, cultured, and devout. The parents of Thomas Boutle, whom she married in 1865, were British by birth; because they were of different backgrounds, both religiously and socially, they had been rejected by their families. They moved to Paris, where they were married at the British Embassy.[18] They were very poor; both died in the cholera epidemic of 1849, leaving Thomas, who had been born in 1839, and four younger sisters. Thomas was taken in by a wealthy and childless woman, Melanie Ballanger.[19] Melanie gave Thomas a good education—in fact, he attended the same school as Mathilde's cousin, Charles—treated him as her son, and made him her heir; however, she never formally adopted him.[20]

Lucie Christine (Mathilde Boutle) holding grandson
Figure 12.1

It was Charles who suggested Thomas to Mathilde's parents as a possible son-in-law; Charles' sister, Marguerite, later described Thomas as a good looking, cheerful, intelligent, witty young man, well thought of by others, a pleasant companion, and a practicing Catholic. Of course he would seem like an ideal son-in-law. His other, less positive qualities did not manifest themselves until later: he was weak and rash, with a violent temper.[21] Melanie, on her part, must have been delighted; it was a better match than Thomas' birth entitled him to, and confirmed beyond all doubt his upper middle class status. Marguerite wrote a description of young Mathilde as well: she was very gentle and calm, never responding to verbal attacks in kind. She was not physically strong and had not grace and suffering strengthened her, might have been rather spineless.[22]

Their first home after their marriage was with Melanie.[23] She was godmother to their first child, a daughter, named after her.[24] A son, Albert, was born two years later, and the family moved into a home of their own, either because they needed more room, or to break away from Melanie's dominating presence, or both.[25] There their third child, Adolphe, was born. However, their fourth child, Eugene, was born at Mathilde's mother's family home outside Paris.[26]

After one more move, the family settled in Vernon, a town about sixty-five kilometers west of Paris. Thomas bought a printing press, and became, for a time, an editor; he had been, until then, a "gentleman of independent means." Before the marriage, Melanie had expressed her intention to have him educated as a notary. However, again according to Marguerite, he was bored by his studies. Knowing that he had a considerable fortune coming to him, and a foster mother who, in spite of being authoritarian and intransigent, loved him to the point of folly, he worked on her in private until he got her consent to abandon his studies.[27] Mathilde deplored this decision, but was unable to persuade him to continue; until Melanie's death it was she, not his wife, who had the last word in all Thomas' decisions.[28]

Mathilde was not yet the recipient of mystical graces; she was a good Catholic wife living what she later described as a "natural, suffering, militant life, which, happily, notwithstanding its mistakes and wanderings, was rooted in God."[29] She loved her husband tenderly and found great joy in receiving the Eucharist with him. Describing one such experience, Easter, 1772, she later wrote, "Never before had I felt so strongly the fusion of our two hearts as at that moment."[30] She prayed for the grace to love God above all things, to bear criticism and injury patiently, to forgive and love even those who caused her the most pain. In March, 1873, she was still asking to accept her crosses generously, and regretting the rebellion and weariness she sometimes felt.[31]

On April 25th, everything changed. During her morning prayer, she suddenly both saw and heard interiorly the words "God alone." Writing about it six years later, at the request of her spiritual director, she recalls: "it was at the same time a light . . . which showed me how I could, though living in the world, belong entirely to God . . . until then, I had not grasped this . . . It was . . . a force which inspired in me a generous resolution, and placed in my hands . . . the means of carrying it out." It was, she continued, "the start of a new life . . . I gave Him my heart irrevocably."[32] The next entry, also written retrospectively, is dated July 16, 1874. She had been ill nearly the whole year (she was pregnant with her fifth child), and was very often deprived of Mass and Communion. Sitting alone with some needlework, she was feeling sad, complaining that God had abandoned her, when her "soul was suddenly taken possession of by the Divine Presence."[33] She could not see him, but felt him as a reality close to her. She adds that this was the first time she had felt the presence of God in this way, but not the last. It endured for about an hour, and greatly consoled and fortified her.

Toward the end of that year she began to experience during communion "the power of Divine love transporting her soul with a force she had never before experienced." She "was terrified lest this might bring on death," but she abandoned herself to God, was calmed by him, and filled with unspeakable peace.[34] It is significant that all of this occurred while Mathilde and Thomas were still sexually active; clearly their marital union was not an obstacle to her growth in prayer. Her last child, Elisabeth, was born in February, 1875.[35] Perhaps it was this which prompted a reflection on the dignity and responsibility of parents; even more than to the parents, the child belongs to God.[36]

In the autumn of 1877 she experienced what Poulain calls "the ligature of the Powers."[37] "my soul, desiring to continue conversing with Our Lord, found herself . . . unable to do so . . . she had lost the power of speech." She was surprised and uncomprehending, but abandoned herself entirely to God, and "remained in that state of deep repose in God in which the soul no longer seeks because she has found."[38] From this time on, this grace was always granted when she received the Eucharist,[39] regardless of whether she was in consolation or desolation, peace or temptation, light or darkness—all the powers of her soul were kept in speechless adoration.[40]

At that time, Mathilde had never heard of passive prayer, and so had no name for the grace given her; nevertheless, since these graces seemed to help her, she had no doubt as to their origin in God.[41] Sometimes the "ligature of the powers" was so strong that she experienced no sensible joy, even in receiving communion;[42] however, this experience gave her "a sense of great security, because I could not attribute the deep recollection in which I found myself to any sensible fervor— which I did not then feel—and therefore I was forced to consider it as the direct action of God."[43] In October, 1879, reading *The Life of St. Chantal*, she found a description of passive prayer, and was confused and troubled by discovering the similarity of her experience to that of a canonized saint. She prayed for guidance, and decided to seek the advice of her parish priest. A wise and holy man, he became her spiritual director,[44] and it was at his request that Mathilde began to keep her journal regularly.[45]

Although at first she felt Jesus' presence without seeing him, he gradually became more visible to her; by 1881 imaginative visions were frequent, especially after Communion.[46] She lost, briefly, all awareness of her surroundings and the passage of time.[47] She attempted to describe one such experience: "The soul sees . . . not herself but only Thee . . . . Naught exists any longer for her, only Thou . . . who art All."[48] In time, her union with God grew more simple—intellectual visions became more frequent than imaginative ones. These she describes as "a sentiment of His Presence which . . . is a complete vision and yet devoid of all form."[49] Yet all was far from rosy: although she does not dwell on her difficulties—after all, her confessor knew of them—Jesus' counsel, to speak to those who persecute her with particular kindness, loving especially those who afflict her, suggests that she was surrounded by lack of understanding and criticism. Jesus also told her—before Thérèse of Lisieux wrote of her "little way"—to do the little tasks requiring daily self-sacrifice, with a love that can be seen and felt, never looking bored with others. She adds, "how often I fail in this with my poor children!"[50]

She had, as do all mystics, recurring temptations against faith, to discouragement, even to despair.[51] There were periods during which God was silent and hidden,[52] when she experienced isolation and emptiness, and feared she was deluding herself.[53] The worst fear, that of being reprobate, she dealt with as her director advised, by begging the Lord at least to let her serve him in this life.[54] Likewise, as were many mystics, she was criticized by others.[55] But few mystics have to endure bitter verbal abuse from a husband and his foster mother. Her main support was Jesus himself; he told her: "I love thee, what matters the rest?" This so consoled and strengthened her that when, immediately afterwards, she "had to hear things calculated to wound profoundly,"[56] she could feel only charity towards the speakers.[57]

Melanie, Thomas' foster mother, was a very dynamic, generous woman, a woman of action, involved in many charitable works. She was, however, authoritarian and not given to self-reflection. Marguerite describes her as a "Martha," quite incapable of understanding, much less appreciating, Mathilde's contemplative spirit. Melanie was a doting and overindulgent mother; her love for Thomas, however, seems to have been possessive and manipulative. Perhaps she grew jealous of Mathilde, because she was, according to Marguerite, given to harsh criticism and stinging jokes.[58] No doubt she was quite unaware of the mixed motives which appear to have lain behind her actions. Nor was Thomas any support to his wife; in any difference of opinion, he sided with Melanie. Mathilde prayed that her distress at these verbal attacks be converted into graces for "their primary source" and "for that other soul who is so dear."[59] Thomas seems to have been at Melanie's beck and call whenever she needed—or thought she needed—him; at times he stayed with her for extended periods. While this would have given Mathilde some respite, he still criticized her as an overindulgent mother in a letter to his oldest daughter.[60] Her cousin, Marguerite, a nun of Adoration Réparatrice, was increasingly a support to her as her family problems increased,[61] and on December 8, 1882 she became a member of the lay fraternity, taking the name Marie-Aimée de Jesus.[62]

In the summer of 1884 Thomas took his two older sons to London; Melanie, not Mathilde, accompanied them. But in the fall, when Mathilde wished to go with her mother and older daughter on a pilgrimage to Lourdes, there was violent opposition. She got a grudging consent only when she suggested that the water might benefit her eyes, which had been afflicted with an unnamed infection for several years.[63] While there she prayed earnestly for the spiritual healing of her beloved husband; Thomas had vowed to mend his ways if her eyes improved.[64]

Mathilde does not specify what bad habits Thomas had vowed to correct, but veiled hints by others suggest that Thomas drank too much.[65] In any case, Thomas himself embarked on a pilgrimage to the Holy Land, without Melanie, in the middle of March the following year.[66] For the first month, his letters home are full of descriptions of his journey and the places he visited; he wrote that he had bought some religious objects for Mathilde, and was looking for more good quality items for them all. However, in his letter of April 12th, he stated that although he was glad to receive Mathilde's letter, he wept that there was none from Melanie, who had not written since March 28th.[67]

This was not neglect on her part; she had died suddenly that very day. Once news of her death reached him, he was overwhelmed with grief.[68] Instead of things growing easier for Mathilde, they became almost unbearable; Thomas went to pieces totally. His drinking increased, and as his physical and moral decline continued he became subject to bursts of violence, during which he was physically abusive to Mathilde.[69] She tried, unsuccessfully, to hide this from her family, more concerned for their suffering on her account than for her own.[70] She had to take charge of the family's finances in order to avoid bankruptcy,[71] and wrote that she "lived in a state of worry which has become habitual."[72] She found support from her director, and from the Superior of the monastery, both of whom believed in her when she was tempted to doubt herself and her spiritual experiences, fearing that she was deluding herself.[73]

Thomas had repeated crises; his great grandson believes that Thomas must have become addicted to absinthe, a popular drink among upper middle class men at the time. It was a very potent poison, causing nightmares, hallucinations, delirium, depression, paranoia, and eventually insanity. But initially it caused euphoria;[74] no doubt it helped Thomas bear the grief of Melanie's death. Often Mathilde was with her husband all night, trying to calm and reassure him.[75] As if this were not enough, she had also to endure the reproaches of others, especially that of Thomas' sisters, who blamed her for their brother's inadequacies.[76] Marguerite defended her, declaring that the ruin of young Thomas was his imprudent weakness in abandoning his studies. By permitting him to do so it was his foster mother who became responsible for his sad future.[77]

As 1887 began, Thomas became increasingly psychotic; Mathilde grieved to see the progressive deterioration of the intelligence and good qualities of her spouse, whom she still loved deeply. She tried to maintain a semblance of normal family life for their children in the midst of her anxieties and financial worries;[78] she reports having sent her two oldest (19 and 17) to their rooms for answering her back, adding, "I will not tolerate that at any age; the fourth commandment was meant to be kept!"[79] (It seems that the charge of being an indulgent mother was unfounded!) Jesus sustained her, asking: "are we not *two* in thy difficulties and perplexities?"[80]

On Christmas Eve, 1887, Thomas entered into his last agony. Except for low Mass Christmas Day, Mathilde was beside him constantly. On the 26th of December, she was able to get to Mass and Communion: "my God took possession of all my being." She offered herself to accept anything, no matter how painful, " if it be to His glory and the best for the soul of my poor suffering one."[81] Thomas died the next day. Sent to get some rest, she could not sleep; after praying for divine guidance in fulfilling her responsibilities to her children, she prayed for Thomas, "for that soul who had always fought so valiantly . . . for God's cause, and led a Christian life without any fear of human respect."[82] So great was her concern for his suffering in Purgatory that she spent several nights in prayer for him. Then she realized that, since this purification was bringing him nearer to God, he himself would be accepting his sufferings.[83] This brought her great peace. Nevertheless, she continued to pray for him, and to have many Masses said "for that soul so dear to me and so full of faith and zeal."[84]

After Thomas' death, life became more normal: Mathilde had more time for prayer, and her mystical life deepened even more. She spent much time and effort ensuring that her children and their friends had "healthy and literary occupation" during vacations by writing and producing plays for them to perform (in addition to being the playwright, she was costumer, fitter, stage manager, impresario, and publicity agent), and arranging outings for them.[85] She stated that she did all this for two reasons: first, they deserve it when they have worked well, and second, "because I have the honor of representing piety to them, I do not want…them ever finding it wearisome."[86]

There were still more human sorrows in store for Mathilde; in November, 1889, her youngest child Elisabeth, not yet 15, died after less than a week's illness.[87] Of this she wrote: "My heart adored even while it broke because it recognized the Will of God. With grace nothing is simpler."[88] Other deaths followed: that of her father,[89] her aunt,[90] and hardest of all, her mother, who had lived with the family since Mathilde's father had become ill, and been a great comfort to her.[91] What Poulain calls "the most cruel trial of her life … an immense sorrow,"[92] but does not specify, occurred just eight months before her own death; it was, in fact, the divorce of her youngest son, Eugene, who had married his first cousin. Perhaps the young man had inherited, or learned, some of his father's bad habits; his wife was not about to stand by him as her aunt had stood by her uncle.[93]

Yet there had been touching consolations also; not only did Mathilde see Jesus, and sometimes his mother; occasionally she saw Thomas and Elisabeth as well. One such vision occurred on her twenty-fifth wedding anniversary: "two years and one month since the death of my husband, and two months since the death of my daughter … Hardly had I begun my morning prayers than my beloved husband … appeared to me … and with him … my little angel. Together we offered to God this … last dear flower of our union … and we three were united with Him like one soul inflamed with His love."[94]

Mathilde's understanding of fraternal charity, seen at first as important for her own spiritual development,[95] had gradually deepened: she came to desire to lead others to love God better. On Christmas, 1883, Jesus revealed to her that the way to do this was to prove to them that God loves them and that the only way to do this was to love them herself.[96] The way in which this was to be accomplished is not clear to her at first; though she perceived that Jesus knows that we need kindness above all, she viewed this as a personal revelation.[97] Seventeen years later, she wrote that she had found the way— "I have been seeking how to make God better loved … and I have found no more powerful means than kindness."[98]

Her eye problems worsened; from October 1889 on she suffered from what Poulain calls a conjunctivitis, which finally caused almost total blindness.[99] This she endured lovingly, saying: "I kiss His Hand which gives me this suffering and that other, harder still, of not being able to see the features of those I love."[100] Traveling with her children, she pretended to see the beauties of nature, so as not to sadden them,[101] but in fact she could not even see to write her journal. Her children gave her a typewriter; Marguerite copied the typed pages into the journal afterwards.[102] When Mathilde learned of the last illness of her spiritual director, she ceased keeping it, since he could no longer read it. Thus there are no entries for the last two months of her life.[103]

In an entry written after Midnight Mass, 1884, eleven years after her first mystical experience, she summed up what had become the basic principle of her life: "I have brought to this Christmas feast a great desire to be, to do, and to suffer, all that God wills. All that matters is that He should be born in us, that He should be in us that which He wishes to be."[104] Sixteen years later, her attitude was unchanged: "in this darkness of the soul accompanied by suffering of the body, with my failing sight, and the impossibility to read or write, I live in a very simple act, always the same, of entire conformity to the will of God."[105]

The last entry in the journal, dated February 8, 1908, concludes: "when the soul is battered to earth, broken, arid . . . then she lives day by day as if each one were to be her last, committing all her care, all her preoccupations to God, and trying only to do His Will from moment to moment.[106] In spite of all her sorrows, her loving surrender to God had not weakened; in spite of her blindness, nothing had dimmed the clarity of her inner sight. She died, as she had predicted, during Holy Week, on Good Friday, April 7, 1908.[107]

Notes

1. Evelyn Underhill, *Mystics of the Church* (New York: Schocken Books, 1964), 244.

2. Auguste Poulain, S. J., ed., *The Spiritual Journal of Lucie Christine* Translated from the French. (St. Louis: B. Herder Book Company, 1920).

3. Auguste Poulain, S. J., ed., *Journal Spirituel de Lucie Christine 1870-1908*, (Paris: Téqui, 1999).

4. Sister Cecelia, A. R., interview on August 3, 2002: cf. Msr. D'Hulst, *Vie de la Vénérable Marie-Térèse du Coeur de Jesus* (Paris: De Gigord, 1935).

5. Alain Le Touzé, "Petit Chronique Familiel" V and VI, (Paris: Author's possession, no date), V; 76, 78.

6. Poulain, *Spiritual Journal*, v.

7. Poulain, *Spiritual Journal*, vi.

8. Poulain, *Spiritual Journal*, v.

9. Le Touzé, "Petit Chronique" V, 77.

10. Le Touzé, "Petit Chronique" V, 79.

11. Poulain, *Spiritual Journal*, xii; Le Touzé, *Petit Chronique*, 70.

12. Poulain, *Spiritual Journal*, xii.

13. Roger Price, *A Social History of Nineteenth Century France* (New York: Holmes and Meier 1987), 317-18; 343.

14. Poulain, *Spiritual Journal*, xii.

15. Price, *A Social History*, 323.

16. Poulain, *Spiritual Journal*, xii-xiii.

17. Poulain, *Spiritual Journal*, 272-73.

18. Le Touzé, "Petit Chronique" V, 55.

19. Le Touzé, "Petit Chronique" V, 54; 61.

20. Le Touzé, "Petit Chronique" V, 64.

21. Le Touzé, "Petit Chronique" V, 70.

22. Le Touzé, "Petit Chronique" V, 70-71.

23. Le Touzé, "Petit Chronique" V, 70.

24. Le Touzé, "Petit Chronique" V, 72.

25. Le Touzé, "Petit Chronique" V, 73.

26. Le Touzé, "Petit Chronique" V, 79.

27. Le Touzé, "Petit Chronique" V, 67.

28. Le Touzé, "Petit Chronique" V, 109.

29. Poulain, *Spiritual Journal*, 3.

30. Poulain, *Spiritual Journal*, 3.

31. Poulain, *Spiritual Journal*, 9.

32. Poulain, *Spiritual Journal*, 10-11.

33. Poulain, *Spiritual Journal*, 12.

34. Poulain, *Spiritual Journal*, 12.

35. Le Touzé, "Petit Chronique" V, 81.

36. Poulain, *Spiritual Journal*, 15.

37. Poulain, *Spiritual Journal*, 16, 1.

38. Poulain, *Spiritual Journal*, 16.

39. Poulain, *Spiritual Journal*, 17,1.

40. Poulain, *Spiritual Journal,* 19-20.

41. Poulain, *Spiritual Journal*, 18.
42. Poulain, *Spiritual Journal*, 19, 2.
43. Poulain, *Spiritual Journal*, 20.
44. Poulain, *Spiritual Journal*, 21-22.
45. Poulain, *Spiritual Journal*, viii.
46. Poulain, *Spiritual Journal*, 38.
47. Poulain, *Spiritual Journal*, 52.
48. Poulain, *Spiritual Journal*, 40-41.
49. Poulain, *Spiritual Journal*, 181-2.
50. Poulain, *Spiritual Journal*, 150.
51. Poulain, *Spiritual Journal*, 119-20; 148.
52. Poulain, *Spiritual Journal*, 64.
53. Poulain, *Spiritual Journal*, 97.
54. Poulain, *Spiritual Journal*, 155.
55. Poulain, *Spiritual Journal*, 186.
56. Le Touzé, "Petit Chronique" V, 85.
57. Poulain, *Spiritual Journal*, 56.
58. Le Touzé, "Petit Chronique" V, 85.
59. Le Touzé, "Petit Chronique" V, 86.
60. Le Touzé, "Petit Chronique" V, 84.
61. Le Touzé, "Petit Chronique" V, 75.
62. Poulain, *Spiritual Journal*, 1; 99.
63. Poulain, *Spiritual Journal*, vii-viii; 276.
64. Le Touzé, "Petit Chronique" V, 91-93.
65. Le Touzé, "Petit Chronique" V, 94.
66. Poulain, *Spiritual Journal*, 204, 1.
67. Le Touzé, "Petit Chronique" V, 95-98.
68. Le Touzé. "Petit Chronique" V, 100; cf. Poulain, 205-6, 1.
69. Le Touzé, "Petit Chronique" V, 102; 109.
70. Le Touzé, "Petit Chronique" V, 103.
71. Le Touzé, "Petit Chronique" V, 107.
72. Poulain, *Spiritual Journal*, 207.
73. Poulain, *Spiritual Journal*, 217.
74. Doris Lanier, *Absinthe: The Cocaine of the Nineteenth Century* (Jefferson, North Carolina: McFarland and Company, 1999), vii; 1-12; 16-41.
75. Le Touzé, "Petit Chronique" V, 105.
76. Le Touzé, "Petit Chronique" V, 106; 108.
77. Le Touzé, "Petit Chronique" V, 109.
78. Le Touzé, "Petit Chronique" V, 107.
79. Poulain, *Spiritual Journal*, 223.
80. Poulain, *Spiritual Journal*, 223.
81. Poulain, *Spiritual Journal*, 242.
82. Poulain, *Spiritual Journal*, 242.
83. Poulain, *Spiritual Journal*, 243.
84. Poulain, *Spiritual Journal*, 244.
85. Poulain, *Spiritual Journal*, 279; 326.
86. Poulain, *Spiritual Journal*, 272-3.
87. Poulain, *Spiritual Journal*, 278.
88. Poulain, *Spiritual Journal*, 280.
89. Le Touzé, "Petit Chronique" V, 124.

90. Poulain, *Spiritual Journal*, 324.
91. Poulain, *Spiritual Journal*, 357.
92. Poulain, *Spiritual Journal*, 359, 1.
93. Le Touzé, "Petit Chronique" VI, 80.
94. Poulain, *Spiritual Journal*, 285-6.
95. Poulain, *Spiritual Journal*, 7.
96. Poulain, *Spiritual Journal*, 166-7.
97. Poulain, *Spiritual Journal*, 23.
98. Poulain, *Spiritual Journal*, 330.
99. Poulain, *Spiritual Journal*, 276, 1; 325, 1.
100. Poulain, *Spiritual Journal*, 341.
101. Poulain, *Spiritual Journal*, 340.
102. Poulain, *Spiritual Journal*, 340, 1.
103. Poulain, *Spiritual Journal*, vii-viii.
104. Poulain, *Spiritual Journal*, 196-7.
105. Poulain, *Spiritual Journal*, 286.
106. Poulain, *Spiritual Journal*, 360.
107. Poulain, *Spiritual Journal*, viii.

PART III

Transforming Interrelationships: Catholic Faith and Secular Society

Overview

Secular Society and the Catholic Imagination

Richard Fossey

I n his apocalyptic novel, *Love in the Ruins*, set in the "dread latter days of the old violent beloved U.S.A and of the Christ-forgetting Christ-haunted and death-dealing Western world," Walker Percy describes a schism in American Catholicism. In Percy's fictional America, an American Catholic Church (A.C.C.) has split with the Roman communion, establishing its own Rome in Cicero, Illinois. Totally accommodating American materialism and patriotism, the A. C. C. celebrates a feast day for property rights and incorporates the national anthem into the liturgy of the Mass.

No doubt, Percy's satiric description of an American Catholic schismatic sect expressed the novelist's misgivings about the direction American Catholicism was moving in the last quarter of the twentieth century. Apparently, in Percy's mind, the Catholic Church in the United States had so accommodated itself to mainstream American culture that it was in danger of becoming simply another religious denomination, not significantly different from mainline Protestantism.

Percy's musings in *Love in the Ruins* is just one expression of ambivalence many Catholics feel about American society. Catholics are thankful that they are no longer the targets of bigotry and even violence, as Catholics were during the Know-Nothing era of the early nineteenth century and the days of the Ku Klux Klan revival of the 1920s. Nevertheless, like Percy, many Catholics worry about becoming so comfortable in contemporary society that the Church becomes simply another civic organization in "post-Protestant America."

If Percy were alive today and were to read the essays that follow, he might be reassured. In these essays, Percy would find ample evidence that many contemporary American Catholics remain unassimilated with contemporary culture—that they continue to stand apart.

In fact, Catholic sociologist Andrew Greeley has argued that American Catholics constitute an "ethnic group," in the sense that they perceive themselves as significantly different from Protestant Americans and retain a self-conscious identity and a "sense of peoplehood" within the larger culture.[1] Moreover, Greeley maintains, American Catholics hold onto a sense of being Catholic ethnics even as their heritage as German Americans, Irish Americans or Italian Americans becomes less important.

What, one asks, are the characteristics of American Catholic ethnicity? What are the attributes of its "sense of peoplehood"? Andrew Greeley might reply that American Catholics (in fact all Catholics) are a people who are distinguished by a "Catholic imagination," an imagination "that views the world and all that is in it as enchanted, haunted by the Holy Spirit and the presence of grace."[2] They are a people who "imagine a world in which God lurks everywhere and people respond to him as a community."[3]

If Greeley is right, then surely the Catholic imagination is derived from the core faith of Catholic believers: their understanding of the sacraments, their devotion to Mary, their reliance on the intercession of the saints, and their steadfast insistence on the dignity of every human life. With regard to all these matters, American Catholics are peculiarly different from most other Americans.

The essays that follow are expressions of the Catholic imagination, testaments to the way many Catholics stand apart from and interact with contemporary culture. First, John Francis Burke of the University of St. Thomas writes on the implications of a Latino spirituality manifested in many of the Catholic Hispanics who have immigrated to the United States in recent years. Burke defines this spirituality as *mestizo*, which he describes partly as an affective appreciation for cultural diversity, a sense of spiritual community that is open to everyone, hospitality toward strangers, and an embrace of the marginalized. Burke sees in this *mestizo* spirituality the possibility of a new model of American politics.

Second, my essay on recent school-voucher litigation describes how nineteenth century conflicts between American Catholicism and mainstream American society over the issue of education continue to resonate and smolder. In 2002, the U.S. Supreme Court put aside its historic antipathy toward religious education and ruled that an Ohio school voucher program may constitutionally direct public money to religious schools, including Catholic parochial schools. Nevertheless, public education's powerful constituency groups continue to oppose public funding for religious schools, a reminder that old animosities toward Catholic education have not yet been laid to rest.

Ruth Kelly of D'Youville College writes of the conversion of Isaac Hecker, founder of the Paulist order, who worshipped first as a Methodist, immersed himself in Transcendentalism, and then converted to Catholicism when he was in his early twenties. Kelly places Hecker in the political and social ferment of the mid-nineteenth century and shows how the events and currents of the day contributed to Isaac Hecker's journey to Catholicism and the formation of the first American Catholic religious order.

In his essay on Catholic boarding schools and Sioux Catholicism, James Carroll of Iona College opens another window for viewing nineteenth-century American Catholicism. Carroll describes the work of three religious orders—the Grey Nuns, the Franciscan Sisters, and the Benedictine Sisters—with the Sioux nation. Carroll contrasts the work of these religious with the missionary approach of contemporary Protestantism and shows how these sisters—many of them European immigrants—shaped a Catholic missionary vision that respected and sought to sustain Sioux culture.

Michele Simms of the University of St. Thomas explains how Catholic doctrine on work and labor—as expressed in a series of papal encyclicals—remains vibrant and relevant in the twenty-first century's global economy. Simms identifies how two moral demands of Catholic social doctrine—the dignity of the human person and concern for the common good—provide a Catholic framework for engaging with a world that is increasingly dominated by corporate manipulations, labor exploitation, and the depersonalization of work.

Next, in her essay on Catholic values and fashion advertising, Janice McCoart of Marymount University shows us that the Catholic Church can still be the subject of ridicule in mainstream popular culture. McCoart documents several instances in which the fashion industry engaged in mocking Catholic values. McCoart's narrative is disturbing in one sense—evidence of prejudice toward our Faith. But in another sense it provides a certain reassurance. Even in this modern age, Catholics are distinctive enough that we can still be scorned for our beliefs; perhaps that is as it should be.

In "Catholic Faith: Between Secularization and Pluralism," Maria Clara Lucchetti Bingemer of Catholic University of Rio de Janeiro describes the "crisis of modernity" that has undermined conventional expressions of religious faith and fostered a "multi-religious explosion" outside traditional Christian worship. These new religious expressions are driven, Bingemer believes, by the need of secular humanity for mystical experience. To have a significant dialogue with secularized culture, Bingemer argues, Christian theology must learn to speak not in terms of abstract speculation but in authentic expressions about the mystical experience of the presence of God.

Finally, Clint Brand of the University of St. Thomas has contributed an essay about Pope John Paul II's Pastoral Provision for the reception of Anglican congregations into full communion with the Catholic Church while retaining elements of their Anglican liturgical tradition. Brand's essay describes events leading up to the reconciliation of several American Anglican congregations with the Roman Catholic Church, including a discussion of the Catholic elements in the Anglican liturgy, a brief overview of the "English Schism," and efforts through the centuries to reunite Anglicans with the Universal Church.

Brand's chapter ends this volume's essays on a triumphant note. As Brand concludes, the Pastoral Provision is

> the fruit of an *American* initiative for reconciling an ecclesial community on the model of incorporation rather than assimilation. . . . The parishes formed so far bespeak in their very existence the grace of charity, openness, and understanding both from those seeking and from those offering a home in the fullness and richness of the Church.

This essay began with a reflection on Walker Percy's *Love in the Ruins*, which subtly challenges American Catholics to reflect on the proper relationship between our Church and contemporary secular society. Perhaps it is appropriate to conclude with a testament from Isaac Hecker, the subject of one of this volume's chapters, who as much as any American Catholic, had a confident vision of what that relationship should be. In a letter to Father Adrien-Emmanuel Rouquette (also the subject of an essay in this volume), Hecker wrote:

> The conversion of the American people to the Catholic faith has ripened into a conviction with me which lies beyond the region of doubt. My life, my labours, and my death [are] consecrated to it. No other aim as an end outside my salvation and perfection can occupy my attention a moment. . . . In the union of Catholic faith and American civilization a new birth awaits them all, and a future for the Church brighter than any past. That is briefly my credo.[4]

Notes

1. Greeley's writing on this topic is contained in *The American Catholic: A Social Portrait* (New York: Basic Books, 1977), 9-31. My discussion of Greeley's thesis relies heavily on Mark S. Massa's *Catholics and American Culture* (New York: Crossroad, 1999) 201-221. Milton Gordon defined ethnicity as a "sense of peoplehood" in *Assimilation in American Life* (New York: Oxford University Press, 1964) as quoted in Massa, *Catholics in American Culture*, 202.

2. Andrew Greeley, *The Catholic Imagination* (Berkeley: University of California Press, 2000), 184.

3. Greeley, *The Catholic Imagination*, 186.

4. Isaac Hecker to Father Adrien-Emmanuel Rouquette, 24 July 1859, in *Documents of American Catholic History,* (Milwaukee: Bruce Publishing Company, 1956), 350.

Chapter 13

The Import of Latino Spirituality for Twenty-First-Century U.S. Culture, Politics, and Religion

John Francis Burke

A t the outset of the historic 1960 presidential election, *Commonweal*, the Catholic lay-run journal, made the following striking observation about the cultural, democratic, and religious challenges posed by the Kennedy candidacy:

> For Protestants the nomination of a Catholic means facing the idea that ours is a pluralistic society with a strong Protestant tradition rather than a Protestant society with a pluralist tradition. . . . On the Catholic side too the issue is a highly emotional one . . . to average Catholics the election of a Catholic President would mean a great deal; they would see it, we think, as the final step to full citizenship for Catholics and a vindication of the American ideal they wholeheartedly endorse.[1]

Indeed, in the same year, John Courtney Murray's *We Hold These Truths* strives to reconcile the basic principles of U.S. American democracy with the Catholic natural law tradition. This ascendance of Catholic identity is one of several key cultural challenges put to the U.S. political consensus during the 1950s and 1960s—the African American civil rights movement, the parallel movement among Chicanos, the women's movement, and the environmental movement, most importantly among others.[2] To recast the ethos of *Commonweal*'s editorial, can the United States be a pluralistic society with a strong white Anglo-Saxon Protestant tradition rather than a white Anglo-Saxon Protestant society with a pluralist tradition? Can we envision and realize a democratic polity whose terms of inclusion are affirming to previously marginalized cultural groups?

In the wake of the multicultural debates that have electrified U.S. politics and society since the 1960s, it is appropriate to revisit these salient questions, especially in terms of the Catholic contribution to the recasting of the U.S. political compact. Indeed, Murray had the good fortune of only having to reconcile atheistic, Catholic, Protestant, and Jewish currents in his work. Today Buddhism, Hinduism, Islam, and other religions and spiritualities based originally in the non-Western world are becoming an integral part of the U.S. religious and cultural landscape. U.S. Catholicism, once centered in European-American ethnic parishes, is increasingly becoming transformed by its vivid African, Asian, and Latino communities. Most notably, Latinos will soon constitute the majority of Catholics, not just in states such as Texas with a longstanding Latino heritage, but nationwide.

Therefore, in this essay I will project the impact of this rising presence of Latino spirituality for U.S politics and culture. Indeed, it is my contention that the Latino spiritual heritage of "crossing borders" and combining multiple heritages has much to offer to us as we wrestle in the United States with the challenges of realizing a multicultural democracy. A growing literature in political science contends that culture, as distinct from class and other political and socioeconomic categories, will "define the great political debates of the twenty-first century."[3] If this be the case, then we need to examine closely the pending contributions of Latino spirituality to the debate about the moral character of the U.S. compact so eloquently pinpointed by Murray over four decades ago.

My presentation will be divided into six sections. Initially I will review Andrew Greeley's contention that one's spiritual imagination has a great deal to say about how one conducts oneself in the world. Second, I will review how the growing Latino presence affords us the opportunity to move beyond the Eurocentrism of Greeley's analysis. Third, I will describe the ethos of "crossing borders" expressed in the *mestizo* spirituality being articulated by U.S. Latino theologians and especially as manifested in Latino popular religion. Fourth, I will review the key implications of this *mestizo* spirituality for the consideration and engagement of multicultural and interreligious issues in the twenty-first century. Fifth, I will illustrate how the grassroots communitarian disposition of Latino spirituality has been effectively utilized in the political and socioeconomic mobilizations initiated by the United Farm Workers and Industrial Areas Foundation groups. Finally, I will project some larger implications of the growing presence of Latino spirituality for contemporary U.S. culture, politics, and religion.

Spiritual Imaginations and Their Import for Politics

Andrew Greeley contends that how one envisions and practices spirituality has a lot to say about how one engages economic, political, and social issues. Drawing from the work of the theologian David Tracy, Greeley distinguishes a dialectical spiritual imagination from a sacramental spiritual imagination. The dialectical imagination, prominent in the Protestant theological tradition, renders God as very distant to and "radically different" from events of the world.[4] Thus, human society is seen as "God-forsaken" and believers can only become redeemed as individuals through their relationship with a sovereign, transcendent God.[5] By contrast, the sacramental imagination, prominent in the Catholic theological tradition, projects a God who is very present in the world. Therefore, the events of this world somewhat reflect God's presence. Catholic tradition "tends to see society as a 'sacrament' of God" and therefore social relationships "reveal, however imperfectly, the presence of God."[6] Political and social community, therefore, are a natural extension of these relationships.

Greeley elicits at least seven dimensions of this sacramental envisioning and engagement of spirituality and reality:

1. The pivotal roles sacred places play in disclosing "the presence of God in all creation"[7]
2. Erotic desire as "good, virtuous, beautiful, and sacramental," especially in contrast to the neo-Platonic and Augustinian legacies in Catholicism that render such desire in immoral and sinful terms[8]
3. The maternal and nurturing dimension of God, especially through the symbolism and stories surrounding Madonnas
4. The critical role of family and neighborhood rituals to the formation of personal character and vibrant community life
5. A vision of order and freedom as complementary to each other[9]
6. A vision of the world as full of enchantment, even amid the most mournful and morose moments: "[Catholics] tend to picture God, creation, the world, society, and themselves the way their great artists do—as drenched with grace, that is to say, with God's passionately forgiving love, His salvation"[10]
7. The cultivation of spirituality through the narratives and stories told by parents, spouses, and neighbors.

Underlying each of these dimensions is Greeley's conviction that as important as formal church teachings are, it is primarily through Catholic popular traditions that Catholics both grasp and in turn project their sacramental spiritual imagination. The high tradition, according to Greeley, is the "teaching of theologians and the magisterium" and is "cognitive, propositional, didactic."[11] The popular tradition, on the other hand, is the "teaching of parents, family, neighbors, and friends" and is "imaginative, experiential, narrative."[12] If the former is "prosaic," the latter is "poetic."[13]

As much as Greeley draws upon the popular tradition to substantiate the sacramental imagination in concrete terms, he does not contend that the two traditions are in conflict with one another or that one is superior to the other—this is not a matter of an "either-or." The high tradition, he accents, enables us to reflect upon and critique the practices of the popular religion, for otherwise the latter run the risk of becoming superstitions. But conversely he adds, if the high tradition becomes too detached from the inclinations of popular religion, it finds "itself cut off from the origins and the raw power of religion."[14]

However, my interest in Greeley's work is more centered on the implications he draws from these two distinct spiritual imaginations for politics. His sociological surveys illustrate that one's spiritual imagination has a significant impact on one's political and social outlook. Protestants—those with a dialectical imagination— seek to bolster the development of free individuals who through their relationship with a transcendent God strive to escape the agony and strife that supposedly characterizes the world. Therefore, Greeley shows, among other matters, Protestants more than Catholics will:

1. Seek contracts and laws to provide a sense of order and shield people from each other
2. Focus more on individual rights
3. See social and governmental bodies as hostile entities.[15]

On the other hand, Catholics—those with a sacramental imagination—view the world as having a natural order and a great deal of goodness; not surprisingly they tend to engage in social relationships as being revelatory of this order and goodness. Consequently, Greeley maintains:

1. Catholics tend to be more conservative than Protestants on issues that undermine family life.
2. Catholics tend to be more liberal than Protestants on the role government programs can play in developing networks of social and economic opportunities for people.[16] Greeley's statistical studies suggest that Catholics do not easily fit the conventional labels of liberal or conservative. Like liberals, Catholics support government intervention into the economy and the role that labor unions have historically played in ensuring decent wages and working conditions for laborers. But like conservatives, Catholics oppose the right to an abortion and are willing to support tough policies on crime.[17] The consistency in the Catholic outlook (and conversely the inconsistency of both the contemporary liberal and conservative positions) derives from its communitarian commitment to the crucial role social and political networks and institutions play in fostering both economic well-being and moral development. Moreover, Catholics are not communitarians because the magisterium

says they are; rather, the high tradition—be it in theology or church documents—evokes communitarianism because of the socialization of Catholics in "grace-full" dense extended networks of family, neighborhood, and popular tradition: "The pertinence of the encyclicals ... is not that the popes have *shaped* Catholic imagination about self and society (though doubtless to some extent they have) but rather that they *reflect* Catholic imagination because they are looking at human life through enchanted Catholic eyes."[18]

The Changing Cultural Landscape

Greeley's exploration of the concrete communitarian sensibilities, as valuable as it is, insufficiently engages the challenges posed by multiculturalism, both within U.S. Catholicism and in the United States at large. First, there is a Eurocentric casting to Greeley's narrative that insufficiently grapples with how multicultural both the U.S. Catholic Church and the United States in general are becoming. For instance, most of the examples he draws upon in his work, *The Catholic Imagination*, to illustrate the power of extended networks of family, neighborhood, and community are drawn almost entirely from the Irish American and Italian American experience. If we are to communicate Catholic social teaching in terms of communitarian sensibilities, then we need to turn to Catholic experiences and heritages that are not exclusively European American in orientation.

Second, Greeley insufficiently wrestles with the philosophical exploration of plurality, especially the fundamental differences between both peoples and cultures that rend community apart. As much as Greeley likes to cite James Joyce's phrase, "Here comes everyone," to describe Catholics or the notion of "a community of communities," to capture the Catholic vision of society,[19] his articulation of order and freedom as being integral to each other remains a very static rendering of plurality. In terms of the focus on cultivating "unity-in-diversity" in Catholic social teaching, Greeley tends to emphasize "unity" more than "diversity."

Considering the spiritual import of the rise of nonwhite cultural groups in the United States will enable us to address these deficiencies in Greeley's argument without abandoning his general insight that one's outlook on spirituality is central to one's politics and personal conduct. Indeed, it only makes sense to ask in what ways the growing presence of Asians, Latinos, and other nonwhite cultural groups within U.S. Catholicism are both enriching and transforming the above sacramental imagination. If there are multiple spiritualities within U.S. Catholicism, then this is of great significance both for charting the direction of the U.S. Catholic Church and for the direction of U.S. politics and society in general.

Although a number of nonwhite groups are gaining in significance in both the U.S. Catholic Church and the country as a whole, the most salient example is Latinos. Therefore, for the purposes of this essay, I will focus on the spirituality being practiced by this group. This is not to minimize the importance of the spiritual practices of Asian, African, and other cultural groups, but simply to provide some scope for my analysis. And in fact, the multicultural integration of diverse spiritual practices within the Latino tradition does draw upon some of these other heritages in significant ways.

Latinos, as acknowledged by the U.S. Census Bureau, are now the largest minority group in the United States. In many locales in the U.S. Southwest, in fact, Latinos are the largest single ethnic/racial cultural group and in some instances constitute an absolute majority. In states such as Texas, that have a historical tie to Mexico and Latin America, Latinos are the majority of Catholics. As noted in the *Exploratory Study on the Status of Hispanic Youth and Young Adult Ministry* by the Institute Fe y Vida (Institute for Faith and Life), the U.S. Catholic Church is already thirty-three percent Latino; and in terms of young Catholics, forty-five percent are Latinos. Furthermore in California, Latino youth comprise seventy-five percent of all Catholics under the age of eighteen.[20]

Nor is this development restricted to the U.S. Southwest; Miami, Florida; or other traditional Latino areas of the United States. One of the greatest challenges in both church ministry and public administration is the rise of Latinos in areas where they heretofore were not present—like *las Carolinas*—and the pressures they bring to bear on the delivery of both ministries and public services. Even in St. Patrick's Cathedral in New York—the "Mecca" of European American immigrant Catholicism—the banner of Our Lady of Guadalupe now hangs prominently on the right side of the altar. Although New York's Latino population has historically been predominantly from Puerto Rico, Cuba, and the Dominican Republic, over the past decade Mexicans have transformed the city's Latino presence.

Acknowledging this growing Latino presence within U.S. Catholicism and the United States is a first step. But to be true to Greeley's contention, we must ask what is the spiritual imagination of Latinos and how does it challenge and recast Greeley's own distinction between the dialectical and sacramental spiritual imaginations? In pursuing this inquiry, we can move beyond the compass of the European American Catholic world that still figures heavily in Greeley's presentation.

An Ethos of *Crossing Borders*

The Latino cultural and spiritual experience has been one heavily characterized by *mestizaje*—a mixing of cultures. Originally, *mestizaje* referred to the mixing of especially European (mostly Spanish) and indigenous peoples in Latin America. However, among U.S. Latinos, it has come to mean a dynamic integration of Latino with African, Asian, and European cultures. Mexican Americans in particular refer to themselves as being products of a double conquest—first by Spain in the sixteenth century and then by the colonization of the U.S. Southwest by U.S. Americans migrating westward in the nineteenth century. Hence, the Mexican American phrase, "We didn't cross the border, the border crossed us." Unlike the longstanding motif of "the melting pot" in the dominant U.S. culture, which essentially assimilates newcomers to the United States to predominant European American mores, in *mestizaje* there is a dynamic conflation of cultures that generates a new culture, but one in which aspects of the contributing cultures can still be identified. Conversely, in contrast to the separatist motifs of some ethnic and racial cultural movements—largely in defensive reaction to the melting pot—*mestizaje*, especially as rearticulated by U.S. Latino theologians, suggests the possibility of a dynamic integration of cultures that does not culminate either in uniformity or divisiveness. Rather than an "either-or" engagement of reality, *mestizaje* stresses "both-and."

Virgil Elizondo has been the foremost theological proponent of considering *mestizaje* as an ethos of lateral, not hierachical, border crossings. For instance, in his autobiography, *The Future is Mestizo*, he pinpoints how as a boy in San Antonio he was caught between cultures. As a Mexican American he was a wetback or a greaser to the Anglos (European Americans) and a *pocho* (a derogatory term for Mexican Americans in Mexico) to his relatives in Mexico. Although initially this predicament of not being at home in either culture was an alienating experience for Elizondo, he came to realize that this capacity to experience and combine cultures was actually empowering.[21]

Elizondo and other U.S. Latino theologians have developed this concrete experience with *mezcolanza* (mixture) and *otredad* (otherness) into a *mestizo* theology that stresses that cultural intersections, rather than necessarily being sources of strife and division, can be a source of unity that ultimately reflects God's presence.[22] Elizondo in particular cites both the examples of Jesus of Nazareth and Our Lady of Guadalupe. He contends that Jesus was a *mestizo* in that as a Galilean he lived in a region where multiple cultures intersected—he could never be Jewish enough for the Jews of Jerusalem nor Roman or Greek enough for the Romans or the Greeks. Likewise, Our Lady of Guadalupe, in her effulgent splendor integrates the Catholic Virgin Mary with the symbols of Nahuatl (Mexican indigenous) mythology—especially that of the feminine figure Tonatzin. In both cases, Jesus and Guadalupe appear to those rejected and marginalized by society and spread a message of hope that could be realized through the integration of diverse traditions.[23] In contrast to an Augustinian rendering of plurality that accents stark irreconcilable differences, Elizondo's theological exegesis acknowledges the distinctiveness of "the other," but suggests that diverse "others" can realize a more bounteous unity through cultural interaction. Genuine "unity-in-diversity" welcomes rather than despairs at the challenges posed by human plurality.

Justo González, in turn, expands upon this ethos of "crossing borders" in *mestizo* theology through his distinction between "frontier" and "border" mentalities. A frontier mentality, as "manifested" by the expansion of the U.S. settlers westward, distinguishes between civilization and the aliens that live "beyond the pale." As the civilization extends its boundaries, the aliens need to be exterminated or assimilated—essentially the historical plight of the indigenous tribes in the United States. By contrast, a border mentality manifests the ebb and flow of cultures across boundaries without any one culture always being in ascendancy and with mutual enrichment being the norm.[24] Although the Spanish conquest of the Americas, as the name suggests, entailed some extermination of indigenous peoples, there was a much more genuine mixing of the European and indigenous cultures than ever ensued through the "manifest destiny" expansion of the United States. It is precisely this Meso-American legacy for mixing cultures without culminating in uniformity that animates the spiritual imaginations and lives of many U.S. Latinos.[25]

In particular, Latino popular religious practices provide very concrete, heartfelt examples of this spirituality of "crossing borders" in practice. Indeed, much of Greeley's articulation of the sacramental spiritual evaluation is steeped in what he terms the popular tradition. By examining the practices of Latino popular religion we can project how the Catholic spiritual imagination is liable to be revitalized and recast in the coming decades in the United States.

In Latino spirituality, popular religion entails long-standing rituals performed by ordinary people: home altars, *el Día de los Muertos* (Day of the Dead) celebrations, personal devotions to the saints, and *las posadas* (a house-to-house pilgrimage held the nine nights before Christmas in which pilgrims join Mary and Joseph in their search for shelter at Jesus' birth), among other examples. In the Caribbean the pursuit of Santeria—a commingling of Christian and especially African rituals—is widespread. As Orlando Espín pinpoints, such popular religion is also a descendent of "the medieval fascination with saints, shrines, relics, miracles, and storytelling."[26] Within mainstream institutional Christian churches in the United States, Mexico, and other parts of Latin America, these popular practices have often been disparaged as unsophisticated, if not uncivilized, supposedly needing purification. Such "civilizing" myopia does not grasp the profound way in which popular religion synthesizes supposedly distinct religious traditions. Furthermore, the inclusiveness, people-centeredness, and the constructive embrace of the marginalized that characterize popular religion suggest a very democratic politics.

In terms of "crossing borders," as Espín relates, Latino popular religion manifests a holistic "sacral worldview" that is a synthesis of African (brought by slaves), medieval Spanish, and indigenous spiritual practices.[27] Indeed this Latino popular religion, in heterogeneous fashion, engages the distinction between the sacred and the profane as a border, not as a frontier—to use González' distinction. This holistic outlook is very much akin to the communitarian sense of the sacramental imagination articulated by Tracy and Greeley, but in turn more *affectively* integrates diverse cultural traditions. Indeed, Espín, in his exegesis of these spiritual practices, makes the provocative claim that the initial religious practices that the Spaniards brought to the Americas were before the Council of Trent and thus are free of the more rigid, doctrinal Catholicism that emerges in the subsequent Reformation-Counter Reformation debate.[28]

Key Implications of *Mestizo* Spirituality

Although a lot more research needs to be done on the practices of Latino popular religion, the crucial implications of this holistic "sacral" Latino spirituality are very heterogeneous in character. First, this grassroots Latino spirituality calls into question what we consider to be Catholicism in the Americas over the past five centuries. At least until the 1960s, the institutional Roman Catholic Church in Latin America had been aligned historically with the political and economic elites of the region. However, the poor, especially among the indigenous peoples, have practiced popular religion alongside the institutional church and in some cases in lieu of it. As noted by González, it was the Catholic orders—Franciscans, Dominicans, Jesuits, and Mercedarians—not diocesan clergy that evangelized the indigenous peoples of the Americas; the diocesan clergy were content to minister to the Spanish colonizers and their indigenous servants in the towns and cities.[29] After the Conquest, popular religion emerges as the heart of the poor peoples' spirituality, an orientation which especially identifies with the suffering, crucified Christ as literally being in solidarity with those who endure poverty, rejection, oppression, and marginalization.

Second, both the heterogeneous and counterinstitutional church orientation of Latino popular spirituality suggests that the growing "conversion" of many Latinos from Catholicism to Pentecostalism both in the United States and across Latin America may actually be a contemporary recasting of this centuries-old spirituality. In other words, the popularity of both the Catholic Charismatic Movement and Pentecostalism among Latinos may very well be due to the fact that Latinos are not finding this holistic affective spirituality in U.S. Catholic and mainstream Protestant churches. It is certainly true, as González acknowledges, that Latin American Pentecostals have historically envisioned their faith as liberating them from a "backward and anti-democractic" Catholic culture as they looked to the Protestant United States as a paragon of modernity and progress.[30] Still, this optimistic assessment subsequently has been revised by some Pentecostals, as they have come to realize the deleterious materialism and consumerism of North American culture. The anticultural stance previously directed at the institutional Catholic Church in Latin America is now being directed by some Pentecostals at Protestant and secular North America.[31]

Third, Latino popular spirituality constitutes a "people's church" that historically has dynamically mixed African, European, and indigenous spiritualities. This spirituality offers a concrete heritage through which Christianity can engage indigenous spiritualities in the Americas and potentially non-Christian spiritualities elsewhere in a constructive, lateral fashion. In contrast to the claim of the Native American scholar, Vine Deloria, that Christianity is an abstract universal religion that violates the sense of geography and place so sacred to indigenous religions in the Americas,[32] Latino popular spirituality suggests that African, indigenous, and European practices have been mixing in the Americas over the past five centuries without losing the sense of place, community, and nature accented by Deloria. In turn, this mixing has not necessarily vitiated the vitality and integrity of each of these intersecting heritages.

Fourth, Latino popular spirituality challenges part of the Herberg-Kennedy thesis that as immigrant groups assimilate to the United States, they are less likely to lose their religion than the ethnicity and language of their native culture. Supposedly, Italian, Irish, and Polish American Catholics lose their distinctive ethnic identities within three generations. Nevertheless, they continue to remain Catholic as opposed to being Protestant or Jewish.[33] However, among Latinos, the spiritual divides of Catholic v. Protestant, Charismatic v. Pentecostal, and indigenous v. Christian spirituality are not hard and fast. Instead, the growing impact of Latino popular spirituality on the United States suggests a different spiritual fault line. On one side stand primarily European American Catholics and Protestants, whose spiritual imagination is rooted in the Reformation-Counter Reformation debate and reflects Tracy's/Greeley's dialectical spirituality. On the other side stand Catholics, Protestants, and practitioners of indigenous rites, primarily Latinos, whose "sacral" worldview is closer to Tracy's/Greeley's sacramental spirituality.

Indeed, when Allen Figueroa Deck refers to the ongoing migration of Latin Americans into the United States as "the second wave," he intends more than just a historic and geographic discrimination from the "first wave" of primarily European immigrants to the United States.[34] Two very different substantive movements are meeting and clashing in the U.S. Southwest. "The first wave"—primarily European migration from east to west across the continental U.S.—was driven by the frontier mentality whose intellectual origins lie in the Reformation and the Enlightenment. "The second wave"—primarily Latino migration from south to north—is keenly oriented by the border mentality whose intellectual origins lie in the heterogeneous and holistic worldview of popular religion. The ability of popular religion to endure—at least five centuries in the Latin American instance—while all the while remaining open to the engagement of other outlooks and other spiritualities—provides a spiritually powerful alternative to the prevailing frontier mentality in the United States, whose benign name is the melting pot.

Fifth, Latino popular spirituality also suggests that we reconsider the categorization of U.S. Catholics in terms of republican, immigrant, and evangelical styles.[35] The republican style, stemming all the way back to John Carroll, is to accept the U.S. American separation of church and state, while striving to bring a Catholic contribution to the formation of the U.S American public character. If the republican style tends to stress the secular side of the church-state dynamic, the immigrant style has focused on building up family, ethnic groups and formal Church networks as a bulwark against the oftentimes hostile reception afforded Catholics by a nativist United States. Finally, the evangelical style finds the republican style too secular and the immigrant style too insular. Instead, the evangelical style beckons a radical reorientation to the Gospel, especially one attentive to the poor and social inequalities—the Catholic Worker movement for instance. However, Latino popular spirituality contains dimensions of all three styles: 1) it is clearly grounded in an ethnic heritage, 2) it pursues a concrete engagement of the preferential option for the poor, and 3) it projects a politics that moves the Catholic republican commitment to pluralism in a more radical heterogeneous direction—a *mestizo* recasting of John Courtney Murray.

Finally, the "sacral" worldview of Latino popular spirituality manifests a capacity for engaging and combining diverse spiritualities in a lateral, not hierarchical fashion. The commingling of multiple cultural traditions in Latino popular religion suggests that the spiritual boundaries for Latino Catholics are not rigid in terms of doctrinal disputes between Catholics and Protestants or for that matter between Christian and non-Christian spiritualities. This capacity for combining opposites is indispensable for effecting an interreligious discourse that moves beyond a Christian-centric discussion of religion in the United States so as to engage Judaism, Islam, and non-Western religions in an inviting way.

To summarize, Latino *mestizo* spirituality is rooted in the dynamic interchange of European, indigenous, and other cultural and spiritual perspectives that has been underway in the Americas for the last five centuries and is becoming part and parcel of the twenty-first century United States (and has already had a longstanding legacy in the U.S. Southwest for the past century and a half). Its ethos of "crossing borders" manifests an *affective* capacity for engaging plurality in a way that revitalizes the Catholic sacramental imagination as realized in families, neighborhoods, and other networks of community life. Some might contend that the aesthetic comportment of this spirituality—*"flor y canto"* [flower and song]—leads to a retreat from the reality of injustice, especially as experienced by most Latinos. However, the vivid family, neighborhood, and community networks in this *mestizo* reckoning of "unity-in-diversity" suggest the potential for a political engagement that genuinely realizes Catholic social teachings on worker rights, solidarity, and the preferential option for the poor.

Grassroots Mobilization Rooted in Latino Spiritual Sensibilities

To illustrate these political implications of Latino spirituality, I would like to focus on the examples of grassroots mobilization by César Chavez and the United Farm Worker movement (UFW) and Ernesto Cortes and the Industrial Areas Foundations (IAF). In particular, as much as Chavez and Cortes may be formally shaped by their training in the Industrial Areas Foundation tradition, I submit that much of their success as mobilizers lies in their recognition of how Catholic communitarian sensibilities, as particularly realized in Latino spirituality, are congenial to the IAF approach.[36]

Without a doubt both of these movements share in common the influence of the grassroots format of community mobilizing established by Saul Alinsky in Chicago. Alinsky's Industrial Areas Foundation practices a mobilization technique that centers on: 1) empowering people to identify the problems they confront in their neighborhoods and communities, and then 2) teaching people how to engender a political network that can put effective pressure on established decision-making structures both in government and the business community. Chavez, under the tutelage of Fred Ross, worked with the Community Service Organization, an IAF-like group, before establishing the United Farm Workers in the 1960s. Cortes, somewhat later, left graduate school at the University of Texas to become an IAF organizer, especially among poor Latinos in the U.S. Southwest, and continues with this vocation. Let us turn to the Latino and Catholic sensibilities that are integral to the mobilizing done by Chavez and Cortes.

In Chavez' case, the connection to Catholic spirituality is very explicit. In his early twenties, Chavez studied the Church's role in labor history, including encyclicals such as *Rerum Novarum*, under the guidance of Father Donald McDonald. As Krier Mich points out, Chavez' use of the tactics of boycott, pilgrimage, and fasting during his leadership of the UFW are rooted both in the nonviolent protest tradition and in Catholic social teaching and spirituality. For instance, Chavez takes the Mexican tradition of making a pilgrimage to the shrine in Mexico City for Our Lady of Guadalupe or to other Marian shrines in Mexico, and transforms it into the 1966 march by the UFW from Delano to the state capital, Sacramento, to draw public attention to the plight of the farm workers and to the justice of the UFW's cause. Indeed, the banner of Our Lady of Guadalupe—traditionally prominent in political struggles in Mexico—is always very visible in UFW activities. In turn, the fast, as Chavez would articulate, is not only a form of protest that similarly gathers public attention to the UFW cause, but is a way of regalvanizing the spiritual strength of the movement.[37]

In Cortes' case, the connection to Catholic spirituality is closer to Greeley's emphasis on how the sacramental spirituality is socialized through dense, extended networks of family, neighborhood, and community. For well over two decades, Cortes has been the "mover and shaker," so-to-speak, in the formation of IAF community organizations in the U.S. Southwest, the most famous being Communities Organized For Public Service (COPS) in San Antonio. These IAF organizations work with primarily poor church and religious communities to cultivate leaders and strategies that enable these communities to become active participants in decision-making forums, both public and private, that have an impact on their communities. Rather than being advocates or spokespersons for poor people, IAF organizers and activists seek to train church community members how to organize, in a lateral and collaborative fashion, so as to be able to engage and transform unjust political, social, and economic forums and outcomes.

Much of the success achieved by Cortes and IAF community organizations has been to take the ethos of the traditional familial networks in Latino culture and make it a basis for collaborative organization and mobilization outside the home. As articulated by Cortes, the institutions that poor people rely on for personal sustenance—especially churches—offer a basis for gaining access to public forums and resources from which they previously had been denied:

> You take institutions—the family, the church—and you use them as a source of power, of confidence, of authority. If you get people to talk about what's in the interest of their families, what are the threats to their families, what are the threats to the churches and community, they're willing to look at things like zoning, and they're willing to look at things like the school.[38]

IAF activists are quite explicit about developing a network of relationships that gives ordinary persons a vivid sense of their own potential and simultaneously develops locales of authentic political community—the Catholic focus on the person and the common good: "The objective [according to Father Leo Penta] is 'to establish islands of political community, spaces of action and freedom in the sea of bureaucrats, political image mongers and atomized consumers.'"[39] In turn, the hope is that these "islands of community" give people a sense of relationships larger than their immediate surroundings and indeed transform how they think about politics.[40]

Ironically, at a time when scholars such as Robert Bellah and Robert Putnam are bemoaning the loss of civic virtues and a sense of public community,[41] these IAF organizations, in admittedly limited ways, are revitalizing civic engagement and the cultivation of political judgment.

Cortes cites Saul Alinsky and such figures as Alexis de Tocqueville and Hannah Arendt as intellectual mentors. But more crucial to the effectiveness of IAF mobilization have been the legacy of Catholic social teaching and the concrete Latino emphasis on extended families and relational networks. The IAF mobilization approach captures the emphasis of Catholic social teaching on the importance of intermediate institutions that connect people to government as well as to private sector organizations. Moreover, Alinsky's insistence that one "Never do anything for someone that they can do for themselves . . . Never" is clearly consonant with the Catholic concept of subsidiarity.[42]

If freedom for Latinos, as Roberto Goizueta suggests, is "grounded in community,"[43] this ontological priority on collaborative relationships provides a fertile basis for successful IAF organizing. The organizers may bring the technical experience necessary for effective mobilizing, but the values of mutual interdependence and commitment to "staying the course," essential to sustaining mobilization, are deeply rooted in the relational ethos of Latino communities, popular tradition, and *mestizo* theology. Both the UFW and IAF mobilizations provide vivid examples of how the *affective* communitarian sensibilities, especially as realized in Latino spirituality and culture, can be transformed into political movements guided by a vision of hope, empowerment, and justice.

Finally, the UFW and IAF examples illustrate the capacity for "crossing borders" accented in the heritage of *mestizaje*. As much as both movements tend to be centered in Latino communities, they have reached out beyond the confines of the Latino community to build bonds of solidarity with non-Latino groups in the pursuit of justice. The UFW would not be where it is today without the successful collaboration between Chavez and the Filipino-American farm workers at the inception of the UFW. In turn, although the UFW has principally organized Mexican-American farm workers, over time it has reached out to new migrant workers coming from Mexico and Central America, a "border crossing" within the Latino community.

The IAF mobilizations, although heavily centered in Latino church congregations in the U.S. Southwest, mobilize church congregations of all racial backgrounds and have historically been located in Protestant and Jewish religious communities in addition to Catholic parishes. Increasingly, IAF mobilizations are also taking into account the necessity of reaching beyond class divides. To address, for instance, the disparity of resources between rich and poor neighborhoods within a school district, the IAF strives to generate dialogue, not division between congregations from both "sides of the tracks." If Greeley is right that one's politics are rooted in one's spiritual imagination and if the U.S. Latino theologians are right that Latinos manifest a holistic spirituality that mixes African, indigenous, and medieval European spiritual practices, the examples of the UFW and the IAF suggest the possibility for a national political movement between the growing number of U.S. Americans whose sacramental spirituality ensues through the integration, not assimilation or separation of ethnic, linguistic, racial, and religious traditions.

Larger Political Prospects

What are the larger implications of this ethos of "crossing borders" for the political landscape of twenty-first century U.S. politics? Although each of the ensuing suggestions needs much more systematic scrutiny, let me project the potential portent of the holistic yet heterogeneous character of Latino spirituality for political parties and movements.

With the exception of Cuban Americans, Latinos in the United States historically have been aligned with the Democratic Party. In recent years, that allegiance has become less clear-cut. Although in California, a preponderant number of Latinos are Democrats, in Florida the situation has been the opposite with Cuban Americans largely siding with the Republicans in opposition to the Castro regime in Cuba. Texas is a middle case: although historically Latinos and Mexican-Americans have been Democrats, there has been a trend of increased partisanship for the Republicans. George W. Bush, for instance, within Texas, has been able to garner as much as half of the Latino vote in elections.

The other stark political reality is that so many Latinos are presently undocumented and therefore are unable to vote. Though the Latinos may actually be the largest group in some cities, it is extremely difficult for many of them to participate in electoral processes. A pivotal contribution of the IAF groups is precisely to train such unempowered persons how to organize with others sharing this plight. In this fashion, not only do the unempowered realize what rights and opportunities are presently available to them, but they learn how to mobilize to change the present laws and political structures that presently keep them on the political sidelines.

As it stands, the major political parties appeal to different aspects of the holistic yet heterogeneous spirituality of Latinos. The Republican accent on antiabortion, family values, and the hard work ethic resonates very well in terms of the Latino strong accent on family and extended networks. Conversely, the Democratic emphasis on providing good opportunities for education, jobs, health care, and housing appeals to these same sensibilities. Assuming the trend of the rising number of Latinos continues and that these persons would actually have access to electoral processes, it is quite possible to envision a political movement that would realize what Joseph Cardinal Bernandin termed the "seamless garment"—one that would integrate the life and poverty issues of Catholic social teaching.[44]

If indeed people act politically, based on their spiritual imaginations, Latino spirituality at minimum will inject into our political debates a greater concern for how public policies affect family, neighborhood, and community networks, especially among the poor and marginalized. On a deeper, normative level the holistic yet heterogeneous disposition of Latino spirituality suggests the potential for a multiethnic, multiracial coalition in twenty-first century U.S. politics that moves beyond the conventional liberal-conservative, Democrat-Republican divides.

Of course, the danger in any political movement that especially invokes aesthetic motifs as norms can quickly degenerate into fascism. Accents upon the organic, the natural order, community, and fraternity can easily be manipulated by unscrupulous leaders into very undemocratic, racist politics.[45] In the 1920s and 1930s, for instance, concepts like José Vasconcelos' *la raza cosmica*—a cosmic race that would integrate the races of the world—were manipulated by Latin American elites to reinforce their own nationalisms, not to further an egalitarian multicultural or transnational politics.[46] In the United States, one only has to recall the appeal of Father Charles Coughlin in the 1930s, who manipulated Catholic communitarian sentiments in a very anti-Semitic direction. Invoking race and culture as a basis for political mobilization is to play "with fire."[47]

Moreover, given that both African Americans and Latinos still significantly lag behind the longstanding European American population in terms of educational and economic success and that the spiritual orientation of these unempowered groups has a holistic, aesthetic cast, the political field is fertile for a mischievous leader who would manipulate these spiritual inclinations toward fascist ends. The concrete reality, especially in those areas of the country that have an extensive population of undocumented workers, is that we are running the real risk of establishing a long-term servant class, largely along color lines, that in some regions could constitute the majority of the population.

The antidote to this fascist scenario is to cultivate a *mestizo* democracy steeped in the ethos of "crossing borders." Indeed, the heterogeneous quality of the Latino spiritual imagination suggests the possibility of a genuine rainbow coalition, bringing together African Americans, Asian Americans, European Americans, and Latinos committed to realizing a democracy in which all peoples, and especially the poor, can gain just and equal access to the political, social, and economic relations that circumscribe their lives. Not since Bobby Kennedy has there been a U.S. politician that has been able to successfully unite poor people across racial lines around a progressive agenda. The rapidly growing Latino presence holds forth the possibility of realizing a multicultural democracy whose terms of inclusion are affirming to previously marginalized cultural groups and to the nascent cultures and creeds that are now integral to U.S. cultural life.

Notes

1. "Catholics and the Presidency," *Commonweal* 71 (1 January 1960): 384.

2. Robert N. Bellah, et. al., *The Good Society* (New York: Vintage Books, 1992), 300.

3. Jo Freeman, "Feminism vs. Family Values: Women at the 1992 Democratic and Republican Conventions," *PS: Political Science and Politics* 26 (1993): 21-28.

4. Andrew Greeley, *The Catholic Myth: The Behavior and Beliefs of American Catholics* (New York: Charles Scribner's Sons, 1990), 45.

5. Greeley, *The Catholic Myth*, 45.

6. Greeley, *The Catholic Myth*, 45.

7. Andrew Greeley, *The Catholic Imagination* (Berkeley: University of California Press, 2000), 24.

8. Greeley, *The Catholic Imagination*, 56.

9. Greeley, *The Catholic Imagination*, 146.

10. Greeley, *The Catholic Imagination*, 168.

11. Greeley, *The Catholic Imagination*, 76.

12. Greeley, *The Catholic Imagination*, 76.

13. Greeley, *The Catholic Imagination*, 76.

14. Greeley, *The Catholic Imagination*, 79.

15. Greeley, *The Catholic Myth*, 45-48.

16. Greeley, *The Catholic Myth*, 45-48.

17. Greeley, *The Catholic Imagination*, 130.

18. Greeley, *The Catholic Imagination*, 125.

19. Greeley, *The Catholic Myth*, 47.

20. Kenneth G. Davis, "Architects of Success: The Promise of Young Hispanic Catholic Leadership," *America 186*, no. 14 (29 April 2002): 7.

21. Virgil Elizondo, *The Future is Mestizo: Life Where Cultures Meet* (Bloomington, IN: Meyer-Stone, 1988), 12, 20, 95.

22. Fernando F. Segovia, "Two Places and No Place on Which to Stand: Mixture and Otherness in Hispanic American Theology," in *Mestizo Christianity: Theology From the Latino Perspective*, ed. Arturo J. Bañuelas (Maryknoll, NY: Orbis, 1995), 31.

23. Elizondo, *The Future is Mestizo*, 57-86.

24. Justo González, *Santa Biblia: The Bible Through Hispanic Eyes* (Nashville: Abingdon, 1996), 85.

25. Duncan Earle, "The Borders of Mesoamerica," *Texas Journal of Ideas, History, and Culture* 20 (Fall/Winter 1997): 61.

26. Orlando Espín, "Tradition and Popular Religion: An Understanding of the Sensus Fidelium," in *Mestizo Christianity: Theology From the Latino Perspective*, ed. Arturo J. Bañuelas (Maryknoll, NY: Orbis, 1995), 154.

27. Orlando Espín, *The Faith of the People: Theological Reflections on Popular Catholicism* (Maryknoll, NY: Orbis, 1997), 122, 124.

28. Espín, *The Faith of the People*, 127.

29. Justo L. González, "Hispanics in the New Reformation," in *Mestizo Christianity: Theology From the Latino Perspective*, ed. Arturo J. Bañuelas (Maryknoll, NY: Orbis, 1995), 240.

30. González, "Hispanics in the New Reformation," 253.

31. González, "Hispanics in the New Reformation," 253.

32. Vine Deloria, Jr., *God is Red: A Native American View of Religion* (Golden, CO: Fulcrum, 1994).

33. Andrew Sung Park, *Racial Conflict and Healing: An Asian-American Theological Perspective* (Maryknoll, NY: Orbis, 1996), 90.

34. Allan Figueroa Deck, S. J., *The Second Wave: Hispanic Ministry and the Evangelization of Cultures* (New York: Paulist Press, 1989), 1.

35. David J. O'Brien, "The Church and American Culture During Our Nation's Lifetime, 1787-1987," in *The Catholic Church and American Culture: Reciprocity and Challenge*, ed. Cassian Yuhaus, C. P. (New York: Paulist Press, 1990), 1-23.

36. William Greider, *Who Will Tell The People: The Betrayal of American Democracy* (New York: Simon and Schuster: 1992), 228; Marvin L. Krier Mich, *Catholic Social Teaching and Movements* (Mystic, CT: Twenty-Third Publications, 1998), 166-67.

37. Mich, *Catholic Social Teaching and Movements*, 168-72.

38. Ernesto Cortes, interview by Bill Moyers, in *A World of Ideas II: Public Opinions from Private Citizens*, ed. Andie Tucher (New York: Doubleday, 1990), 147.

39. Greider, *Who Will Tell the People*, 223.

40. Greider, *Who Will Tell the People*, 226, 240.

41. Robert N. Bellah, et. al., *Habits of the Heart: Individualism and Commitment in American Life* (New York: Harper and Row, 1985). Robert Putnam, Bowling Alone (New York: Touchstone Books, 2001).

42. Greider, *Who Will Tell the People*, 225.

43. Roberto S. Goizueta, *Caminemos Con Jesús: Toward a Hispanic/Latino Theology of Accompaniment* (Maryknoll, New York: Orbis, 1995), 17.

44. Mich, *Catholic Social Teaching and Movements*, 218-24.

45. Francine Muel-Dreyfus, *Vichy and the Eternal Feminine: A Contribution to a Political Sociology of Gender*, trans. Kathleen A. Johnson (Durham, NC: Duke University Press, 2001).

46. Joseba Gabilondo, afterword to *The Cosmic Race: A Bilingual Edition, by José Vasconcelos*, trans. Didier T. Jaén (Baltimore: Johns Hopkins University Press, 1997), 100.

47. Ana Maria Díaz-Stevens and Anthony M. Stevens-Arroyo, *Recognizing the Latino Resurgence in U.S. Religion: The Emmaus Paradigm* (Boulder, CO: Westview, 1998), 7.

Chapter 14

"False Generosity" Toward Inner-City School Children: Why the Fierce Opposition to Vouchers for "Sectarian" Schools?

Richard Fossey

In *Zelman v. Harris-Simmons*,[1] decided in June 2002, the United States Supreme Court repudiated its old hostility to public aid for religious schools, hostility that Justice Clarence Thomas once described as being rooted in nativist bigotry toward Catholicism. By a five to four vote, the Court upheld an Ohio voucher program for Cleveland school children, a program that allows students in a crumbling public school system to attend private schools at public expense—either secular or religious.

Zelman was almost universally condemned by public education's major constituency groups—the National School Board Association, the National Parent Teacher Association, public school administrators groups, and the teachers unions. Almost with one voice, these groups denounced the Supreme Court's decision and vowed to continue fighting vouchers in state courts and legislatures.

This vehement opposition is puzzling in light of the deplorable conditions that exist in the nation's inner-city schools. In fact, it was the dreadful state of Cleveland's public schools that led the Ohio legislature to create a voucher program that would allow Cleveland's inner-city children an avenue of escape.

This essay asks why public education's major stakeholders are so deeply hostile to public aid for religious education, given the fundamental problems of the inner-city public schools. It concludes that voucher opponents reflect Paulo Freire's notion of "false generosity" in their unwillingness to allow impoverished families to make their own educational choices. Moreover, evidence suggests that part of the opposition to public aid for religious schools can be traced to anti-Catholic prejudice.

Background to *Zelman*
The Deeply Troubled Cleveland Public Schools

In the early 1960s, Cleveland was a prosperous midwestern city with thriving industry and business enterprises. Cleveland's school system had over 150,000 students and was predominantly white.[2] However, the district was starkly segregated by race, with the Cuyahoga River serving as the dividing line between black and white school children.

In 1973, a desegregation suit was filed in federal court, commencing more than twenty-five years of litigation. A federal judge divided the district into 190 attendance zones, imposed busing, and issued more than 500 orders in an effort to promote racial integration.[3] Nevertheless, by the time the Sixth Circuit Court of Appeals brought the desegregation case to a close in 1999,[4] the system was predominantly African American; and enrollment had shrunk to around 75,000.

Moreover, although the Cleveland system spent $1.1 billion on desegregation programs between 1978 and 1998,[5] student performance was abysmal. According to a special report published by *Education Week* in 1998, only seven percent of a 1991 cohort of eighth graders passed the twelfth grade proficiency exam and graduated on time in 1995.[6] In 1996-1997, only four percent of Cleveland's eighth graders passed the state proficiency exam in algebra; and, on any given day, one in six Cleveland school students was absent.[7] A national report on urban dropout rates, published by the Manhattan Institute in late 2001, reported that only twenty-eight percent of a cohort of eighth graders graduated on time in 1998, the lowest graduation rate among all the urban districts that the report examined.[8]

In March 1995, after hearing testimony and evidence, a federal judge declared that a "crisis of magnitude" existed in the Cleveland schools.[9] The federal judge ordered Ohio's State Superintendent of Education to take control of school operations, effectively putting the district into receivership.

Startled into action by the federal court order, the Ohio legislature voted to approve a voucher program for Cleveland, allowing students to leave the public school system and go to a neighboring public school system or enroll in private schools—including religious schools. One parent, who used a voucher to put her youngest child in a Catholic kindergarten, described the system her family had fled. "The school was a zoo," she said. "There's no learning. You had three kids sharing one book."[10]

The Cleveland Voucher Program

Created by the Ohio legislature in 1995, the Cleveland voucher program offers vouchers to children in Cleveland's public school system, which they can use to attend private schools. Under the program, children can also use their vouchers to attend nearby public school systems; but, as of 2002, no public system had agreed to take them.

Vouchers are distributed to families according to financial need. "Families with incomes below 200 percent of the poverty line are given priority and are eligible to receive 90 percent of private school tuition up to 2,250 dollars."[11]

In 1999, about 3,700 of Cleveland's 75,000 students participated in this voucher program. Most children were from minority and low-income families, and sixty percent came from families living below poverty level. Ninety-six percent of the voucher recipients enrolled in religious schools, many of them Catholic.[12]

Voucher Opponents Challenge Cleveland's Voucher Program in Court

Although only a few voucher programs have been introduced in the United States, all have been challenged in court, often by the teachers unions. The Cleveland program is no exception. In 1996, voucher opponents filed suit in an Ohio state court, attempting to wipe out the program. Ultimately, they were unsuccessful.[13] At the end of lengthy litigation, the Cleveland voucher program continued to operate.

After losing in the state courts, voucher opponents sued again in federal court, claiming that the Cleveland voucher program violated the Establishment Clause of the U.S. Constitution because it allowed public funds to go to religious schools. A federal trial court agreed and enjoined the program.[14] (The Supreme Court stayed the trial court's injunction pending full appellate review.)

Ohio education officials appealed to the Sixth Circuit Court of Appeals; but in December 2000, a Sixth Circuit panel of three judges upheld the trial court's ruling.[15] The Sixth Circuit concluded that the voucher program had the "primary effect" of advancing religion and violated the Establishment Clause.

In a bitter dissenting opinion, Sixth Circuit Judge Ryan accused the court majority of "nativist hostility" to religious schools.[16] In striking down the voucher program, Judge Ryan said, the majority had sentenced "nearly 4,000 poverty-level, mostly minority children in Cleveland to return to the indisputably failed Cleveland public schools."[17]

Ohio education officials appealed the Sixth Circuit opinion to the U.S. Supreme Court, and the Supreme Court agreed to hear the case. On June 27, 2002, the Supreme Court issued its decision. By a five to four vote, it reversed the Sixth Circuit.[18]

Justice Rehnquist wrote the majority opinion, which rejected the Sixth Circuit's conclusion that the voucher program impermissibly aided religious schools. On the contrary, Justice Rehnquist wrote, the Cleveland program was "entirely neutral with respect to religion."[19] The program provided vouchers to "a wide spectrum of individuals, defined only by financial need and residence in a particular school district." Cleveland families are permitted to "exercise genuine choice among options public and private, secular and religious." Therefore, the program was one of "true private choice."[20] As such, Justice Rehnquist concluded, the Cleveland voucher program did not violate the Establishment Clause.

Although the *Zelman* decision was decided on legal grounds, the Court took note of the desperate condition of the Cleveland public schools. "For more than a generation," Justice Rehnquist wrote, "Cleveland's public schools have been among the worst performing public schools in the nation." Rehnquist noted that a federal district court had declared a "crisis of magnitude" and placed the school system under state control in 1995.

> Shortly thereafter, the state auditor found that Cleveland's public schools were in the midst of a "crisis that is perhaps unprecedented in the history of American education." The district had failed to meet any of the 18 state standards for minimal acceptable performance. Only 1 in 10 ninth graders could pass a basic proficiency examination and students at all levels performed at a dismal rate compared with students in other Ohio public schools. More than two-thirds of high school students either dropped or failed out before graduation. Of those students who managed to reach their senior year, one of every four still failed to graduate. Of those students who did graduate, few could read, write, or compute at levels comparable to their counterparts in other cities.[21]

Justice Clarence Thomas joined the majority opinion, but he submitted his own concurring opinion. School choice programs that involve religious schools, Thomas argued, only appear unconstitutional to those who distort constitutional values in a way that disserves those Americans who are in greatest need. Thomas concluded his concurring opinion by quoting Fredrick Douglass: "[N]o greater benefit can be bestowed upon a long benighted people, than giving to them, as we are here earnestly this day endeavoring to do, the means of an education."[22]

Public Education in the Inner Cities is Deeply Troubled

As the Supreme Court described it in *Zelman*, the Cleveland school district is a disaster; but it is not atypical of inner city school systems. In 1998, *Education Week* published perhaps the most comprehensive report on urban public schools that had ever been compiled. *Education Week* acknowledged the heroism and commitment of many urban educators and recognized that there were some "islands of achievement" in an "ocean of failure."[23] Nevertheless, *Education Week*'s assessment of the urban public schools was somber and bleak. "It's hard to exaggerate the education crisis in America's cities," the report began.[24]

Education Week singled out the Cleveland district as a school system that was particularly distressed. However, the evidence is indisputable that most inner-city public school systems are deeply troubled. Even the Democratic Leadership Council, a body that is particularly sympathetic to urban constituencies, acknowledges a crisis in urban education. An article appearing in *New Democrats Online* (the online commentary for the Democratic Leadership Council) admitted that "time is running out on the urban school reform movement." Plagued by a "miasma of underperformance," the writer said inner-city schools were threatening to drag down efforts to reinvigorate cities as attractive places to live.[25]

These observations are corroborated by numerous respected commentators. Jonathan Kozal's *Savage Inequalities* describes conditions in several inner-city schools, which are fairly typical. On the whole, it is accurate to say that inner-city public school systems are characterized by racial isolation, high dropout rates, low student achievement, and ineffective governing boards.[26]

"False Generosity" of Voucher Opponents

Given the abysmal condition of inner-city public schools, it is hard to understand why the most powerful stakeholders in public education stridently oppose voucher programs that would allow inner-city children to attend religious schools. Their opposition is particularly puzzling when one reviews the research that shows that religious schools—Catholic schools, in particular—do a good job of educating inner-city children.[27]

Nevertheless, virtually all of public education's major professional organizations oppose vouchers or any other program that would allow government funds to aid religious schools. This opposition was dramatically illustrated by an *amici curiae* brief filed by the National School Board Association in the *Zelman* case, in which the NSBA urged the Court to declare the Cleveland voucher program unconstitutional. NSBA was joined in its brief by several education organizations including: National Parent Teacher Association, American Association of School Administrators, National Association of Secondary School Principals, National Association of Elementary School Principals, American Association of University Women, National Association of Elementary School Principals, National Association of Federally Impacted Schools, and National Association of Bilingual Education.[28]

Education historian Diane Ravitch, in a 1997 essay, expressed the basic unfairness of the voucher opponents' position. "[W]hat I argue," Ravitch wrote,

> is that it is unjust to compel poor children to attend bad schools. It is unjust to prohibit poor families from sending their children to the school of their choice, even if that school has a religious affiliation. It is unjust to deny free schooling to poor families with strong religious convictions. . . . It is unjust that there is no realistic way to force the closure of schools that students and their parents would abandon if they could.[29]

Paulo Freire's work, *Pedagogy of the Oppressed*, may help us understand why self-avowed children's advocates are so bitterly hostile to allowing poor families to choose their own schools. According to Freire, oppressors (in this case public education's various special interest groups) can never be relied upon to liberate the oppressed. "The oppressors," Freire writes:

> who oppress, exploit, and rape by virtue of their power, cannot find in this power the strength to liberate either the oppressed or themselves. . . . Any attempt to "soften" the power of the oppressor in deference to the weakness of the oppressed almost always manifests itself in the form of false generosity; indeed, the attempt never goes beyond this. In order to have the continued opportunity to express their "generosity," the oppressors must perpetuate injustice as well. An unjust social order is the permanent fount of this "generosity," which is nourished by death, despair, and poverty.[30]

Thus, to use Freire's language, inner-city school systems have become "instrument[s] of dehumanization," which satisfy "the egoistic interests of the oppressors" and make the oppressed the objects of paternalistic humanitarianism.[31]

It may not seem fair to accuse voucher opponents of "false generosity," which is simply another way of saying that they are arrogantly paternalistic. But it is difficult to understand the stubborn opposition to better educational opportunities for the urban poor. Although voucher opponents base their position on high-minded regard for the democratic ideals of public education, their position condemns inner-city school children like the ones who reside in Cleveland to receive a shockingly inadequate education in the nation's deficient urban school systems.

Are Voucher Opponents Anti-Catholic?

Of course there may be other explanations for public education's implacable opposition to public aid for religious schools, and Supreme Court Justice Thomas has suggested one of them—anti-Catholic prejudice.

Thomas wrote the plurality opinion in *Mitchell v. Helms*,[32] the Supreme Court's last significant Establishment Clause decision prior to *Zelman*. In *Mitchell*, the Court ruled that a federal aid program that benefited religious schools was constitutionally permissible. Dissenting Justices argued that the Constitution barred government aid from flowing to "pervasively sectarian" schools; but Justice Thomas rejected this argument out of hand.

"[H]ostility to aid to pervasively sectarian schools has a shameful pedigree," Justice Thomas wrote, "that we do not hesitate to disavow."[33] Moreover, Thomas continued:

> Although the dissent professes concern for "the implied exclusion of the less favored," . . . the exclusion of pervasively sectarian schools from government-aid programs is just that, particularly given the history of such exclusion. Opposition

to aid to "sectarian" schools acquired prominence in the 1870s with Congress's consideration (and near passage) of the Blaine Amendment, which would have amended the Constitution to bar any aid to sectarian institutions. Consideration of the amendment arose at a time of pervasive hostility to the Catholic Church and to Catholics in general, and it was an open secret that "sectarian" was code for "Catholic."[34]

Thomas concluded that "nothing in the Establishment Clause requires the exclusion of pervasively sectarian schools from otherwise permissible aid programs, and other doctrines of this Court bar it. *This doctrine, born of bigotry, should be buried now.*"[35]

Justice Thomas has acknowledged anti-Catholic bigotry in the federal courts, but the same bigotry also lurks in the public education industry. As Andrew Greeley wrote in 1977, "the reaction of the American educational enterprise to [white ethnics and Catholic schools] has been shaped in great part by anti-Catholic nativism." By "educational enterprise," Greeley made clear, he did not mean American school teachers. Rather, he saw bigotry in the upper ranks of public education: "upper level school administrators, professors and deans of education" and state- and national-level educational bureaucrats.[36]

In fact, antipathy to Catholic schools runs deep in American education. In the early nineteenth century, Protestant Americans, who had hitherto been the dominant cultural force in American society, saw their hegemony threatened by an influx of Catholic European immigrants, particularly the Irish. The common schools movement that began in that period was partly a response to this threat. By providing nonsectarian public schools, it was hoped, Catholic immigrant children would be assimilated into American society.

But, as education historian Diane Ravitch pointed out, the common schools were not truly nonsectarian schools. "The goal of the common school movement," Ravitch wrote, "was not to create secular schools but to assure that all public funds were devoted solely to non-denominational Protestant schools and that no public funds could be used for 'sectarian' schools. Catholic schools were, of course, sectarian."[37]

During the 1830s and 1840s, Catholics began objecting to putting their children into public schools where the King James Bible was read and where blatantly anti-Catholic textbooks were often used. In New York City, Bishop John Hughes led an effort by the city's Catholics to obtain a portion of the public school funds for the parochial schools. This endeavor failed, and Hughes ultimately urged Catholics to "leave public schools to themselves" and nurture a system of parochial schools instead.[38]

Later in the nineteenth century, anti-Catholic sentiment led many states to amend their constitutions to bar any public aid for religious institutions—and religious schools in particular. These constitutional amendments are collectively referred to as Blaine Amendments, in reference to James G. Blaine, a Republican leader of the U.S. House of Representatives during the Grant administration.[39] In 1875, Blaine sought to insert an amendment into the U.S. Constitution prohibiting public funds from coming "under the control of any religious sect."[40] This effort, scholars have shown, was motivated by Blaine's desire to capitalize on a wave of anti-Catholic feelings that swept through the United States in the years following the Civil War.[41]

Although Blaine's proposed amendment narrowly failed, similar provisions were added to many state constitutions; several western territories were required to insert a Blaine-type amendment into their proposed state constitutions as a condition of achieving statehood.[42] By 1890, twenty-nine states had adopted constitutional provisions barring public aid to religious schools.[43]

Paul Viteritti, in an exhaustive study that appeared in the *Harvard Journal of Law and Public Policy*, sketched the history of the so-called "Blaine Amendments."[44] Viteritti's research clearly shows that many of these provisions were enacted during a period of intense religious bigotry toward the Catholic Church.

Most scholars agree that anti-Catholic prejudice was a major factor in the adoption of these constitutional amendments.[45] Toby Heytens summarizes the scholarly consensus on this point:

> [T]he conclusion that [the Blaine Amendments] were driven by the Protestant/ Catholic divide is unmistakable, despite the fact that none of the amendments refer specifically to Roman Catholics or Catholic schools. This appears to be the scholarly consensus. It is also supported by the statistics regarding private school religious affiliation at the time, the Senate debate over the Federal Blaine Amendment, and the breakdown of social and political groups that supported and opposed the measure.[46]

Interestingly, some states approved constitutional provisions banning aid to religious schools even before Blaine's effort to amend the federal Constitution. For example, in 1854, the Massachusetts legislature, dominated by the virulently anti-Catholic Know-Nothing Party, approved a state constitutional amendment that barred aid to religious schools. This provision was approved by the voters the following year.[47] In addition, the Massachusetts legislature considered legislation (not passed) that would have prevented any foreign-born person from voting or holding public office.[48]

What Lies Ahead

Now that the Supreme Court has held that publicly funded voucher programs may legally include religious schools, one might hope that some of the virulent opposition to vouchers would subside. One might even hope that some voucher opponents would withdraw their opposition in acknowledgement of a Supreme Court decision that is now the law of the land.

But this has not been the case. Public education's major stakeholders remain fiercely and almost unanimously opposed to vouchers for religious schools. In fact, most of public education's powerful interest groups wasted no time in criticizing the Supreme Court's *Zelman* decision. Within a few days after the Supreme Court ruled, the following organizations issued press releases expressing disappointment with *Zelman*: National Association of Elementary School Principals,[49] National Parent Teacher Association,[50] National School Boards Association,[51] National Association of State Boards of Education,[52] National Association of Secondary School Principals,[53] and the Association for Supervision and Curriculum Development.[54]

In fact, some groups not only expressed disappointment with *Zelman*, they pledged to continue fighting vouchers both politically and in the courts. In particular, the nation's two largest teachers unions vowed to oppose voucher programs by every means available to them. Bob Chase, president of the National Education Association, the nation's largest teachers union, issued a press release saying NEA would continue to fight vouchers for private and religious schools "at the ballot box, in state legislatures, and in state courts."[55] Indeed, NEA had previously raised its membership dues for the specific purpose of fighting voucher proposals.[56] Sandra Feldman, president of the American Federation of Teachers, issued a press release echoing the same sentiment. Feldman said that AFT would fight any future efforts to enact voucher legislation in the United States.[57]

In addition to the unions, public education's administrators and school board groups are continuing the fight to stop public funding for religious education. For example, the executive director of the American Association of School Administrators, a national group dominated by public school superintendents, announced that his organization would "continue to oppose any proposed law and/or referendum that would direct public tax funds to religious and other private K [through] 12 schools."[58]

Most commentators agree that the next major battleground over vouchers will be the state courts, particularly courts in jurisdictions that have Blaine Amendments, which, as we have seen, are rooted in nativist bigotry.[59] There are more than thirty such states.[60]

The Blaine Amendments pose a particular threat to voucher programs because the U.S. Supreme Court may not have the last word as to the legality of state voucher laws. It is well established that state courts may interpret their own constitutions to define constitutional guarantees more broadly than the Supreme Court interprets the federal constitution.[61] Thus it is possible that a state court would declare a voucher program unconstitutional under its own state constitution, even though the program is valid under the federal constitution as interpreted in *Zelman*. This possibility is most likely in states that have Blaine Amendments in their constitutions.

On the other hand, state courts may choose not to interpret their own constitutions in a way that infringes upon rights that the U.S. Constitution guarantees. At least one scholar has argued that the Blaine Amendments are unconstitutional on their face because they purposefully discriminate against Roman Catholics.[62]

In any event, there is no doubt about the voucher opponents' post-*Zelman* strategy. They will continue to fight voucher programs in the state courts, utilizing Blaine Amendments when feasible, to strike down programs that are constitutionally valid according to *Zelman*. If this strategy succeeds, voucher opponents can ignore the U.S. Supreme Court.

This strategy was made clear on August 5, 2002, when a Florida trial judge struck down Florida's voucher program as a violation of the Florida Constitution.[63] Like the Cleveland program, the Florida voucher program permitted children in failing public schools to use state-funded vouchers to attend private schools— both secular and religious.

Voucher opponents, supported by the state teachers unions, attacked the Florida program, and a Florida trial judge ruled that the program violated Article I, Section 3 of the Florida Constitution. That provision states (in pertinent part): "[N]o money shall ever be taken from the public treasury directly or indirectly in aid of any church, sect or religious denomination or in aid of any sectarian institution."

The Florida opinion was issued less than six weeks after the Supreme Court's *Zelman* ruling; and within forty-eight hours after it was released, the National School Board Association, the American Federation of Teachers, National Education Association, and the National Parent Teacher Association issued statements praising the Florida judge's decision.[64]

No in-depth study has been done on the motivation behind Florida's anti-religious aid provision, but commentators have identified it as a Blaine Amendment.[65] It was enacted in 1885[66] during a time of intense Catholic prejudice in the United States, and its language is in harmony with the Blaine Amendments that were adopted by other state legislatures during the last quarter of the nineteenth century and with Congressman Blaine's original 1875 proposal.

Of course, the fact that voucher opponents used Florida's Blaine-type constitutional provision to stop a voucher program does not mean in itself that organizations and individuals involved in such efforts are bigoted toward Catholics. They may simply be using a convenient means at hand to stop a program they view as threatening to their interests. Nevertheless, it seems fair to conclude that at least some of the strident efforts to stop vouchers for religious schools are based on antipathy to Catholic education, Catholic doctrine, and Catholic values.

Conclusion

Public education in the inner cities is a calamity, and it will remain a calamity until poor urban families have the power to throw off oppression—-the power to choose an alternative to public education. In *Zelman v. Simmons-Harris*, the Supreme Court attempted to give them that power when it ruled that the Cleveland voucher program is constitutionally valid.

Voucher opponents—virtually all of the professional organizations that represent public education's powerful constituencies—vow to fight in state legislatures and state courts in an effort to stop any proposal to provide public funding for religious schools.

A Florida trial court opinion—striking down a state voucher program less than six weeks after the Supreme Court's *Zelman* decision, shows that antivoucher groups will utilize the Blaine laws—those "repellant residues of nineteenth-century nativism"[67]—to stop children from having a religious-school alternative to failing public schools. It may be too much to charge contemporary voucher opponents with bigotry toward the Catholic faith. But it is certainly fair to say that the anti-voucher stance of public education's professional groups demonstrates the "false generosity" that Freire described—an arrogant refusal to let poor families make their own educational choices.

Notes

1. Zelman v. Simmons-Harris, Nos. 00-1751, 00-1777, and 00-1779, 2002 WL127 8554 (U.S. June 27, 2002).

2. Beth Reinhard, "Cleveland: A Study in Crisis," *Quality Counts 98, Education Week Special Report, Education Week Online,* http://www.edweek.org/sreports/qc98/challenges/cleveland/cl-n.htm (14 Aug. 2002).

3. Reed v. Rhodes, 179 F.3d 453, 457-58 (6th Cir. 1999).

4. Reed v. Rhodes, 179 F.3d at 457-58.

5. Reinhard, "Cleveland: A Study in Crisis."

6. "Cleveland's Lost Generation: A Staggering Dropout Rate," *Quality Counts 98, Education Week Special Report, Education Week Online,* http://www.edweek.org/sreports/qc98/challenges/cleveland/cl-c3.htm (14 Aug. 2002).

7. Reinhard, "Cleveland: City in Crisis."

8. Jay P. Green, "High School Graduation Rates in the United States," *Manhattan Institute,* http://www.manhattan-institute.org/html/cr_baeo.htm (18 July 2002).

9. Reed v. Rhodes, No. 1:73 CV 1300 (N.D. Ohio March 3, 1995).

10. Reed v. Rhodes (N.D. Ohio March 3, 1995).

11. Zelman v. Simmons-Harris, slip opinion at 4.

12. Zelman v. Simmons-Harris, slip opinion at 5.

13. Simmons-Harris v. Goff, 711 N.E.2d 203 (Ohio 1999).

14. Zelman v. Simmons-Harris, 54 F. Supp. 2d 725 (N.D. Ohio).

15. Simmons-Harris v. Zelman, 234 F.3d 945 (6th Cir. 2000).

16. 243 F.3d at 973 (Ryan, J., dissenting).

17. 243 F.3d at 974 (Ryan, J., dissenting).

18. Zelman v. Simmons-Harris.

19. Zelman v. Simmons-Harris, slip opinion at 21.

20. Zelman v. Simmons-Harris, slip opinion at 21.

21. Zelman v. Simmons-Harris, slip opinion at 2.

22. Zelman v. Simmons-Harris, slip opinion at 9 (Thomas, J., concurring).

23. "The Urban Challenge," *Quality Counts '98, Education Week Special Report. Education Week Online,* http://www.edweek.org/sreports/qc98/intros/in-n.htm (14 August 2002).

24. "The Urban Challenge."

25. Richard Whitmire, "Time is Running Out on Urban Schools," *Blueprint Magazine, June 29, 2002, New Democrats Online,* http://www.ndol.org ndol_ci.cfm?kaid=110&subid=181&contentid=250686 (2 Aug. 2002).

26. Richard Fossey, "Desegregation Is Over In the Inner Cities: What Do We Do Now?" in *Reinterpreting Urban School Reform,* ed. Louis F. Miron and Edward P. St. John (Albany, NY: SUNY Press, 2003), 15-32.

27. Anthony Bryk, Valerie E. Lee, and Peter B. Holland, *Catholic Schools and the Common Good* (Cambridge, Mass.: Harvard University Press, 1993); David E. Campbell, "Bowling together: Private schools, Public Ends," *Education Next* 1(3): 55-66; Valerie E.

Lee, "Catholic Lessons for Public Schools," in *New Schools for a New Century: The Redesign of Urban Education*, ed. Diane Ravitch and Joseph Viteritti (New Haven, Conn.: Yale University Press, 1997).

28. "Brief of *Amici Curiae* National School Boards Association, National Parent Teacher Association, etc.," *National School Board Association* (10 December 2001), http://www.nsba.org/novouchers/vsc_docs/zelman_brief.pdf (14 Aug. 2002).

29. Diane Ravitch, "Somebody's Children: Educational Opportunity for all American children," in *New Schools for a New Century: The Redesign of Urban Education*, ed. Diane Ravitch and Joseph P. Viteritti (New Haven, Conn.: Yale University Press, 1997), 257.

30. Paulo Freire, *Pedagogy of the Oppressed* (1970; New York: Continuum, 2000), 44.

31. Freire, *Pedagogy of the Oppressed*, 54.

32. 530 U.S. 793 U.S. 793, 120 S.Ct. 2530 (2000).

33. Mitchell v. Helms, 530 U.S. at 828.

34. Mitchell v. Helms, 530 U.S. at 828-29.

35. Mitchell v. Helms, 530 U.S. at 829 (emphasis added).

36. Andrew M. Greeley, An *Ugly Little Secret: Anti-Catholicism in North America* (Kansas City, Mo.: Sheed, Andrews and McMeel, 1977), 63.

37. Diane Ravitch, "Somebody Else's Children," 262.

38. Lawrence A. Cremin, *American Education: The National Experience 1783-1876* (New York: Harper and Row, 1980), 168.

39. For an excellent and thorough discussion of the proposed constitutional amendment sponsored by Congressman Blaine in 1875 and 1876, see Steven K. Green, "The Blaine Amendment Reconsidered," *American Journal of Legal History* 36 (1992), 39-69.

40. "The Blaine Amendment," *Becket Fund for Religious Liberty*, http://www.blaineamendments.org/ (15 Aug. 2002).

41. Steven K. Green, "The Blaine Amendment Reconsidered," *American Journal of Legal History* 36 (1992), 39-69. Other commentators agree with Green's conclusions. See Tony Heytens, "School Choice and State Constitutions," *Virginia Law Review*, 117, 134; 86; Richard Komer and Clint Bolick, "School Choice: The Next Step," *Institute for Justice* (July 1, 2002), http://ij.org/editorial/choice_next.shtml (14 Aug. 2002).

42. Joseph P. Viteritti, "Blaine's Wake: School Choice, the First Amendment, and State Constitutional Law," *Harvard Journal of Law and Public Policy* 21 (1998): 657-718.

43. Viteritti, "Blaine's Wake," 673.

44. Viteritti, "Blaine's Wake," 657-718.

45. Richard Komer and Clint Bolick, "School Choice: The Next Step."

46. Troy, Heytens, "School Choice and State Constitutions," *Virginia Law Review*, 86, 117, 138.

47. The history of Massachusetts' anti-aid amendment is set forth in a memorandum in support of a motion for summary judgment filed by the Becket Fund in Boyette v. Galvin, No. 98-CV-10377-GAO filed on 7 November 2002. George Will also discusses the Massachusetts anti-aid provision in "A Choice for Children," *Washington Post*, 29 Nov. 1998, C7.

48. Joseph P. Viteritti, "Blaine's Wake," 669.

49. "Principals Discouraged by Supreme Court's School Voucher Decision," *National Association of Elementary School Principals* (27 June 2000), http://www.naesp.org/comm/prss6-27-02.htm (14 Aug. 2002).

50. "National PTA Vows to Continue Fighting Private School Vouchers," *National Parent Teacher Association* (27 June 2002) http://www.pta.org/aboutpta/pressroom/pr020627.asp (14 Aug. 2002).

51. "Court Ruling Still Leaves Flaws in Vouchers: Voucher Programs Bad Idea for Students, Says School Boards President," *National School Board Association* (27 June 2002), http://www.nsba.org/pressroom/pr062702-2.htm (14 Aug. 2002).

52. Brenda Welburn, "Statement by Brenda Welburn on the U.S. Supreme Court's Cleveland Voucher Decision," *National Association of State Boards of Education* (2002), http://www.nasbe.org/Press_Release.html (14 Aug. 2002).

53. Gerald Tirozzi, "Statement on the Supreme Court Ruling on the Cleveland Voucher Program," *National Association of Secondary Principals* (2002), http://www.nassp.org/publicaffairs/pr_clvlndvchrs.html (14 Aug. 2002).

54. Gene Carter, "Statement by Gene Carter, Executive Director, Association for Supervision and Curriculum Development," *Association for Supervision and Curriculum Development* (27 June 2002), http://www.ascd.org/educationnews/sc_voucher_decision_statement.html (14 Aug. 2002).

55. Bob Chase, "Statement of Bob Chase, President of the National Education Association on the U.S. Supreme Court Decision on Private School Tuition Vouchers," *National Education Association* (27 June 2002), http://www.nea.org/nr/nr020627.html (14 Aug. 2002).

56. Editorial, "Without Merit," *Wall Street Journal*, 10 July 2002, A34.

57. Sandra Feldman, "Statement by Sandra Feldman, President, American Federation of Teachers, on the Supreme Court's Ruling on School Vouchers," *American Federation of Teachers* (27 June 2002), http://www.aft.org/press/2002/062702.html (17 July 2002).

58. Paul Houston, "Statement of AASA Executive Director Paul Houston on the Cleveland Voucher Case," *AASA Online,* http://www.aasa.org/News_Room/2002/june/6-27-02.htm (17 July 2002).

59. See for example, Monte Whaley, "Old Law May Be Voucher Stopper," *Denver Post*, 22 July 2002; Laurie Goodstein, "The Nation: In States, Hurdles Loom," *New York Times*, 30 June 2002; Richard Komer and Clint Bolick, "School Choice: The Next Step," *Institute for Justice* (1 July 2002), http://ij.org/editorial/choice_next.shtml (14 Aug. 2002).

60. Heytens, "School Choice and State Constitutions," 123.

61. See Viteritti, "Blaine's Wake," 680 and sources cited in footnote 107.

62. Heytens, "School Choice and State Constitutions," 140-60.

63. Dana Canedy, "Florida Court Bars Use of Vouchers," *New York Times*, 6 Aug. 2002, A10.

64. "NSBA Hails Fla. Court Ruling That Vouchers Are Unconstitutional," *National School Boards Association* (5 Aug. 2002), http://www.nsba.org/pressroom/pr080502.htm (14 Aug. 2002); "NEA Hails Florida Voucher Decision," *National Education Association* (5 Aug. 2002), http://www.nea.org/nr/nr020805.html (14 Aug. 2002); Sandra Feldman, "Statement by Sandra Feldman, President, American Federation of Teachers, on Florida Court Ruling on the Unconstitutionality of Vouchers," *American Federation of Teachers* (5 Aug. 2002), http://www.aft.org/press/2002/080502.html (14 Aug. 2002).

65. The Becket Fund for Religious Liberty maintains a web site providing information about Blaine amendments. It includes Florida as a Blaine Amendment state. "Blaine Amendment." *Becket Fund for Religious Liberty*, http://www.blaineamendments.org/ (15 Aug. 2002). The Becket Fund's web site address is http://www.becketfund.org/ (15 August 2002). Heytens, "School Choice and State Constitutions," 126 identifies Florida as a state

with a Blaine Amendment.

66. Florida Constitution of 1868, Declaration of Rights, section 6 stated "No preference shall be given by law to any church, sect or mode of worship and no money shall ever be taken from the public treasury directly or indirectly in aid of any church, sect, or religious denomination or in aid of any sectarian institution." Article 1, section 3 of Florida's current constitution contains slightly different language. It states in pertinent part: "No revenue of the state or any political subdivision or agency thereof shall ever be taken from the public treasury directly or indirectly in aid of any church, sect, or religious denomination or in aid of any sectarian constitution."

67. George Will, "A Choice for Children," *Washington Post*, 29 Nov.1998, C7.

Chapter 15

Journey to Faith:
Isaac Hecker and Nineteenth-Century American Reform

Ruth M. Kelly

Too often when we look at the history of the American Catholic Church we separate the American from the history. However, there are many ways that "mainline" American history and American Catholic history intersect. An example of this integration is the nineteenth-century Age of Reform, and the journey of faith of the nineteenth-century American convert, Isaac Hecker. Isaac Hecker, a Protestant convert to Roman Catholicism, founded the first American order of priests, the Congregation of Missionary Priests of St. Paul the Apostle (the Paulists), in 1858. Father Hecker saw his ministry to be the conversion of non-Catholic America. Hecker was optimistic about the evangelization of America, and was convinced "that every American would in time become a Roman Catholic."[1] He believed that the Catholic Church was essentially democratic, and especially suited to democratic America.

Hecker also saw his mission as one to renew Catholicism worldwide. Like the Puritans who saw their settlement as a "city on a hill" reforming the Old World, Hecker saw the renewal of the universal Church coming from a Catholic America. The combination of the "Catholic faith and . . . the energy and youthfulness of the American people" would transform "American culture and ultimately the entire

Catholic world." He wanted to "build a Catholic America which would lead to a Catholic World."[2]

Isaac Hecker is representative of the liberal Catholics of the late nineteenth century who sought to "fashion a more American style of Catholicism."[3] Roman Catholicism was identified in the United States with the social and political patterns of Europe, and Hecker presented Americans with a different model of Catholicism. Hecker's liberal, American style of Catholicism was an alternative to the devotional Catholicism of immigrant Catholics that many Americans found objectionable. Hecker's liberal Catholicism is described by his biographer David O'Brien as a combination of

> orthodox faith with the simple conviction that the Church had to learn to be at home in America. Hecker took for granted the value of freedom of conscience, self-reliance and democratic government . . . he saw these as America's providential gift to the world. He hoped his Catholic Church would eventually come to appreciate and accept these gifts.[4]

Hecker's vision of American Catholicism was not appreciated or understood by members of the conservative wing of the American Catholic Church or the European church. This idea of a uniquely American, democratic, Catholic Church was labeled a heresy, the Americanist heresy, and condemned by Rome in 1895.[5] Hecker's vision of the American Church was deemed dangerous by the nineteenth-century European Church, which was petrified by the term, "democracy." While democracy seemed an outrageous and dangerous ideology to the Church in the nineteenth and early twentieth centuries, by the late twentieth century, some of Hecker's ideas for the Catholic Church had been realized in the promises of Vatican II.

The focus of this chapter is not to examine the Americanist heresy associated with Hecker or to look at Isaac Hecker's distinguished career as founder of the Paulist Fathers and editor of the *Catholic World*. Hecker, like all people, is a product of his time and place. Isaac Hecker came of age during the first half of the nineteenth century. This was a very exciting period in American history and many changes in American life and politics were ushered in during these years. This was the Age of Reform, the Age of Jackson. During this time, America was radically changed by a democratization of politics, religion, and markets.

This chapter, therefore, will look at the nineteenth-century American world of Isaac Hecker, the Protestant reform movements, the political movements, and the intellectual movements that were his frame of reference. How did these cultural and societal forces ultimately lead Isaac Hecker to the Catholic Church? How does his background explain his mission to convert America to Catholicism?

The political and social tensions of mid-nineteenth-century America were caused, according to historians Charles Sellers, by the collision of "history's most revolutionary force, the capitalist market" and "history's most conservative force, the land."[6] While the commercial boom after the War of 1812 presented Americans with unlimited opportunities for economic advancement, it meant the destruction of the way of life of the subsistence farmer and the urban mechanic, both sharing the quality of life available in a subsistence culture. This culture is idealistically portrayed by Sellers as having "fostered family obligation, communal cooperation, and reproduction over generations of a modest comfort." The boom introduced the farm household to the market and to farming for profit; this ultimately led to an inability to reproduce the family farm into the next generation. The commercial boom also affected the urban mechanic. It "shattered the mechanics' unity by extending markets for their products beyond their locality" and "inaugurated an irreversible proletarianization of the mechanic class."[7]

The boom after the War of 1812 was followed by the Panic of 1819. This was the year Isaac Hecker was born in New York City, into a German-American Methodist family.

The Panic of 1819 was the first economic crisis that affected the entire United States and was the beginning of the modern business cycle of boom, crisis, depression, and recovery. Unlike previous economic crises, the Panic of 1819 could not be explained by acts of nature or governments, such as crop failures or war. Rather it appeared out of nowhere, mysteriously from within the economic system itself.[8] The Panic was part of an international depression following years of war; it was severe in the United States because of the reckless expansion of credit by banking institutions. When the banks suspended specie payments, bank notes—the only circulating currency—were worthless. Merchants went bankrupt, city workers lost their jobs, and the economy ground to a standstill. The paralysis maintained its grip through the early 1820s, and not until after mid-decade did prosperity return.

The psychological and political effects of the panic were just as important as its economic effects. Americans had left the settled ways of the old agrarian order and jumped into a market revolution of unlimited prosperity and optimism; then they were just as suddenly plunged into poverty and despair. As historians Charles Sellers, Henry May, and Neil McMillen explain:

> The shock of this experience made the 1820s a decade of soul-searching and tension. . . . Class antagonisms sharpened as impoverished farmers and urban workers blamed political and business leaders . . . for the disaster. And finally, there was a growing interest in politics, a dissatisfaction with the political leadership that had allowed hard times to come, and a demand for new leaders who would be more responsive to the popular will and use government to relieve distress.[9]

This was the world of Isaac Hecker and of his brothers born in New York City—John in 1812, George in 1818, and Isaac in 1819. Their father, John Hecker, operated a brass foundry in New York. While John Hecker survived the panic, he was out of business by 1828.[10] The brothers, beginning with John, joined an uncle in the bakery business and they became the sole support of the family. Soon, young John Hecker owned the bakery, then expanded and opened another store. When it became difficult to obtain flour during the Panic of 1837, he built a flour mill. By 1843, Hecker & Brothers ran a flour mill and three bakeries.

The Hecker brothers were typical of successful, modern New York business-men in the Jacksonian era. New York City, after 1840, was the fastest growing large industrial area in the world. New York City's industrialization, however, was radi-cally different from industrialization in the rest of the country. It is described by one scholar of the period as "metropolitan industrialization," a pattern of industrial transformation much more like London or Paris than the New England towns of Lowell or Lynn.[11] New York was a "metropolitan labyrinth of factories and tiny artisan establishments, central workrooms and outworkers' cellars, luxury firms and sweatwork . . . shops." New York's industrial growth did not mean the end of small producers like the Hecker operation. The success of small businesses was not de-pendent on adapting modern and expensive machinery, but on an "intensified divi-sion of labor."[12] The Hecker operation followed this industrial pattern of growth and success without a significant change in the production process. That is not to say, however, that the Heckers did not modernize their production. John and George Hecker were "inventive." John developed a machine that mixed and rolled the bread dough, and George invented a floating grain elevator.[13]

Small businesses like the Heckers were also successful because of the popula-tion growth in New York City. The city was the fastest growing area in the world. Between 1800 and 1850, New York's population grew seventy percent.[14] This in-crease in population created a large and diverse consumer market as well as a concentrated source of wage labor. As the city grew and prospered, the gap be-tween the "mercantile bourgeoisie" like the Heckers and the working class deep-ened. As the middle class gained hegemony over the economy and the culture, the lower class sank ever lower into "disease, filth, and mortality."[15]

Many of the New York bourgeoisie who dominated manufacturing were com-mitted evangelical Protestants, who believed they had a duty to be not only per-sonally successful, but to save souls as well. These men combined, "artisan repub-lican emphasis on rights, virtue, independence, and the masters' obligation with. . . the evangelical. . . argument" of perfectionism.[16]

The most prominent American proponent of perfectionism in the United States was the preacher, Charles Finney. While Finney was nominally a Presbyterian, his methods and message transcended denominational boundaries. Beginning in 1821 and for the next fifteen years, Charles Finney traveled from New England to New York City, and across New York State, preaching his message of perfectionism. He followed the Erie Canal and this part of New York State became known as the "burned-over district," for it was as if a fire had consumed and renewed the towns Finney visited. Finney demanded that after a sinner was converted, some kind of "relevant social action" must follow for "entire sanctification."[17] The Second Great Awakening had arrived.

Successful American entrepreneurs like the Heckers were affected by these doctrines. Finney,

> offered businessmen who surrendered . . . both domestic and social tranquillity. He
> promised to Christianize a fractious populace . . . by making individual conversion
> the only means of social improvement. What sealed his alliance with businessmen

and carried the refocused Moderate Light to hegemony was his unconscious equation of Christian virtue with their capitalist asceticism.[18]

As they became more and more successful, the Heckers realized, like many of the successful Protestant bourgeoisie of New York, that they had a responsibility to correct the conditions facing the working class in New York City. However, the Hecker brothers did not follow the evangelical model, at least not at first. They identified both the source of the problem and the solution to the problem to be the political system, and therefore worked to reform New York politics. The party the Heckers became active in was the Locofoco Party.[19] This party arose in New York in the 1830s and consisted of disgruntled Tammany Democrats and a few Whigs. The political agenda of the Locofocos was

> primarily to purify government and eliminate aristocratic corrupt influences, particularly Tammany [politicians] and their banker friends; their program . . . was vitriolic in its denunciation of monopolies, banking, and paper money.[20]

The party appealed to "petty entrepreneurs in search of wider business opportunities and . . . exploited workers in search of a deflationary currency and an end to banks." The party was led by "professionals, petty and middling merchants, and disgruntled renegades from the Democrats."[21] The Locofocos were for equal rights and equal laws; therefore they were opposed to any state granted "exclusive privileges, special advantages, or any form of monopoly." The party believed that inequality resulted from the actions of the "positive state." It was only through the destruction of the "authority and prestige of the state and its officers" that equality could be achieved. The Locofocos "affirmed unqualified and uncompromising hostility to bank notes and bank papers."[22]

John Hecker, the only brother old enough to vote, was a leader in the Locofoco party. He was especially concerned with the issue of paper money. George and Isaac helped their older brother spread the Locofocos' message; they set up a printing press in their home and printed an anti-paper message on the back of all paper received at the bakery.[23] In 1837, the year of the major economic panic, the Heckers worked actively for the Locofoco candidates in the city election. They, "organized meetings, arranged for speakers, and posted handbills."[24] Their party lost, but so did the Tammany Democrats. Gradually the Locofocos returned home to the Democratic Party and the Democrats adopted some Locofoco issues.

The events of 1837 had a great effect on Isaac Hecker. He had placed great hopes on reform through the political process. He later wrote that what he learned was that

> not much was to be hoped from political actions, as politicians were governed more by selfishness and a thirst for power than by patriotism and the desire of doing good to their fellow citizens.[25]

After the demise of the Locofocos, the Heckers were still active in reform move-ments. It was during this period that they followed the perfectionist businessman model discussed earlier. They established a reading room for their employees' im-provement, and they dealt with the immediate plight of the less fortunate by offer-ing free bread to the unemployed. They sought answers to the social problems around them by "reading reform papers and attending reform lectures." They were intrigued with the "activist democratic Christianity that would overcome injustice, greed, and ambition."[26]

The most prominent reformer of the time was Orestes Brownson, the Boston Unitarian minister and editor. The Heckers attended Brownson's lectures in New York in 1841. They were impressed by Brownson and his message of worker rights; they invited him back to New York in 1842 and sponsored four more of Brownson's lectures.

Like the Heckers, Brownson had invested his hopes for reform on the political process and had been badly disappointed in the presidential race of 1840. After the election he "began to reexamine his political convictions and to focus more exclu-sively on religious questions."[27] Orestes Brownson was now "convinced that the hopes invested in America could not be fulfilled by people alone; they needed divine assistance."[28] Brownson lived with the Heckers while he lectured in New York and he developed a friendship with the young Isaac. Orestes Brownson

> had a profound influence on the course of Hecker's life. It broadened his horizon, introduced him to new realms of thought, and turned his attention to philosophy and religion as effective agents for social change.[29]

The "new realms of thought" that Orestes Brownson introduced the young man to was the philosophy/religion of Transcendentalism. The study of Transcen-dentalism was an important event in Isaac Hecker's journey of faith.

The origins of Transcendentalism, according to religious historian Sidney Ahlstrom are "unfathomable"; its causes are "beyond explanation."[30] While the beginnings of Transcendentalism in the United States can be traced to the study of Kant, the accessibility of European Romantic texts, and German biblical criticism, American Transcendentalism "did not just spring to life magically"[31] out of Eu-rope. Transcendentalism grew out of the New England Unitarian faith. The Tran-scendental Club first met in Boston in 1836. Present at the meeting were George Ripley, Bronson Alcott, Orestes Brownson, James Freeman Clarke, Ralph Waldo Emerson, Convers Francis, and Frederic Henry Hedge. All but Alcott were Unitar-ian ministers.[32] The club met for four years. Eventually twenty-six people, includ-ing Nathaniel Hawthorne, Margaret Fuller, Elizabeth Peabody, and Henry David Thoreau became members of the club. Usually "a dozen or so men and women [met] to discuss the various aspects of the new philosophy."[33] The main activity of this young group was publishing, (a rather complete literary history of New En-gland during this period could be written just using the members of the club) and they all published works that aggressively promulgated the new philosophy.

These "new views" signaled a break with the Unitarianism of their fathers. The Transcendentalists found the liberal religion of the previous generation too formal and too rational; it was not meeting their spiritual and emotional needs. The answers to life's fundamental problems, these young people believed, were to be found within themselves, through their intuition. They shared common beliefs that individuals contain within themselves godlike attributes, that the senses and emotions are superior to reason and intellect, and that it was through the study of nature that man could commune with the supernatural. The Transcendentalists "emphasized the individual, the subjective, the imaginative, the personal, the emotional, and the visionary."[34]

In 1842, Isaac Hecker was affected by a mystical experience that "shook the center" of his life. Isaac lost all interest in the family business and could no longer work. He could not communicate or relate to those around him. The family alternated between Susan Hecker's opinion that her son was going through a spiritual transformation in preparation for becoming a Christian, to John Hecker's opinion that his brother was suicidal. The Hecker family asked Brownson to help their son and brother regain normalcy, and in December 1842 Brownson invited Isaac to Boston. During his stay with Brownson, Isaac decided to move to Brook Farm until his mind "became perfectly settled in my present state or returns to its former state."[35]

Brook Farm was founded in 1841 by Brownson's Transcendental friend, George Ripley. The longer Ripley was involved in the Transcendental Club, the more he became dissatisfied with his Unitarian ministry in Boston. Like the evangelicals who peopled the reform movements of the era, Ripley believed that, "some practical application should be made of the fresh views of philosophy and life." That practical application was Brook Farm, a Transcendental community set up outside Boston in West Roxbury. The residents of Brook Farm supported themselves by farming, teaching, woodworking, and sewing.[36] Isaac Hecker would support himself at Brook Farm by baking the daily bread.

The farm was a place where

> conversation abounded, distinguished visitors came and went, and the community managed to maintain its morale . . . Many who studied in its schools gratefully remembered Brook Farm as an enduring inspiration. Nobody seemed the poorer for having participated in its common tasks and partaken of its fervent, hopeful spirit.[37]

Brook Farm was a "community where the central questions of nineteenth-century American culture were actively engaged."[38] Hecker had been exposed to much in the middle-class culture of his time: Finney's crusade for religious perfection, evangelical reform, and Jacksonian democracy; and he had "learned something of religious philosophy" from Brownson. Now he was at Brook Farm, an "open-minded, unprejudiced seeker after truth." He had experienced a calling to a higher life but, "he had no clear idea of what that might be, no words with which to describe, and control, whatever was at work within."[39]

At Brook Farm Hecker baked bread in the early morning and then spent the rest of the day in prayer and study. Methodism, his mother's faith, had given him a framework of "basic Christian themes and . . . a specifically Methodist concern to live fully under the influence of divine grace." Now he seriously studied Christianity and "regularly prayed that he might find a church."[40]

Isaac Hecker found himself drawn more and more to the Episcopal Church; its rituals, authority, and doctrine appealed to him. He thought it was providential when he learned that his brother John had joined the Episcopal Church, and that Brownson too, was leaning in the Episcopal direction. Isaac kept studying and looking; he was conflicted because, although he decided that he needed a Church, "to select any one church would cheapen his experience, compromise the Gospel, and perpetuate the scandalous divisions within what should be the body of Christ."[41]

In July of 1843, Hecker left Brook Farm. Life at Brook Farm was a valuable experience to Hecker and he was always grateful for the valuable lessons he gained with the Brook Farm community. Later he wrote that Brook Farm had, "collected the dreamers . . . it was the realization of the best dreams these men had of Christianity."[42] But like his experience with politics and reform, Transcendentalism did not give him what he was seeking.

Isaac Hecker agreed with the Transcendentalist belief that men were good, and given the right environment, they would strive for the better goal. He also agreed with the Transcendentalist notion that inside every human was a seed of divinity. However, Transcendentalism did not answer Hecker's question of how does one cultivate that seed? Hecker looked at the reform movements of his day, the philosophical movements, the social movements, the political movements, and the religious movements. He plotted the reforms on a triangle and discovered that all the reform movements had religion at their centers. He agreed with Brownson's contention that a church was needed to "arouse desire for reform and to successfully effect it."[43]

But which church would fulfill that need? Hecker started again on his journey of faith to find that church. He returned home to New York and visited churches there: a Methodist Church, a Mormon Church, his brother's Episcopal Church, and a Catholic Church. He found the Episcopal bishop, Samuel Seabury welcoming and gracious. His visit to a Catholic Church was a disaster. The first Catholic Hecker spoke to, New York Bishop John Hughes, was just the opposite of his Episcopal counterpart. Bishop Hughes did not welcome this young man and did not eagerly and respectfully enter into a dialogue about the attributes of the true Church as had Bishop Seabury. Rather, Bishop Hughes submitted Hecker to a lecture on church discipline. Hecker was insulted, and he left the meeting with Hughes "irritated" and unimpressed.

He still struggled with his decision: which church to join? The Episcopal Church was socially acceptable to American society; the Catholic Church was not. The Catholic Church was maligned and persecuted in nineteenth-century America because it was seen as foreign and contrary to American culture. Hecker agonized over this question of a church; he could not make up his mind. The Episcopal

Church asked so little of him, but the Catholic Church asked so much of him.[44] Isaac Hecker's solution to his dilemma was to submit his will to God and wait and see where the spirit would lead him.[45]

What is amazing and speaks to the complexity of Hecker's journey of faith, was that during this time of searching for a church, Isaac Hecker had decided to study for the ministry. He began his studies of Latin and Greek in preparation for seminary, still uncertain which church was the true church of Christ.

While Hecker struggled with his decision, Orestes Brownson surprised all with his declaration of his intention to become a Catholic. He urged Isaac to do the same. Brownson advised Hecker to set aside the "repugnance and lack of respect that their intellectual friends" felt for the Church and place himself under its direction.[46] That was the fundamental question that plagued Hecker: he knew the Catholic church was the body of Christ and the channel of the Holy Spirit, but was he willing to submit his will to the direction of the church?[47]

On August 2, 1844, almost a year after leaving Brook Farm, Isaac Hecker became a Catholic. He decided to become a Catholic even though he was unfamiliar with church doctrine, ignorant of how the church operated, and without close personal ties to any Catholics. Like Brownson, Hecker had been convinced through studies and investigations that the Catholic Church was the church that provided its members a way to holiness and perfection. However, unlike Brownson, Hecker's decision for the church had an added mystical dimension. He became a Catholic as a result of "following his higher convictions and deepest wants," and placing himself "unreservedly in submission to the Holy Spirit."[48] Hecker's "journey inward" had led him to find his church, the Catholic Church.

Isaac Hecker did not reject his particular American experience after entering the Church—he embraced it. The Protestant reform environment that Hecker came from insisted that religious conversion be accompanied by a response, an action. His response to his conversion experience was to dedicate himself to convert America to Catholicism.

Isaac Hecker trained for the priesthood and was ordained a Redemptorist priest in London in 1849. He returned to the United States with fellow American priest converts in 1851 and began a series of successful missions in American cities. These missions used a modified model of the Protestant revival meetings popularized earlier by Charles Finney. Hecker and his group of American Redemptorists traveled from Watertown, New York to New Orleans, preaching to thousands of Catholics. James Gibbons, later Cardinal Gibbons, credits one of these missions that he heard as a young man as a factor in his decision to enter the priesthood.

Hecker was convinced that the Catholic Church offered America the way to fully develop its unique nature and destiny, and he was optimistic that America was ripe for conversion to the Catholic faith. According to Martin Kirk, Hecker felt that, "all earnest Americans, should they follow their convictions, and should they be given an unbiased presentation of the Catholic Church, would find themselves drawn into her fold."[49]

The benefits to America and to the Church were mutual:

Catholicism would lead the American people to the fulfillment of its most cherished images of itself as a religious people seeking to realize its destiny before God and man. In turn, America would offer the Church her greatest opportunity, not only for numerical and material growth, but for the development of a most spiritual and progressive civilization.[50]

In 1855, Hecker wrote *Questions of the Soul* to address seekers like himself—middle-class Americans who had "outgrown dogmatic Protestantism" and then found Unitarianism and Transcendentalism wanting. One of America's "chief characteristics" Hecker wrote was this quest for "a more spiritual and earnest life."[51] He wrote this book with his Transcendentalist friends in mind because as Joseph Gower writes in the introduction to *Questions of the Soul*:

Hecker shared many of the values held by the Transcendentalists, he believed that if he could make Catholicity intelligible to them, he would promote their conversion and through them the conversion of the country.[52]

However, the conversion of middle-class Protestant Americans was not the mission that the Redemptorists had in mind for Isaac Hecker and his fellows. The Redemptorists felt their best use was in ministering to Catholics, specifically, German immigrant Catholics. This issue and others led to conflicts between the priest converts and their Redemptorist superiors, and Isaac Hecker was expelled from the order. In 1858, with special permission from Rome, Hecker established the first American religious order, the Congregation of St. Paul, popularly known as the Paulists. Hecker saw the mission of the Paulists was to present "Catholic teaching to the non-Catholics of their native land and it was for this specific purpose"[53] that the order was established.

Hecker was constantly looking for ways to share his faith with his fellow Americans. In 1858, he began the Paulist Press, and today that publishing house is the largest Catholic publisher in North America. The Paulists who followed Hecker continued in that tradition, and in 1925 the Paulists entered the broadcast media bringing the message of the Church to Americans with their own radio station, WLWL in New York. They continued with innovations to evangelize America, such as outfitting mobile homes as traveling chapels. In 1958, the order founded Paulist Productions, which produces made-for-television movies, documentaries for the History Channel, and feature length films. The Paulists perpetuate the mission of Isaac Hecker by evangelizing through print, radio, television, video, and the Internet.[54]

All the events and movements of the mid-nineteenth century contributed to Isaac Hecker's journey to the Church and the formation of the first American religious order. The Market Revolution, the panics, the reform movements, Jacksonian politics, all disrupted the settled agrarian, Protestant way of life in America. Americans became optimistic seekers, developing new strategies, new ways, and new thoughts to deal with modernity. An environment was created that made it possible for one of these Protestant seekers to find his philosophical and spiritual questions answered in the Roman Catholic Church.

Notes

1. Paul Robichaud, "What Isaac Hecker Can Teach Us About America," *The Catholic World*, 238, No. 1423, (2 January 1995): 41.

2. David O'Brien, *Isaac Hecker, An American Catholic* (Mahwah, NJ: Paulist Press, 1992) 2-7.

3. Jay Dolan, *American Catholic Experience, A History from Colonial Times to the Present* (Notre Dame: University of Notre Dame Press, 1992) 235.

4. O'Brien, *Isaac Hecker*, 7.

5. This was the so-called Americanist heresy addressed by Pope Leo XIII in 1895 in his letter *Longinqua Oceani* and in the 1898 the letter, *Testem Benevolentiae*.

6. Charles Sellers, *The Market Revolution, Jacksonian America, 1815-1846* (New York: Oxford University Press, 1991) 4.

7. Sellers, *The Market Revolution*, 15, 17, 25.

8. Murray N. Rothbard, *The Panic of 1819: Reactions and Politics* (New York: Columbia University Press, 1962) 7.

9. Charles Sellers, Henry May, and Neil McMillen, *A Synopsis of American History* (Chicago: Ivan R. Dee, 1992) 126.

10. Hecker's biographer, Vincent F. Holden, hints that John Hecker might have lost his business due to alcoholism. Vincent F. Holden, *The Yankee Paul, Isaac Thomas Hecker* (Milwaukee: The Bruce Publishing Co., 1958) 8.

11. Sean Wilentz, *Chants Democratic, New York City and the Rise of the American Working Class, 1788-1850* (New York: Oxford University Press, 1984) 107-142.

12. Wilentz, *Chants Democratic*, 107.

13. O'Brien, *Isaac Hecker*, 15.

14. Willentz, *Chants Democratic*, 109.

15. Willentz, *Chants Democratic*, 109.

16. Willentz, *Chants Democratic*,149.

17. Willentz, *Chants Democratic*, 461.

18. Sellers, *The Market Revolution*, 230.

19. The party received its name from the name of the matches the party faithful used for light at their meetings.

20. Wilentz, *Chants Democratic*, 235.

21. Willentz, *Chants Democratic*, 235.

22. Lee Benson, *The Concept of Jacksonian Democracy, New York as a Test Case* (Princeton, New Jersey: Princeton University Press, 1973) 94-95. Holden, *Yankee Paul*, 13.

23. Holden, *Yankee Paul*, 14.

24. O'Brien, *Isaac Hecker*, 16.

25. Isaac Hecker, "Dr. Brownson and the Workingman's Party Fifty Years Ago," *Catholic World*, XLV (May 1887), 203.

26. O'Brien, *Isaac Hecker*, 18.

27. O'Brien, *Isaac Hecker*, 19

28. O'Brien, *Isaac Hecker*, 19.

29. Holden, *Yankee Paul*, 17.

30. Sidney Ahlstrom, *A Religious History of the American People* (New Haven, Conneticut: Yale University Press, 1974) 599.

31. Charles Capper, *Margaret Fuller, An American Romantic Life* (New York: Oxford University Press, 1992) 182.

32. Ahlstrom, *A Religious History*, 600.

33. Capper, *Margaret Fuller*, 182.

34. James Martin, Randy Roberts, Steven Mintz, Linda O. McMurry, and James Jones, *America and Its People* (New York: Harper Collins, 1993) 348-349.

35. Letter of Isaac Hecker to family, January 7, 1843. Quoted in O'Brien, 23.

36. The most famous resident of Brook Farm was Nathaniel Hawthorne. He was on the Agriculture Committee of the commune. The locale of his novel, *The Blithedale Romance*, was Brook Farm.

37. Ahlstrom, *A Religious History*, 501.

38. O'Brien, *Isaac Hecker*, 29.

39. O'Brien, *Isaac Hecker*, 29.

40. O'Brien, *Isaac Hecker*, 31.

41. O'Brien, *Isaac Hecker*, 32.

42. Isaac Hecker, undated memorandum on Brook Farm. Quoted in Holden, 63.

43. Holden, *Yankee Paul*, 73.

44. Martin Kirk, *The Spirituality of Isaac Hecker, Reconciling The American Catholic Character and the Catholic Faith* (New York: Garland Publishing, 1988) 74.

45. O'Brien, *Isaac Hecker*, 54-55.

46. Kirk, *Spirituality of Isaac Hecker*, 80.

47. Diary, 7 June 1844, quoted in Kirk, 81.

48. Kirk, *Spirituality of Isaac Hecker*, 83; O'Brien, *Isaac Hecker*, 65.

49. Kirk, *Spirituality of Isaac Hecker*, 202.

50. Kirk, *Spirituality of Isaac Hecker*, 202.

51. Isaac Hecker, *Questions of the Soul* (New York: D. Appleton, 1855) reprint. Arno, 1978. 55.

52. Joseph F. Gower, *Introduction, Questions of the Soul*, Isaac Hecker reprint 1978 by Arno Press, Inc., Published 1855 by D. Appleton, New York. 3.

53. James M. Gilles, *The Paulists* (New York: Macmillan Co., 1932) 2.

54. *The Paulist Fathers* http://www.paulist.org/ (11 November 2002).

Chapter 16

Catholic Indian Boarding Schools and Sioux Catholicism[1]

James T. Carroll

The interaction between the native peoples of North America and representatives of the Roman Catholic Church began in the eighteenth century when missionaries arrived in western Canada to serve a growing number of French traders and the emerging *Métis* population. Over the next century the frontier missionaries developed a missiology that emphasized acculturation, accommodation, and syncretism to secure the "souls" of the Native American population. One important element of this approach to conversion was the creation of boarding schools where students could receive instruction in the Catholic faith and learn how to become self-sufficient farmers. These institutions contributed to the success of Catholic missionary efforts which depended upon the elimination of traditional practices and the promotion of a sedentary existence. In the nineteenth century the Roman Catholic Church established more Native American boarding schools than any other denomination and received financial support from the federal government.[2]

In order to reveal social, cultural, and religious dynamics at Catholic Indian boarding schools this analysis will employ a case study approach and focus on four Catholic Indian boarding schools on the northern Great Plains: Fort Totten Indian Industrial School (Devils Lake, North Dakota), Fort Yates Indian Industrial

School (Fort Yates, North Dakota), Saint Francis Mission School (Rosebud Reservation), and Holy Rosary Mission School (Pine Ridge Reservation).[3]

In general terms, the findings reveal many cultural parallels between the church workers and native students attending the boarding schools. More specifically, the following theoretical principles help explain the relationships at these institutions:

1. There existed a religious, cultural, and emotional middle ground at these boarding schools. On the middle ground no group possessed the strength to force others to abandon ingrained cultural ideals and practices.
2. The four boarding schools were "wood and mortar" manifestations of "frontier Catholicism," where rigidity evaporated and mutual accommodation was the norm.
3. All those connected with the boarding schools—the Native American students and their religious teachers—possessed a resilience that thwarted government efforts to eliminate cultural uniqueness.
4. The social environment at the schools was bicultural, where accommodation replaced assimilation and cooperation eclipsed force.

The remainder of this article will expand on these ideas by probing social constructs at these schools and providing historic examples of cultural interaction and syncretism.

The Middle Ground

Between 1874 and 1926 these four schools encountered shifts in government policy, cultural identity, and institutional life. The sisters and Indian students who shaped this institutional history gradually adjusted to cultural differences, negotiated major obstacles in order to create a cultural and religious middle ground, and, in the end, established an educational setting where secular curriculum and religious indoctrination were well integrated. While this work examines four Catholic Indian boarding schools in the present-day states of North and South Dakota in the late nineteenth and early twentieth centuries, many of the characteristics that surfaced can be expanded to other Indian boarding schools. In the final analysis, the ideas revealed in this study are critical when considering the role of Catholicism in the Christianization and Americanization of the Indian.

Change and adaptation were two conspicuous dynamics at the four schools. All of the constituencies—Indian students, religious sisters, and federal and church officials—experienced three distinct periods of change: Grant's Peace Policy (1873-1887), the Dawes Severalty Act (1887-1933), and the Indian New Deal (1933-1953). In the decade after the American Civil War, Indian experts and government officials concluded that Indian affairs should be the domain of various religious denominations. When Ulysses S. Grant was elected president he assigned reservations to specific religious groups in the hope that they would successfully assimilate the native peoples by establishing mission outposts and schools. With the rapid immigration to the American West in the last two decades of the nineteenth century and a reemergence of nativism, federal policy shifted to land allotment for native peoples and a more secular system of education. The election of Franklin Delano Roosevelt in 1932 ushered in an *Indian New Deal* where self-determination and tribal autonomy became the focus of federal-Indian relations. These schools succeeded throughout the entire period because the Indian students and religious sisters adapted successfully to shifts in federal policy and brokered compromises that satisfied external prescriptions while protecting important cultural and religious distinctions. Despite fifty years of education and acculturation, the Sioux students were still strongly attached to their tribal culture and identity. The sisters for their part were subject to intense government scrutiny and vocal opposition, yet never wavered on their primary goal of religious indoctrination.

Fort Totten, Fort Yates, Saint Francis, and Holy Rosary served as a middle ground between Sioux cultural identity and forces aimed at complete assimilation. The atmosphere at these schools was such that Indian adults and children, representatives of the Roman Catholic Church, and those charged with Indian assimilation were able to function in an effective manner. In short, no single group was powerful enough to coerce the others into completely abandoning their ideals or cultural constructs. Some concrete examples of the middle ground at the boarding schools included: the willingness to allow frequent interaction between school and "camp"; the existence of a bilingual school environment; the efforts to involve Indian adults in the life of the school; and the sincere attempts to blend Catholic beliefs with Sioux culture. Both the Indian students and religious sisters moved towards cultural accommodation[4] through the medium of on-reservation boarding school living. These characteristics contributed to the positive Indian response of these four Catholic Indian boarding schools and toward the long-term success that they enjoyed.

The establishment of the middle ground at the four schools was, in part, a product of the Catholic approach to mission and evangelization. The sisters who taught at these schools believed that the positive aspects of Sioux culture should be cultivated and preserved and incorporated with the essential tenets of Roman Catholicism. "By building on what they believed was good in Lakota culture, they sought to perfect the good tendencies with Church teaching."[5] The missionaries learned to speak the Sioux language, made an effort to visit and minister with all tribal constituencies, and cultivated a mission school environment that encouraged cross-generational involvement. Establishing the main church near the boarding schools, opening hospitals, visiting the various Indian camps, and seeking adult conversion were some manifestations of this approach to mission.

By placing Indian identity in a Catholic context, these missionaries avoided a pitfall of Christian activity among the Indians: "Any single comment on the relative failure of North American missions must focus on what proved to be an incompatibility between mission policy and *Indian feelings about their own identity and future*[6] [italics in original]." The sisters at these schools, and Catholic missionaries in general, combined major Catholic feast days with important events in Indian culture, participated in traditional tribal events, used the *Two Roads*[7] to communicate the faith in a culturally appropriate manner, and incorporated many Indian practices into Catholic liturgical life of the reservations. While some critics claimed that this approach to Indian conversion bordered on syncretism, it was, in fact, an example of missionary adaptation that had a long history in the Roman Catholic Church.

> Though the Lakota Catholics' participation in traditional Lakota ceremonies led some to think that they were superficial Catholics, this was not the case, and those who made this error confused syncretism with missionary adaptation. Native participation in these ceremonies was actually an indication of the Church's tolerant attitude at this time towards indigenous cultures that were not antagonistic to the Catholic faith.[8]

By avoiding the white-centered forms of religious and cultural compliance that characterized many Protestant and government efforts, these four schools evangelized large segments of the tribe, enjoyed an unusual level of support among the Indians, and were able to execute their mission effectively.

Creating a middle ground and executing the religious mission of these schools was the work of the Grey Nuns, Benedictine Sisters, and Franciscan Sisters. With few exceptions, the sisters were recent arrivals from French Canada (Grey Nuns) and Germany (Benedictines and Franciscans). These immigrant sisters were called upon to become "westering women" who carried the beliefs and structures of Catholicism and formal education to various Sioux bands in Dakota Territory. Unlike teachers who worked at government and Protestant schools, these women faced the dual task of adjusting to a foreign culture as well as implementing a program of Americanization at their schools. This challenge, particularly apparent among the Grey Nuns and Benedictine Sisters, resulted in boarding school environments that reflected Indian, American, and European cultures.

Since immigrants or second-generation Americans staffed all four schools, the process instituted to assimilate the Indians was less radical and more culturally sensitive than efforts at other Indian schools. By the mid-1880s the pathways to American identity were clearly articulated: formal education, rigid separation of students from the larger Indian population, exclusive use of English, inculcation of a patriotic spirit, and a total repression of tribal practices and culture. The immigrant experience of the sisters argued against this abrupt transformation, favoring instead a gradual and moderate approach that would result in cultural accommodation. The sisters learned the Sioux language, allowed the students to participate in important tribal events, tacitly endorsed biculturalism, and permitted Indian adults to visit the schools. Since the four institutions were on-reservation boarding schools staffed by immigrant women, accommodation, as opposed to assimilation and acculturation, was the method favored by the missionaries. Since the sisters did not impose a system of forced assimilation, they avoided the rejection and conflict that affected other schools and were able to cultivate a healthy creative exchange that generated positive feelings between the Indians and the sisters.[9]

In nearly all respects the sisters who opened these schools and worked at creating a middle ground with the Indians resembled the stereotypes of women on the western frontier: "The Madonna of the Prairie," the submissive dove, and the "Goddess of the Schoolbook." While none of these descriptions were completely inaccurate, the religious sisters who went to Dakota Territory were too complex to be represented in a cultural bromide. These women negotiated contracts, built schools and developed curricula, made their own decisions, and were relatively independent of male dominance. By committing themselves to the vow of chastity, focusing on a particular work, and pooling their financial and intellectual resources, these sisters "were among the most publicly active of the late nineteenth- and early twentieth-century women. In many ways women religious had freedoms unknown to most other nineteenth-century women."[10] Very few "westering" women built thriving educational institutions, negotiated various federal imbroglios, moved freely among the Sioux and their leaders, experienced tribal uprisings, or responded courageously to fire and pestilence.[11] This was, however, the legacy of the Grey Nuns, Benedictines, and Franciscans who staffed these schools and epitomized the spirit of the frontier.

Catholic Boarding Schools and Frontier Catholicism

These religious women were part of a vanguard that transplanted Roman Catholicism to the American frontier in the late nineteenth century. In 1943, Father Thomas T. McAvoy, CSC, (reasserted more recently by Brother Tomas Spalding, C.F.X.), outlined five tendencies in American Catholicism that were products of the "frontier"[12] and which were institutional dynamics at these schools:

1. *An inclination to downplay doctrinal differences between Catholic and non-Catholic*—There were many parallels between Indian religious ideas and the practices of Roman Catholicism that emerged at the four boarding schools. By way of example, a young girl died at Fort Totten in 1877 and her pagan parents were comfortable with the actions of the sisters because "prayers over the dying, dressing the dead in fine attire, and ceremonies to mark the passage between this life and the next were common elements of both Catholic and Indian religious practice."[13]
2. *A self-directed individualism that had small need for external direction*—During the Ghost Dance of 1890, William "Buffalo Bill" Cody arrived at Fort Yates to arrest Sitting Bull and conflict was imminent. Sister Gertrude McDermott, superior of the Fort Yates Industrial School, took it upon herself to visit the Sioux leader in an unsuccessful effort to defuse a volatile situation.[14]
3. *A ready acceptance of the natural and active virtues that were part of the American scene*—The sisters who conducted the four boarding schools embraced the frontier virtues of aggressiveness and political

astuteness. At Fort Totten the sisters secured the removal of an unacceptable Indian agent and those working at Saint Francis and Holy Rosary negotiated *a thicket* when Thomas Jefferson Morgan, a rabid anti-Catholic, became Commissioner of Indian Affairs in 1889 and proposed the elimination of federal monies to denominational boarding schools.

4. *An inclination of vowed religious toward a more active life*—After arriving at Fort Totten, "not having horse or carriage, the Sisters remained at home busily working. However, some of the Indians complained to an [Indian Bureau] employee at the Fort, saying: 'The black robe and women of prayer are here for us. Our children are sick and dying, still no one comes to see them.' In a few days a carriage was offered by the Fort, and two sisters began to visit the homes accompanied by an interpreter."[15]

5. *A modification of the liturgical and devotional practices that differentiated Catholic from Protestant*—All four schools used Father Albert Lacombe's *The Two Roads*, which communicated the tenets of Catholicism in a metaphor familiar to the Sioux Indians—both pictures and the idea of a road emerge in many native stories about their history and culture.[16] The willingness to attach Catholic beliefs to existing cultural practices is a hallmark Catholic missiology and the most obvious difference between Catholic and Protestant approaches to the Native American apostolate.

McAvoy, and later Thomas Spalding, argue that these tendencies contributed to the Americanist crisis that shook the Catholic Church at the beginning of the twentieth century. When these characteristics are analyzed within the geographic context of Dakota Territory in the late nineteenth and early twentieth centuries at four Catholic Indian boarding schools, concrete manifestations of "frontier" Catholicism emerge.

The other distinctions attributed to "frontier" Catholicism—self-directed individualism, acceptance of active and natural virtues, and the inclination to activity by vowed religious—were present among the Grey Nuns, Benedictines, and Franciscans. The sisters came to the frontier with broad directives to establish schools. However, with the exception of canonical visitations, they were left to their own devices when it came to practical modifications of conventual rules and the day-to-day operations of these institutions. In large measure, the women selected to operate these institutions, especially the foundresses, were self-directed individuals who instilled this spirit among the sisters who worked for them. There was ample opportunity for all four schools to fail and the sisters to return to their motherhouses—yet missionary zeal, practical leadership, and communal cooperation overcame many obstacles and contributed to the growth and success of these institutions.

While the religious staff at all four schools were cognizant of Church doctrine and attempted to avoid the worst dangers of syncretism, a good deal of devotional and liturgical accommodation took place to appeal to Indian sensibilities. The Catholic Sioux Congress was started in 1890, which allowed the Sioux to demonstrate their religious unity; the Saint Mary and Saint Joseph Societies allowed the Sioux to harmonize Catholic devotional practices with Indian traditions; and Indian music, dances, and customs were blended with the sacred mysteries of Catholicism. The devotional and liturgical life at all four schools reflected the doctrines of Catholicism, the ethnic traditions of the missionaries, and the vitality of Sioux traditions and culture. Newcomers to Indian missionary work were immediately struck by the differences between Eurocentric Catholicism and Sioux Catholic expressions of faith.

Biculturalism

Accommodation was important at the four schools because the medicine men and traditional Sioux religion still held sway. The missionaries wanted to convert a large segment of the tribe. These on-reservation schools could not escape Indian culture, since the students came directly from the "camps" infused with a healthy cultural identity. These practices are examples of the downplaying of doctrinal differences and modification of religious expression.

Practicality, self-direction, and frontier conditions convinced the sisters that many of their conventual norms were not suitable on the Indian frontier. In order to gain the support of the adult Indians for the boarding schools, to attend to the sick and dying, and to win adult converts, the sisters traveled frequently, remained overnight in the Indian camps, and used their own discretion to respond to the conditions they encountered. There were very few American sisters in the late nineteenth and early twentieth centuries who enjoyed the independence of Sister Lajemmcrais Chenier at Fort Totten, Sister Gertrude McDermott at Fort Yates, or Sister Kostka Schlaghecken at Saint Francis and Holy Rosary. These pioneers set a standard, which was adopted by many of the sisters who ministered on the reservations. The sisters' willingness to adapt to conditions on the reservations enhanced the success of the boarding schools, earned the respect of the Indians, and provided a healthy balance between independence and communal responsibilities. The communal spirit enabled the sisters to help each other adjust to the new environment,

> endure the hardships of isolation, to persevere in the face of the harsh reality of life on the frontier. Even when circumstances forced the sisters to modify their rules for living, they persisted in structuring their lives around the welfare of the group.[17]

This characteristic separated the efforts at Fort Totten, Fort Yates, Saint Francis, and Holy Rosary Missions from other on-reservation school environments and the governing philosophy of Protestant and government schools among the Indians.

The sisters who established these schools, while cultivating a middle ground between the structures of assimilation and Sioux culture, and exhibiting many of the positive characteristics associated with "frontier Catholicism," represented one side of boarding school life, while the Indians who attended these schools represented the other. The students who attended these four boarding schools faced a variety of cultural challenges that were negotiated through a process best described as selective accommodation. A lifestyle governed by regular schedules, indoor activities, and a steady regimen of labor was contrary to traditional cultural patterns among the Sioux Indians. While the students at these schools visibly absorbed the dictates of assimilation, at a deeper level they retained and cultivated many cherished Sioux traditions. The presence of a strong system of peer support, the close proximity of the schools to the centers of Indian culture, and the practice of harmonizing the Catholic faith with local culture preserved Sioux identity and fostered selective accommodation.

> Reformers could not anticipate that many students caught between the contesting claims of native and white outlooks, were not prepared to abandon one in the process of acquiring the other, that just as an assimilationist education might win converts to white civilization, so it was just as likely to produce the bicultural personality.[18]

The active participation of the Indian students in their cultural formation and the middle ground that existed at the four boarding schools produced a bicultural school identity.

The tacit acceptance of a bicultural identity was, in part, a cause for the positive response that these schools experienced throughout their institutional existence. There were many examples at all four schools where the school leaders permitted students to return to their camps for important cultural events, allowed parents to participate in the life of the boarding schools, and accepted an indigenized environment among their students. Sitting Bull (Standing Rock), Chief Red Cloud (Pine Ridge), and Chief Waanatan (Devils Lake) were very supportive of these schools and were utilized by school officials to encourage the students and to advance the mission of education. This type of interaction was not encouraged at most Indian schools because the presence of Indian culture went against official policy and was viewed as antithetical to civilization and education.

Conclusion

Between the implementation of Grant's Peace Policy and the publication of *The Problem of Indian Administration*, Indian culture underwent a major transformation and the role of Indian boarding schools changed accordingly. By the mid-1920s the Sioux Indians in North and South Dakota were interacting with a growing white population, transacting business outside the reservation, and attending public educational institutions up to the college level. Given these cultural changes, Saint Francis and Holy Rosary Missions were in a position to assume a degree of cultural resonance because they served only Sioux Indian students. During the

Indian New Deal, however, both boarding schools were exposed to increasing criticism by certain segments of the Indian population. On the one hand, Indian cultural decline, doubts about the efficacy of Indian boarding schools, and efforts to rekindle Indian culture contributed to this change in viewpoint. On the other hand, the sisters who were assigned to these missions according to the tradition of their community may have lacked the zeal for Indian education, were caught between the labor demands of running a boarding school and the regulations of convent life, and were unable to broker a middle ground. All of these factors contributed to the criticism leveled against Catholic Indian boarding schools after 1920.

In short, the era of widespread Catholic-Indian support and cooperation came to a close after the *Meriam Investigation* highlighted the shortcomings and problems of Federal-Indian policy and rejected the policy of total assimilation in 1928.

Notes

1. An earlier version of the paper—"Plains Indian Education: The Catholic Perspective"—was presented at the Circles of Knowledge—Plains Indian Education Conference, Buffalo Bill Historical Center, Cody, Wyoming, September 29, 2001. This paper benefits from the comments and rich discussion that occurred at that conference. In addition, notes and citations have been updated to include recent historiography on the topic.

2. The policy of assigning Indian reservations to specific religious denominations was the official policy in Canada and the United States between 1870 and 1900.

3. See James T. Carroll, *Seeds of Faith: Catholic Indian Boarding Schools* (Garland 2000) for a full treatment of this topic.

4. Richard White, *The Middle Ground: Indians, Empires, and Republics in the Great Lakes Region, 1650-1815* (New York: Cambridge University Press, 1991), 52. In White's argument, cultural accommodation was a "bridge" to the middle ground. For a more recent account of the middle ground that includes the place of women in native societies and the central role of Catholic kin networks in Indian-white relations see Susan Sleeper-Smith, *Indian Women and French Women: Rethinking Cultural Encounter in the Western Great Lakes* (Amherst: University of Massachusetts Press, 2001).

5. Ross Enochs, *The Jesuit Mission to the Lakota Sioux* (Kansas City: Sheed and Ward, 1996), 104.

6. George Jennings, "The American Indian Ethos: A Key for Christian Missions?" *Missiology: An International Review* 5 (October 1977): 490. For additional consideration of church-Indian relations see C. L. Higham, *Noble, Wretched, and Redeemable: Protestant Missionaries to the Indians in Canada and the United States, 1820-1900* (Albuquerque: University of New Mexico Press, 2000); Mary Cochran, *Dakota Cross-Bearer: The Life and World of a Native American Bishop* (Lincoln: University of Nebraska Press, 2000), and Robert Kapitzke, *Religion, Power, and Politics in Colonial Saint Augustine* (Tallahassee: University Press of Florida, 2001).

7. This refers to Father Alfred Lacombe's "Catholic Ladder," a pictorial catechism developed in 1865 where two roads are presented to the neophytes: the Catholic road leading to heaven and the (presumably) Protestant road which ends in hell. This small masterpiece of pedagogy was present at virtually every Catholic Indian mission in Canada and the United States.

8. Enochs, *The Jesuit Mission to the Lakota Sioux*, 136.

9. See Edward P. Dozier, "Forced and Permissive Acculturation," *The American Indian* 7 (Spring 1955): 38-44 for a brief discussion of the implications of forceful patterns of assimilation.

10. Carol Coburn and Martha Smith, "Creating Community and Identity: Explaining Religious and Gender Ideology in the Lives of American Women Religious, 1836-1920," *U.S. Catholic Historian* 14 (1996): 104. See also their full-length treatment *Spirited Lives: How Nuns Shaped Catholic Culture and American Life*, 1836-1920 (Winston-Salem: University of North Carolina Press, 1999).

11. For specific references to the role of women on the frontier see Glenda Riley, *Women and Indians on the Frontier, 1825-1915* (Albuquerque: University of New Mexico Press, 1984) and *The Female Frontier: A Comparative View of Women on the Prairie and the Plains* (Lawrence: University of Kansas Press, 1988).

12. Thomas McAvoy, C.S.C., "Americanism and Frontier Catholicism," *Review of Politics* 5 (1943): 292-301 quoted in Thomas W. Spalding, C. F. X., "Frontier Catholicism," *Catholic Historical Review* 77 (July 1991): 474. For a full analysis of this topic see Anne Butler, Michael Engh, and Thomas Spalding (ed.), (Maryknoll, NY: Orbis Press 2000).

13. "Excerpts from the Grey Nuns Annals," 7, Archives Diocese of Fargo.

14. "A Short Sketch of Mother Gertrude," Archives Sacred Heart Monastery, Yankton, South Dakota.

15. "Excerpts from the Grey Nuns Annals," Grey Nuns Annals Folder, 3, Archives Diocese of Fargo.

16. Francis Paul Prucha, "Two Roads to Conversion: Protestant and Catholic Missionaries in the Northwest," *Pacific Northwest Quarterly* 79 (1988): 133.

17. Susan Peterson, "A Widening Horizon: Catholic Sisterhoods on the Northern Plains, 1874-1910," *Great Plains Quarterly* 5 (1985): 131.

18. David Wallace Adams, *Education for Extinction: American Indians and the Boarding School Experience, 1875-1928* (Lawrence: University Press of Kansas, 1995), 301.

Chapter 17

Catholic Insight on Workplace Human Rights and Corporate Humanism

Michele Simms

nvironmentalism. Globalization. Biotechnology. Bioterrorism. The issues of the day form a dialectic and taken together invite age-old questions of what it means to be human, and what forms and informs humanity. By extension, these issues invite questions about what constitutes ethical business practice and the evolving role of corporate social responsibility.

Questions prompted by this dialectic crystallize the issues of morality and justice and "every issue of morality and justice is an issue of the person."[1] Any discussion about environmentalism, globalization, biotechnology-terrorism is about human value. Since all "human lives are situated within broader structures of meaning,"[2] of specific time, space, and history, the task is to articulate those structures, to give and find meaning. The business enterprise is no exception to this quest where work itself is the "essential expression of the person"[3] and the "business enterprise economy is at the root of human freedom with and orientation toward the common good."[4]

This chapter presents the relationship between Catholic thought and business practice. It utilizes the encyclicals as support for human rights, a trend in business that forms a humanistic framework grounded in the social teachings of the Catholic Church. Specifically, part I introduces the encyclicals and outlines how Catholic thought informs levels of substance and process. Given this context, part II identifies the practices of workplace human rights and its corresponding relationship to corporate humanism.

Background and Role of the Catholic Encyclicals

Catholic social doctrine is comprised of official teachings on the economic and political dimensions of the social order. These doctrines were formalized during Pope Leo XIII's reign at the end of the nineteenth century. It was the Pope's encyclical *Rerum Novarum* ("The Condition of Labor," 1891) that initiated the Catholic Church's articulation of a systematic theology of social justice.

Catholic social doctrine provides a broad theological and philosophical framework of social analysis developed in three stages. Stage one was a response to problems posed by the industrial revolution. The key texts are Leo XIII's *Rerum Novarum* and Pope Pius X's *Quadragesimo Anno* ("Reconstructing the Pope Social Order," 1931). The key issues addressed are government's role in society and the economy, labor's right to organize, just wages, and a Christian critique of capitalism and socialism.

Stage two emerged during World War II and continues to the present. It is a response to the internationalization of life. The key issues addressed involve the growing material interdependence of the world and the identification of a moral framework for addressing the political, strategic, and economic issues facing all of humanity. Examples of key texts, although not used in this analysis, are Pope John XXIII's *Mater et Magistra* ("Christianity and Social Progress," 1961); *Pacem in Terris* ("Peace on Earth," 1963), the Second Vatican Council's *Pastoral Constitution on the Church in the Modern World* (*Gaudium et spes*, 1965), and the Synod of Bishops' *Justice in the World* (*Iustitia in mundo*, 1971).

Stage three is the response to new social questions posed by technology in post-industrial societies. The key text is Pope Paul VI's *Octagesima Adveniens* ("The Eightieth Year," 1971) that introduces new social questions about how post-industrial and developing societies are internationally related and how new forms of organization and intelligence seek to legitimate social and political orders. Pope John Paul II's *Laborem Exercens* ("On Human Work," 1981) and *Centesimus Annus* ("The Hundreth Year," 1991) are integral to this stage.

Critical to this analysis are two of the moral demands of Catholic social doctrine. The first is the dignity of the human person, created in the image of God with human rights and duties that protect and enhance this dignity. The second moral demand is concern for the common good: the social nature of humanity and the nature of the relationship between the state and society (i.e., concerns with solidarity and socialization), and with voluntary associations (i.e., labor unions).

Catholic social doctrine provided by the Magesterium is rich in content, substance, and history. The four encyclicals used in this analysis—On Human Work: *Laborem Exercens* (1981); On the Hundreth Anniversary of *Rerum Novarum: Centesimus Annus* (1991); On Reconstruction of the Social Order: *Quadragesimo*

Anno (1931); and On Capital and Labor: *Rerum Novarum* (1891)—illuminate ap-proaches to addressing contemporary business practice by providing direction at a substantive and at a process level.

In regard to *substance*, the encyclicals inform on four levels:

1. *On Being a Person*—A consistent theme of the Church's social doc-trine is a "correct view of the human person and of his unique value."[5] The primacy of the person connects and reinforces John Paul's distinc-tion between the objective and subjective meanings of work. The objec-tive meaning of work relates to productive action, including the tech-nology of production and its outcomes; the subjective meaning of work expresses and embodies the worker as person,[6] whose rights "flow from his essential dignity as a person."[7]

2. *Person-to-Work Link*—The encyclicals establish the universal relation-ship between the person and his/her work. Labor and capital are "in-separably linked"[8] and *together* become the link to the greater good.

3. *Social Connection/Life Ethic*—The Church helps order social relation-ships and responsibilities. Cardinal Bernardin identifies five "bedrock" convictions or fundamentals that are consistent with a life ethic (as noted in Part II).

4. *Corporate Humanism and Human Rights*—Corporate moral agency requires the "work-contract be modified by a partnership-contract."[9] This partnering extends to multinational corporations "with a united purpose and effort to promote by wisely conceived pacts and institu-tions a prosperous and happy international cooperation in economic life."[10] Human rights flow from work "as part of the broader context of those fundamental rights of the person."[11]

In regard to *process*, the encyclicals inform on three levels:

1. *Dialogue*—The call for dialogue as a specific form of communication with others that teaches about one's self, about God, and all of human life, goes beyond tolerance and respect. The goal of dialogue is to collectively define common goods: "then only will true cooperation be possible for a single common good when the constituent parts of soci-ety deeply feel themselves members of one great family and children—that they are one body."[12]

2. *Dialectical Relationship*—Moral theology that offers a way to deter-mine how to live and what to do—is an essential part of integrating theory and practice in a dialectical relationship between the divine and the human. The process of a dialectic offers the perspective of *kairos* which signifies a "right" or special time when important things are immi-nent or already occurring. By framing 'new social questions' as *kairos* allows a way for the dialectic—the human and divine—to emerge in a mutual response.

3. *Praxis Cycle of Faith Reflection*—The model of action-reflection combined with social analysis that forms the praxis cycle provides a method
and a framework for approaching ethics in today's business environment. The cycle is part of the dialectic that frames the *kairos* perspective.[13]

This is most significant. A *kairos* perspective: (1) places business in a humanistic framework. Listening and seeing through the eyes of others promotes the role
of business as a society of persons which is part of corporate moral agency; (2) is
a call to organizational conversion; (3) primes business to create structures of
meaning that address structural concerns; and (4) as a construct associated with
liberation theology, "it is not merely the shape of a particular social institution and
structures that must be analyzed but the shape of the entire age or epoch."[14]
The interdependent relationship between globalization and environmentalism,
with the attending issues of biotechnology and bioterrorism, comprise the social
order that influences contemporary business practices and corporate social responsibility. The depth and breadth of what Catholic social teaching offers to
business practice today cannot be underestimated.

Globalization, Environmentalism, Bioterrorism, and Biotechnology

Mahoney describes globalization as economic growth and dislocation whose impact on the worker results in "three economies living side-by-side."[15] The first
economy workforce is prospering in the information and global age. Second economy
individuals are doing "well by some measure but are squeezed" with increasing
health and education costs, and declining incomes. The third economy "touches a
substantial number of people," left without access and/or training for the "new
economy."[16] The global workplace has renewed the focus on the worker by surfac-
ing sweatshop and labor issues of the 1990s that continue today. Globalization
makes corporate citizenship an international concern and progressive global businesses realize the "shared bottom-line" that comes from partnering with all stakeholders.
With the impact of economic globalization, the profound connection between
the issues of ecology and social issues are emerging,[17] implying that environmental
problems, at their root, are social problems.[18] Environmental issues are broadly
categorized as those that pose threats to public health not answerable by medicine.
These include, but are not limited to, chemical hazards in workplaces, polluted air
and water in residential communities, contaminated food in supermarkets and res-
taurants, and the spread of infectious diseases by people, animals, and food. An
increasing public awareness of and focus on sustainability of the earth is a major
development and trend that is a part of environmentalism. The "cry of the earth is
the cry of the poor; there is no true separation between how we support life economically and ecologically."[19]

The events of September 11 shifted the focus from the broad public health agenda to bioterrorism: the release of biological agents and toxins "to terrorize a civilian population or manipulate a government."[20] Advances in biotechnology and easy access to necessary equipment and material to establish labs, make biological agents "attractive weapons for terrorists."[21] Whether the risk of a major attack is high or low, bioterrorism has its psychological impact. Covert dissemination of a biological agent in a public place (i.e., chemical agents disseminated through contaminated food and water) will not have immediate impact due to the delay between exposure and illness where "day after relentless day, additional cases could be expected, and in new areas."[22] Every act of bioterrorism cannot be prevented. This reality is juxtaposed with a time when biotechnology offers the "promise of control" through reproductive technologies, cloning, DNA banks, and genetic engineering.

To this end, biotechnology stands to redefine persons by fostering feelings of invincibility and immortality. Yet the very advances in biotechnology contribute to the reality of bioterrorism. The two together evoke international and global concern that portends broad environmental consequences while requiring a local, community response of which the business enterprise is a part.

The intricate web between the environment and globalization serves as a backdrop to the role of biotechnology and bioterrorism and surfaces the tensions of today's "age" or "epoch." Taken together, they contribute to the shift from worker rights to civil rights to human rights. In Jungian terms, it is part of the soul/image work that is done individually and collectively.[23] It is what Werhane cites as the method of moral imagination.[24] Greenleaf offers the model of servant leadership for changing systems by tapping into the human condition.[25] In referencing the Catholic Encyclicals, such ethical concerns are grounded in the Catholic tradition of virtue, obligation, and mutual responsibility extended into notions of human rights.

Workplace Human Rights and Corporate Humanism

The "universal destination" of the earth's goods assumes the relationship that through work, a person uses intelligence and freedom but not just for herself/ himself. "Whoever has received from the divine bounty a large share of temporal blessings, whether they be external and material, or gifts of the mind, has received them for the purpose of using them for the perfecting of his own nature, and at the same time, that he may employ them, as the steward of God's providence, for the benefit of others."[26] The role of the Church, itself an international institution, "is to raise up the dignity and value of all workers and to seek universal human progress . . . by raising the moral and human dimensions of issues in an ever-changing workplace."[27] How the Church helps order social relationships and responsibilities rests on what Bernardin identifies as five "bedrock" convictions or fundamentals that are consistent with a life ethic in the broadest context:[28]

1. There are basic goods and values humans share through the gift of life and such goods and values serve as a common ground for public morality.
2. These goods and values express an inalienable human dignity with corresponding rights and duties for each individual.
3. Rights and duties form within the individual human community as "recognition and pursuit" of the common good: "a good to be pursued in common with all society; a good that is ultimately more important than the good of any individual."
4. This good is actualized in living community which itself becomes a form of protection for the individual.
5. As part of this community, both individuals and institutions (including government, business, education, labor, and other mediating structures) have "an *obligation* which is rooted in distributive justice to *work to pursue this common good*; this is how we go about meeting the reasonable claims of citizens striving to realize and experience their fundamental human dignity."

What does this imply for business specifically? The themes of personhood, community, and common good, subsumed under mutual, reciprocal, and open systems, converge into a different structure of meaning. What is pursued are "institutions in which spiritual development and economic benefit are happily combined"[29] to fulfill the impetus behind *Rerum Novarum*: to "adjust this economic system according to the norms of right order."[30] Church teaching moves us away from the polarization of labor and capital and rather suggests there is a right relationship and social order assuming "managerial ability that foresees accurately human needs and that organizes others to work together to satisfy those needs."[31]

The notion of rights, then, is not an isolated event discussed in the context of the individual. Rather, it comes out of this notion of corporations/businesses as open systems attentive to the person; as corporate moral agency and human (person) rights.

Rights as Context

Worker/workplace rights emerge from two obvious premises. First, businesses function in part because there are employees/people to do the work. Employee rights, although constitutionally guaranteed, are not universally honored in business. Some of the "absence of legal rights in the workplace is paralleled with the absence of recognition that these rights are moral rights and as such should be honored with or without legal mandate."[32] Second, persons create the business world— business activity, as the Church states, has impact on the lives of people beyond their borders and therefore has moral obligations.

A moral right (or a natural right) is a right that is neither conventional nor institutional. Such rights cannot be created or conveyed, as they are endowed rights by virtue of being human. Moral rights include equal consideration, security and subsistence, life and the right not to be tortured, freedom of choice, action and privacy, and private ownership. (These are in contrast to constitutionally and/or legislatively based U.S. employee rights to due process, freedom, privacy, safe working conditions, fair pay, participation, and meaningful work.) Moral rights are called human rights and are distinct from legal rights; although conferred on all humans they are not necessarily respected nor acknowledged. Human rights are rights all possess despite particular customs and laws but are not necessarily universally recognized, honored, or practiced.

Corporate moral agency[33] is a construct to describe those corporations that acknowledge the premises of natural rights or human rights in the workplace. The posture of corporate moral agency views the corporation as a "distinct functional entity with a deliberate disposition to do something in a certain way or to realize a certain state of affairs."[34] It requires corporate intentionality: an act that "involves both beliefs and desires and a self-conscious tendency to act in a certain way to realize an outcome based on these beliefs and desires."[35] With this view, the corporation becomes an intentional system; it is more than an individual behavioral action of intent.

Further, as a moral agent, the corporation "may ascribe secondary moral agency."[36] A corporation functions as a result of the individual action that occurs but the corporation is not simply an aggregate of individual actions—it is something more (in the same way a person is not merely a collection of images). It is an outcome of group choices and decision-making by individual actions on behalf of the corporation—this is what Werhane proscribes as secondary action and therefore secondary moral agency—but moral agency none the less. Because such actions are secondary does not mean they are less than, and therefore by extension less than responsible if they were, in fact, acting as individuals. Further, although secondary actions are collective they still originate in actions of persons and can be actions that are either moral or immoral.

Corporate moral agency requires the "work-contract be modified by a partnership-contract"[37] and that this partnering extend to multinational corporations "with a united purpose and effort to promote widely conceived pacts and institutions as prosperous and happy international cooperation in economic life."[38] This is cited as well in *Centesimus Annus*, in which Pope John Paul II recognizes multi-national corporations as partners in an ethic of developmental responsibility. Perhaps it is through corporate moral agency that business joins those "who, understanding what the times require have striven . . . to better the condition of the working class by rightful means . . . [to] better the condition both of families and individuals; to infuse a spirit of equity into the mutual relations of employers and the employed . . . and [to] enable them to obtain fitting and profitable employment."[39]

Corporate moral agency appears to follow a natural law perspective where "business enterprises are morally justified—indeed, they are morally praiseworthy—to the extent that the products and services business enterprises provide promote the fundamental goods that fulfill human nature."[40] This stands in sharp contrast to structures that alienate

> [which] happens in consumerism, when people are ensnared in a web of false and superficial gratifications rather than being helped to experience their personhood presented in an authentic and concrete way. Alienation is found also in work, when it is organized so as to ensure maximum returns and profits with no concern whether the worker, through his own labor, grows or diminishes as a person, either through increased sharing in a genuinely supportive community or through increased isolation in a maze of relationships marked by destructive competitiveness [41]

Market-justice forces also contribute to this alienation that emphasizes "individual responsibility, minimal collective action and freedom from collective obligations except to respect other person's fundamental rights."[42]

This is viewed as a particular challenge: creating a sustainable new vision of economic justice and corporate social responsibility adequate to the challenges of the emerging global economy.[43] Required are intentional structures and structures of meaning bringing together corporate moral agency and the person.

Intentional Structures/Structures of Meaning

What might these structures look like? Part of the structures are outlined in *Rerum Novarum*:

> duties that bind; not to look upon their work people as their bondsmen, but to respect in every man his dignity as a person ennobled by Christian character . . . to misuse men as . . . things in pursuit of gain, or to value solely for their physical powers—that is truly shameful and inhuman; religion and the good of his soul must be kept in mind . . . his great and principal duty is to give every one what is just.[44]

In *Laborem Exercens*, Pope John Paul II speaks of the organization of work into right relationships and meaningful structures so that wages and other social benefits (rest, health benefits, pension, and insurance) are included.[45] In this way, the organizational ethic, as the "articulation, application, and evaluation of the consistent values and moral positions of an organization by which it is defined, both internally and externally"[46] reflects the corporate structure.

Including an integrated aspect of corporate moral agency while respecting human rights and dignity is a form of total ethics management.[47] This management philosophy views organizations as open systems comprised of fiduciary relationships.[48] By functioning as moral agents, corporations can intentionally create ethical climates, which parallel the notion of "individual character." This brings the theological foundations to business ethics and forms corporate humanistic models.[49]

Further, ethical climate itself gets defined relative to the relationships in which the organization is embedded politically, socially, economically, and religiously. "No organization or institution is morally self-contained."[50] The goal is to collectively define common goods and "then only will true cooperation be possible for a single common good when the constituent parts of society deeply feel themselves members of one great family."[51] In fact, the whole act or process of defining "common good" is a good: it provides a framework and an opportunity for the "inner life" and meaning of a company to emerge.

Corporate moral agency, the correct view of the person and work's product as common good, are not new principles. Rather, they inform and reinstate the deeply human aspects of rights and responsibilities in business practice. By placing these principles in the context of the times, biotechnology and bioterrorism can be viewed as less chronological historical fact and more as the *kairos* that propels business to a human rights focus and a reengagement of humanistic organizational systems.

Models and Links:
From Worker to Civil to Human Rights in Business

Rerum Novarum explicitly states the worker condition as the social question tied to nineteenth-century events. With the advent of the industrial revolution, worker rights emerged in this country and were adopted through statutory protections circa 1935-1981.[52] Simultaneous to the emergence of worker and civil rights was an emerging consciousness of human rights. The Universal Declaration of Human Rights was formalized by the United Nations General Assembly and adopted in 1948 to establish an International Bill of Rights following World War II. Its genesis is linked to a 1941 radio address by Pope Pius XII calling "for an international bill recognizing the rights that flowed from the dignity of the person."[53] The United Nations established a Human Rights Commission composed of members from eighteen countries, chaired by Eleanor Roosevelt and spearheaded by a group of American nongovernmental organizations (NGOs). The framers of the Declaration pulled from many sources, to be sure, but clearly a Catholic presence is felt.

There is a pervasive emphasis on the person as manifest in the language of "inherent dignity" and "worth of the human person"; affirming the human person "endowed with reason and conscience"; the right to form trade unions and associations; rights to remuneration for the person and his/her family; the family as "the natural and fundamental group unit of society" entitled to "protection by society and the state;" a priori rights of parents to choose their children's education and a provision for special care and assistance for women and children." Many of these ideas about family, work, civil society, and the dignity of the person are taken from the encyclicals *Rerum Novarum* and *Quadragesimo Anno* and reinforced as the "lively attention to and concern for human rights" in *Centesimus Annus*.[54]

Catholic teaching and perspective look at certain common goods as rights. Everything the Church says about human rights has its foundation in the dignity of the person made in the image of God. The Church teaches solidarity not as a policy but as a virtue requiring personal reform; that universality does not mean homogeneity; and the Holy See "consistently lifts up the original vision of the Declaration—a vision in which political and civil rights are indispensable for social and economic justice and vice versa."[55] The worker movement itself is part of what the Church sees as a general movement "among workers and other people of good will for the liberation of the human person for the affirmation of human rights."[56] Such development must always be understood not solely in economic terms but in a way that is "fully human."[57]

The Church continues that "ultimately a correct understanding of the dignity and rights of the person"[58] and "the human rights that flow from work are part of the broader context of those fundamental rights of the person."[59] This is what Mele calls structural needs: what every person needs to achieve human development through humane living; true knowledge; and proper relationships with others, God, environment, and self. All "structural needs are human rights."[60]

Business and Human Rights

Hence, it seems fitting that a convergence of business practice with human rights would occur. In the first four decades, following the adoption of the Universal Declaration of Human Rights, the Cold War was the central political framework for viewing the world. Human rights were considered a state issue requiring state action; the private sector was not involved. With the Cold War effectively at an end, the world perspective has shifted and the debate concerning human rights has become a clear concern of business. Three historical events explain the evolving relationship between business and human rights: the environmental movement, which surfaced issues of nuclear proliferation, sweatshop, and labor issues; the emergence of a global society; and the human rights movement itself identifying "multinational companies as the most powerful nonstate actors in the world."[61]

These trends result in businesses recognizing their impact on individuals, communities, and the environment:

> It is clear that one of the central measures of a company's social responsibility is its respect for human rights. And while most companies recognize the moral imperative to operate consistent with human rights principles, recognition is growing that respect for human rights also can be a tool for improving business performance.[62]

Businesses incorporating a human rights perspective take on many forms. These include public acknowledgment of responsibility for human rights (by such companies as Royal Dutch Shell and Novo Nordisk); pilot projects; institutionalizing efforts through board level oversight and human rights training; and projects sponsored and partnered on ethical trading, fair labor practices, and efforts to maximize personal and economic development for workers in the global supply market.

Back to *Rerum Novarum*: New Reform, New Things

What is also emerging from individual efforts is the movement to working collaboratively on these issues. Private sector collaboration is occurring (i.e., business organizations provide tools and assistance to enhance awareness and develop the skills and relationships needed to address human rights issues effectively). Companies are developing reporting and verification measures crossnationally (Novo Nordisk). Companies based in developing countries focus on community development and social infrastructure as human rights (The Tata Group and Levi-Strauss). Several promote a human rights agenda by educating the public on such issues (Bennington and Reebok).

Note that several of these initiatives are cross-sector partnerships. They involve nongovernmental organizations working with private corporations, religious efforts teaming with business efforts as new ways to collaborate and cooperate, and community development and social infrastructure being tied to economic gain. Having a human rights perspective at the core with focus on the individual and the larger system, constitutes the essence of corporate humanism.

In many ways, one could read these initiatives as coming from *Rerum Novarum*. Businesses must attend to principles that directly affect the worker and the company's public and private business partners. The "condition of the worker" impacts the community and environment in which the business operates. Finally, businesses as well as public institutions involve the care and concern for individual human rights, the environment, and the community.

Conclusion

This paper presents the salience of Catholic insight in today's business environment. The focus on the person is deliberately chosen to view the emerging practice between business and human rights. By extension, corporate moral agency provides a way of creating a humanistic approach.

Regardless of all differences, one thing is certain: "the moral world is grounded in the reality of the person."[63] And what "we" may lose sight of in the day-to-day practice of living, and making a living, is that of which Catholic tradition serves to remind us:

> A business cannot be considered only as a society of capital goods; it is also a society of persons in which people participate in different ways and with specific responsibilities. To achieve these goals there is still need for a broad associated worker's movement, directed towards the liberation and protection of the whole person.[64]

The Catholic encyclicals offer both substance and a process to guide and support workplace human rights and corporate humanistic approaches as models of business practice. Understanding Catholic social teaching helps place the business community in the correct posture of humility, interdependence, and anticipation, as both inclusive and intentional. It allows for a right relationship to those whom the business community ultimately serves, always with the correct view of the person.

Notes

1. John Kavanaugh, *Who Count as Persons?* (Washington D.C.: Georgetown University Press, 2001), 21.
2. Carl Elliott, *Bioethics, Culture and Identity: A Philosophical Disease* (New York: Routledge, 1999), xxxv.
3. John Verstraeten, Michael Naughton and Simona Betetta, "Work as Key to the Social Question: The Great Social and Economic Transformations and the Subjective Dimensions of Work," *Conference Background Paper* 2001, http://www.stthomas.edu/cathstudies/cst/mgmt/le/background.htm (15 Dec. 2001).
4. Domenec Mele, "A Humanistic Framework For The Corporation of the 21st Century" (paper presented for the Center for Business Ethics, University of St. Thomas, Houston, TX., December 2001), 1.
5. John Paul II, *Centesimus Annus: On the Hundredth Anniversary of Rerum Novarum* (Washington, D.C.: United States Catholic Conference, 1991), 11
6. John Paul II, *Laborem Exercens: On Human Work* (Washington, D.C.: United States Catholic Conference, 1981) 5, 6.
7. *Centesimus Annus*, 11.
8. *Laborem Exercens*, 13.
9. Pius XI, *Quadragesimo Anno: On Reconstruction of the Social Order*, 1931, http://www.vatican.va/holy_father/pius_xi/encyclicals/documents/hf_p-xi_enc_19310515_quadragesimo-anno_en.html (8 Dec. 2000).
10. *Quadragesimo Anno*, 89.
11. *Laborem Exercens*, 16.
12. *Quadragesimo Anno*, 137.
13. See Robert McAfee Brown, *Kairos: Three Prophetic Challenges to the Church*, (Grand Rapids, MI: Eerdmans Publishing, 1990) for a detailed discussion with examples.
14. Karen Lebacqz, "Bioethics: Some Challenges from a Liberation Perspective," in *On Moral Medicine: Theological Perspectives in Medical Ethics*, eds. Stephen Lammers and Allen Verhey (Grand Rapids, MI: Eerdmans Publishing, 1987), 66.
15. John Cardinal Mahony, "A Jubilee for Workers: Challenges and Opportunities for the New Millennium," *Social Development and World Peace, U. S. Conference of Catholic Bishops*, 2000, http://www.usccb.org/comm/archives/2000/00-212.htm (8 Oct. 2002).
16. John Cardinal Mahony, "A Jubilee for Workers," 2.
17. See "Assemblee des eveques du Quebec," *Message of May 1, 2001*, http://www.cvcques.qc.ca/aeqdoc_cas_2001.html (8 Oct. 2002) and Theodore Panayotou, "Globalization and Environment," *CID at Harvard University Working Paper No. 53*, July 2000, http://www.cid.harvard.edu/cidwp/053.htm (10 Oct. 2002).
18. Michele Simms, "Emerging Trends/Ethics in Corporate Social Responsibility," *Center for Business Ethics Working Paper*, December 2002, http://www.stthom.edu/cbe
19. Assemblee des eveques du Quebec, 1.
20. TIHPR, "Bioterrorism Preparedness Policy Brief," *Texas Institute for Health Policy Research* 2001, http://www.healthpolicyinstitute.org (1 Feb. 2002).
21. TIHPR, 2.
22. TIHPR, 2.

23. Anthony Storr, *The Essential Jung* (Princeton, NJ.: Princeton University Press, 1983), 69-70.

24. Patricia Werhane, *Moral Imagination and Management Decision-Making* (New York: Oxford University Press, 1999).

25. Robert Greenleaf, *Servant Leadership: A Journey into the Nature of Legitimate Power and Greatness* (New York: Paulist Press, 1991).

26. Pope Leo XIII, *Rerum Novarum: On Capital and Labor*, 1891, http://www.vatican.va/holy_father/leo_xiii_enc_rerum-novarum_en.html (2 Oct. 2001).

27. John Cardinal Mahony, "A Jubilee for Workers," 2.

28. Joseph Cardinal Bernardin, *A Moral Vision for America* (Washington, D.C.: Georgetown University Press, 1998), 109-110. The convictions are echoes of *Rerum Novarum*: the common good finds its origin in a vision of the person as one grounded in community, who understands the mutual relationship between society and government as one where rights are religiously respected wherever they exist.

29. *Quadragesimo Anno*, 37.

30. *Quadragesimo Anno*, 101.

31. Barbara Andolsen, "Roman Catholic Tradition and Ritual in Business Ethics: A Feminist Perspective," in *Spiritual Goods: Faith Traditions and the Practice of Business*, ed. Stewart Herman (Philosophy Documentation Center: Library of Congress, 2001), 73.

32. Patricia Werhane, *Persons, Rights and Corporations* (New Jersey: Prentice-Hall, 1995), 3.

33. Peter French, "The Corporation as a Moral Person," *American Philosophical Quarterly* 16 (1979): 210; Kenneth Goodpaster, "Morality and Organizations," in *Ethical Issues in Business Second Edition*, eds. Thomas Donaldson and Patricia Werhane (Englewood Cliffs, NJ: Prentice-Hall, 1982), 137-44; Michael Keeley, *A Social Contract Theory of Organizations* (IN: Notre Dame University Press, 1988); L. May, *The Morality of Groups* (IN: Notre Dame University Press, 1987); Manuel Valasquez, "Why Corporations Are Not Morally Responsible for Anything They Do," *Business and Professional Ethics Journal*, no. 2 (1983): 1-18; Patricia Werhane, *Persons, Rights and Corporations*, 34-40.

34. Edward M. Spencer, Anne E. Mills, Mary V. Rorty and Patricia H. Werhane, *Organizational Ethics in Health Care* (NY: Oxford University Press, 2000), 16.

35. Edward M. Spencer, *Organizational Ethics*, 36.

36. Patricia Werhane, *Persons, Rights and Corporations*, 59.

37. *Quadragesimo Anno*, 65.

38. *Quadragesimo Anno*, 89.

39. *Rerum Novarum*, 55.

40. Manual Valesquez, "Why Corporations?" 121.

41. *Centesimus Annus*, 41.

42. Dan E. Beauchamp, "Prevention and Its Limits," in *New Ethics for the Public's Health*, eds. Dan E. Beauchamp and Bonnie Steinbock (New York: Oxford University Press, 1999), 103.

43. Dennis McCann, "Catholic Social Teaching in an Era of Downsizing: A Resource for Business Ethics," in *Spiritual Goods: Faith Traditions*, 94.

44. *Rerum Novarum*, 20.

45. *Laborem Exercens*, 45.

46. Edward M. Spencer, *Organizational Ethics*, 5.

47. F. Navran, "Twenty Steps to Total Ethics Management," 1997, http://www.navran.com?Products/DTG/part07.html (12 Nov. 2001).

48. Edward M. Spencer, *Organizational Ethics*, 23.

49. Mele cites examples of these shifts with business focus on corporate vision and mission, knowledge worker, learning organizations, social capital and social marketing, and corporate values. See Domenec Mele, "A Humanistic Framework."

50. Patricia Werhane, *Organizational Ethics*, 30.

51. *Quadragesimo Anno*, 137.

52. Michele Simms, "A Critical Analysis of Workplace Medical Screeening Practices, Privacy and Self-Disclosure: Assessing Individual and Organizational Concerns in the 1990s," Doctoral Dissertation, Wayne State University, Detroit, MI (1991).

53. Mary Ann Glendon, "The Sources of 'Rights Talk': Some are Catholic," *Commonweal* (12 October 2001): 11.

54. *Centesimus Annus*, 47.

55. Mary Ann Glendon, "The Sources," 13.

56. *Centesimus Annus*, 26.

57. *Centesimus Annus*, 29.

58. *Centesimus Annus*, 47.

59. *Laborem Exercens*, 16.

60. Domenec Mele, "A Humanistic," 5.

61. Bennett Freeman, "Corporate Responsibility and Human Rights," 2001, http://www.globaldimensions.net (13 Nov. 2001).

62. UNCHR, "Business and Human Rights: A Progress Report, *Office of the High Commisioner for Human Rights*, 2001 http://www.unchr.ch/business.htm (13 Nov. 2001).

63. John Kavanaugh, *Who Count*, 139.

64. *Centesimus Annus*, 43.

Chapter 18

Image and Social Responsibility:
Catholic Values and Fashion Advertising

Janice G. McCoart

I n the age of the megabrand, global expansion of business, keen competition, and the search for the new have driven the trend in recent years to cultivate controversial images and ad concepts meant to remain in the minds of consumers. These ads sail into our lives and our homes, on the sides of buses, in the pages of magazines, and plastered across billboards. They may perpetuate unwanted stereotypes, bring undesired values into our lives, or disrespect religious standards and beliefs. The controversies of the Benetton and Calvin Klein campaigns are notorious and so has been the trend for drug and heroin-chic photography in the editorial pages of magazines.

The focus of this discussion is on the anti-Catholic sentiment that has surfaced in the fashion industry. The first discussion centers on the shock-tactic images of the Benetton advertising campaign. Abercrombie & Fitch, probably the more unexpected company of the two, publishes a quarterly catalogue that challenges the boundaries of propriety in many arenas. Among the most surprising and repetitious are those relating to Catholic values. Finally, we examine Jean Paul Gaultier's fall 1989 couture collection, which featured clothing inspired by nun's habits. In all cases, the campaigns claim motives of the highest standards for their actions, but resulting controversy suggests that they must take responsibility for any disrespect, divisiveness, or infringement of societal values.

In the first case, Luciano Benetton started with a small, family owned sweater-knitting business in Italy, which has become the largest knitting manufacturer in the world. Today Benetton has more than 7,000 licensed stores in 120 countries including Japan, China, Russia, The Czech Republic, Poland, Turkey, and Egypt. Its product line extended into men's, children's, and infant apparel, shoes, underwear, perfumes, watches, sunglasses, toys, skiwear, and even condoms.

Originally, Benetton was best known for its brightly colored sweaters, the look of the shops, and the Benetton ad campaign, carrying the "United Colors of Benetton" slogan and highlighting multiracial children-of-the world motifs. The September 1989 *Time* magazine praised Benetton for their "multi-ethnic rainbow book," a campaign of models of various skin colors, emphasizing society's multi-ethnicity.[1] It even won praise from the United Nations, for whom the manufacturer designed uniforms for tour guides. In those days, their ads ran in *Mademoiselle*, *YM*, and *Seventeen*. As the company expanded its market from fifteen to twenty-five-year-old females to include thirty- to fifty-year-olds, it ran ads in *Vogue*, *GQ*, *Rolling Stone*, *Essence*, *Glamour*, and *Details*.

Then the company chose Eldorado, a Paris agency, to develop its advertising, while J. Walter Thompson placed the ads in American publications. The Paris firm tried a new approach: productless ads, a method meant to market company philosophy or designer image. Without emphasis on product characteristics, the ads attempted to predispose the consumer to what makes one manufacturer distinctive from another. Without any merchandise or copy, the impact of the ads rested solely on the unexplained visual image. What followed was a series of artistically composed ad layouts featuring images meant to reflect social issues in contemporary society. The pictures were credited to photographer Oliviero Toscani, who received as much praise for his work as he did criticism. The images were either provocative because of their ambiguity or because they symbolized societal standards that the ads challenged.

An ambiguous image characterized the first ad of the campaign, which ran in *Rolling Stone*, *GQ*, and billboards across the country in fall 1989 and winter 1990. It pictured two male arms, one white and one black, handcuffed together at the wrist, both garbed in light blue denim work shirt sleeves. "Which is the criminal? Which is the captor?" asked *Mother Jones* writer Dennis Rodkin.[2] "Handcuffs do not convey brotherhood," objected Donald Polk, president of the *New York Urban League*, in *Time* magazine.[3] "They're both criminals; that's an interesting view of equality!" said Clarence Smith, President of *Essence*, a magazine targeted at black women. In fact, the ad was totally nixed in the United Kingdom.[4]

Another ambiguous ad pictured a white roll of toilet paper on a white background, despite the "colors" theme of the campaign. It was believed to be a unique symbol of universality. In 1991, an ad showing a newborn baby girl with its placenta and umbilical cord attached was rejected by *Cosmopolitan*, *Essence*, and *Elle*, but accepted by *Vogue*, *Self*, and *Parenting*. Mary Anne Sommers, publisher of *Child*, said she would not run the ad, because Americans view childbirth as an "extremely private and personal subject," and she felt the ad could offend some of her readers.[5] I experienced a surprise when a *Vogue* magazine dropped off the sofa and opened to the page of this ad. My then eight-year-old daughter flinched and said "eeeoooo," and I was in a position to have a discussion that I had not planned to have.

Juxtapose such ambiguous images to one that pictured a nun and priest kissing on the lips. Perhaps the biggest outcry was caused by this ad, because it appears to challenge Catholic beliefs. This was rejected by all American publications but *Rolling Stone* magazine. Especially without the aid of copy, what is the message this image sends? It certainly appears to challenge the vows of celibacy. The viewer also recognizes the individuals in the picture as religious because of their attire. In the article "Habit and Habitus: Current Legislation," Elizabeth McDonough writes that "the primary function of the habit is to serve as a sign of consecration and a witness to poverty. That is to say, the habit is consistently understood to be indicative of a way of life with transcendent and immanent consequences."[6] So, does the image challenge not celibacy alone but "a way of life"? In an even broader sense, these individuals in their roles are symbols of Catholicism. Does the image, then, question Catholic beliefs? Most interesting is the reaction of others to the image; it then becomes a basis for discussion. For instance, the Anti-Defamation League of B'nai B'rith said that the company

> has lost sight of simple standards of propriety. In what seems to be a campaign underscoring shock and attention-getting devices, Benetton is now trivializing, mocking, profaning, and offending religious values—in this case, especially the Catholic Church.[7]

In the midst of the Persian Gulf conflict another ad pictured a cemetery with one white Star of David among a field of white crosses. They are actually gravestones located at the cemetery for the Battle of Normandy during World War II. Some people puzzled over its symbolism in relation to the Middle East conflict. In Italy, a Milan jury deemed it offensive to religion.[8]

Another image that prompted a broad response was a family grieving at the bedside of a sunken-cheeked young man who had died of AIDS moments earlier, certainly a very Christ-like man in appearance. The picture stirred questions about whether the ad raised awareness of the disease or exploited it. Like the others, there was no copy in the ad except the Benetton logo and a line telling what number to call for the nearest store. Had the ad included an AIDS hotline number to call for information or urged support for local AIDS organizations, it would have appeared to serve a purpose beyond the promotion of the Benetton name.[9]

Luciano Benetton explained that these shock-tactic themes "depended on social issues of the moment."[10] Oliviero Toscani, the photographer and creative director of Benetton's advertising during this campaign, claimed he came originally from photojournalism. So he takes the "reality" from the editorial side of a magazine and mixes it into the advertising side, instead of what is expected—beauty and the unreal.[11]

It is important to note that the advertising campaign was worldwide. As mentioned, the United Kingdom found some images to be unacceptable. An Italian court found them offensive. French AIDS organizations sued Benetton for defamatory advertising and breach of privacy. The French court found the company guilty of exploiting AIDS in 1995 and ordered the company to pay $30,000 in damages.[12]

The ad campaign affected Benetton's business operations in other ways. In 1995, twelve German retailers withheld payments for merchandise, because they maintained the controversial ads had hurt their sales. Benetton sued in the Italian courts and won the case against the first retailer, which signaled similar results with the others.[13]

American sales dropped from a mere 15 to less than 10 percent of corporate sales over the duration of the controversial campaign.[14] The American market did not respond with their dollars to shock-tactic images that were potentially divisive to races, religions, and nations.

In regard to the ethics of images and concepts in advertising, the American store chain Abercrombie & Fitch is not expected to be a bedfellow of Benetton's, but it is. The store was founded by David Abercrombie in 1892. It was dedicated to selling only the highest-quality camping, fishing, and hunting gear. In 1900 a very loyal customer, Ezra Fitch, convinced Abercrombie to let him buy into the business and become a partner. The two conflicted, however, and by 1907 Abercrombie resigned. Shortly after his resignation, Abercrombie & Fitch began publishing a catalog. It featured 456 pages of outdoor gear and clothing and was distributed to 50,000 customers around the world. As orders came in, the store achieved international status.

Abercrombie & Fitch outfitted Theodore Roosevelt for trips to Africa and the Amazon and Robert Peary's expedition to the North Pole. Earnest Hemingway bought guns there. Presidents Hoover and Eisenhower obtained fishing equipment. The list of distinguished customers includes Amelia Earhart, Presidents Taft, Harding, and Kennedy, The Duke of Windsor, Clark Gable, and Cole Porter.

Abercrombie & Fitch was acquired by Limited Inc. in 1988 and in 1992 was repositioned as a more fashion-oriented casual apparel business. It became independent in 1998 and is based in Reynoldsburg, Ohio, from which 230 stores are managed.

Since the mid-nineties, Abercrombie & Fitch's chief competitor has been American Eagle Outfitters, where the same clothing styles sell for less money. In an effort to combat that type of competition, the store introduced *A&F Quarterly* in 1998, a racy publication that is half lifestyle magazine and half catalog. Each issue consistently displays several pages of scantily clad or naked models. Its layouts are similar to *Sports Illustrated* meets *Playboy*.

Since its origin, *A&F Quarterly* managed to raise the ire of several groups, which are usually not spoken in the same breath: Mothers Against Drunk Driving, the National Organization for Women, Michigan Attorney General Jennifer Granholm, Illinois Lieutenant Governor Corinne Wood, Citizens for Community Values, the American Decency Association, the Chicago City Council, the State of

Utah, Concerned Women for America, the Illinois State Legislature, South Carolina's Lieutenant Governor Bob Peelers, and the Catholic League.

Here are examples of their objections to the publication: the 1998 back-to-school *Quarterly* included "Drinking 101," a crash course in binge drinking, complete with sexually named recipes and party games.

The Christmas 1999 catalog, *Naughty or Nice*, includes a cartoon of Santa and Mrs. Claus engaging in sadomasochism, several nude models, vulgar language, and sex tips from a porn star.

After the Michigan Attorney General raised her objections, Abercrombie & Fitch recalled an issue, which then became a collector's item, and paid circulation soared from 75,000 to 100,000. The company agreed to shrink-wrap it, require proof-of-age eighteen, and place a warning label on it.

Upon evaluating one photograph of a nude young man with plaid slacks wrapped around the neck and shirt tucked to hide genitalia, one may wonder what is wrong with the clothing, as they are not seen well by the viewer, or whether the fashion is to wear apparel that is very wrinkled.

The company says the catalog is marketed to college students, but Abercrombie & Fitch's target customer is age 15 to 22. Of course, the legal drinking age is 21. Middle school students wear the clothes in addition to high school teenagers. Michigan Attorney General Jennifer Granholm's children, ages 10, 13, and 14, were able to obtain the catalog without a problem. After that, clerks in all 230 stores nationwide carded anyone requesting a catalog.

By the way, formal boycotts of the stores were instigated by both Illinois Lt. Governor Corinne Wood and the Catholic League. Boycotts and media comment do not seem to be the answers, because young people are often drawn to whatever incites disapproval from parents.

Ironically, Abercrombie & Fitch's clothes are not much sexier than the camping, fishing, and hunting gear the firm originally sold. Khakis, T-shirts, and button-down shirts are the chief merchandise.

The 2001 Spring Break issue incited attention for challenging Catholic beliefs in several places. In a hypothetical expert advice column, Jason, from Bryn Mawr, Pennsylvania, writes:

> I am graduating from a Catholic high school this year, and I'm in love with one of my sisters. No, not *my* sister (that would really be a sin) but one of the sisters who teaches me English. I fantasize about taking her away from these stone buildings and barren courtyards to a small island down in the Caribbean where we can be together. Am I going to hell for this?

The answer states:

> Dear Jason,

Probably. But why not ask her anyway? That's the only way you'll get her to kick the habit. Ha ha. Get it? Kick the habit?

Another question:

Dear A&F,
Someone recently told me that my favorite teacher is gay. This is particularly weird because I go to a Catholic high school. What should I say to him (the teacher)?

And the answer:

Dear Mark,
The thing is, if you're gay and you're Catholic, you have a strong chance of becoming a priest. (If you're gay and you're Jewish you have a strong chance of writing Broadway musicals.) You don't have to say anything. Unless, that is, you want to ask him out. And that *would* be weird, wouldn't it?[15]

The tone of the letters and answers smack of rebellion, youthful judgment, and ignorance. They also perpetuate stereotypes and challenge Catholic values.

In an article titled "Convert Your Hotel," the writer makes suggestions for decorating the spring break hotel room: "Lots of palm fronds are a great way to execute this eco-friendly flair, and you might be able to get them for free if you crash a Catholic mass on Palm Sunday."[16]

The article "Cults of Personality" reviews films to make your "Saturday nights a little wilder." The review of *Cemetery Man* states the plot as: "Caretaker of a cemetery full of zombies is destined to be with a beautiful mystery woman. Or maybe not:"

Cult Status:
Bridges the gap between film grad students, comic book geeks, and horny teenagers by referencing cult faves both silly (The Three Stooges) and sublime (painter René Magritte).

Causes of Cult Following:
Pre-stardom [Rupert] Everett walks around with his shirt off; painfully beautiful and voluptuous [Anna] Falchi walks around with her shirt off; zombies get their heads blown off; surreal ending blows your mind.

How to Join:
One viewing is all it'll take, but learning to make wry comments after bashing in a dead nun's head to a pulp couldn't hurt either.[17]

Here is a better synopsis of the plot in *Cemetery Man*: *Cemetery Man* is based on the Italian horror comic strip "Dylan Dog." The character of Francesco Dellamorte was originally conceived with English actor Rupert Everett in mind. Dellamorte is a grave keeper in an Italian village. For some unexplainable reason, the dead have the habit of rising from their graves during the night a week after they died, and it is up to Dellamorte and his misshapen and retarded assistant Naggi to put them in their graves. Somehow Dellamorte gets tied up romantically with a mysterious woman (played by supermodel Anna Falchi) who keeps appearing as different characters in his life. A series of bizarre circumstances befall Dellamorte, as he tries to make sense out of a world falling apart around him (and his sanity with it).[18]

My research shows no connection between "a dead nun" and the movie plot. Here as in the previous example the writer is purposely over the edge in this reference to Catholic beliefs and includes a violent tone as well.

After initial criticism of this catalog, Abercrombie & Fitch released a disclaimer that the catalog's remarks about Catholics were "completely tongue in cheek" and "meant to be funny." The concept for *A&F Quarterly* began with the company's President Michael Jeffries, but Sam Shahid is the man behind the layout and execution. Shahid is best known as the author of many of Calvin Klein's advertising campaigns, including the one that was criticized as child pornography. In a *New York Post* interview in 1999 Shahid said, "When people make something out of a thing that's not there, they're reading their own problems into it, or their fears or what they may be guilty of."[19] But I think the most telling fact is that the writers are made up of recent graduates, college students, and a few MTV writers. So the most youthful and ignorant individuals are writing to appeal to a market of their peers.

William A. Donohue writes in *America* that anti-Catholic incidents of this type are "the result of ignorance" or "a function of malice." In addition:

> Within the church, there is a disconnect between many lay Catholics and the Catholic-bashing that is targeted specifically at church teachings, beliefs, and practices. Some lay Catholics feel that defending their church is the province of the clergy and religious. Chapter 5 of the NATO charter says that an attack on one nation is an attack on all member nations. If lay Catholics were to internalize their logic and apply it to their own religion, the scourge of Anti-Catholicism would retreat with their efforts. The time is past when the priests, sisters, and brothers in our church can fight this battle by themselves.[20]

Here is the concern about these concepts and images in fashion advertising: in *The Sponsored Life*, author Leslie Savan warns about "the growing tendency to define our sense of self by the images of advertising. Advertising is working constantly to make us think that by buying certain products our lives are going to be changed in some radical wonderful way. . . . By the time children are twenty years old, they have been shaped and conditioned to believe that something material, something they can buy will be the fastest, easiest route to making them happy."[21] In his book, *The Process of Argument*, Michael Boylan points out that an advertising picture in itself is an argument of persuasion—it persuades a segment of people about an idea, a product, or service.[22] Both observations teach us that advertising makes material goods the most desired values, as opposed to the values of goodness, love, religion, etc. and that the ad itself persuades the consumer by image, for instance, that the lifestyle described in *A&F Quarterly* is the most desirable one.

Another avenue through which the fashion industry may communicate an anti-Catholic message is design. Ironically, the level of the industry in which design may challenge values to the greatest degree is the long established French *couture*. Couture means "the art of dress making," while *haute couture* implies clothing that is reserved for the best design and highest quality of fashion and workmanship. Couturiers have been the major influence on fashion design for the last one hundred years.

Couture fashions are produced on a made-to-order basis, where the fittings to the client's measurements may occur over several sessions. These clothes are priced between $5,000 and $50,000 for a single garment. Fewer than 1,000 women in the world can afford such prices. Couturiers are happy if they sell 200 garments per season.

Yet it can cost one to two million dollars-a-year for a design house to produce a collection. These costs include fabrics, labor, and the expense of the fashion shows. So the French government provides compensatory support. One design house may generate extensive publicity for all of the rest, and thus, the extensive sales of ready-to-wear, fragrances, accessories, and licensing businesses.

Therein lies the motivation to design the audacious and extreme for the runway. While couture is regarded as offering the opportunity for the purest form of creativity, thereby providing a laboratory for research and development, designers may perceive that boldness and rebellion attract the very valuable attention that will create free publicity and support the greatest number of sales.

Jean Paul Gaultier is one of these designers. After formal couture training during his employment with Cardin, Esterel, and Patou, he became the "bad boy" designer when he turned to freelance work, using his considerable dressmaking and tailoring skills to produce garments that were irreverent to the fashion establishment.

The marketing of Gaultier's fall 1989 couture collection carried an anti-Catholic message. He sent models down the runway in nun's habits and garters. The reactions to and descriptions of the collection provide some explanation for the stunt. *People Weekly* described them as "ecclesiastically clad model 'nuns' [coming] down the runway in garter belts."[23] *The Houston Chronicle* said: "Jean Paul Gaultier chose an unholy theme of good nuns and bad nuns, all ascending from some subterranean hell, rotating in presentation and descending again."[24]

When he was told that some in the audience were offended by the nun's garb the models wore, Gaultier said, "But I'm Catholic!" *The Globe and Mail* suggested that the attempt was to attract "those who renounce the world and those who can't get enough of it."[25] That is what my mother used to refer to as "making trouble."

Like the Benetton ad of the nun and priest kissing and the weak efforts at humor of the hypothetical expert advise column in *A &F Quarterly*'s Spring Break issue 2001, Gaultier's fashions depict a rebellion against the "way of life" of the religious, as it is defined by Elizabeth McDonough in *Canonical Counsel*. The juxtaposition of sexually suggestive garters with the habit appears to challenge the vows of celibacy, as was the case with the previously mentioned sales promotions. The defiance of both "the way of life" and celibacy expresses the same for Catholic beliefs, since the religious in their roles are symbols of Catholicism. It is time for each of these businesses to take responsibility for their disrespect of Catholic values.

Notes

1. Scott, "It's a Small World After All," *Time.* 25 September 1988, 56.

2. Dennis Rodkin, "How Colorful Can Ads Get?" *Mother Jones*, January 1990, 52.

3. "Picture Imperfect," *Time*, 4 December 1989, 69.

4. Rodkin, "How Colorful," 52

5. "Benetton ads: a Risqué Business," *Time*, 25 March 1991, 13.

6. Elizabeth McDonough OP, JCD, "Habit and Habitus: Current Legislation," *Canonical Counsel* (November–December 1997): 651-52.

7. J. Trescott, "Benetton ads: Clashing Colors," *Washington Post*, 10 August 1991, C1, C5.

8. "Picture Imperfect," 69.

9. P. Span, "Colored with Controversy," *Washington Post,* 13 January 1992.

10. "Picture Imperfect," 69.

11. T. Rich, "Toscani and His Critics," *PRINT*, 52, No.2, (1998): 174-77.

12. "Italy Refuses to Censor Benetton Ads," *Women's Wear Daily*, February 1994, 2.

13. "Benetton Scores in Ad Lawsuit," *Women's Wear Daily*, 26 April 1995, 10.

14. M. Blonsky, and C. Calligaris, "At Benetton, a Retreat From Revolution," *Washington Post*, 30 April 1995, H2.

15. "XXXPert Advice, Ask A&F," *A&F Quarterly*, Spring Break Issue 2001, 58.

16. "XXXTra Ambience, Convert Your Hotel," *A&F Quarterly*, Spring Break Issue 2001, 61.

17. "XXXTra Time, Cults of Personality," *A&F Quarterly*, Spring Break Issue 2001, 110.

18. Mutant Reviewers from Hell Do "Cemetery Man," http://www.geocities.com/~aral/rcemetary.html (2 April 2002).

19. Boycott Abercrombie & Fitch, http://www.safeplace.net/ccv/docs/AbercrombieFitch.htm (26 March 2002).

20. William A. Donohue, "The Ten Worst Anti-Catholic Atrocities of 2001," *America*, 18 February 2002, 14.

21. Rich, "Toscani and his critics," 174-177.

22. Michael Boylan, *The Process of Argument*, (Englewood Cliffs, NJ: Prentice Hall, 1993).

23. Karen S. Schneider, "After Decking Out Madonna and Losing His Closest Friend, Jean Paul Gaultier Softens His Fashion Cutting Edge," *People Weekly*, 12 December 1990, 123.

24. Linda G. Griffin, "Avant–garde Fun/New Styles Playful; More Wearable," *Houston Chronicle*, 2 November 1989, 6.

25. David Livingstone, "Showmanship on Display at Gaultier Presentation," *The Globe and Mail*, 26 October 1989, C3.

Chapter 19

Catholic Faith
Between Secularization and Pluralism

Maria Clara Lucchetti Bingemer

T he Western world is living in a time that is only comprehensible within the context of secularization, experienced as a crisis of models, paradigms, and values. This modern crisis has impacted all who live in it but especially the generations who previously experienced a more stable state of affairs and who find their certitude and the fundamental values of family and religion threatened.

The purpose of this work is to analyze one aspect of the crisis of modernity, namely its impact on religious identity and religious experience. The analysis begins with a short description of what constitutes the so-called crisis of modernity, conscious, however, of the fact that any attempt to describe such a complex subject will necessarily be limited. Next, the chapter presents two responses to this crisis: the "return to the sacred," represented by the multi-religious explosion within secularized society; and the efforts of Christianity since the years prior to Vatican Council Two to deepen its own identity and discover an adequate way of communicating with a world that is simultaneously secularized and multireligious.

Since the experience of God appears to hold the only possibility of a "common ground" for dialogue between Christianity and such a broad range of religious groups, both traditional and contemporary, this analysis will focus on both divergent understandings of this experience and the means to witness to its truth claims.

The Modern Situation: Attempting a Description

Even as paradigms and models have fallen or changed in today's society, cultures have reawakened to the awareness that human persons are essentially relational, and that even as autonomous beings they are governed by "otherness." This "otherness" is named differently within various religious traditions: Transcendence for some, the divine otherness, or the completely Other, or plural and countless divinities. In the Christian faith this personal Otherness is called God.[1]

While modernity stripped the world and societies of ties to the sacred, a reaction from within society itself sought to resacralize the world, challenge modernity's presuppositions, and nullify its impact on living out religion, on the profile of religious identity, and on contemporary religious experience. The reappearance of the religious or the sacred, as well as the thirst for mystery and for the mystic in different forms, denotes a return (or the permanent need for) contemplation.[2]

A new religiosity has emerged, a product of the complexity of our times, a new way of living religion. At the peak of secularization, we experience what is referred to as a return to the sacred, a postmodern phenomenon.[3] In spite of the whole process of secularization and the categorical dismissal of religion by the "masters of suspicion," some people still spend hours of time in cults, celebrations, and praise ceremonies. Some invest all their affective potential as well as their time, energy, creativity, and resources in religious rituals, participating in long assemblies, looking for corporal and spiritual cure, searching for communion with the universe and nature, reciting mantras, or looking for therapy to achieve integration of the self.

Consciously or unconsciously, people are affected by the conjoining of secularization and the multireligious explosion; they begin to assume different paradigms of perception and analysis, as well as a new world vision. Activities and religious practices that once were carried out within personal enclosures can now be observed in city squares, shopping centers, stores in middle-class neighborhoods, and on highways. The most intimate restlessness and deep secrets of human beings (regarding their futures, health, and happiness) are shared in the public square, and are no longer shared in places that are discreet and favorable to mystery.

It is not clear that this almost wild drive of our contemporary culture for religious experiences corresponds to a real search for a deep encounter, or a desire to be affected by an "other." To search for religious or spiritual sensations does not necessarily imply a desire to experience otherness, and may not even leave room for otherness and difference.

Confronted with a multireligious explosion that has attracted many away from participation in traditional forms of religion, Christianity finds itself dealing with the question of its own identity, within an ocean of varying religious experiences— experiences that do not necessarily include the Otherness who in absolute liberty reveals itself as Holiness, that is to say, as the Absolute Other. When every search for spiritual sensation demands equal recognition in terms of mystical experience—

gotten sometimes through artificial resources, other than and not in relation with what is established and deepened only in gratuity, in hearing and in desire—the Western mystical tradition is betrayed. If every experience of seduction of the Sacred is legitimized, humanity runs the risk of baptizing many divinities with this name reserved for the True One, who doesn't surrender his sacred name in vain.[4]

Christianity and Dialogue among Religions

Another challenge addressed to Christianity today from religious pluralism concerns ecumenism and ecclesial dialogue. It is not only about intra-ecclesial dialogue among the various denominations found inside of one Church, but even more about a dialogue in which Christianity and other religions (both traditional world religions as well as new religious movements) together seek points of reference for a convergence of conflicting beliefs and practices that can lead to a common ground.[5]

Though new religious movements have been criticized many times for morals that do not conform to the doctrinal and ethical principles of Judaism and Christianity, the fact is that several new religious movements have a rather strict moral code, sometimes even more than the one found in the Judeo-Christian frame of reference. The figure of Jesus, central to Christianity, also appears in these movements, but from a different point of view than in the Christian tradition; his death and resurrection are questioned, and consequently so is his divinity. Other figures of Christianity, such as Mary and the saints, are invoked by several of these movements, but these figures do not fulfill the same role as they do in Catholicism.

In the analysis of new religious movements, the sects constitute a phenomenon apart.[6] Showing a rather fundamentalist stamp, they always keep, though in a veiled way, a protesting attitude towards traditional Christianity, especially with regard to the Catholic Church, which is reproached for soiling the purity of the Gospel. By accentuating the eschatological principle of a millenarist shape and the pneumatic spiritual principle (in opposition to the preponderant role of dogma in the Church), the sects enjoy a very marked seductive power and gain increasingly more people who participate in their rituals in an intense way.

While acknowledging all their ambiguous aspects, one can legitimately wonder if the seduction—increasingly strong, exerted by the sects even to former members of the historical Christian Churches—might not be a legitimate questioning of the methods they use to evangelize. Also one may wonder if the success of these religions in the diffusion of their message does not have something to say to the historical Christian Curches about the coldness of their liturgies, about the bureaucratization of their institutions, about the necessity of reconsidering the affective dimension of the communication of their teachings.

In these movements the communitarian dimension strongly links the members of the group. It is surprising to note that certain new groups of Christian communitarians (the Charismatic Revival and other groups formed by Catholics and non-Catholics, like for instance Pentecostal Protestantism) are similar both in terms of motivation (marked by a strong affectivity) and in the expression of strongly connected relationships. It should however be recognized that these groups, while remaining inside the institution of the Church, show several similarities to the so-called new religious movements, and like them, have a great capacity for attracting new recruits.

Basically, the great challenge, the great scandal of Christianity to the multi-religious world today continues to be faith in Jesus Christ, Son of God and Univer-sal Savior. Recognizing and proclaiming the singularity of the event of the Incarna-tion of the God whom no one has ever seen, and yet who is revealed in the historical particularity of Jesus of Nazareth, is an inescapable requirement of Christianity. This is what is more and more contested by other religions, who support the thesis that there are mediations other than that of Jesus for the revelation of God. And the same thing can be found in those currents inside Christianity, that propose to reconsider the unicity of Jesus.[7]

While the above-mentioned differences of belief and conflict of interest are great, the dialogue among religions is not without an offer of hope. Without making concessions about the central point of the Incarnation, Christians, today as al-ways, are called to find in the secularized, postmodern and multireligious world, a new but faithful way of experiencing God who is at the center of their identities, and of calling them forth while nurturing them into further integrity.

From Religious Seduction to Experience

Karl Rahner affirmed that the Christian of the future (we would add, of the present) will be a mystic, that is to say, somebody who has experienced something, or he/she will be nothing at all, even less a Christian.[8] Since time immemorial, and today more than ever, speaking of God from the perspective of the Christian faith, means speak-ing about an experience, or, better, starting from an experience. While this experi-ence is divine, it is also profoundly human ever since the moment when, in the fullness of time, as the Christian faith proclaims, God Himself was made flesh, was made human, the Word Incarnate, Jesus Christ.

If it suddenly seems—rightly or not—that Christianity may have partially lost the possibility of expressing itself through words, of proclaiming before the world of today with a loud and understandable voice the God who is at the heart of its experience, it would, to a great extent, be the result of the divorce between the experiences and practices of the Faith on the one hand, and on the other hand, of the significant human experiences that move and mobilize what is most profound in the human being. To the degree that these human experiences lose their analogy with the Christian experience—personal, communal, and ecclesial—they cease to be salvific. In short, they do not deserve being called, strictly speaking, experiences of God.

At the present time, the quest for dialogue among religious traditions is finding in the experience of God a fertile soil for possible progress. Although one cannot, with regard to the experiences that occur within several religions, simply reduce them one to another or identify them one with the other, it is undeniable that religious and mystical experience can be used as a privileged ground for theological dialogue, insofar as it returns the human being to fundamental questions of significance: Where do we come from and where will we go? What is the meaning of human existence, with its burden of suffering and death? What is the source of this movement that we share, which brings us into relationship, which carries us out of ourselves into solidarity and communion with the other, and which is the response to the interpellation by an Absolute of which we are aware and in which we believe?

The answer—though mysterious and veiled—to these questions, and the simple fact that it concerns us, signals the experience of God as the indispensable criterion for Christianity, not only for advancing in the understanding of its identity, but moreover for going forward toward the different which challenges it and paradoxically renders it increasingly faithful to the core of its fundamental truth.

As a starting point for dialogue in a multireligious world, the experience of God also presents nothing less than the possibility, for the human being, of living out the fundamental anthropological dimension of gratitude. While walking on the road of the experience of God, man notes that The One whom his heart desires does not at all surrender to the immediacies of his needs, and even less to the consuming "frenzy" of certain psychological states and emotional conquests. The experience of God, while occurring on the level of desire, can only occur gratuitously, always leaving him or her in the grip of unappeased desire, and thus always capable of desiring and, consequently, of experiencing.[9]

The Judeo-Christian tradition recognizes the natural presence of this desire in the human being. Scripture does not fail to take into account this human desire deeply rooted in the vehemence of the aspiration for life in its fullness, in which the fundamental element is the establishment of personal relations with God.[10] However, this experience does not consist, for Judaism and even less so for Christianity, in a permanent satiety or in the unfinished enjoyment of all desires.

If, on the one hand, it is certain that "only the desire is capable of qualifying the relationship of God with man,"[11] on the other hand, the relation established by this desire places man before the very "difference" of God: a difference of the desire of the Other, the encounters with whom can be made only by renouncing oneself, in conversion, in the examination of one's own desires. It is the only way, in the Christian experience, of opening a space so that God can desire in man and consequently for allowing man to desire only God, by increasingly identifying his desire with the divine desire. It is thus the human being who, in experience, is seized by God, and not the other way around. And his experience, if it is true, entirely escapes his control.

So, if the experience of God occurs on the level of desire—not being able to occur otherwise—it is also necessary to say that it occurs as a mystery—a revealed mystery, undoubtedly the Mystery of Love that comes close in saving but yet remains a mystery. There is no natural logical transition between the daily experience of life and the experience of God, although the former is the place where the latter occurs. One may speak of an analogical knowledge, on the basis of the fundamental perception that nothing, no reality, is able to express Transcendence. With regard to any human experience of Transcendence, the term "mystery" is the most appropriate one for defining the discovery of God as the Absolute who attracts and invites to experience.

And yet the Incarnation of the Word in Jesus of Nazareth says to the Christian that, purely by the grace and mercy of God, time itself has received a new significance and this "subsequence" has been redeemed, and thus his religious experience consists in the insoluble union of two seemingly irreconcilable poles: the theological fact that God lets himself be experienced while at the same time being Absolute and Father. Defined as love from the very beginning of Christianity, this God reveals himself as a Father in the personal and intimate relationship that he maintains with humankind, a relationship whose primary point of reference is the loving union maintained with Jesus of Nazareth, in whom the Christian faith has recognized the Beloved Son of the God never seen by anyone.

The mystery of the Incarnation of God in Jesus Christ thus reveals, not only that the Divine Absolute is experienced by humankind as fatherhood, but moreover that this experience makes it possible to glimpse a difference and a plurality even in the interior of God's existence, experienced as Father, Son, and Holy Spirit.

The great difficulty of speaking intelligibly today to postmodern, and/or post-Christian ears, about the God of Christian revelation, perhaps results, not only but mainly from the fact that, for some time, historic Christianity attached only little importance to experience and even to a *pedagogy* of the experience of God.[12] Fearing the intimacy and the subjectivism engendered by modern individualism, which could lead to alienation, to a disengagement from community and history—which, to a certain extent has already occurred and still occurs—Christians became suspicious of everything that came from the domain of religious experience and would have the appearance—however remote—of being near to so-called mystical experience. Apparently, mystical experience was reserved only for privileged people, almost always dedicated to contemplation in a cloister.

The ethical attitude that the Church calls love (*agape*) neither finds itself at odds with the experience of God nor denies the assertion that this God, revealed by grace, would be an object only of desire, never of necessity. Humanity, in the grace of contemplation and at the deepest level of the experience of God, can feel the proximity of the Ineffable Absolute never seen by anyone. Humans can perceive a depth—the home of him who challenges one by coming from the heart of reality— that he experiences as an authentic manifestation of the Divine.

There is more: it is this dialectical movement (the experience of the infinite in the finite, through the challenge that comes from the heart of the finite and leads up to the ethical act; the infinite intervenes in the finite and transforms it, and touches the finite which is at the same time the fringe of the infinite) that allows man to become aware of this Absolute which lovingly governs life for him, the Same who reveals, in Jesus Christ, his name of Father. In going to the foundations of his human existence, poor and limited, marked by many conflicts, by injustices and restrictions of all kinds, man becomes aware of a divine origin which withdraws from the field of experience, or better, from awareness, from the knowledge that one might have from this experience.

Conclusion: Theology—Vulnerability of Reason

At this moment, as the crisis of modernity and the diversification of the field of religion become more and more complex, theology is in turn questioned concerning its identity and the very meaning of its existence. If the identity of Christianity is at this time problematic, what about the language of theology, which claims with extreme boldness to organize the discourse on God using poor, limited, and now somewhat distorted human reason?

And yet it is perhaps more urgent than ever that theology rediscover its primordial vocation and significance in order to be able to pronounce the word that is proper to it. More concretely, theology must, here and now, concentrate its attention in a special way on that which is the central object of its content, the frame of its method: God himself. This is the only way that will lead theology to really become what it is and what it is called to be: that is, theo-logical.

Thus, when it comes to true theology, reason has its citizenship, though this citizenship is, even wishes to be, auxiliary, secondary, like that of a handmaiden. While daring to look into and reflect on the mystery that graciously reveals itself, reason (which modernity has set up as a definitive protagonist that has arrived at the height of instrumentality and of claiming to explain everything) will have no other path, than the one of vulnerability, which allows itself to be unceasingly demolished and reconstituted by the revelation of the mystery which always exceeds it.[13]

Thus, by assuming this constituent and foundational vulnerability, theology will fall in step with him who, throughout his encounter with humanity, never preserved, never clung to his prerogatives, who laid himself bare and who could be encountered in all that is smaller, more humble, and less important according to the criteria of this world (cf. Phil 2:5-1). Thus, if the experience of God is basically an interrelational experience and vulnerability with regard to an Otherness which, from its absolute difference in revealing itself, does not do so by overwhelming but in serving and in saving, then the discourse on this experience will not have any other choice than the way of encounter with the same vulnerability, in letting itself be unceasingly influenced by the otherness inevitably present in the relationship that is grounded there.[14]

It is necessary however to pay attention to the symbolic, "sacramental" dimension that theological discourse entails today, which is perhaps different from yesterday. At the apogee of modernity and secularization, theology sought indirect ways of speaking, in the name of respect for plurality and religious freedom, trying the path of dialogue with modern atheism and agnosticism, and opting many times for mute testimony where only the gesture counted, and where ethics was the sole common denominator driving toward this dialogue. Today the situation no longer appears the same.

It could be that the major and more demanding part of vulnerability at this moment consists in taking up again the explicit proclamation, in using religious and mystical discourse when speaking about God. The field of religion has been transformed into an immense supermarket of opportunities where each can choose a recipe according to individual taste. A pluralism of sects invokes the thirst for transcendence and spirituality in which humanity is caught up. It is here that the Name that continues to love and call humankind to the permanent dialogue of love and communion must be made to resound by Christian theology.

It is this name that Jesus of Nazareth specified as Father. And it is this name that, by taking root inside the most intimate core of the human being, expresses the most transcendent Divine Being—the Wholly Other. To name God as Father, to recognize his paternity and to really express it, is to recognize him both as the foundation and origin of the human being as well as something outside of oneself. It is to allow all dimensions of life to freely organize themselves for relationships of true solidarity and fraternity. It is, in addition, to proclaim that divine paternity is not a projection of insecurity, frustration, or a human construction, as has been endlessly repeated in so many critiques of religion, but the Revelation of God as the Father by an only Son, the Savior of humankind.[15]

Insofar as we do not confuse this experience with the simple search for feelings or emotional compensation that characterizes many religious manifestations today, theology will be put on the defensive by the fundamental question of God, the center of its discourse, and by this way of talking about him to contemporaries.

Other sects will criticize Christian theology's claim to speak about the personal characteristics of the Unutterable and Inexpressible God. But, if this same God lets himself be experienced in spirit and truth and even in human flesh assumed and redeemed by the Incarnation of the Word, it is possible to talk about this experience. This is what should be, at the present time, the primary occupation of theology, which may be more and more a mystical theology, not only because it is centered upon the reflection of what is proper to it, but because it will increasingly take on the form, not of abstract speculation, but of a testimony to the interdependent, sympathizing, and loving relationships of humans with God.

Notes

1. Some of the reflections contained in this chapter are presented in a more complete form in a previous work, named "Sacramental presence in a postmodern context" in *Post modernity and sacramentality*, ed. Lieven Boeve and Limen Leussen (Leuven-Paris-Sterling, VA, Leuven University Press and Uitgeverij Peeters, 2001), 65-105.

2. The question of God shows itself today as the path of possibility for the dialogue among religions. Cf. the reflections on *Theo centrism* which succeeds *Christ centrism* in the attempts of Christianity to dialogue with other religions, in some recent works: Jacques Dupuis, *Jesus Christ à la rencontre des religions* (Paris: Desclée, 1989); Michael Fitzgerald, "Panorama du dialogue inter-religieux et questions théologiques," in *Spiritus* 33 (1992): 92-103. See also Jacques Dupuis, *Vers une théologie du dialogue interreligieux*, (Paris: Cerf, 1997).

3. "Let's take here the term post-modern in one of its technical meanings: as cultural paradigm, in relative contrast, although coexistant with nonmodern and modern paradigms. Due to a question of space and time, we don't specify contents and expressions of those two other paradigms. But we use the term postmodern as an expression of the exotic or psyche-delic, as it has been done by some publications or by the media." Cf. Marcelo Carvalho Azevedo, "América Latina: perfil complexo de um universo religioso," *Cadernos Atualidade em debate*, n. 26 (1996): 12-13.

4. Cf. Jean. Ladrière, "Approcio filosofico alla mistica," in *La mistica* (ed.) Jean Marie van Cangh (Bologna: Dehoniane, 1992), 83.

5. Cf. the ever more numerous works over the last years on this subject. We cite the following: Hans. Kung, *El Cristianismo y las grandes religianes* (Madrid: Europa, 1987); Adolphe, Gesché, "Le Christianisme et les autres religions," *Revue théologique de Louvain* 19 (1988): 315-41; Jacques Dupuis, *Jesus Christ à la rencontre des religions*; *Vers une théologie chrétienne des religions* (Paris: Cerf, 1998) among others.

6. We employ here the term "sects" according to the definition of Max Weber, who opposed the concept of "sect" to that of the "church," but in ascribing to it the characteristic that seems to fit better with the mode of organization of religious groups, in Brazil and in other parts of the world, which are called "sects" people who believe in Jesus, gather together around the Bible, with ritual that is marked by the affective and emotional, claiming direct inspiration from the Holy Spirit who speaks through the mouth of the faithful, whoever that might be, without hierarchical rigorism.

7. Cf., for example, such works as the one of Paul Knitter, *No other name? A critical survey of Christian attitudes toward the world religions*, (Maryknoll: Orbis, 1985). Cf. also the writings of Michael Amaladoss, Ramón Pannikar and others.

8. Cf. Karl Rahner, *Escritos de teología VII*, (Madrid: Taurus, 1972): 75-81.

9. Cf. the number of biblical texts that express the even corporeal repercussions of human desire: Ps 42; Ps 123, 3; Ps 63, 2; Ps 130, 6; Ps 73, 25-28 and others. Jesus himself speaks to his disciples in terms of desire (cf. Ic 12, 49-50; 22, 15). The Bible itself ends with the cry of impatient desire of the Bride who calls for her Beloved: Maranatha! Come, Lord! (Ap 22, 17.20).

10. Cf. on this subject what is said by Michel Meslin, *L'expérience humaine du divin*, (Paris: Cerf, 1992), 386.

11. Michel Meslin, *L'expérience humaine du divin*, 404-405.

12. There is no lack of accusations on this matter, be they from within the Christian world, like Joseph Sudbrack, *La nueva religiosidad* (Madrid: San Pablo, 1990), 99 or from outside, like Jacob Needleman, *Lost Christianity*, (San Francisco: Harper and Row, 1985), 102-103. "While Catholic monks and nuns are teaching all kinds of things, from botanics to business, they are not so many those who are teaching people how to pray."

13. Cf. on the impossibility of reason accounting for the mystery of God: Maria Clara Bingemer, "A post-christian and postmodern Christianism," *Liberation Theologies, Postmodernity, and the Americas* (London-New York: Routledge, 1997): 83-94.

14. On this subject, see what is said by François Varillon, *L'humilité de Dieu*, (Paris: Centurion, 1978), 84: "Il faut une longue expérience, il faut peut-etre toute une vie, pour comprendre un peu que, dans l'ordre de l'amour, comme la richesse est pauvrete, la puissance est faiblesse. L'homme s'incline toujours, quand il pense a son Dieu, a sortir de la sphere de l'amour, a imaginer des attributs qui ne seraient pas ceux de l'amour. Il a fallu des siècles pour que le Dieu des armées soit enfin adoré comme le Dieu desarmé."

15. On the experience of divine paternity, cf. the important text of Meslin, "Désir du Père et paternité divine," *Expérience humaine*, 297-320.

Chapter 20

Restoring All Things in Christ:
Some Reflections on the Pastoral Provision
for the Anglican Use of the Roman Rite

Clinton A. Brand

In June of 1980, Pope John Paul II approved a special Pastoral Provision for the reception of converted Episcopalian priests together with their congregations into full communion with the Catholic Church while retaining elements of their Anglican liturgical tradition. Though ratified with little fanfare and attracting scant attention at the time, this Pastoral Provision represents the first tentative steps toward fulfilling a set of possibilities with roots deep in the Anglican schism of the sixteenth century. At last, belatedly, auspiciously, converts from Anglicanism were coming home to Rome, not as scattered individuals but as a body of the faithful, bringing with them their shared gifts and offering—indeed restoring—to the Catholic Church their distinctive spiritual patrimony.

Responding to petitions from a group of American Anglicans who sought a canonical means of reunion with the Holy See, the Pastoral Provision was promulgated by decree of the Sacred Congregation for the Doctrine of the Faith and issued through the National Conference of Catholic Bishops (NCCB).[1] The decree provided for the ordination of Anglican clergymen (even married ones) to the Catholic priesthood, for the confirmation of Anglican laity so disposed, and for the establishment of "common identity" parishes preserving those features of the Anglican liturgical heritage compatible with Catholic faith and doctrine. Toward this end, the

Pastoral Provision established a framework for developing a distinct Anglican us-
age of the Roman Rite, composed from sources in the Book of Common Prayer and
Anglican traditions of worship. In 1987, the Vatican's Congregation for Divine
Worship approved the liturgical texts of the Anglican Use under the title of *The
Book of Divine Worship*.[2] Today, there are some half-dozen active Anglican Use
Catholic congregations, all in the United States, and most of those in Texas, including my own parish, Our Lady of Walsingham in Houston.[3] Though these "common
identity" parishes are as yet few in number and while their future is still unfolding,
the Pastoral Provision represents something more than the concession of a "halfway house" for "recovering" Anglicans. It is a remarkable ecclesial and liturgical
development in its own right, and however "provisional" it may be the Anglican
Use can be understood as one of the fruits of post-conciliar renewal with intriguing
implications for understanding the progress of liturgical reform, the pontificate of
Pope John Paul II, and the dynamics of Catholic tradition.

On the evening of 19 August, 1980, the day before the press conference an-
nouncing the approval of the Pastoral Provision, Archbishop John R. Quinn of San
Francisco, then President of the NCCB, is reported to have said, "I'm not sure what
all this means."[4] Twenty-two years later, the meaning of the Pastoral Provision is
still far from obvious, but already the Anglican Use has established itself as an
important model of "reconciled diversity" with further promise of enriching the
Church and building up the Body of Christ. Here I want to reflect on the fascinating
story of how the Anglican Use came to be and to assess its importance as a liturgical and ecclesial development, one that is uniquely English in origin, yet decidedly
American and pervasively Texan in character. It is, as we shall see, a story fraught
with irony and riddled with paradox. In order to appreciate what England, America,
and Texas have to offer the Universal Church through the organic development of
this local and particular usage, we need first to understand the larger context of
Anglican conversions to Catholicism, some of the anomalies of the English Reformation and its aftermath, as well as the evolution of a Catholic and sacramental
sensibility through worship with the Book of Common Prayer. Finally, then, to
glimpse how this sensibility has been restored to its proper origins and authenti-
cated in the Catholic Church, it is worth offering a brief descriptive overview of the
Anglican Use liturgy as celebrated in the "common identity" parishes, together
with some comment on their distinctive ethos of congregational worship.

The record of Anglican conversions to the Catholic Church stretches back to
the seventeenth century—nearly to the beginnings of Anglicanism itself—but the
number and pace of these conversions picked up after the Oxford Movement stimulated a revival of Catholic faith and practice within the Church of England. Especially since the reception of John Henry Newman in 1845, a steady stream of converts from Anglicanism has immeasurably enriched the Catholic Church. Counting
among their number such figures as Henry Manning, Gerard Manley Hopkins, G.
K. Chesterton, Ronald Knox, Robert Hugh Benson, Christopher Dawson, Evelyn
Waugh, and Graham Greene, these and other converts, both clerical and lay, from
the Church of England as well as the Episcopal Church in the United States, contributed significantly to the Catholic intellectual revival in the English-speaking

world.[5] As they embraced the Roman Catholic Church, they brought with them into the Church and offered in service to the Church their remarkable literary and artistic talents, their wit, their apologetic zeal, and their vigorous and articulate sense of Catholic Faith and Truth. They also carried with them a special temperament forged as Anglicans and honed on worship according to the Book of Common Prayer. Anglicanism served them in a way quite distinct from the experience of other converts, as a kind of nursery or seedbed in which a distinctively "Catholic" religious sensibility grew and matured. Their faith and their gifts were fertilized in the soil of ground laid waste at the Reformation but subsequently reclaimed and recultivated with the rich humus of a sacramental and incarnational religious tradition.

However much these Anglican converts contributed to the Catholic Church, what they received was infinitely greater—the fullness of communion, the voice of authority, and the assurance of grace. But their experience was, as it remains for many Anglican converts today, marked with a certain ambivalence. Cardinal Newman's semiautobiographical novel narrating an Anglican layman's anguished path to Rome is aptly titled *Loss and Gain*.[6] In Newman's time, the sense of loss was mostly social, cultural, and aesthetic in character: often estranged from friends and family, leaving behind the traditions and associations of Anglican parish life, and turning wistfully away from the familiar cadences of the Prayer Book, English converts found themselves in a Church that seemed "foreign" and—worse—predominantly Irish! But the loss was not only or exactly a loss of "Englishness."

Newman and many of his fellow converts began their trek to Rome with the recognition of an authentic tradition of residual Catholicism within the Anglican Church. This tradition, while often obscured and at moments seemingly moribund, found its living expression in the Prayer Book and in a devotional ethos stretching back to the seventeenth-century Caroline divines and beyond to the color and vitality of English Catholicism before the Reformation. Because of the peculiar circumstances of the English schism and owing to the subsequent persecution of recusant Catholics, something of the native genius of late medieval English Catholicism was effectively lost to the Roman Catholic Church. Much was destroyed, but much was also preserved and submerged within the Church of England, later to be reclaimed, even coopted, by those Anglicans who forged and followed the Oxford Movement.[7] First, the Tractarians (focusing on doctrine) and, then, the Anglican ritualists (emphasizing liturgy) fashioned an articulate and energetic Anglo-Catholic movement, undertaking in the nineteenth century their own work of Catholic *ressourcement*. They virtually disowned their Protestant lineage and instead sought to recover the resources of patristic and medieval Catholicism and to enrich the Anglican vernacular liturgy with the whole heritage of Catholic devotion and sacramental worship. The effects of this Catholic revival in the Anglican Communion were curious and even counterintuitive: while the logic of Anglo-Catholicism pointed ineluctably to Rome and reunion with the Holy See, the accomplishments of the revival, however limited, convinced many of its adherents that they were already truly "Catholic" (or at least on par with the Eastern Orthodox churches) and encouraged them to work from within in hopes of a long-range, corporate *rapprochement* with the Roman Church. The sequence of "defections" to

Rome, beginning with Newman, far from undermining the Anglo-Catholic position, as often as not challenged those who remained behind to demonstrate ever more clearly and prayerfully the conviction of their own "Catholicism." With each high-profile conversion, "swimming the Tiber" became more natural but also, paradoxically, more difficult.

"Submitting to the Roman obedience," as Anglo-Catholics sometimes described conversion with a sigh of gloomy inevitability, came to involve, then, a sense of loss that was not only cultural but also poignantly *religious*. To become fully Catholic they had to give up much that seemed authentically Catholic, including a vernacular liturgy with patristic and medieval roots, the habit of active participation in congregational worship, and a dynamic traditionalism extraordinarily receptive to the riches of the Christian past, particularly those of the Eastern churches. But this story of loss and gain is even more complicated. Many Anglo-Catholics, often embattled and isolated in their own communion, perceived the weaknesses of their position. In the absence of an authoritative magisterium and lacking an altogether coherent dogmatic theology, they could not resist the corrosive effects of liberalism and modernism, even in their own ranks. While they succeeded in enriching the sacramental and devotional life of the Anglican Church, theirs was something of a "paper religion," and in practice could occasionally sink into the decadent aestheticism of "dressing up and playing church." Still, at its best, Anglo-Catholicism was a genuine force of renewal, often countercultural in effect, proclaiming a kind of radical orthodoxy and unsettling conventional Anglican propriety with a real call to holiness. But at its heart, the movement felt the wound of schism and increasingly came to be animated by a longing for the fullness of communion in the Universal Church.

By the beginning of the twentieth century, Catholic-minded Anglicans in Britain and the United States regularly prayed for the reunification of the Church and offered at mass (as they pointedly called the Anglican eucharist) suffrages for the Pope as the "the Patriarch of the West." With the advent of the modern ecumenical movement, many hoped for some form of corporate reunion and a few even dreamed of an Anglican uniate church in communion with the Bishop of Rome. Such dreams were to prove shortsighted and premature, not the least because those bent on reunion with Rome never amounted to more than a small minority in the Anglican Communion.

For those Anglo-Catholics who had managed to study, argue, meditate, and pray themselves into a theological position largely consonant with Roman Catholicism (in all things save the final—and fundamental—acceptance of the Petrine office), the Second Vatican Council seemed both to encourage and inhibit visions of corporate reunification. On one hand, the Council's Decree on Ecumenism offered an olive branch to the Church's separated Anglican brethren, if only in acknowledging a distinction between the status and claims of Anglicans, in particular, and those of Protestants, at large. And the Constitution on the Sacred Liturgy suggested a program of liturgical reform reminiscent of what Anglicans themselves had long ago pioneered.[8] But in the giddy aftermath of the Council, it seemed to many conservative Anglo-Catholics that the Roman Church herself was giving way to the same liberalizing tendencies that were progressively attenuating Catholic faith and doctrine in the Church of England and in the American Episcopal Church. Thus many Anglicans rationalized their position, and even though individual converts continued to walk their solitary way to Rome a great many chose to sit tight, hunkering down in their own Anglo-Catholic "fortress parishes." Notwithstanding their high-minded notions of church polity, they were little more than congregationalists practicing a religion of desperate wishful thinking. As the dust settled from the Council, it became clear that the Catholic Church went on being Catholic, but all the smoke from Anglo-Catholic thurifers could not conceal the fundamentally Protestant character of the Anglican schism.

Our story brings us, then, to the papacy of Pope John Paul II and the initiative of a group of American Anglicans that resulted in the Pastoral Provision. In 1976, the General Convention of the Episcopal Church unilaterally voted to ordain women to the priesthood, thereby dealing a deathblow to the prospects of ecumenism and decisively rejecting the Catholic understanding of the apostolic ministry. But women's ordination was only one issue among many and symptomatic of a larger, long incubating Anglican departure from the historic content of Christian faith and doctrine. Traditionalist Anglicans, both of the catholic and the evangelical variety, found themselves at sea, tossed overboard from a ship that had been highjacked by those who put their own cultural agenda before the mission and identity of the Church as the Bride of Christ. Well before the Convention, Pope Paul VI had addressed a cautionary letter to the Episcopal Church, but this letter and its contents were deliberately withheld from the Convention's delegates meeting in Minneapolis.

Not long after the 1976 General Convention, Catholic-minded Anglicans began concerted efforts to establish links with the Holy See. In the leadership of the heroic churchman Canon Albert Julius du Bois, longtime president of the American Church Union (the association of American Anglo-Catholic clergy committed in principle to reunion since its founding in 1859), Anglicans seeking communion with Rome found a Moses to lead them out of Egypt.[9] The contacts forged through Canon du Bois and the discussions that ensued for the next several years, from the last days of Pope Paul VI through the first year of the pontificate of Pope John Paul II, met with favorable reception from several members of the American Catholic hierarchy and from Franjo Cardinal Seper, then head of the Sacred Congregation for the Doctrine of the Faith. On the Solemnity of All Saints, 1 November 1979, Father du Bois and the contingent he led signed a formal petition for reunion on the altar of the North American Martyrs at the North American College in Rome. From there, the petition was received by Cardinal Seper and warmly approved by Pope John Paul II. The result of this extraordinary convergence of good will, faith, and prayer on all sides was the Pastoral Provision, which was officially ratified and announced just weeks after Canon du Bois's death in 1980. Three years later, after a process of assessment and discernment for priests, catechesis and preparation for laity, and much consultation on the liturgy, the first "common identity" parish was erected with the ordination of Father Christopher Phillips and the formation of the Church of Our Lady of the Atonement in San Antonio, Texas.

As Canon du Bois and his fellow converts knew very well, the roots of this ecclesial and liturgical development lie deep in the anomalous character of the English schism and in the peculiar historical dynamics whereby Catholic sacramental worship survived and then came to assert itself in the Anglican religious tradition. It is well beyond the scope of this paper to narrate the whole complex history of the Protestant Reformation in England, but let me suggest the outlines of a framework of interpretation that may help make sense of the Pastoral Provision and explain how the Anglican Use of the Roman Rite came to assume its place in the Church's patrimony of worship.

The sequence of events by which England fell out of communion with the See of Peter—King Henry's defiance of papal authority, the declaration of royal supremacy, and the final break with Rome in 1534—forever and tragically changed the religious and cultural landscape of England. But these events, it is worth remembering, were hammered out of historical and political contingency, and the schism, at least in its initial stages, did not represent a movement of popular rebellion or even much disaffection from traditional Catholic doctrine or practice. Kings and popes had quarreled before, kings and popes would quarrel again. Though the martyrs Saint Thomas More and Saint John Fisher shrewdly perceived the implications of Henry's usurping of ecclesial and spiritual authority, that the king had declared himself the "Head" of the Church in England did not necessarily preclude reconciliation with Rome, and, at first, Catholic life went on much as it had before.[10] King Henry's daughter, Mary Tudor would during her short reign exercise royal supremacy to restore Catholicism in England. For more than a century the nation's religion hung in the balance with the hopes of some and the fears of others that this or that monarch would turn "papist." While King Edward VI and Queen Elizabeth I unambiguously proclaimed their Protestantism, King James I and King Charles I (both married to Catholics) seemed at moments to flirt with Catholicism; King Charles II died a Catholic, King James II reigned briefly as a Catholic, and only with the so-called "Glorious Revolution" of 1688 was the Protestant religion firmly and constitutionally established. The political contingency of the schism both shaped and reflected a deeper set of conflicts in a nation that came to define its identity in opposition to "popery" but which could not entirely expunge the legacy of "popishness" from its religious and cultural life.

The English Reformation, forged in equivocation, compromise, and ambiguity, was a process that lasted across a century and involved both a systematic attack on traditional religion and the simultaneous preservation of a strong current of vestigial Catholicism. The contradictory character of the Reformation in England has occasioned great debate among historians and generated some complex and contentious historiography venturing to trace and apportion elusive relations between causes and effects.[11] Yet an impressive and growing consensus of historians, including J. J. Scarisbrick, Christopher Haigh, and Eamon Duffy, now argue convincingly that the Reformation from its inception was imposed on a largely resistant population by an alliance of avaricious, power-hungry politicians and a small cadre of militant Protestant agitators seeking to exploit the king's conflict with the papacy.[12]

The successive waves of state-sponsored Reformation under King Henry VIII, King Edward VI, and Queen Elizabeth I amounted to a wholesale assault on the cultural vitality and spiritual richness of late medieval Catholicism. Power and Greed joined hands with Sacrilege and Iconoclasm to work the burning of missals and breviaries, the desecration of shrines and chantries, the despoliation of the monasteries, and the smashing of altars, rood screens, statues, and stained glass windows. Such destruction entailed not only a massive loss of artifacts but also an attack on a distinctively English Catholic spirituality, an ethos of prayer, a culture of devotion, and a particular kind of Marian and eucharistic piety. By Shakespeare's time the English landscape was littered with "Bare ruined choirs, where late the sweet birds sang" (Sonnet 73), and already folks spoke of "the old religion," sometimes with contempt but as often with nostalgia.

The impulse toward destruction was consistently met with a countervailing, though often quiet, ethic of preservation. But quite aside from the holy things that were hidden away or salvaged, something of the spirit of "the old religion" was retained and internalized among the faithful to live on within the walls of the old churches and cathedrals under the dispensation of the new order. For Englishmen of the late sixteenth century the alternatives were stark: they could embrace persecution and martyrdom, on one hand, or, on the other, choose conformity, however grudging or merely nominal, to the established church. Most opted for the latter, and the Church of England included among its clergy and laity a considerable though indeterminate number of so-called "church papists," those who remained Catholic at heart but who outwardly or minimally conformed to the state religion.[13] While the degree of their influence in the English church is virtually impossible to assess, the very category of "church papists" and the fears they aroused in doctrinaire Protestants bespeak the undisputed reality of a widespread conservative sentiment in the church, or at least a disposition willing to accommodate contingent circumstances in hopes of better days.

Such ambiguities and the difficulties of defining the exact character and content of early modern Anglicanism point to another important dimension of post-Reformation English church history. The Sovereign Power in England could command public conformity to the state church, but it could not beyond certain limits compel or probe the depths of conscience—nor did it even seek to do so. The Articles of Religion, eventually codified as thirty-nine in 1563, railed against "Romish" abuses but were so ambiguously worded as to admit a wide latitude of interpretation and, with some mental gymnastics, could accommodate a broad spectrum of belief, including much that was genuinely Catholic.[14] The Elizabethan Settlement settled very little, in fact, but rather had the effect of displacing religious conflict from overt disputes over theology to noisy quarrels over worship and ceremonial. Thus liturgy became the great battlefield of Anglicanism, and thus, to paraphrase Christopher Haigh, at the beginning of the seventeenth century England was a nation neither fully "de-Catholicised" nor completely "Protestantised."[15]

The tangled history of Anglicanism is closely bound up with the development of Anglican traditions of worship and the evolution of the Book of Common Prayer.[16] For most of the first fifteen years after the schism, until after the death of King

Henry VIII, the Mass and offices continued to be said in Latin according to the traditional English variations of the medieval Roman Rite (the "uses" of Salisbury, Hereford, York, Bangor, and Lincoln). In 1544, the Archbishop of Canterbury, Thomas Cranmer was commissioned to translate and adapt the liturgy from the Salisbury missal and manual (the Sarum Use) in the composition of the first English Prayer Book. Imposed in 1549, this first Book of Common Prayer incited armed rebellion throughout the west of England (as the decree of royal supremacy had not), and the good men of Cornwall rejected the new liturgy on the grounds that they couldn't understand English! But despite the shock of the vernacular and some departures from the old rite—the elaborate ceremonial of the Sarum Use was proscribed and veneration of the saints repressed—Cranmer's Order of Holy Communion, "Commonly called the Masse," represented a fairly faithful, though streamlined rendering of the essential elements of the Latin Mass. When Cranmer's rival, the conservative Stephen Gardiner, Bishop of Winchester, insisted that the 1549 Prayer Book was fully compatible with the theology of the Catholic Mass, he only expressed what many thought—or hoped—to be the case. But such ideas were hardly a source of comfort since these sentiments provoked Protestantizers in the church to demand a thoroughly reformed service book, resulting in the Prayer Book of 1552. With its "black rubric," emphatically denying the Real Presence, the 1552 book marks a kind of low point of Anglican regression. The "black rubric" disappeared from every subsequent edition of the Book of Common Prayer, and the fitful trajectory of Prayer Book revision thereafter (beginning with the Elizabethan Prayer Book of 1559) was in the direction of restoring the substance of the 1549 book and reintroducing language more consonant with a theology of the Real Presence and Eucharistic Sacrifice.

Despite the contention it aroused, the Book of Common Prayer served the Anglican Church as the source and seal of unity—or as sign of as much unity as Anglicans could ever claim—and from its Catholic origins it carried and conveyed through the centuries the memory and the possibility of sacramental participation in the Body of Christ. Throughout the seventeenth century, Puritans in the English church fumed against lingering vestiges of "popishness" in the Prayer Book and sought to reduce its rites to a platform for preaching and Bible reading, but on the whole the language and ritual of the Prayer Book came to inspire a broad following and a deep attachment.

Yet the accomplishment of the Book of Common Prayer owes not only to the elements of continuity it provided with pre-Reformation worship but also to the particular vernacular medium in which that continuity was expressed. In translating the Roman Rite and borrowing features from the Greek liturgies, Cranmer made the most of his classical and humanist education, and he seized the full resources of the English language at a remarkable stage of its development. With astonishing linguistic skill and literary talent, he fashioned a vernacular liturgical idiom capable of expressing with euphony, precision, and clarity the subtle and supple richness of the Latin rite and some of the Greek.[17] Cranmer's translations of the Roman collects, for example, are one of the undisputed glories of the Prayer Book and unrivalled as works of beauty, capturing in limpid rolling periods much of the concision, emotional range, and theological nuance of the Latin originals.[10] Arguably, what was preserved in the Prayer Book was deeper and truer than anything else in Anglican experience.

Lacking a clear structure of authority and a coherent body of doctrine, Anglicans perforce were thrown back upon the flexible resources of their liturgy to expound their faith. In both its strengths and limitations, Anglicanism became a particular testing ground, a five-hundred-year laboratory for the principle of *lex orandi, lex credendi*. The offices of the Prayer Book could be recited with Calvinist austerity, but its rites would also be celebrated with Tridentine panoply. The Catholic core of the Book of Common Prayer provided the context and something of a stimulus for a series of Catholic revivals, beginning with the Caroline divines of the seventeenth century. Their association with currents of Counter-Reformation spirituality and their (falsely) alleged "crypto-popery" helped provoke the English civil wars and the Puritan revolution. Quite apart from the ensuing conflict, the revival shaped by Lancelot Andrewes and John Cosin, among others, enriched the Anglican devotional ethos, anticipating the Oxford Movement and influencing what would become the Episcopal Church in the United States.[19]

In adopting the 1637 Scottish Prayer Book (the version informed by the Caroline revival) as the model for the first American Book of Common Prayer, Episcopalians on these shores acquired some rich resources for sacramental worship. In the nineteenth and twentieth centuries, American Anglo-Catholics shared with the Oxford Movement the challenge and the opportunity of recalling the Anglican Communion to its Catholic roots. American Anglo-Catholicism grew in tandem with its British counterpart, but freed from associations with the monarchy and the established church it also developed its own independent character and robust spirit. (It is perhaps a tribute to this character and to an American sense of openness, on the part of Anglicans and Catholics alike, that an American initiative led to the Pastoral Provision and that the Anglican Use has yet to be instituted in the country from whose history it takes its origins.) Yearning for the fullness of communion yet deeply attached to their own spiritual tradition, English and American Anglicans did what they could within their own churches to rectify the damage done at the Reformation.

In an effort further to enrich, supplement, and correct the Book of Common Prayer and to bind themselves more closely to the central liturgical tradition of Western Christendom, some Anglicans beginning in the late nineteenth century produced complete English translations of the *Missale Romanum*, using the Prayer Book as a stylistic template. These "Anglican Missals," in both English and American editions,[20] represent the penultimate stage of development in the long and fitful Anglican pilgrimage to reclaim the spirit and the substance of the Catholic faith first planted in England when Saint Augustine of Canterbury arrived in Kent with his commission from Pope Saint Gregory the Great in the year of Our Lord 597. But this work of restoration only came to its proper fulfillment in 1979, All Saints' Day, when Father du Bois and his delegation signed the petition for reception into the Catholic Church on the altar of the North American Martyrs and then made their way to the Church of St. Gregory, the very place from which the Roman pontiff had sent his missionary to England almost fourteen-hundred years before. There, taking nothing for granted and feeling the full historical weight of the moment, they knelt and prayed for the complete reunion of Christ's Church.

Such, sorely abbreviated, is the essential historical background for understanding how and why in the waning years of the twentieth century a small band of American Anglicans approached the Holy See seeking incorporation back into the Universal Church. And such is a brief account of the historical experience necessary for appreciating the special character of the Anglican Use parishes formed under the auspices of the Pastoral Provision. But that character is also significantly the result of some important developments within the Roman Catholic Church and of their convergence with the modern growth of English-speaking Catholicism. The way to the Second Vatican Council was paved in the nineteenth and early twentieth centuries with the advent of the liturgical movement, the Catholic intellectual revival, and the work of theological *ressourcement*. Simultaneously, the Church in Britain, after Catholic emancipation and the restoration of the hierarchy, emerged from centuries of legal persecution, and the Church in America came together and developed its own character from the diversity of its immigrant communities. All of these vectors of influence, like so many beams of light, refracted through the prism of the Council and focused by the pontificate of John Paul II, combine with the Anglican inheritance to constitute the witness of a particular kind of dynamic traditionalism that is the special charism of the Anglican Use congregations. Insofar as the Anglican convert Cardinal Newman is rightly hailed one of the spiritual fathers of Vatican II, something of his vision and temperament has come to fruition in the Holy Father's provision for "the common identity" parishes of the Anglican Use.

This "common identity," then, is rich and multifaceted and defies easy definition. It involves much more than the accommodation or "inculturation" of a peculiar Anglo-Saxon "ethnicity." Rather and more fundamentally, it represents a fully earned realization of, and a particular way of living out, the Catholic symbiosis between the rule of prayer, an ethos of worship (*lex orandi*) and the rule of belief, a body of doctrine (*lex credendi*). If the history of the Anglican tradition teaches anything, it instructs us that modes of liturgical prayer do indeed shape, prompt, and reflect habits of belief and focal points of truth, but it also teaches that even deeply engrained customs of worship require for their authentication the abiding, living voice of authority in the fullness of communion. Anglican Use Catholics seek, then, to be faithful to the rule of Holy Scripture, Sacred Tradition, the Chair of Peter, and the Church's Magisterium and to demonstrate that fidelity in and through their dedication within their local parish communities to a particular liturgical apostolate.

Yet the phrase "liturgical apostolate" sounds perhaps grander and loftier than what most Catholics of the Anglican Use perceive themselves as doing in living the Catholic faith through their diverse gifts and callings. The "common identity" parishes are, in many respects, much like other parishes in their dioceses. Formed around a small nucleus of Anglican converts, each of the "common identity" parishes now includes several converts from other religious traditions and a considerable number of lifelong Catholics, men and women of various backgrounds, and many large families. They are active in all the religious life and charitable work of their diocesan communities, but what draws them together and gives them their special character is a common reverence for the liturgy of the Roman Rite in its Anglican Usage and with this reverence a shared style of congregational worship and parish life.

With the best of Catholic liturgy through the ages, congregational worship in the Anglican Use parishes is stately and dignified, rich and clear, simple and ceremonious. The Divine Liturgy, celebrated as Solemn Mass at the principal Sunday service and major Holy Days, aims to work the sanctification of time and space and souls through a liturgical ethos that is catechetical, kerygmatic, eschatological, mystagogic, iconic, dramatic, and always incarnational—qualities that would require a dissertation to explain in detail! Ritual actions and gestures are clear, precise, and deliberate. The language is robust and hieratic. The active participation of all the faithful is normative with a clear delineation of the roles and functions of the celebrant, deacon, servers, kantor, choir, and congregation. Music is integral to the unfolding of the liturgical action (it never consists of "performance pieces"), and Anglican Use parishes delight in congregational singing, with a rich repertory of traditional hymns carefully chosen to fit the propers of the day and season. Vigorously making a joyful noise, the people sing every last verse of every hymn, and seldom does the choir sing or chant anything that is not also sung or chanted by the whole congregation. Plainsong and Anglican chant feature prominently. Hymnody and psalmody are carefully balanced and integrated.

When the Divine Liturgy does not open with the chanting of a processional Introit followed by the Asperges (from Easter through Pentecost), Solemn Mass on Sundays often begins with some other preparatory service of psalms and canticles. In penitential seasons, the liturgy starts with the singing of Psalm 51 (*Miserere mei, Deus*) and Psalm 43 (*Judica me, Deus*), or else the office of sung Morning Prayer with the Invitatory Psalm (the *Venite*) and the Song of Zechariah (the *Benedictus Dominus Deus*), together with the psalms appointed for the day, a lesson, and responsorial suffrages. The Holy Eucharist proper commences with the celebrant's greeting ("Blessed be God: Father, Son, and Holy Spirit"), followed by the Collect for Purity, taken originally from the Sarum Use and featured in the Anglican Prayer Book as an introductory invocation for the entire rite:

> Almighty God, unto whom all hearts are open, all desires known, and from whom no secrets are hid: Cleanse the thoughts of our hearts by the inspiration of Thy Holy Spirit, that we may perfectly love Thee, and worthily magnify Thy holy name, through Christ our Lord.[21]

Then follows the Summary of the Law and the *Kyrie*, sung in Greek or English, and the *Gloria*, in English or Latin, then the Collect of the day, the lessons, gradual psalm, and the Gospel (typically chanted by the deacon from the center of the nave). After the homily and the Nicene Creed, the Prayers of the People next take place, followed by the Penitential Rite consisting either of the Prayer Book's General

Confession or the *Confiteor*, concluding then the Liturgy of the Word with the exchange of the Peace (in a location here different from its placement in the *Novus Ordo* of the common Roman Rite). The Liturgy of the Faithful opens with an offertory anthem, the offertory responses, and the celebrant's preparation of the altar and the gifts. The Eucharistic Prayer proceeds with the celebrant facing the people, intoning the *Sursum corda*, and then turning toward the altar, *ad orientem*, for the Preface, Sanctus, and the Canon of the Mass. The Anglican Use Canon is the traditional Gregorian Canon of the Roman Rite, in the translation from *The English Missal*, a vernacular rendering that bears affinities to the sixteenth-century English translation commonly attributed to Miles Coverdale. The sanctus bell rings at the elevations of the Sacred Body and the Sacred Blood. The consecration is interpolated with the contemporary Roman Rite's proclamation of the Mystery of Faith. Following the *Our Father*, the priest breaks the host, saying "Christ our Passover is sacrificed for us," and the people respond, "Therefore let us keep the feast." After the *Agnus Dei*, the entire congregation says the Prayer of Humble Access, a distinctively Anglican prayer composed by Cranmer with phraseology from medieval collects and from the Greek Liturgy of Saint Basil:

> We do not presume to come to this Thy Table, O merciful Lord, trusting in our own righteousness, but in Thy manifold and great mercies. We are not worthy so much as to gather up the crumbs under Thy Table. But Thou art the same Lord whose property is always to have mercy. Grant us therefore, gracious Lord, so to eat the flesh of Thy dear Son Jesus Christ, and to drink His blood, that we may evermore dwell in Him, and He in us.[22]

With the invitation and communion antiphon, the congregation communicates, kneeling at the communion rail, and receiving the sacrament from the hands of the priest or deacon, by intinction. A prayer of thanksgiving and the blessing draws the Mass to a close, and the rite concludes then with a recessional hymn or else the Sarum Recessional Chant, consisting of the Last Gospel, as the priest and servers make their way from the sanctuary to the sacristy.

The Divine Liturgy according to the Anglican Use contains all of the essential elements of the post-conciliar Missal of Pope Paul VI, together with components and ceremonial from the Roman Missal of 1962, and the medieval Use of Sarum, not to mention echoes here and there of the Byzantine Rite and the Eastern Catholic liturgies, all woven seamlessly together in the prayerful vernacular of the historic Book of Common Prayer. The Anglican Use liturgy offers, in fact, a compact résumé of the history of the Catholic Mass, with strata from the whole sequence of its long and organic development from patristic to modern times. It also contains within itself the whole Anglican story of loss and gain, of destruction and preservation, attenuation and restoration, and of vestigial Catholicism attacked, afflicted, and then reclaimed and refined. But the Anglican Use liturgy is hardly an archaeological relic, nor is it a contrived museum piece; it is rather very much a living liturgy, newly adapted to be sure, but substantively continuous with the order of Mass celebrated by the "common identity" parishes long before their reception into the

Catholic Church. As the Congregation of Divine Worship prepared to draft the liturgical texts of the Pastoral Provision in consultation with their Anglican peti-tioners, the Vatican made it clear that the "common identity" liturgy should grow from the actual, recent, and ongoing liturgical practice of those seeking to translate their own religious heritage and sensibility into the context of Roman Catholic wor-ship. For all its distinctiveness, the Anglican Use liturgy is still an embodiment of the Church's historic Roman Rite, and one, moreover, that fulfills to a singular de-gree the norms for the restoration and renewal of the Roman Rite contained in the Council's Constitution on the Sacred Liturgy, *Sacrosanctum Concilium*, and one that accords fully with the most recent Vatican directive on the translation of litur-gical texts, *Liturgiam Authenticam*.[23] On the principle of "restoring all things in Christ," the Pastoral Provision has effected in the "common identity" congrega-tions of the Anglican Use a remarkable enrichment of the Church's liturgical and ecclesial life.

But the Pastoral Provision remains provisional—it was issued *ad tempus non determinatum* and subject to juridical modification—and its future depends not only on the good graces of the bishops who have approved the formation of the "common identity" parishes in their dioceses but on the ability of Anglican Use Catholics to remain true to their distinctive identity and tradition while proving themselves faithful and integral to the Universal Church. The accomplishments to date give reason for cautious optimism: six thriving congregations, others taking shape, the construction of several handsomely appointed churches, one splendid parochial school, some seventy Episcopal priests ordained to the Catholic priest hood under the auspices of the Pastoral Provision (though obviously only a few of these actually serve "common identity" congregations), not to mention an impres-sive number of vocations and seminarians. There are also long-range plans and hopes of organizing a "common identity" religious order and of establishing a house of study to assure the continued growth and vitality of the Anglican Use.

The Pastoral Provision is a remarkable development for several reasons. First, quickly and graciously approved by Pope John Paul II, it is illustrative of the Holy Father's approach to carrying out the mandates of the Second Vatican Council, both in spirit and substance. Second, the Pastoral Provision is also significant as a precedent for licit liturgical diversity. The Anglican Use is the first canonically certified variation on the common Roman Rite approved for parishes especially designated for its celebration. It is also noteworthy as the fruit of an *American* initiative for reconciling an ecclesial community on the model of incorporation rather than assimilation. (For complicated reasons, proposals for a version of the Pastoral Provision for Great Britain have come to nothing, owing in part to some resistance from the Catholic hierarchy in England and Wales.)[24] The contrast with Britain is instructive and points to another important implication of the Pastoral Provision's adoption in America, namely the challenge and opportunity of collegi-ality. As the decree specifies, Anglican congregations and their priests seeking reception under the terms of the Pastoral Provision must do so with the permission of the local ordinary, and the "common identity" parishes formed thereby fall under the jurisdiction of the diocesan bishop working in concert with the Vatican-appointed Ecclesiastical Delegate for the Anglican Use. The parishes formed so far bespeak in their very existence the grace of charity, openness, and understanding both from those seeking and from those offering a home in the fullness and richness of the Church.

Cardinal Newman suggested that the Anglican Church, with all its flaws and imperfections, nevertheless carried within itself just enough residual Catholicism to serve as a providential blessing for the deliverance of her stepchildren back into the arms of Holy Mother Church.[25] Countless other Anglican converts would surely concur. Now we also wait to see if such providential grace refracted through the converts' experience of loss and gain may bear further fruit through the Anglican Use to redound to the greater gain and more perfect good of the whole Church. In the meantime, those Roman Catholics of the Anglican Use can sing with a newfound gusto and a particular resonance the words of Psalm 122 (reclaiming its language from its Anglican associations as the text of the British coronation anthem), singing thus with a proud American accent:

> I was glad when they said unto me, we will go into the house of the Lord.
> Our feet shall stand in thy gates, O Jerusalem.
> Jerusalem is builded as a city that is at unity in itself.
> O pray for the peace of Jerusalem; they shall prosper that love thee.
> Peace be within thy walls, and plenteousness within thy palaces.

Notes

1. The text of the decree of the Sacred Congregation for the Doctrine of the Faith promulgating the Pastoral Provision is most readily available as Appendix A of Father Jack D. Barker's "The Pastoral Provision for Roman Catholics in the U.S.A.," http://www.stmarythevirgin.org/jackbarker.html. Father Barker's essay provides a detailed history of the Pastoral Provision from the petitions to the Vatican from Anglican clergy—Father Barker was one of the signatories—through the erection of the first Anglican Use Catholic parishes. For many details of this essay, I am indebted to Father Barker's account.

2. The full text of *The Book of Divine Worship* can be found in pdf format at http://www.bookofdivineworship.com/, and hereafter will be cited as *BDW*.

3. The principal Anglican Use Catholic congregations to date are Our Lady of the Atonement (San Antonio, Texas), Our Lady of Walsingham (Houston, Texas), St. Mary the Virgin (Arlington, Texas), St. Anselm of Canterbury (Corpus Christi, Texas), and St. Athanasius (Boston, Massachusetts). See the official website of the Pastoral Provision at http://www.pastoralprovision.org. The websites of these congregations contain a wealth of information about the history, development, and character of the Anglican Use.

4. As reported by Barker, "The Pastoral Provision for Roman Catholics in the U.S.A.," *loc. cit.*

5. For the stories of such converts, see Joseph Pearce, *Literary Converts: Spiritual Inspiration in Age of Unbelief* (San Francisco: Ignatius Press, 2000); and Patrick Allitt, *Catholic Converts: British and American Intellectuals Turn to Rome* (Ithaca, NY: Cornell University Press, 1997).

6. John Henry Newman, *Loss and Gain: The Story of a Convert*, ed. Alan G. Hill (Oxford: Oxford University Press, 1986).

7. There are several useful studies of the Oxford Movement; especially commended is Christopher Dawson's *The Spirit of the Oxford Movement* (London: Sheed and Ward, 1945). See also Geoffrey Rowell, *The Vision Glorious: Themes and Personalities of the Catholic Revival in Anglicanism* (Oxford: Oxford University Press, 1983).

8. See the Decree on Ecumenism, *Unitatis redintegratio*, and especially the "Joint Declaration on Cooperation, Pope Paul VI and Archbishop Michael Ramsey," 24 March 1966; as well as the Constitution on the Sacred Liturgy, *Sacrosanctum concilium*, in *Vatican Council II: The Conciliar and Post Conciliar Documents*, ed. Austin Flannery, O.P., Revised Ed. (Northport, NY: Costello, 1988).

9. For an appreciation of Canon du Bois, with an overview of his ministry and an account of his role in the development of the Pastoral Provision, see Father James T. Moore, "The Anglican Use: Some Historical Reflections," *The Catholic Social Science Review* 5 (2000): 401-407. See also Barker, *loc. cit.*

10. See Henry Chadwick, "Royal Ecclesiastical Supremacy," in *Humanism, Reform and Reformation: The Career of Bishop John Fisher*, ed. Brendan Bradshaw and Eamon Duffy (Cambridge: Cambridge University Press, 1989), 169-203.

11. For an overview of this historiography, see Rosemary O'Day, *The Debate on the English Reformation* (London: Methuen, 1986).

12. See J. J. Scarisbrick, *The Reformation and the English People* (Oxford: Blackwell, 1985); Christopher Haigh, *English Reformations: Religion, Politics, and Society Under the*

Tudors (Oxford: Oxford University Press, 1993); and Eamon Duffy, *The Stripping of the Altars: Traditional Religion in England 1400-1580* (New Haven: Yale University Press, 1992).

13. See Alexandra Walsham, *Church Papists: Catholicism, Conformity and Confessional Polemic in Early Modern England* (Woodbridge: Boydell Press, 1999).

14. Yet it needs saying that the Thirty-Nine Articles have always been a stumbling-block for Catholic-minded Anglicans; the Articles have been tortured into some semblance of conformity with Catholic belief, but more often they have been quietly ignored or defied. As Father Daniel Callam points out in his essay for this collection ("Jane Austen's Catholic Sensibility," note 7), "The plot of Newman's novel *Loss and Gain* pivots around the hero's inability to swear to, or even to comprehend, the Thirty-Nine Articles." Famously, Newman's own Tract 90, "Remarks on Certain Passages in the Thirty-Nine Articles," ventured unsuccessfully to interpret the Articles from a Catholic perspective and provoked such a flurry of response that it helped precipitate Newman's conversion.

15. Haigh, *English Reformations*, 288-90

16. On the history and development of the Anglican liturgy and its relation to the Roman Rite, see Dom Gregory Dix, *The Shape of the Liturgy* (Westminster: Dacre Press, 1945), particularly Chapter XVI. Useful resources for understanding the development and evolution of the Book of Common Prayer include F. E. Brightman, *The English Rite*, 2 vols. (London: Rivingtons, 1915); E. C. Ratcliff, *The Booke of Common Prayer of the Church of England: Its Making and Revisions 1549-1661* (London: SPCK, 1949); and Massey Shepherd, *The Oxford American Prayer Book Commentary* (New York: Oxford University Press, 1950).

17. Even Hilaire Belloc, never accused of being soft on anything from the reformed tradition, acknowledged the compelling style with which Cranmer captured and incorporated Catholic liturgical tradition in the Prayer Book. See *Characters of the Reformation* (Garden City, NY: Image Books, 1958), 78-79.

18. For a short study and appreciation of Cranmer's rendering of the Roman collects, see Eamon Duffy, "Rewriting the Liturgy: The Theological Implications of Translation," in *Beyond the Prosaic: Renewing the Liturgical Movement*, ed. Stratford Caldecott (Edinburgh: T. & T. Clark, 1998), 110-122. See also Edward Meyrick Goulbourn, *The Collects of the Day: An Exposition Critical and Devotional of the Collects Appointed at the Communion*, 2 vols. (New York: E. & J. B. Young, 1881).

19. On the character of seventeenth-century Anglicanism, see *Anglicanism: The Thought and Practice of the Church of England, Illustrated from the Religious Literature of the Seventeenth Century*, ed. Paul Elmer More and Frank Leslie Cross (London: SPCK, 1935).

20. See *The English Missal* (London: W. Knott, 1933) and *The People's Anglican Missal in the American Edition* (Long Island, NY: Frank Gavin Liturgical Foundation, 1946).

21. *BDW*, 291.

22. *BDW*, 322.

23. The text of *Liturgiam Authenticam*: "On the Use of Vernacular Languages in the Publication of the Books of the Roman Liturgy" is available at http://www.ewtn.com/library/CURIA/CDWLITAU.HTM.

24. For an account of why the model of the Pastoral Provision has not, to date, proved viable in Britain, see William Oddie, *The Roman Option: Crisis and the Realignment of English-Speaking Christianity* (London: Harper-Collins, 1997).

25. See, in particular, Newman's *Certain Difficulties Felt by Anglicans in Catholic Teaching* (London: Longmans, Green, 1918).

Appendix A

Darkness into Light:
Guadalupe, Mother of All Mexico

A Film Produced by
Patricia Lacy Collins and Robert S. Cozens

Veneration of the Virgin Mary has been a vital part of Mexican life for almost a hundred years. Today, millions of Mexican devotees make their way to shrines to the Virgin throughout the country. They travel in busses and cars, on bicycles, and on foot. They walk to the sound of Indian drums, oompah bands, and mariachi brasses. Some pilgrims are barefoot. Some enter the shrines on their knees.

Guadalupe, Mother of All Mexico is a groundbreaking documentary on Mexican popular culture that was shown at *Mapping the Catholic Cultural Landscape* Conference at the University of St. Thomas in April 2002. The film explores the histories and miracles associated with the Virgin Mary as she is honored under the titles of Our Lady of Guadalupe (in Mexico City), Our Lady of Remedies (in Comonfort, Guanajuato), Our Lady of Solitude (in Oaxaca), and Our Lady of San Juan de los Lagos (in Jalisco). The four Marian celebrations examined all date from the Transition period of the sixteenth and seventeenth centuries, and each illustrates syncretic joinings of vastly different cultures.

The film weaves together scenes from pilgrimages, feast day celebrations, and other public and communal events with commentary by devotees, observers, and scholars. It vividly illustrates how spiritual life has shaped Mexican culture throughout history—including in pre-Christian times—and continues to do so today. Music is basic to the culture and the story—Indian music for dance, and music with Nahuatl and Spanish lyrics.

Guadalupe, Mother of All Mexico can stimulate reflection and discussion in any course studying Mexican culture and in a variety of courses in Catholic Studies, cultural anthropology, Latin American studies and history, popular culture, and religions. It was produced by Patricia Lacy Collins and Robert S. Cozens.

Collins and Cozens are developing a series of three films that treat the spiritual journey of the Mexican people. The series is entitled *Darkness Into Light. Guadalupe, Mother of All Mexico* tells the earliest part of the story. It is followed by *Semana Santa, San Miguel*, the centerpiece of the historical and liturgical set. Model study guides are being developed to accompany this series of three films.

The third and final film, *Following the Spirit*, is in preparation for edit. It examines Mexico's long and difficult struggle for a just separation of church and state and the ultimate establishment of freedom to live according to conscience, the condition necessary for human dignity and for maintaining all human rights.

Throughout the series, events of popular piety reflect the vitality of faith and spirituality in the culture of Mexico today—a valuable consideration for today's audiences, both academic and general.

Father J. Michael Miller, President of the University of St. Thomas, described *Guadalupe, Mother of All Mexico* as "a great contribution toward understanding the role and importance that the Virgin of Guadalupe plays in Mexican culture. The film adds to an understanding of Latin American culture that should be basic to the study of Latin-American history."

> *Guadalupe, Mother of All Mexico* is a 56-minute documentary produced by San Rafael Films and is available from the University of California Extension Center for Media. The Center can be contacted at *cmil@uclink.berkeley.edu*. San Rafael Films can be reached at *sanrafaelfilms@hotmail.com*.

About the Editors

Sister Paula Jean Miller, FSE, is director of Catholic Studies and associate professor of theology at the University of St. Thomas in Houston, Texas. She specializes in moral theology and marriage and family studies. As director of Catholic Studies, Sister Paula Jean concentrates on multidisciplinary and multicultural approaches to the Catholic intellectual tradition. She has developed study abroad programs for the university in Rome and the Holy Land, through which students can experience the Catholic heritage.

Sister Paula Jean Miller is a member of the Franciscan Sisters of the Eucharist. She received her licentiate and doctorate in sacred theology from the John Paul II Institute for Studies on Marriage and Family in Washington, D.C., in 1993. Other publications include:

Members of One Body, Prophets, Priests and Kings: An Ecclesiology of Mission (1999).

Marriage: The Sacrament of Divine-Human Communion, A Commentary on Saint Bonaventure's Theology of Marriage (1996).

Richard Fossey is a professor in the College of Education at the University of Houston and Fondren Research Fellow at the Center for Reform of School Systems in Houston, Texas. He teaches courses in education policy, school law, and higher education law. Before arriving at UH, he was associate dean of the College of Education at Louisiana State University.

Dr. Fossey earned a B.A. from Oklahoma State University, a J.D. degree from the University of Texas School of Law, and an Ed.D. degree from Harvard University. Before beginning his doctoral studies, he practiced education law in Alaska, representing Alaska Native school districts in Inuit, Athabaskan, and Aleut communities. Other publications include:

Condeming Students to Debt: College Loans and Public Policy (1998, co-edited with Mark Bateman).

Crime on Campus: Legal Issues and Campus Administration (1995, co-authored with Michael Clay Smith).